MAHATMA GANDHI

A Biography

MAHATMA GANDHI

A Biography

Complete and unabridged

_____

B. R. NANDA

DELHI
OXFORD UNIVERSITY PRESS
CALCUTTA   CHENNAI   MUMBAI

Oxford University Press, Walton Street, Oxford OX2 6DP

Oxford   New York
Athens   Auckland   Bangkok   Calcutta
Cape Town   Chennai   Dar es Salaam   Delhi
Florence   Hong Kong   Istanbul   Karachi
Kuala Lumpur   Madrid   Melbourne   Mexico City
Mumbai   Nairobi   Paris   Singapore
Taipei   Tokyo   Toronto

and associates in
Berlin   Ibadan

First published by George Allen and Unwin Ltd, 1958
Reissued by Oxford University Press, 1981
Fourth impression 1989
Oxford India Paperbacks 1996
Third impression 1997

ISBN 0 19 563855 7

Printed at Wadhwa International, New Delhi 110 020
and published by Manzar Khan, Oxford University Press
YMCA Library Building, Jai Singh Road, New Delhi 110 001

To The Memory Of
My Mother
and
My Brother A. P.

Preface

FEW men in their lifetime aroused stronger emotions or touched deeper chords of humanity than Gandhi did. 'Generations to come, it may be,' wrote Einstein of Gandhi in July 1944, 'will scarcely believe that such a one as this ever in flesh and blood walked upon this earth'. While millions venerated Gandhi as the Mahatma, the great soul, his political opponents saw in him only an astute politician. Not until 1946-7 (when the transfer of power enabled them in their minds to disengage Mr Gandhi the man from Mr Gandhi the arch-rebel) were the British able to see him in a gentler light. And it was his tragic death which finally convinced his Pakistani detractors that his humanity encompassed and transcended his loyalty to Hinduism.

It is not easy to write the life-story of a man who made such a strong impact on his contemporaries. Yet it is important that the image of Gandhi does not become that of a divinity in the Hindu pantheon, but remains that of a man who schooled himself in self-discipline, who made of his life a continual process of growth, who shaped his environment as much as he was shaped by it, and who tenaciously adhered to certain values to which civilized humanity pays lip-service while flouting them in practice.

Though the arrangement of this biography is necessarily chronological, I have attempted, at appropriate points, to analyse Gandhi's attitude to important issues. The background of Indian nationalism, the Indian political scene when Gandhi returned from South Africa, his religious evolution, the transformation in his mode of life and acquisition of new values, his ethics, economics, and political movements, his attitude to war, and untouchability— all these have been treated in separate chapters. This combination of the chronological and the analytical methods has facilitated the discussion in a single volume of Gandhi's long and many-sided life in some detail, and the correlation of the story of his life with the evolution of his ideas. Gandhi was no theorist; his principles evolved in response to his own needs, and the environment in which he found himself. In fact, it is as difficult to assess the events of his life without understanding the ideas which inspired him, as it is to interpret his ideas on religion, morals, politics, or economics without reference to the context of his own life.

I know how hard it is for one who has lived through the last forty years, to be completely objective about the events of which Gandhi was the centre, but in assessing and reassessing events and personalities, it has been my endeavour to understand and to interpret in the historical perspective, rather than to uphold or to condemn. How far I have succeeded in this endeavour it is for the reader to judge.

I am grateful to the Government of India and the Director of the National Archives for permission to examine and use material from contemporary records which have enabled me, I believe, to present for the first time, a two-dimensional story of Gandhi's relations with the government. Any account of Gandhi's struggles which is wholly, or even largely based on official sources is, however, apt to be lopsided. I have therefore used these sources only to illuminate some of the obscurer spots, and to see events in their proper perspective.

The material for a biography of Gandhi is enormous. It is no easy task to try to sum up his long, rich and varied life in a single volume. I owe a heavy debt of gratitude to authors of numerous works on Gandhi and on the Indian national movement; acknowledgements have been duly made in the text, the footnotes and in the selected bibliography at the end of the book. I am grateful to the Navajivan Trust for permission to quote from Mahatma Gandhi's writings. I would also like to thank the following for according permission to reproduce brief extracts: Messrs Victor Gollancz Ltd., from W. C. Smith's *Modern Islam in India*, Messrs Cassell and Company from Vincent Sheean's *Lead Kindly Light*, Messrs Curtis Brown Ltd., from *Nine Troubled Years* by Lord Templewood, Oxford University Press, from *India: A Re-*

statement by Reginald Coupland, and Messrs. Jonathan Cape Ltd., and Philip Mason from *The Guardians* by Philip Woodruff.

For assistance given to me in preparation of this book my thanks are due to the Gandhi Memorial Museum Library, New Delhi, particularly to Mr Avanibhai Mehta; to Mr Girja Kumar, Librarian, and his assistants in the Indian Council of World Affairs Library; and to the staff of the Central Secretariat Library.

I am grateful to Mr V. K. Krishna Menon, Mr Pyarelal and Kaka Saheb Kalelkar, who were good enough to discuss and elucidate certain points. Among those who evinced keen interest in the progress of this book I must mention Mr Devadas Gandhi who unfortunately did not live to see it, and Mr N. C. Chaudhuri. Mr K. P. Mushran and Mr M. K. Kaul gave me much encouragement.

Mr B. N. Khosla read the entire book in manuscript and made useful suggestions. Mr Satya Prakash gave me ungrudging assistance in correcting the proofs and preparing the Index. I alone, however, bear responsibility for the views expressed in the book and for its shortcomings.

I am indebted to my wife for her encouragement and patience during the long hours of silence in which this book was composed.

B. R. NANDA.

A*

Contents

BOOK I

FORMATIVE YEARS

Chapter 1

CHILDHOOD

'WHY were you absent from the gymnastics class on Saturday?' asked the headmaster, as he looked severely from the attendance register to the fourteen-year-old boy, who had been brought before him.

'I was nursing my father,' replied the boy, 'I had no watch and the clouds deceived me. When I arrived all the boys had gone.'

'You are lying,' said the headmaster curtly.

The year was 1883. The place was Rajkot, a small princely state in Western India. Dorabji Edulji Gimi, the headmaster of the Alfred High School, was a strict disciplinarian; he had made games compulsory for the students of the upper forms and accepted no excuses from those who failed to attend. The boy was Mohandas Gandhi. That he should have been convicted of lying was more than he could bear. He cried helplessly. He knew he was right but he did not know how to convince the headmaster. He brooded on the incident until he came to the conclusion that 'a man of truth must also be a man of care'. Never again, he said to himself, would he put himself in a position in which his explanations would be dismissed as lies.

He shone neither in the classroom nor in the playground. Quiet, shy and retiring, he was tongue-tied in company. He did not mind being rated as a mediocre student, but he was jealous of his reputation. He was proud of the fact that he had never told a lie to his teachers or classmates; the slightest aspersion on his character drew his tears.

This moral sensitiveness may seem precocious in a boy of fourteen, but it was part of the tradition of the Gandhi family. Mohan's father Karamchand and grandfather Uttamchand had been known for their integrity and for the courage of their convictions.

Bania by caste, the Gandhis were grocers and hailed from Kutiyana in Junagadh State. An enterprising member of the Gandhi clan, Harjivan Gandhi, bought a house in the year 1777 in Porbandar where he and his children set up as small traders. The family, however, came into prominence when Uttamchand, a son of Harjivan Gandhi, made such a striking impression on Rana Khimaji, ruler of Porbandar, that he was appointed as the *Diwan*.

Porbandar was one of some three hundred states of Kathiawar Gujerat which were ruled by princes whom the accident of birth and the support of the suzerain power kept on the throne. Kathiawar, though feudal in structure and politically backward, had not remained impervious to currents of social reform which have given India her fundamental unity over the centuries. Some of the famous places of Hindu pilgrimage are situated in Gujerat: Dwarka in the extreme west, hallowed by association with the life and death of Lord Krishna, and the historic temple of Somnath. The teachings of Buddha, Mahavira, and Vallabhacharya, have mingled in common emphasis on the sacredness of all that lives, and the songs of Mirabai and the poems of Narsinh Mehta have inspired the people. Gujerat has been noted for its enterprising businessmen, but it has also produced religious and social reformers; one of them Swami Dayanand, an apostle of reformed Hinduism, was a contemporary of Karamchand Gandhi. There is a certain tenacity in the Gujerati character which, when allied to a sense of mission, can sweep everything before it. Perhaps it was not an accident that Gandhi and Jinnah, the two men who in different ways most influenced the history of India in this century, had Gujerati blood in their veins.

To be a *Diwan* of one of princely states was no sinecure in those days. To steer one's course safely between the wayward Indian Princes, the overbearing British Political Agents of the suzerain power, and the long-suffering subjects required a high degree of diplomatic skill and practical sense. Uttamchand Gandhi proved a

brilliant administrator and rescued Porbandar from the mis-
management and insolvency into which the state had drifted.
Unfortunately for him, Rana Khimaji died young, and the Queen
Regent, into whose hands the reins of administration fell, did not
appreciate the virtues of integrity and independence in her *Diwan*.
The inevitable clash came when Uttamchand gave his personal
protection to Kothari, a minor but honest official of the state
treasury, who had refused to oblige the Queen Regent's maid
servants. The enraged Queen sent a contingent of troops to
surround and shell the house of her chief minister; for long the
ancestral house of the Gandhis bore the marks. Luckily the
British Political Agent heard of these operations and had them
stopped. Uttamchand left Porbandar for his native village in
Junagadh, where he was kindly received by the *Nawab*. Observers
noted, however, that the fugitive minister saluted the *Nawab* with
his left hand. Questioned on this discourtesy, he replied that, in
spite of all that had happened, his right hand was pledged to
Porbandar. Uttamchand had to atone for the breach of the court
etiquette by standing barefooted in the sun for ten minutes, but
the *Nawab* was chivalrous enough to commend his loyalty by
exempting him and his descendants from payment of customs duty
if they traded in their native village.

When the Queen Regent's rule came to an end and Rana
Vikramjit came to the throne, efforts were made to get
Uttamchand Gandhi back to Porbandar as the *Diwan*. He declined
and the post was given in 1847 to his twenty-five-year-old son
Karamchand Gandhi, who served as *Diwan* for twenty-eight years.
Like his father, Karamchand was an upright and fearless minister;
in due course, he too incurred the displeasure of the ruling prince,
and leaving the ministership to his brother Tulsidas, moved to
Rajkot where he became the *Diwan*. It was in this capacity that he
had the temerity to reprimand the Assistant British Political Agent
for speaking insultingly of the ruler of Rajkot; he was arrested
but refused to apologize to the British officer who, though taken
aback by the intrepidity of a native minister, thought better of it,
and let him go.

Karamchand Gandhi married four times, death having claimed three wives in succession. Putlibai, the fourth wife, was nearly twenty years younger than her husband. She bore him three sons, Lakshmidas (Kala), Karsandas (Karsania) and Mohandas (Mohania) and a daughter Ralitabehn (Goki) who survived all the brothers. Karamchand had also two daughters from his earlier marriages.

Mohandas, the youngest child and the future Mahatma, was born on October 2, 1869.

Even as the chief minister of Porbandar, Karamchand continued to share the three-storeyed ancestral house with his five brothers and their families. The suite allotted to him was on the ground floor and had two rooms, besides a tiny kitchen and a verandah, one of which was 20 feet long and 13 feet wide, and the other 13 feet long and 12 feet wide. It was in this house, with his brothers and sisters, and numerous uncles and cousins that Mohandas Gandhi grew up. The town of Porbandar, with its narrow lanes and crowded bazaars, surrounded by massive walls which have since been largely demolished, is no more than a stone's throw from the Arabian Sea. The buildings, though by no means architecturally distinguished, are built of a white soft stone which hardens with the years, shines like marble in the sunlight, and has given to the town the romantic name of the 'White City'. The streets are dotted with temples; the ancestral house of the Gandhis itself was built around two temples. But the life of this port was and is necessarily centred on the sea. Even in the latter half of the nineteenth century there were scores of families with business contacts overseas, and it was to one of these contacts that M. K. Gandhi owed his introduction to South Africa.

When he was seven Mohan's parents moved 120 miles east to Rajkot; though the family link with Porbandar remained, Rajkot became henceforth the Gandhis' second home. Rajkot had no sea-beach where the children could play; it lacked the picturesque panorama of the 'White City', but politically and socially it was less of a backwater and had better facilities for education. In Porbandar, Mohan had attended a primary school where the children wrote the alphabet in dust with their fingers. Rajkot boasted of a high school.

Mohan's mother Putlibai was a capable woman who made herself felt in court circles through her friendship with the ladies of the palace. But her chief interest was in the home. When there was sickness in the family she wore herself out in days and nights of nursing. She had little of the weakness, common to women of her age and class, for finery or jewellery. Her life was an endless chain of fasts and vows through which her frail frame seemed to be borne only by the strength of her faith. The children clung to her as she divided her day between the home and the temple; her fasts and vows puzzled and fascinated them. She was not versed in the scriptures. Except for a smattering of Gujerati, she was practically unlettered; her knowledge of religion was acquired at home or from discourses heard at religious gatherings. She was orthodox, even superstitious. She would not let the children touch an 'untouchable' or look at the lunar eclipse. Mohan was more curious than the other children and asked searching questions. How did contact with Uka, the household sweeper, contaminate? How could the eclipse harm the onlooker? Her explanations did not always carry conviction. But for all this scepticism he was bound to her by bonds the strength of which he felt throughout his life. 'His voice softens when he speaks of his mother,' wrote an observer in 1908, when Mohan was thirty-nine years old, 'and the light of love is in his eyes.' She could not satisfy his curiosity nor stop him from rushing headlong into the secret atheism of his adolescence, but her abounding love, her endless austerities and her iron will left a permanent impression upon him. These qualities proved an undying source of inspiration for one whose life was to be one long struggle for self-mastery, and whose battles were to be waged and won in the hearts of men. The image of woman he imbibed from Putlibai was that of love and sacrifice. Something of her maternal love he came to possess himself, and as he grew it flowed out in ever increasing measure, bursting the bonds of family and community until it embraced the whole of humanity. He owed to his mother not only a passion for nursing which made him wash lepers' sores in his *ashram*, but also an impetus for his technique of appealing to the heart through self-suffering—a technique which wives and mothers have practised from time immemorial.

Mohan's father Karamchand Gandhi was a man of little academic education but rich in experience of men and affairs. He was, in the words of his son, 'a lover of his clan, truthful, brave, generous'. He had little interest in piling up money and left hardly any property for his children. The epics, the *Ramayana* and the *Mahabharata* were recited in the house, and occasionally there were discussions with Jain monks and Parsi and Muslim divines. But religion was for Karamchand mostly a matter of ritual. 'Whatever purity you see in me,' recalled his son at the age of sixty-two, 'is derived from my mother, not from my father.'[1]

The half-century which divided Karamchand from his youngest son made the father not so much an affectionate companion as an object of reverence. It was a child thus predisposed who read the ancient play *Shravan Pitribhakta* portraying the boundless love of the mythical boy Shravan for his parents. The picture of Shravan carrying his blind parents on a pilgrimage by means of slings fitted to his shoulders was indelibly printed on Mohan's mind. The story moved him deeply and Shravan became his model. Obedience to parents became his motto. The rule of implicit obedience was extended from the parents to the teachers, and from the teachers to all 'elders'. This surrender of the privileges of childhood may have contributed to an excessive passivity, passing into a morbid diffidence and preventing him from playing with, and even speaking to, other children. If a prize or a medal came his way at school, he took it to be beyond his deserts; he carried the distinction in his inner pocket, as it were, lest others should discover his poor worth.

And as if this was not sufficient handicap for a boy in his teens, he was married at the age of thirteen. For the greater economy and convenience of the parents, it was a triple wedding in which Mohan, his brother Karsandas and an elder cousin were married

[1] *The Diaries of Mahadev Desai*, Vol. I, entry dated March, 31, 1932.

off. Mohan's bride, Kasturbai, was the daughter of Gokaldass Makanji, a merchant of Porbandar and a friend of the Gandhi family. Love came to these children, and more so to Mohan, with the hurricane force of adolescent awakening. From a Gujerati pamphlet he had imbibed the ideal of life-long fidelity to his wife; from this he deduced his right to exact a similar fidelity from her and to exercise a surveillance over her movements. To visit friends or the temple, she had to have his permission. The fact that he was under the influence of a vicious companion who fanned his jealousy made matters worse. Kasturbai, the proud little girl, chafed under these arbitrary restrictions, and in her own quiet and determined way resisted them. These 'dark days of doubts and suspicions' proved to be a useful education to the young husband. 'I learnt,' he told John S. Hoyland many years later, 'the lesson of non-violence from my wife when I tried to bend her to my will. Her determined resistance to my will on the one hand, and her quiet submission to the suffering my stupidity involved on the other, ultimately made me ashamed of myself and cured me of my stupidity in thinking that I was born to rule over her; and in the end she became my teacher in non-violence.' The immediate effect of the marriage was that Mohan lost a year at school, though he made it up later by skipping a class. Luckily for him marriage did not mean, as it meant for his elder brother and cousin who had been married at the same time, the end of his education.

Mohan had secretly prided himself on being an obedient child. He had learnt 'to carry out the orders of the elders, not to scan them'. But there came a time when this want of independence began to hurt. The form which adolescent revolt takes depends upon the strength of the taboos which are broken. In the Vaishnava community in which the Gandhis lived meat-eating and smoking were horrible sins. There is little wonder, therefore, that Mohan should in this rebellious phase have been enticed into them. Mehtab, one of the schoolmates, filled the role of the Machiavellian tempter. He argued in favour of meat-eating. He claimed that many people in the town, including the teachers in the school, secretly took meat in spite of their pretence to the contrary; that the British, being meat-eaters, were hardy and could not be overthrown by the vegetarian Indians. Meat was in fact a cure-all; it could prevent boils and tumours and drive off the ghosts which troubled little Mohan in his sleep.

The subtle sophistry of this friend overthrew Mohan's last defences but, in order to spare a shock to his parents, he consented to a meat feast in a lonely spot by the river. He had a bad night after the first feast, 'the goat bleating inside me'. The dinners were repeated at suitable intervals and gradually he overcame his early disgust. One complication, however, remained: after joining in these furtive feasts, he had to invent apologies to his mother for lack of appetite at mealtime. Since lying went against the grain, he was driven to the conclusion that the change in his diet would have to wait until he grew up and became accountable to no one except himself.

Smoking was another transgression of this period. With another boy Mohan began to pilfer stumps of cigarettes thrown away by his uncle. This was of course unsatisfactory. As the children had no money to buy cigarettes, they began to steal the servants' coppers, but that did not take them far. Then they started smoking the stalks of a wild plant. Their young spirits at last felt thwarted. One evening, in sheer despair, they slipped into a temple for a final ceremony to cut the Gordian knot by committing suicide. Their courage failed them at the critical moment; rather than quit the world, they decided to give up smoking.

Another escapade of the period was the theft of a bit of gold to pay off a debt incurred by his brother. The guilt weighed upon him until he could bear it no longer. He wrote out a confession and presented it to his father; their simultaneous tears at once marked the atonement by the son and forgiveness by the father.

The adolescence of Mohan was no stormier than that of many of his contemporaries; adventures into the forbidden land of meat-eating and smoking and petty pilfering were, and are not un-common among boys of his age. What was extraordinary was the way his adventures ended. In every case he posed for himself a problem for which he sought a solution by framing a proposition in moral algebra. 'Never again' was his promise to himself after each escapade. And he kept the promise.

There was nothing to mark him off from other boys of his age except perhaps an unnatural seriousness and passivity. He did not seem to be a child who could elbow his way forward. But under his cold unprepossessing exterior there was a burning passion for self-improvement. It was his habit 'to forget what he did not like and to carry out what he liked'. What others read for pleasure he read for instruction. Millions of children—and adults—in India have heard the stories of Prahlad and Harishchandra. The boy Prahlad, who suffered untold hardships without faltering in his faith in God, and King Harishchandra, who sacrificed all he had for the sake of truth, are heroes of Hindu mythology, the creatures of poetic imagination, and have been treated as such. But for Mohan they became living models. History or literature were for him not merely an unminted mine of wonder, but an inspiration for a better and purer life. While children of his age competed for the conventional prizes and trophies in the school, this sensitive child posed and puzzled out moral problems for himself.

Chapter 2

OFF TO ENGLAND

MOHAN passed the matriculation examination in 1887. His father's death a year earlier had strained the means of the family. Being the only boy in the family who had persevered in his studies, its hopes rested on him and he was sent to Bhavnagar, the nearest town with a college. Unfortunately for Mohan, the teaching in the college was in English. He was unable to follow the lectures and despaired of making any progress.

Meanwhile, Mavji Dave, a friend of the family, suggested that Mohan should go to England to qualify at the bar. It was easy enough to become a barrister; in contrast, the degrees of Indian Universities consumed more time, energy and money and had less value in the market. A Bombay degree was likely to produce nothing better than a clerical post. Mavji Dave argued that if Mohan aspired like his father and grandfather to be the *Diwan* in one of the states of Kathiawar, he needed a foreign degree. Karamchand and Uttamchand Gandhi had held high posts and managed with very little education, but times had changed. The universities were now producing Bachelors of Arts and Law by the thousand, products of the English education for which Macaulay had planned. There were, however, too many of them. It was, therefore, a definite advantage in the competition for the plums of public service to be able to sport a foreign degree.

Mohan jumped at the idea of going abroad. Not only was he anxious to see England, 'the land of philosophers and poets, the very centre of civilization', but also because it offered him an immediate escape from the agony of attending the classes in Bhavnagar College where the teachers seemed to be talking over his head. His elder brother had no doubt that the proposal was

attractive but wondered how they could afford it. Mother
Putlibai felt lost. How could she let her youngest boy sail to an
alien land to face unknown temptations and dangers? She wished
her husband had been living to take a decision to which she felt
unequal. She asked Mohan to seek the advice of his uncle, who was
the eldest member of the Gandhi family. Mohan trekked by cart
and camel to Porbandar to see his uncle, who was courteous but
visibly reluctant to bless the unholy trip across the seas. Another
disappointment was in store for him when he approached Mr
Lely, the British Administrator of Porbandar, a state which the
Gandhis had served so well, to grant him a scholarship for studies
in England. The British officer treated him with scant courtesy,
asked him to take a degree at Bombay University and then ask
for a scholarship. All this was depressing enough, but Mohan did
not lose heart. He knew that if the trip to England fell through, he
would have to return to the classrooms of Bhavnagar, a none too
pleasant prospect. He thought of selling his wife's jewellery. This
desperate course was rendered unnecessary when his generous
brother undertook to find funds. The misgivings of the mother
were set at rest when a Jain monk, Becharji Swami, made the boy
take a solemn vow that he would not touch wine, woman or meat
while he was away from the shores of India.

A fresh hurdle appeared just when Mohan was about to sail.
The elders of the Modh Bania caste to which the Gandhis
belonged summoned him before the caste tribunal and
declared that the trip to England was a violation of the Hindu
religion. The nineteen-year-old boy, who had been unable to
stammer a few words of thanks at a farewell party at his school,
mustered the courage to resist the browbeating of the bearded
leaders of his caste. Infuriated at this defiance, the caste tribunal
issued a fiat of excommunication against Mohan. But before this
order could become a real nuisance, he sailed from Bombay on
September 4, 1888.

From the rural surroundings of Rajkot to the cosmopolitan
atmosphere of a steamship was a tremendous change for Mohan.
Adaptation to western food, dress and etiquette was a painful

process. He felt tongue-tied when accosted by fellow-passengers. The slender hold on the English language which he had acquired in school and college nearly gave way. He could hardly speak without being weighed down with a feeling that he was making a fool of himself. The vegetarian vow added to his embarrassment. Afraid to question the waiters on the composition of the menu, he lived on the fruits and sweets he had brought with him. He received much gratuitous advice. One passenger told him that he would not be able to do without meat after leaving Aden. When Aden had been safely passed, he was warned that meat would be indispensable after crossing the Red Sea. In the Mediterranean, a prophet of doom announced grimly that in the Bay of Biscay he would have to choose between death on the one hand and meat and wine on the other.

His sense of isolation increased after he landed in England. A terrible feeling of loneliness gripped him. It was partly the usual nostalgia of the Indian student as he begins his self-imposed exile. To it were added the misgivings of an exceedingly diffident and sensitive boy. His thoughts wandered back to his home in Rajkot, his beloved mother, his wife, his baby boy. The prospects before him appeared to be bleak. He must acclimatize himself to another climate, strange surroundings and a new mode of living. Vegetarianism to which he was vowed seemed to condemn him not only to perpetual semi-starvation, but also to public ridicule. Indescribably lonely, he wept as he lay awake in bed, and thought of the three long years which must run their weary course before he could return home.

The vegetarian vow became a continual source of embarrassment to him. Friends in England feared that his food fads would ruin his health, and make of him, socially, a square peg. He could not rebut the arguments of advocates of meat eating; secretly he had always wanted to take meat but felt bound by the vow. When he felt puzzled or weak he went on his knees and prayed to God to help him keep the word he had given to his mother.

One day, while roaming about in London, he stumbled upon a vegetarian restaurant in Farringdon Street. The sight of this restaurant,' he recorded later, 'filled me with the same joy that a child feels on getting a thing after its own heart.' He had his first hearty meal since he had sailed from India. In the restaurant he also bought a book entitled 'Plea for Vegetarianism' by Salt whose arguments went home. A meatless diet had been hitherto a matter of sentiment to him; henceforth it was one of reasoned conviction. Vegetarianism, adopted out of deference to his parents, had been an inconvenient obligation, but before long it became a mission, the starting point of a unique discipline of body and mind, which transformed his life. The discovery of this restaurant was an event more significant than he could see at the moment. There was a long and hard but sure road which led from Farringdon Street in London to the Phoenix and Tolstoy Settlements in South Africa, and to the Sabarmati and Sevagram Ashrams in India.

The conversion to vegetarianism brought a new self-assurance to Gandhi. Henceforth, he might appear a crank, but he did not feel like one. His friends, however, feared that by insisting on meatless meals he would make a mess of his health as well as his studies. To disarm his critics, and to prove that, vegetarianism apart, he was not impervious to the new environment, he began to put on a thick veneer of 'English culture'. There was a lot he had to cover up. Used to his native Kathiawari costume in school and college, he had felt palpably awkward in English dress while travelling aboard ship and stepping ashore. His hold on the English language was tenuous and even ordinary conversation entailed a laborious mental rehearsal from his mother tongue.

Having made up his mind to become an 'English Gentleman', he spared neither time nor money. Whatever the cost, the veneer had to be the best in the market. New suits were ordered from the most fashionable tailors in London; the watch was adorned with a double gold chain from India; under expert tuition lessons began in elocution, dancing, and music. The product of these sartorial and cultural exercises was later described by a contemporary. This is how the twenty-year-old M. K. Gandhi struck Sachchidanand

Sinha in February 1890, when he saw him in Piccadilly Circus: 'He was wearing a high silk top hat burnished bright, a Gladstonian collar, stiff and starched; a rather flashy tie displaying almost all the colours of the rainbow under which there was a fine striped silk shirt. He wore as his outer clothes a morning coat, a double-breasted vest, and dark striped trousers to match and not only patent leather boots but spats over them. He carried leather gloves and a silver-mounted stick, but wore no spectacles. He was, to use the contemporary slang, a nut, a masher, a blood—a student more interested in fashion and frivolities than in his studies.'[1]

Gandhi could not, however, throw himself into this experiment with complete self-abandon. The habit of introspection had never deserted him. English dancing and music did not come easy to him. Drapers and dance halls could turn him into an English gentleman, but only an English gentleman about town. His brother was straining the slender resources of the family, perhaps incurring debts to enable him to continue his studies in England. As he brooded over it all, he realized the folly of chasing the will-o'-the-wisp of an English gentleman.

After a brief three months' excursion, the introvert returned to his shell. There was a rebound from extreme extravagance to meticulous economy. He kept an account of every farthing he spent. He changed his rooms, cooked his own breakfast, and to save bus fares walked eight to ten miles daily. He was able to pare down his expenses to £2 a month. He began to feel keenly the obligations to his family and was glad that he had reduced the calls on his brother for funds. Simplicity harmonized his inward and outward life; the dandyism of the first three months had been only a defensive armour against those who considered him a misfit in English society.

The connection between dietetics and religion may seem far-fetched, but the two were intimately related in the evolution

[1] Article in the *Amrit Bazar Patrika*—Republic Day Souvenir, January 26, 1950.

of M. K. Gandhi. His early vegetarianism was part of his Vaishnava heritage; he had abstained from meat because it was repugnant to his parents. Sheikh Mehtab, a clever schoolmate, had coaxed him into meat-eating for a while; but he had given it up when obliged to tell lies to his parents to ward off their suspicions, and decided to defer the enjoyment of this delicacy till he was old enough to be independent of parental authority. In England he scrupulously observed the promise he had given to his mother not to touch meat, but he was conscious all the time that sentiment rather than reason was on his side. Not until he read Salt's book did he discover the virtues of vegetarianism. With the zeal of a new convert he devoured books on dietetics, developed an interest in cooking, outgrew the taste for condiments, and came to the sensible conclusion that the seat of taste is not in the tongue but in the mind. The control of the palate was one of the first steps in that discipline which was to culminate many years later in total sublimation. The dietary experiments, dictated by considerations of health and economy, were to become a part of his religious and spiritual evolution.

The immediate effect of vegetarianism was to give a new poise to him in England, and to draw him out of his shell. He made his first venture into journalism by contributing nine articles to the *Vegetarian*. These articles, largely descriptive, dealt with the diet and habits of the Indian people, their social system and festivals, and had occasional flashes of humour. That he should have sent these articles for publication is a notable achievement, if we recall that in Bhavnagar College he had been unable to follow lectures in English. He became a member of the executive committee of the London Vegetarian Society and took an interest in designing its badge. In Bayswater, where he stayed for a short time, he founded a vegetarian club. He came into contact with at least one eminent vegetarian, Sir Edwin Arnold, the author of the *Light of Asia* and *The Song Celestial* two books which moved him deeply. In vegetarian restaurants and boarding-houses of London he came across not only food faddists but also a few devout men of religion. He owed his introduction to the Bible to one such contact.

His excessive shyness was not, however, shaken off by three years in England. Apart from the Vegetarian Society, the only organization which drew him was the *Anjuman Islamia*, an organization of Indian Muslims, mostly students, who debated political and social questions over light refreshments. Non-Muslim students were permitted to join these discussions which brought together a number of Indian students in England who were later to make their mark in India's public life. Among these were Gandhi, Abdur Rahim, Mazharul Haq, Muhammad Shafi, Sachchidanand Sinha and Harkishan Lal Gauba. Gandhi (along with Sinha and Harkishan Lal) held nationalist views on political questions, but he spoke little and unlike some others, lacked the faculty for vehement assertion.

New literary, social and political forces were stirring in the England of the eighties and nineties but there is little evidence of Gandhi having been susceptible to them. He does not refer in the course of the forty page account of his stay in England to Karl Marx, Darwin or Huxley. Science, literature and politics did not excite him. He was wholly preoccupied with personal and moral issues. The crucial problem for him was how to marshal his inner resources in order to keep the promise he had given to his mother, to fight the recurring temptations of 'meat, wine and woman', and to inject into his daily life simplicity, economy and purpose. His efforts at journalism were confined to the columns of the *Vegetarian* and his reading to religious texts such as the *Gita* and the New Testament. If any subject seemed to strike a vital chord in him, it was religion. Nevertheless, at this stage his acquaintance with religion, even with Hinduism, was quite elementary.

In an article in the *Vegetarian* of June 20, 1891, Gandhi gave his own assessment of what the stay in England had meant to him: 'In conclusion I am bound to say that during my nearly three years' stay in England I have left many things undone . . . yet I carry one great consolation with me that I shall go back without

having taken meat or wine, and that I know from personal
experience that there are so many vegetarians.'

Here was an earnest but diffident young man with a definite
but limited range of interests. Not even the most partial observer
could have detected in this young barrister-at-law any promise of
distinction when he sailed for India. He did not seem to be cut out
for a brilliant career, least of all in law or politics.

Chapter 3

BRIEFLESS BARRISTER

As Gandhi gave up the cultivation of the social graces and turned his attention to his studies, he felt that the law course could not engage him fully and that he had time to improve his basic education. His high school training had been indifferent; the lack of fluency in English troubled him in particular. Since he could spare neither the time nor the funds to go to Cambridge or Oxford, he decided to prepare for the matriculation examination of the London University. Undismayed by the first attempt in which he was ploughed in Latin, he passed the examination. Knowledge of Latin proved useful to him in the study of law; it was an asset to him when he practised in South African courts where Roman Dutch was the common law. Latin also helped to fashion his simple and crisp English prose.

Law Examinations at this time were not difficult; the examiners were generous and percentage of successes was high. Most law students crammed summaries of their text-books for the examination; but Gandhi was too conscientious to use these short cuts. He read the Roman Law in Latin, and laboriously studied Broom's *Common Law*, Snell's *Equity*, Tudor's *Leading Cases*, William's and Edward's *Real Property*. Thanks to his conscientiousness and diffidence he turned even the bar examination into an arduous affair; when he got through it, he was assailed by fresh doubts and anxieties. He had read the law, but could he practise it? He found it hard enough to speak to strangers even in a small party. How would he be able to cross swords with his rivals in the court room? He had heard of legal luminaries like Sir Pherozeshah Mehta, and could well imagine the sorry figure he would cut in comparison. Frantically, he looked for advice. He could not venture to meet the great Indian lawyer and statesman, Dadabhai Naoroji who was in England at the time. An English lawyer, however, advised the Indian youth to widen his reading, to improve his knowledge of history, and to study human nature. Naïvely, Gandhi hastened to buy a book on physiognomy and to equip himself for the difficult role of a practising lawyer. He distilled what consolation he could from the opinion of this English lawyer that exceptional acumen, memory and ability were not the only prerequisites for success at the bar, that honesty and industry could also go far. Thus, 'with just a little leaven of hope mixed with despair', he sailed for India.

A great shock lay in store for him, when he landed at Bombay. His mother had died while he was in England. The news of the tragedy had been deliberately withheld from him. It was a cruel blow. Many years later, he recorded in the autobiography, that 'most of my cherished hopes were shattered'. The austere life, the immutable faith and the abounding love of his mother were, nevertheless, indelibly imprinted on him. She was perhaps the biggest single influence in shaping the Mahatma of the future, the man in the loin-cloth, vowed to days of silence and fasts, waiting upon God for guidance, and answering hate with love.

He had now to reckon with the Modh Bania caste which had excommunicated him when he had sailed for England. As a sop to orthodoxy, he was persuaded by his brother to visit Nasik to wash off his transgression with a dip in the holy waters of the Godavari. This atonement appeased only one section of the Modh Banias; the other section stubbornly declined to lift the ban. Gandhi met this tyranny in an unorthodox manner. He did not protest nor betray any rancour against his opponents; indeed he co-operated in the enforcement of the boycott against himself. This attitude blunted the edge of caste-tyranny; the appeal to the heart went home. Many of his critics among Modh Banias later whole-heartedly supported his social and political movements. These early experiences did not sour him. He continued to defend the institution of caste, 'the Varnashramdharma', without, of course, its later incrustations.

B

Gandhi was anxious to justify the hopes of his family which had invested so much on his foreign education. His brother expected rich dividends in the form of 'wealth, and name and fame'. The barrister's degree, however, was not an open sesame to the top of the bar. The law course in England had not included Hindu or Muslim law: Gandhi noticed that the home-bred *vakils* of Rajkot knew more of Indian law and charged lower fees than barristers. To practise in Rajkot was thus to invite sure ridicule; Gandhi therefore accepted the advice of his friends that he should go to Bombay to study Indian law, to gain experience of the High Court and to secure what briefs he could. He threw himself with gusto into legal studies, digested the Evidence Act, skimmed Mayne's *Hindu Law* and grappled with the Civil Procedure Code.

His knowledge of Indian law began to grow but not his income. Brokerage to 'touts' for briefs secured through them was an accepted mode of building up practice, but to Gandhi it was something beneath the dignity of his profession. Briefs were slow in coming. After waiting unconscionably, he got his first brief from Mamibai, a poor woman whom he charged thirty rupees. As he rose in the small-causes court to cross-examine a witness, he was unable to collect his thoughts, collapsed into his chair and refunded the fee to his client. This was a disgraceful début, which filled the young barrister with black despair as to his future in a profession he had entered at such a heavy cost.

The straits to which he had been reduced may be surmised from the fact that he applied for a part time job as teacher in a Bombay High School with the modest salary of seventy rupees a month. He had passed the London matriculation examination with Latin as his second language. But he lacked what the school wanted, an Indian University degree. London matriculation could not secure him a teacher's post, but it had brushed up his English. It was with some relief that he discovered that he had a flair for drafting memorials and petitions, and that he could make a living out of it. To set up as a petition writer, it was not necessary to prolong his stay in Bombay. He wound up his little establishment

and returned to Rajkot, where petition writing brought him an
income of 300 rupees a month.

He might have settled down as a barrister scribe but for a
predicament into which he was pitchforked. His elder brother,
Lakshmidas, who had once held a political appointment, was
under a cloud and persuaded him to see the Political Agent whom
he had met in England. The Political Agent resented this
intervention and had the young barrister turned out of the house.
Gandhi's cup of humiliation was full. He thought of filing a suit
against the British officer for insulting him. Those who knew the
world, the British bureaucratic world, advised him that such a
procedure could only be ruinous to himself. The great lawyer of
Bombay, Sir Pherozeshah Mehta was consulted. 'Such things,' he
commented, 'are the common experience of many *vakils* and
barristers. Gandhi is still fresh from England and hot-blooded.
If he would earn something let him pocket the insult.' This was
the heyday of British rule in India, before the political awakening.
The professional classes were painfully conscious of their dependence upon local officials. The angry breath of a British officer
had shrivelled the career of many a hot-headed young man.

With the continual tug of war among its petty princes and
their favourites, the atmosphere of Kathiawar was too full of
intrigue and corruption to be congenial to Gandhi. Most of his
work lay in the court of the Political Agent who was now
irreconcilably prejudiced against him. So when an offer of a job
came to him from South Africa, he gladly accepted it. The
contract was for a year in connection with a civil suit involving
£40,000. The remuneration was £105, a first-class return fare
and actual expenses. The fee was modest, and it was not quite
clear whether he was engaged as counsel, or as a clerk, but he was
in no position to pick and choose. Without seeking any elaboration
of the offer, he accepted it.

A second voyage was in store for him. Ironically enough, like
the first it provided an escape from immediate difficulties. In
1888 he had welcomed the trip to England because he had been
unable to get on in the Bhavnagar College. Five years later he

had welcomed a year's exile in South Africa because his *amour-propre* and professional fortunes had suffered rude buffets in his homeland.

He could hardly have imagined the new vistas of maturity and public service which the South African adventure was to open to him. The conceited British officer who had bundled the young Indian barrister out of his house had unwittingly done a disservice to the British Empire.

Chapter 4

A FATEFUL JOURNEY

GANDHI landed at Durban in May 1893. He was received by his employer Abdulla, one of the wealthiest Indian merchants in Natal. The western dress and the urbane manner of the young barrister set the shrewd old merchant thinking. Had he hired a white elephant? Could this young man be trusted to resist the baits which the other party might throw in his way at Pretoria, where the suit was being contested? These misgivings soon vanished when the young lawyer and the old merchant discovered a common interest in religion.

After a week's stay in Durban, Gandhi left for Pretoria to take up the assignment which had brought him to South Africa.

His brief stay at Durban had given him disconcerting evidence of colour prejudice. He was taken by Abdulla to see the Durban court. The European magistrate ordered him to take off his turban. Gandhi refused, left the court room and wrote a letter of protest in the local press in which he was mentioned as 'an unwelcome visitor'. It was a new experience for him. He had never before encountered blatant racial prejudice. The arrogance of British officials in India he had attributed to individual aberrations. And in England he had come into contact with many Englishmen whose courtesy and goodwill he treasured.

The experience in Durban, however, was nothing compared with what befell him in the course of his journey from Durban to Pretoria. When his train reached Maritzburg late in the evening, he was ordered to shift to the van compartment. He refused but was unceremoniously turned out of the first-class carriage. It was a bitterly cold night as he crept into the unlit waiting-room of Maritzburg station and brooded over what had happened. His

client had given him no warning of the humiliating conditions
under which Indians lived in South Africa. Should he not call
off the contract and return to India? Should he accept these
affronts as part of the bargain? He had already left India because
his position in Rajkot had become untenable after he had incurred
the displeasure of the Political Agent. Was he now to flee back to
India because South Africa was too hot for him? He felt he had
to draw the line somewhere. Determined to face whatever
happened, he resumed his journey.

At Charlestown, then a rail terminus, he had to take a stage
coach for Standerton. He was told he could not sit inside the
coach with European passengers and was seated with the driver.
A little later he was asked to travel on the footboard. He refused
and suggested that he might be given the seat due to him in the
coach box. This impertinence was too much for the white official
in charge of the coach, who fell upon Gandhi and belaboured him
mercilessly until some of the European passengers intervened.
Gandhi had borne the beating but had not budged from his seat.
It was a classic scene, a fit subject for a great artist: quiet courage
and human dignity pitted against racial arrogance and brute
strength.

On arrival at Standerton Gandhi met some Indian merchants.
They explained to him that what had happened to him was the
daily lot of Indians in Transvaal. He reported the incident to the
Agent of the Coach Company, though he made it clear that he
did not wish to proceed against his assailant. At Johannesburg he
drove to the Grand National Hotel only to be told that Indians
were barred; moreover, it required extensive quotations from
railway regulations and special pleading with the Station Master
of Johannesburg before he was able to buy a first-class ticket for
Pretoria, and but for the intercession of a European fellow
passenger he would again have been pushed out of the first-class
compartment.

The five days' journey from Durban to Pretoria was a long
drawn out agony. But it dramatized for Gandhi the condition of
Indian immigrants in South Africa. Indian merchants had learnt to

pocket these humiliations as they pocketed their daily earnings. What was new was not Gandhi's experience, but his reaction to it. So far he had not been conspicuous for assertiveness; on the contrary, he had been pathologically shy and retiring. But something happened to him in that bleak windswept waiting-room of Maritzburg railway station as he smarted under the insult inflicted on him. The iron entered his soul. In retrospect, this incident seemed to him as one of the most creative experiences of his life. From that hour, he refused to accept injustice as a part of the natural—or unnatural—order in South Africa. He would reason; he would plead; he would appeal to the better judgment and the latent humanity of the ruling race; he would resist, but he would never be a willing victim of racial arrogance. It was not so much a question of redeeming his own self-respect as that of his community, his country, even of humanity. The helpless resignation of the mass of Indian settlers, the fact that they were illiterate, had few rights and did not know how to assert the rights they had—all this had the miraculous effect of dissipating his own diffidence. The feeling of inferiority which had dogged him as a student in England and as a budding lawyer in India vanished. In Bombay he had been unable to face a small-causes court, but one of the first things he did on arrival at Pretoria was to invite its Indian residents to a meeting 'to present to them a picture of their condition in Transvaal'. The meeting was a great success. Gandhi suggested the formation of an organization to voice the grievances of the Indian community. A token of this practical leadership was his offer to teach English to those Indian merchants who wanted to learn it. His first three pupils were a barber, a clerk and a petty shopkeeper who received the honorary tuition at their places. He came to know every Indian in that town. He brought the disabilities of the Indian community to the notice of the British Agent in Pretoria, who was sympathetic but pleaded helplessness because Transvaal was a Boer State outside the orbit of the British Empire. The Boer Government had already chased most of the Indian settlers out of Orange Free State. South Africa seemed to have no room for a self-respecting Indian. Gandhi's mind became more and more exercised with the question as to how this state of affairs could be put right.

Meanwhile, he had to attend to the civil suit which had brought him to South Africa. In this suit were involved the huge sum of £40,000 as well as trade rivalry and family feuds between two of the biggest Indian merchants in South Africa, Abdulla of Natal and Tyeb Sheth of Transvaal. True to the litigious tradition of their native land, these two merchants were resolved to fight it out to the bitter end. Gandhi was assigned the modest role of examining the books of Abdulla's firm and serving as a link with its lawyers. The young barrister did not disdain the duties of an accountant-clerk. What may have appeared to another as an affront struck him as an opportunity. He dug deeply into the details of the case, acquired a knowledge of book-keeping and trade practices and improved his English by copious translations from Gujerati in which the firm's accounts were kept. He carefully observed how the material prepared by him was sorted by the attorney and how the brief itself was prepared.

The high water mark of the legal profession had once appeared to him to consist in feats of forensic eloquence or facile quotations from law manuals. After a year's hard labour on this suit he learnt that the function of the lawyer is to sift the facts and to find out the truth. He was conscious that he was neither eloquent nor learned, but he could depend for success upon his integrity and industry. This case taught him what a junior barrister learns in a senior barrister's chamber; it also gave him the confidence that he should not, after all, fail as a lawyer, that facts were three-fourth of law and that 'once we adhere to truth, the law comes to our aid naturally'.

On a close examination of the facts, Abdulla's case appeared to him to be strong in fact as well as in law. But he saw that the suit was ruinous to both the parties. The mounting fees of the lawyers, the inevitable dislocation in the normal work of the firms, and the bad blood engendered all round, dictated the wisdom of a settlement out of court. Not without reluctance did the two firms accept arbitration. The arbitrator's verdict went in favour of Abdulla. If it had been enforced immediately, Tyeb Sheth would have faced bankruptcy. Gandhi persuaded his client to be magnanimous in his hour of triumph and agree to payment by instalments. He could look back on his first important brief with satisfaction: 'I had learnt the true practice of law. I had learnt to find out the better side of human nature and to enter men's hearts. I realized that the true function of a lawyer was to unite parties riven asunder.'[1]

Henceforth it was his constant endeavour to reconcile opponents outside the court room rather than let them fight it out. It was not only the litigants who gained in the process. 'I lost nothing,' he recorded many years later, 'not even money, certainly not my soul.'

---

[1] Gandhi, M. K.: *Autobiography*, Ahmedabad (1945), p. 168.

B*

Chapter 5

PLUNGE INTO POLITICS

THE civil suit at Pretoria having happily concluded, Gandhi's contract was over, and he returned to Durban to catch a steamer for India. At the farewell party which Abdulla, his grateful client, gave in his honour, Gandhi happened to glance through the pages of the *Natal Mercury* and read a news item entitled 'Indian Franchise'. A bill was being introduced in the Natal Legislature to disfranchise Indian settlers, but Gandhi's host and other merchants attending the party were unable to throw any light on this measure. They knew enough English to be able to converse with their white customers, but few of them could read newspapers, much less follow the proceedings of the Natal Legislature. They had come to Natal for trade, and politics did not interest them. They had not yet realized that politics could affect their trade. Only recently, Indian traders had been hounded out of the Orange Free State, and now Natal was enacting a racial measure. 'This is the first nail into our coffin!' was Gandhi's comment. The Indian merchants pleaded with him to stay on in Natal to take up the fight on their behalf. They had so far relied on European barristers, and were therefore glad to have an Indian barrister in their midst. He agreed to defer his return to India for a month, and hoped that by then a decision on the disfranchisement of Indian voters would be taken.

Gandhi lost no time in settling down to work: the farewell party converted itself into a political committee to plan Indian opposition to the bill. A sound instinct seems to have guided the twenty-five-year-old barrister in organizing his first political campaign. The insight he had acquired, while at Pretoria, into the Indian settlers' problems stood him in good stead. His strategy was threefold. In the first place, a spirit of solidarity had to be infused into the heterogeneous elements composing the Indian population. The Muslim merchants and their Hindu and Parsi clerks from Bombay, the semi-slave 'indentured' labourers from Madras, and the Natal-born Indian Christians had all to realize their common origin. On the Indian Christians it was to be impressed that because they were Christians they did not cease to be Indians. The merchants had to accept their kinship with the poor indentured labourers whom extreme poverty had brought to a life of toil in far-off Natal. Secondly, the implications of the disfranchising measure had to be brought home to the Indian community, as well as to the saner section of the European public opinion and the Natal Government. Finally, the widest publicity must be given to the Indians' case to quicken the conscience of the peoples and governments of India and Great Britain. The Government of India was not autonomous; it had, however, some moral responsibility for the lot of those whose emigration it had permitted for the greater prosperity of the Europeans of Natal. The Imperial Government in London had the authority, if it thought fit, to withhold assent from bills passed by the Natal Legislature, and Gandhi hoped that it might be persuaded to intervene against racial discrimination affecting Her Majesty's Indian subjects in South Africa.

It is a measure of Gandhi's success as a publicist that the Indian National Congress in its annual session in December 1894 recorded its protest against the disfranchising bill, and in the next three years the London *Times* devoted eight leading articles to the Indian problem in South Africa. A petition drafted by Gandhi and signed by 400 Indians was presented to the Legislative Assembly of Natal. The petition created a stir in the Natal Legislature and the Government, but the bill was passed nevertheless. The Indians were not dismayed by their failure; they had at least been roused from their political lethargy. As for Gandhi, this first experience of political agitation into which he had been pitchforked cured him of what once had seemed an incorrigible self-consciousness. Not that he had a sudden attack of egotism.

He explained his limitations in a letter dated July 5, 1894 to Dadabhai Naoroji, the eminent leader of the Indian National Congress, and at that time a member of the British Parliament: 'A word for myself and I have done. I am inexperienced and young and, therefore, quite liable to make mistakes. The responsibility undertaken is quite out of proportion to my ability. So you will see that I have not taken the matter up, which is beyond my ability in order to enrich myself at the expense of the Indians. I am the only available person who can handle the question. You will, therefore, oblige me very greatly if you will kindly direct and guide me, and make necessary suggestions which shall be received as from father to his child.'[1]

The concept of inferiority is a relative one; in a community looking to him for leadership, Gandhi forgot his own limitations. As 'the only available person', he undertook a task from which elsewhere he may have shrunk.

One last chance remained. The bills passed by the Natal Legislature required the Queen's assent before they became law. Gandhi decided to send a monster petition to the Colonial Secretary in London. The petition bore 10,000 signatures, covering almost the entire population of free Indians in Natal. It was part of Gandhi's technique to use every move in this campaign for the political education of the community. For example, no one was allowed to sign the petition until he had understood and accepted its contents. A thousand copies were printed and mailed to prominent politicians and newspapers. Both in India and Britain, the case of the Natal Indians had a good press.

Meanwhile the month for which Gandhi had postponed his departure for India came to an end. The Indians of Natal begged him to stay on. It was not certain that the British Government would veto the offending measure. Moreover, had he not warned them that this was the first nail in their coffin? Would he leave them in the lurch and see his own work undone? Gandhi agreed to prolong his stay, but how was he to make a living? Since he would not hear of payment for public work, twenty merchants

[1] Masani, R. P.: *Dadabhai Naoroji*, London; p. 468.

offered him retaining fees to produce a minimum of £300 a year which he reckoned enough to pay his way in Durban.

The Bar Society of Natal opposed Gandhi's admission as an advocate to the Supreme Court. The Chief Justice admitted him, but in keeping with the etiquette of practising barristers, ordered him to take off his turban. A year ago, as a visitor in a lower court in Durban, Gandhi had walked out rather than give in to this humiliation. Now, as an advocate of Supreme Court, he swallowed the bitter pill with the reflection that, if he was to fight colour prejudice, he must choose bigger issues and other occasions.

Gandhi felt that what the Indians urgently needed was a permanent organization to look after their interests. Out of deference to Dadabhai Naoroji, who had presided over the Indian National Congress in 1893, he called the new organization Natal Indian Congress. He was not conversant with the constitution and functions of the Indian National Congress. This ignorance proved an asset, as he fashioned the Natal Congress in his own way to suit the needs of the Natal Indians. The Indian National Congress of this period was a debating society of the intelligentsia which was hardly heard of between its annual pageants of speeches and petitions and protests. The Natal Indian Congress was, however, designed as a live body, functioning throughout the year and dedicated not only to politics but to the moral and social uplift of its members. Though it served a community which had very little political experience, it was not a one-man show. An indefatigable secretary though he was, Gandhi enlisted popular interest and enthusiasm at every step. He made the enrolment of members and the collection of subscriptions into something more than a routine. He employed a gentle but irresistible technique for exerting moral pressure on half-hearted supporters. Once in a small village, he sat through the night and refused to take his dinner until at dawn his host, an Indian merchant, agreed to raise his subscription for the Natal Indian Congress from three to six pounds.

Since his student days in London Gandhi had kept a meticulous account of his daily expenses. He exercised a similar vigilance on the finances of the Natal Indian Congress. So efficiently were its accounts maintained that thirty years later he could write; 'I dare say, the account books of the year 1894 can be found intact even today in the records of the Natal Indian Congress'. For himself he refused to accept anything from public funds. He felt that if he became a paid advocate of the Indian community, he could not remain its fearless servant; honorary public service was thus not only a duty to his people, but also a safeguard of his own independence. In these early years of his political apprenticeship, he formulated his own code of conduct for a politician. He did not accept the popular view that in politics one must fight for one's party right or wrong. The passion for facts, which he had recently cultivated in his practice of law, he brought to bear on politics; if the facts were on his side, there was no need to embroider on them. He avoided exaggeration and discouraged it in his colleagues. The Natal Indian Congress was not merely an instrument for the defence of political and economic rights of the Indian minority, but also a lever for its internal reform and unity. He did not spare his own people and roundly criticized them for their shortcomings. He asked them to improve their standard of living and integrity in business. He was not only the stoutest champion of the Natal Indians, but also their severest critic.

To appreciate the role which Gandhi and the Natal Indian Congress were to play in the Dark Continent, it would be well at this stage to look back and to see the problem in its historical perspective.

'The Asiatics,' wrote Lord Milner, 'are strangers forcing themselves upon a community reluctant to receive them.' In fact, the Indian emigration to South Africa in the sixties started at the instance of the European settlers who were in possession of vast virgin lands ideal for tea, coffee and sugar plantations, but lacked manpower. The negro could not be compelled to work after the abolition of slavery. The Government of India was therefore approached by the Europeans of Natal for Indian labourers to be permitted to emigrate to that country. Recruiting agents of the planters toured some of the poorest and most congested districts of Madras and Bengal and painted rosy prospects of work in Natal. Free passage, board and lodging; a wage of ten shillings a month for the first year, rising by one shilling every year; and the right to a free return passage to India after five years' 'indenture' (or, alternatively, the option to settle in the land of their adoption), drew thousands of poor and illiterate Indians to distant Natal.

The first shipload of 'indentured labourers' from India arrived in Durban in November 1860. By 1890 nearly 40,000 Indians had been imported as indentured labourers. Theirs was, to use Sir W. W. Hunter's phrase, a condition of semi-slavery. Not all employers were cruel, but it was difficult to change employers on the plea of ill-treatment, and if a labourer did not renew his 'indenture' after five years, he was hemmed in by all sorts of restrictions. Nevertheless, many of these labourers already cut off from their roots in India, preferred to settle in Natal. They bought small plots of land, grew vegetables, made a decent living and educated their children. This excited the jealousy of the European traders who began to agitate for the repatriation of every Indian labourer who did not renew his term. In other words, the Indian was wanted in Natal as a slave or not at all. In 1885 a commission on Indian immigration found European public opinion heavily weighted against the presence of free Indians whether in agriculture or in trade. The commission considered the ex-indentured Indian an asset and his repatriation not only unjust to him but ruinous to the economy of the colony. The argument of enlightened self-interest did not, however, appeal to those who were haunted by the fear that the Indian would under-live and under-sell the European.

The grant of responsible government to Natal in 1893 removed whatever little restraint the Colonial Office in London exercised on the policy of racial discrimination. A delegation from Natal took to India proposals for compulsory indenture or compulsory repatriation of all Indian labourers; alternatively it suggested an annual poll tax of £25 per head. The British Indian officials' ignorance of the conditions in Natal was equalled only by their eagerness to help the European planters in that country. The Government of India agreed to the levy of a £3 tax payable by every member of the family of the ex-indentured labourer who was merely exercising his right to settle in Natal in terms of the agreement which had governed his emigration from India. It was a crippling tax for the poor wretches whose wages as indentured labourers ranged between ten and twelve shillings a month. Poor, illiterate and unorganized, they were helpless and the only quarter from which they could hope for sympathy and support was the Indian merchant.

The Indian merchant had followed the Indian labourer to South Africa and found a ready market among the Indian labourers and the negroes; the latter found that the Indian merchant was more courteous and a little less rapacious than the European merchant. The growing prosperity of the Indian merchant, however, became an irritation to his European rivals. The legislation to disfranchise Indians which had led Gandhi to prolong his stay in Natal was aimed at the Indian trader. The possession of immovable property worth £50 or an annual rental of £10 being the minimum qualification for a vote, only 250 Indians were on the electoral list as against 10,000 European voters. The enrolment of even a few Indians as voters appeared a danger signal to the Europeans, who would not admit the 'niggers' —black, brown or yellow—to a share in the wealth or government of Natal. The politicians of Natal made no secret of their object which, as one of them put it, was 'to degrade the Indian to the level of the Kaffir' and 'to prevent him from forming part of the future South African nation that is going to be built'. The measure was designed, declared another politician, 'to make the Indians' life more comfortable in their native land than in Natal'.

The bill disfranchising the Indians was passed by the Natal Legislature and received the assent of its Governor. The Colonial Office in London, largely influenced by the agitation organized by Gandhi, vetoed the bill on the ground that it discriminated against the inhabitants of another part of the British Empire. The Europeans of Natal were not discouraged by this veto; they sought their object without avowing colour bar as such. An amended bill was passed according to which, 'no natives of countries (not of European origin) which had not hitherto possessed elective representative institutions founded on parliamentary franchise were to be placed on voters' list unless they obtained an exemption from the Governor-General'. Though the amended bill was as effective a check on the Indian franchise as the one which had been vetoed by the British Government, it was something of a gain that racial discrimination had not been written into the statute-book.

Indian trade and immigration also came under galling restrictions. No one could henceforth trade in Natal without a licence which a European could have for the asking and an Indian only after much effort and expense, if at all. And since an educational test in a European language was made a *sine qua non* for an immigrant, the door was barred and bolted against the majority of potential immigrants from India, except, of course, the semi-slave indentured labourers who continued to be imported.

In this anti-Indian campaign, the Europeans of Natal were only following in the footsteps of their Boer neighbours in the Transvaal and Orange Free State. Krüger, the bellicose President of Transvaal (Boer) Republic, had told an Indian deputation: 'You are the descendants of Ishmael and, therefore, from your very birth bound to slave for the descendants of Esau.' A representative of the British Government was stationed in Pretoria, but he pleaded helplessness. When the Boer War broke out, the maltreatment of Indians was part of the indictment against the Boers. The Indians had still to learn that in South Africa they could get no more justice from the Briton than from the Boer.

The legal disabilities on Indians were bad enough, but the daily humiliations they suffered were worse. Every Indian without distinction was called 'a coolie'—a contemptuous word for a labourer. Indian schoolmasters were 'coolie school masters'; Indian store-keepers were 'coolie store-keepers'. Gandhi was 'a coolie barrister'. Even the steamers owned by Indians were called 'coolie ships'. Indians were commonly described as 'Asian dirt to be heartily cursed, chokeful of vice, that lives upon rice, and the black vermin'. In the statute-book they were described as 'semi-barbarous Asiatics, or persons belonging to the uncivilized races of Asia'. They were not allowed to walk on footpaths or to be out at night, without a permit. First and second-class tickets were not issued to them. If a white passenger objected, they could be unceremoniously bundled out of a railway compartment; they had sometimes to travel on footboards of trains. European hotels would not admit them. 'Natal,' wrote the *Cape Times*, 'presents the curious spectacle of a country entertaining a supreme contempt for the very class of people she can least do without. Imagination can only picture the commercial paralysis which would inevitably attend the withdrawal of the Indian population from that colony. And yet the Indian is the most despised of creatures.'

In Transvaal, Indians could not trade or reside except in specified locations which the London *Times* described as ghettoes. In Orange Free State, there was a law prohibiting Asiatics and other coloured persons from trading or carrying on any business whatsoever. 'Wherever the Indian goes,' wrote the *Cape Times*, 'he is the same useful well-doing man, law-abiding under whatever form of government he may find himself, frugal in his wants and industrious in his habits. But these virtues make him a formidable competitor in the labour markets to which he resorts.' As Lionel Curtis told Gandhi many years later, it was the virtues, rather than the vices of the Indians, which had aroused the jealousy of the European and exposed them to political persecution.

Chapter 6

LYNCHED

WHAT with his public activities and what with his legal work it looked as if Gandhi was now settled in Natal. In the middle of 1896 he visited India to fetch his family, and incidentally, to canvass whatever support he could for the Indian cause in South Africa.

From Calcutta, where he landed, he took a train for Bombay *en route* to Rajkot. When the train reached Allahabad, he utilized the forty-five minute halt for sight-seeing in the town and returned to the railway station just in time to see his train steam away. During this enforced stay at Allahabad, he called on Chesney, the editor of the *Pioneer*, who did not disguise his sympathy with the South African whites, but was sporting enough to promise that the columns of his paper would be open to the Indian point of view.

On arrival at Rajkot, Gandhi devoted the better part of a month to the writing of a pamphlet on the Indian problem in South Africa and had it printed and despatched to influential public men and newspapers all over the country. This pamphlet covered, though more cautiously, the same ground as his earlier pamphlets in Natal, *An Appeal to Every Briton in South Africa* and *The Indian Franchise*.

He followed up this pamphlet with a country-wide tour to educate public opinion. In Bombay he had an audience with the 'uncrowned king' of that town, Sir Pherozeshah Mehta, whom he had regarded since his student days in London with a reverence bordering upon awe. Under the distinguished patronage of Sir Pherozeshah, a meeting was called to hear Gandhi on South Africa. As he rose to read the script he had been warned to prepare, the crowded hall seemed to whirl before him, his hands trembled and his voice trailed away into nothingness. The rest of the speech was read with good effect by Wacha, a local orator.

In Poona, he met the two giants of Maharashtrian politics—Gokhale and Tilak. Gokhale who had devoted himself whole-heartedly to public life, was always on the look-out for patriotic young men; the earnestness of the young barrister from South Africa impressed him at once. On Gandhi's side it was a case of 'love at first sight'. Immediately, the interesting fact was that Gokhale and Tilak, who disagreed about almost everything agreed jointly to sponsor a public meeting in Poona to hear the grievances of the Indians in South Africa. The great Tilak, a politician to his finger tips, could not help observing that the young lawyer from Natal was hopelessly unfamiliar with Indian politics.

The poise and leadership which had come so naturally to Gandhi in South Africa was missing on Indian soil. He became morbidly conscious of his youth and inexperience. Sir Pherozeshah Mehta reminded him of the Himalayas, Tilak of the ocean and Gokhale of the holy Ganges. The 'debacle' at the meeting in Bombay, when he was unable to finish his speech, was painfully reminiscent of the break-down four years earlier in a local court which had compelled him to quit Bombay and the profession of a solicitor for that of a scribe at Rajkot. It was a fortunate circumstance that his political career began in South Africa. If he had entered politics in India at that time, the odds were heavy that he would have floundered hopelessly. Apart from the sense of immaturity which haunted him in the homeland, Indian politics at this time offered few outlets for his constructive genius, and were beginning to be riddled with personal and factional rivalries. The uniform kindness which he received from prominent politicians was due to the fact that the cause he championed, that of Indians overseas, was common ground among politicians of all shades.

The Presidency of Madras, from which the majority of indentured labourers in Natal hailed, gave Gandhi a very warm welcome. He received unstinted support from leaders of public opinion and the Press, particularly the influential *Hindu*. The pamphlet on the Indians' condition in South Africa sold like hot cakes and a reprint became necessary. In Calcutta, the response from the local leaders and the Press was not so cordial. Nevertheless, two British owned papers, the *Statesman* and the *Englishman*, featured interviews with him.

While plans were afoot for holding a public meeting in Calcutta, Gandhi received a cable from Natal urging him to return immediately. The trip ended abruptly, but it had served the cause nearest to his heart. It had stimulated the interest of the homeland in the condition of Indians overseas. Public meetings had been held under influential auspices in the principal towns, and the Press, including its Anglo-Indian section, had pulled out the skeleton in the imperial cupboard.

One definite disappointment of the tour must, however, be recorded. Gandhi's efforts to induce some educated young men to throw in their lot with him in the service of the Indians in South Africa bore no fruit. One of his friends in fact advised him not to fritter away his life in far-off Natal in fighting a hopeless cause on behalf of its tiny Indian minority while the millions of Indians were still without the blessings of self-government. Gandhi was, however, not the man to give up a cause once he had taken it up. To him South Africa offered a field for public service, as active as any, and with its own peculiar risks and rewards. As he wrote to a young barrister whom he was urging to come to Natal: 'In any case I cannot be too plain in saying that no one in our position should go to South Africa with a view to pile money. You should go there with a spirit of self-sacrifice.'[1]

The spirit of sacrifice for which he was pleading, he was to need himself on his return to South Africa. Distorted versions of his activities and utterances had reached Natal and inflamed Europeans of that colony. A four line cable from Reuter's London office was featured prominently in Natal papers. It ran:

[1] Quoted in *Mahatma* (Volume I) by Tendulkar—letter dated October 18, 1896.

'September 14. A Pamphlet published in India declares that the Indians in Natal are robbed and assaulted and treated like beasts and are unable to obtain redress. *The Times of India* advocates an inquiry into these allegations.'

The reference was to the pamphlet which Gandhi had published in India. The leading paper of Johannesburg, The *Star*, had once complimented Gandhi for 'writing forcibly, moderately and well', and the *Natal Mercury* had commended 'the calmness and moderation' of his writings. The pamphlet published in India was, if anything, more subdued in tone than what Gandhi had said and written in Natal. His speeches in India had been delivered from carefully prepared texts. So transparent was his sense of fairness that the editor of the *Englishman* of Calcutta had let him see the draft of an editorial on the Indian question in South Africa.

The truth about Gandhi's activities in India did not, however, percolate to Natal. Meanwhile, the cable from London made him the most hated man in the colony. He was accused of smearing the country which had harboured him and of 'dragging the Europeans of Natal in the gutter and painting them as black as his own skin'. He was alleged to have organized an agency to flood Natal with Indian immigrants. It so happened that the s.s. *Courland*, by which the Gandhi family travelled, and another ship the s.s. *Naderi* had left Bombay for Natal about the same time. Gandhi's first client and friend Abdulla was the owner of one ship and the agent of the other. The two ships had about 800 passengers on board, half of them bound for Natal. It was just a coincidence that the two ships had sailed almost at the same time at the end of November 1896, and that they arrived together in Durban harbour on December 19. To the Europeans of Natal, already excited by Reuter's report, the coincidence looked like a conspiracy. Two thousand Europeans met in the town hall of Durban and called on the Natal Government to prevent the 'free Indians' from disembarking. They took a pledge that 'every man at this meeting agrees and binds himself with a view to assisting the Government to do all his country may require of him'. There

was more than a veiled hint of the use of force against the Indians
in the two ships. When another meeting was held a few days later,
the hall resounded with the cries of 'Sink the ship'.

After the ships had cast anchor in the port, the Europeans did
their best to coax, cajole or coerce the Indians. A free return
passage was dangled before those who would agree to go back;
and those who declined were threatened that they would be
pushed into the sea. The shipowners were warned to return their
unwelcome cargo to India or incur the implacable wrath of the
Government and Europeans of Natal. The ships were placed under
quarantine; when the duration of quarantine was prolonged from
five days to three weeks, its political use was obvious. These
tactics had the support of influential Europeans, including Harry
Escombe, the Attorney-General of Natal. If the Indians, most of
whom were illiterate and on their first voyage with their families,
did not succumb to these threats, it was due to Gandhi's infectious
courage and optimism. For him these were anxious days. The
lives of these passengers, most of whom he did not know, and
those of his own family were in jeopardy on his account; it was
he who was *bête noire* of the Europeans of Natal. On Christmas
Day, 1896, there was a small party in the Captain's cabin and
somebody asked Gandhi what he would do if the Natal Europeans
were as good as their word and forcibly prevented the landing of
Indians. 'I hope,' he said, 'God will give me the courage and
sense to forgive them, and to refrain from bringing them to law.
I have no anger against them. I am only sorry for their ignorance
and their narrowness.'

When twenty-three days of this political quarantine and
threats failed to browbeat the Indians, the ships were permitted to
enter the harbour on January 13, 1897. Escombe, who had done
much to fan the fanaticism of the Europeans, now tried to check
it. In the name of the Queen he commanded the mob of nearly
4,000 men, who had collected to oppose the landing, to disperse.
The Indians were allowed to disembark with the exception of
Gandhi, who had received a message from Escombe to wait till
the evening, when he would be escorted by the Superintendent of

the Water Police. In the afternoon, however, Laughton, a European lawyer and friend of Gandhi, came aboard and announced that all danger was at an end and that in any case it was undignified for Gandhi to slip into Durban 'like a thief in the night'. It was therefore decided that Mrs Gandhi and children would immediately drive to the house of Rustomji, the Gandhis' host, and Gandhi and Laughton would join them later on foot. They had not walked far when some European boys recognized Gandhi. A crowd began to collect; as it swelled, it became more and more menacing. Laughton hailed a rickshaw to save his friend, but the Zulu boy pulling the rickshaw was scared away. Laughton and Gandhi began to walk together followed by the mob. When they reached West street, Laughton was torn away. A hailstorm of rotten eggs and brickbats raged round Gandhi. 'Are you the man who wrote to the Press?' shouted a European and gave a brutal kick. Gandhi nearly fainted, held the railings of a house to regain his breath and staggered along. He had given up hope of reaching home alive; he recalled later that even at this critical moment his heart did not arraign his assailants. 'Then a beautiful and brave thing happened'. Mrs Alexander, the wife of the local Superintendent of Police, came on the scene. She recognized Gandhi, began to walk alongside him and opened her sunshade to keep off the flying missiles. The Europeans had run amuck, but they dared not raise their hand against a white woman. Meanwhile, a few constables arrived and escorted Gandhi to the house of his host.

Hardly had Gandhi's wounds been dressed when a European mob surrounded the house and threatened to burn it if Gandhi did not surrender. Superintendent Alexander posted himself at the gate and began to humour the mob to gain a little time. Meanwhile, he sent word to Gandhi to agree to being smuggled out of the house if he did not want to have all the inmates, including women and children, roasted alive. Dressed as an Indian constable, with a metal saucer under his turban, and attended by a detective dressed as an Indian merchant, Gandhi slipped through the crowd and after jumping fences, squeezing between rails and passing through a store, reached the police station.

He did not have to remain in the police station for long. The Natal Europeans had been provoked by Reuter's brief and somewhat garbled report of Gandhi's activities in India. On the morning of the day on which he was assaulted, in an interview with a Press correspondent, he had explained away the various charges against him. There was a belated recognition that he had been the victim of a misunderstanding. 'Mr Gandhi is within his rights,' wrote the *Natal Mercury*, no sympathiser of the Indian cause, 'and so long as he acts honestly, and in a straightforward manner, he cannot be blamed or interfered with. So far we know, he has always done so, and his latest pamphlet, we cannot honestly say, is an unfair statement of the case from his point of view. Reuter's cable is a gross exaggeration of Mr Gandhi's statement.'

The Secretary of State for Colonies in London cabled to the Natal Government to prosecute Gandhi's assailants. Gandhi's reaction was characteristic. It was, he said, a principle with him not to seek redress of a personal wrong in a court of law; and in any case it was hardly fair to haul up a few hot-headed young men for acts of violence without calling influential Europeans to account, including members of the Natal Government who had worked up the Europeans of Durban to white heat.

That day, January 13, 1897 was fateful. Gandhi had escaped from the very jaws of death. His poise and magnanimity had raised him not only in the affections of the Indians, but in the esteem of the saner Europeans in Natal. He continued to serve the Natal Indian Congress and to organize the Indian community. In 1899, when the Boer War broke out, he was faced with a major decision on the attitude which the Indian community should adopt towards the conflict which was to change, for better or for worse, the history of South Africa.

Chapter 7

STONES FOR BREAD

THE outbreak of the Boer War in 1899 was the final phase in the struggle between the Boer and the British for hegemony in South Africa. The Indians had been badly treated by both Boers and British, though more blatantly by the former, and some of them were not sorry at the prospect of the two races bleeding each other white. Gandhi's own ideas on non-violence and pacifism had not yet matured. It was, he felt, neither possible nor desirable for each citizen to determine in such a crisis on which side the balance of justice lay. The Indians in Natal had been denied elementary rights as citizens, but Gandhi argued that those who even claimed rights could not escape corresponding obligations. The suggestion that the Boers were likely to win and that Indian neutrality would pay dividends after the war he dismissed as downright cowardice. Twenty years later, when he had completed the transition from the loyalist to the rebel, he was unrepentant for his decision in 1899 to support the British in the Boer War: 'If I had today the faith in the British Empire which I had then entertained, and if I now cherished the hope which I did at that time of achieving our freedom, under its aegis, I would advance the same argument today.'[1]

He succeeded in swinging the majority of the Indians in Natal to his point of view. The Government was, however, in no hurry to avail of the Indians' co-operation. Jameson, a member of the Natal Legislative Council, told Gandhi: 'You Indians know nothing of war. You would only be a drag on the army; you would have to be taken care of, instead of being a help to us.' 'But,' pleaded Gandhi, 'Is there nothing we can do? Can we not do

[1] Gandhi: *Satyagraha in South Africa*, Madras, 1928. p. 116.

ordinary servants' work in connection with the hospitals? Surely, that will not demand very great intelligence?' 'No,' replied Jameson, 'it all needs training.' It was only when General Buller's forces were suffering heavy casualities on the banks of the river Tugela and British morale touched a low ebb that the Indians' offer was accepted, and the formation of an Indian Ambulance Corps permitted. The corps consisted of nearly 1,100 Indians with Dr Booth of the Indian Anglican Mission as Medical Superintendent and Gandhi its *de facto* leader. The corps reached the front on the eve of the action at Colenso, where it spent a strenuous week. The next summons came on the eve of the battle of Spionkop. The corps was in the field for about three weeks. It was the duty of the 'bearers', as the rank and file of the Indian Ambulance Corps were known, to receive the wounded outside the line of fire, and to tramp with them to the base about twenty miles away. Even though their terms of service did not require them to serve within the firing line, the Indians did so cheerfully on several occasions.

Vere Stent, the editor of the *Pretoria News* has left a pen-portrait of Gandhi in the battlefield: 'After a night's work which had shattered men with much bigger frames, I came across Gandhi in the early morning sitting by the roadside—eating a regulation army biscuit. Every man in (General) Buller's force was dull and depressed, and damnation was heartily invoked on everything. But Gandhi was stoical in his bearing, cheerful and confident in his conversation and had a kindly eye.'

The ambulance corps consisted of 1,100 men out of whom 300 were free Indians and the rest indentured labourers. It was a motley crowd; barristers and accountants, artisans and labourers; it was Gandhi's task to keep them together and to charge them with a spirit of service in the cause of those whom they regarded as their oppressors.

The work of the Indian Ambulance Corps was mentioned in General Buller's despatches and the thirty-seven 'leaders' of the Indian Ambulance Unit received war-medals. The Indian effort, considered as a contribution to the British victory in the Boer

War, may have been, as Gandhi would have been the first to admit, insignificant, but it was a fine gesture on the part of an oppressed minority. For a while the Indians were flattered by being greeted in the European Press as the 'Sons of the Empire'. And among those who personally complimented Gandhi were a number of Europeans who had been the ring-leaders of the anti-Indian demonstration in Durban which nearly ended in the lynching of Gandhi in January 1897.

When the issue of the war was no longer in doubt Gandhi felt that the change in the political climate had made it possible for him to return to India. The Natal Indians relieved him reluctantly and on condition that he would return if they required him within a year.

He landed at Bombay at the end of 1901, just in time to attend the Calcutta session of the Indian National Congress. He was shocked at the lack of organization in the Congress camp; the sanitary conditions were exactly ideal for an epidemic. An unfamiliar figure among Indian politicians, he could move about unnoticed, and with characteristic modesty served as 'a clerk and a bearer' to the Secretary of the Congress. He piloted a resolution through the Congress on the condition of the Indians in South Africa. After the Congress session he stayed on for a month with Gokhale whose kindly interest in Gandhi had not abated since they first met during Gandhi's visit to India in 1896. It was Gokhale's ambition to launch Gandhi into Indian public life. There was a strong bond of mutual respect between the two men; Gokhale was fascinated by Gandhi's sincerity, zeal and method, and Gandhi by Gokhale's complete dedication to the service of India.

Gandhi paid a flying visit to Rangoon, where he saw the golden pagoda, the foongis, 'the freedom and energy of the Burmese women', and 'indolence of the men'. Back in Calcutta, he travelled by train to his hometown Rajkot, visiting Banaras, Agra, Jaipur and Palanpur *en route*. He chose to travel third class and stayed mostly in 'dharamshalas'; the journey was devoid of comfort, but it enabled him to see for himself the hardships of the third-class passenger and the corruption which disfigured the places of Hindu pilgrimage.

After practising for a while in the Rajkot courts, he moved down to Bombay, where Gokhale had urged him to settle and to take a hand in the affairs of the Indian National Congress. He moved into a fine bungalow in Santa Cruz, and quickly built up a good practice. Gokhale was happy; an able and earnest worker had been added to the not-too-thick phalanx of Indian patriots. But all the plans, Gandhi's and Gokhale's, went by the board when a cable arrived from South Africa, urging Gandhi to return to lead the Indian settlers in the crisis that faced them.

The occasion for the urgent summons from South Africa was the visit to that country of Chamberlain, the Colonial Secretary in the British Cabinet, and the opportunity it provided for representing the grievances, new as well as old, of the Indian settlers.

When the Boer War had broken out, Lord Lansdowne, the British Secretary of State for War, had declared that of all the misdeeds of the Boers, none filled him with so much indignation as their treatment of 'British Indians' in Transvaal. The Boer Governments of Transvaal and Orange Free State had made no secret of their racial arrogance and freely enacted discriminatory laws against Indians, but they had far too many preoccupations, including the recurring threat to their existence, to be able to enforce these laws rigorously.

At the end of the Boer War, the British Government appointed a committee to scan the Boer statute-book, and to repeal the laws which were repugnant to the spirit of the British Constitution and inconsistent with the liberty of Queen Victoria's subjects. The committee interpreted the liberty of the subject as the liberty of the white subject; the Indians thus remained outside the pale of the reformed code. In fact, all the anti-Indian laws of the Boer régime were compiled in a handy manual. 'The British rulers of Transvaal', declared Sir Henry Cotton, the President of the Indian National Congress in 1904, 'had applied themselves with British vigour and precision to the task of enforcing the Boer laws. In dealing with Indian colonists their little finger has been thicker than Mr Krüger's loins and where he had whips, they have chastised with scorpions.' A new department, largely manned by British officers who had served in India, was set up to deal with the Asiatics in Transvaal. It became an instrument of bureaucratic tyranny and used the emergency powers, assumed by the Government during the period immediately following the war, to shut out even returning refugees who had spent many years in Transvaal and had left the country on the outbreak of the war.

When Gandhi landed at Durban in December 1902, he found that the Indians had to free themselves not only from the old chains fastened on them in Natal, but also the new chains being forged for them in Transvaal. He headed a deputation of Natal Indians, which waited on the Colonial Secretary at Durban. Chamberlain gave the usual 'patient hearing' to the Indian deputation, but argued that the colonies were self-governing and the Indians had better come to terms with the colonists.

From Natal the Colonial Secretary was to visit Transvaal. Through his old friend Alexander, Superintendent of Police in Durban, Gandhi secured a permit to enter Transvaal to represent to the Colonial Secretary the case of Transvaal Indians, but the Transvaal Government excluded him from the Indian deputation which was to wait upon the Colonial Secretary. This was not only an insult to Gandhi; it was a portent of what was in store for the Indians in Transvaal.

The assignment for which he had been recalled from India— the interview with the Colonial Secretary—was over. For Gandhi the temptation to return to his family, and professional and public activities in India was strong; but the peril to the Indian community was so palpable and its trust in him so great that he decided to prolong the self-imposed exile. In 1893 he had come to South Africa for a year and stayed for eight years; in 1902 he had come for six months and was to stay for twelve years. He resolved that he must live in South Africa until 'the gathering clouds were dispersed or until they broke upon and swept all away, all our counteracting efforts notwithstanding'.

He had himself enrolled as an attorney of the Transvaal Supreme Court and set up his office at Johannesburg, which was henceforth to be the centre of his activities.

A new phase opened in Gandhi's career. The racial and anti-Indian policies of the European colonies in Natal and Transvaal, far from being reversed by the victory of the British over the Boers, were receiving a new impetus. The Indians had to fight not for equality with Europeans but even for elementary civic rights, and for preservation of interests which they had built by dint of hard work over a quarter of a century. Evidently the struggle was an unequal one and there was no knowing how long it would be protracted. Gandhi, by taking upon himself the responsibility of leading it, had burnt his boats; his own career and family were as nothing beside the cause he had taken up. His life underwent a transformation, not only in externals, in his style of living, but also in the acquisition of new values.

The story of this transformation is not only fascinating in itself, but reveals the springs of that moral and spiritual strength which enabled him to play a unique role in the public life of two continents.

Chapter 8

THE RELIGIOUS QUEST

GANDHI's father Karamchand, the *Diwan* of Porbandar and later of Rajkot, was a man of the world without much of the spiritual in his make-up. He possessed, however, the religious culture which was part of the equipment of his age and class. During his long illness, he occasionally invited to his bedside Hindu pundits, Jain monks, and Parsi and Muslim divines, for discussions on religious matters. Mohan, as his father's nurse, was often present at these discussions and though he could hardly have followed them, the fact that men of different faiths joined in a friendly debate gave him an early lesson in tolerance.

Gandhi's mother Putlibai was completely wrapped up in religion. Her life was an interminable round of fasts and religious observances. There was, however, no provision in the Gandhi household for a regular instruction in religion, a serious omission for a child like Mohan whose interest in moral and religious questions was, to say the least, precocious. The glitter and pomp of religious ritual did not satisfy him. Looking through the books in his father's library, he came across in the *Manusmriti* the story of the Creation; it sounded apocryphal to him, but nobody bothered to resolve his doubts. His confusion increased when, contrary to the practice at home, meat-eating seemed to have the imprimatur of Manu, the law-giver. He began to gravitate towards atheism which, as we have already noted, was a part of his adolescent rebellion against all authority.

When at the age of eighteen Gandhi arrived in London, his acquaintance with the religion of his birth was of the meagerest. It was with some embarrassment that he owned to his Theosophist friends, who had invited him to read Sir Edwin Arnold's *The*

Song Celestial that he had never read *Bhagavad Gita* in Sanskrit, or even in Gujerati, his mother tongue. This was his introduction to a book which was to become his 'spiritual reference book'. Another book of Sir Edwin's *The Light of Asia*, also fascinated him; the story of Gautama Buddha—his life, renunciation and teaching—stirred him to his depths.

Gandhi did not join the Theosophical Society, but its literature stimulated his interest in religion. It was in England too that he was introduced to the Bible by a fellow vegetarian-enthusiast. The New Testament, particularly the Sermon on the Mount, went straight to his heart. The verses, 'But I say unto you that ye resist not evil; but whosoever shall smite thee on thy right cheek, turn to him the other also. And if any man will sue thee at the law, and take away thy coat, let him have thy cloke also', reminded him of the lines of the Gujerati poet, Shamlal Bhatt, which he used to hum as a child:

> For a bowl of water give a goodly meal ;
> For a kindly greeting bow thou down with zeal ;
> For a single penny pay thou back with gold ;
> If thy life be rescued, life do not withhold.
> Thus the words and actions of the wise regard ;
> Every little service tenfold they reward.
> But the truly noble know all men as one,
> And return with gladness good for evil done.

The teachings of the Bible, the Buddha and Bhatt fused in his mind. The idea of returning love for hatred, and good for evil captivated him; he did not yet comprehend it fully, but it continued to ferment in his impressionable mind. Before Gandhi left England, he had already crossed 'the Sahara of atheism'[1] into which he had strayed in his adolescence.

During his first year in South Africa he came across some ardent Quakers who perceived his religious bent and decided to annex him to Christianity. They loaded him with books on Christian theology and history; they preached at him, and

[1] *Autobiography*, p. 92.

C

prayed with him and for him. Finally, they took him to a Convention of Protestant Christians in the hope that mass emotion would sweep him off his feet. Gandhi was lavish in praising the nobility of the Quakers' character, but said blandly that he felt no inner call to renounce Hinduism and to embrace Christianity.

It appeared to Gandhi's Christian friends that he had been on the brink of a conversion, but had, for some unknown reasons, stepped back. The first impact of Quaker proselytizing in a strange country was doubtless strong on him, but he was in no greater hurry to become a Christian in Pretoria than he had been to become a Theosophist in London. His knowledge of Hinduism was yet superficial, but he felt with the religion of his birth a strong bond of sentiment. One of his Quaker friends, Coates, asked him to cast off his necklace of *Vaishnava* beads. 'This superstition does not become you. Come, let me break the necklace,' suggested Coates. 'No you will not,' replied Gandhi, 'it is a sacred gift from my mother.' 'But do you believe in it?' asked Coates. 'I do not know its mysterious significance,' rejoined Gandhi, 'I do not think I should come to harm if I did not wear it. But I cannot without sufficient reason give up the necklace that she put round my neck out of love.'[1] The necklace was a symbol; he could no more discard Hinduism, without sufficient reason, than the necklace, both having come down to him from his beloved parents. Again, if certain aspects of Christianity—the life and death of Jesus, the Sermon on the Mount and the crystalline purity of some Christians—appealed to him, there were other aspects of Christianity which repelled him. As a child he had heard a Christian missionary in Rajkot ridicule Hindu gods and goddesses at street corners, and had also learnt to associate conversion to Christianity with meat-eating, smoking and drinking—terrible sins in the eyes of the *Vaishnava* community to which the Gandhis belonged. He had noticed that children of Indian labourers who had been born in Natal and converted to Christianity were under the thumb of European clergymen.

[1] *Autobiography*, p. 154-155.

Apart from these associations with conversion, he had what may be called doctrinal difficulties. He came across interpretations of Christianity which contradicted current beliefs. When he had read Tolstoy's *Kingdom of God is Within You*, he felt he had learnt more from it than from all the books which his Quaker friends had given him. Tolstoy had condemned Christian churches of all denominations for perverting the true teaching of Christ to maintain their power over the masses, and had drawn pointed attention to the contradiction between Christ's teachings and the daily life of Christians. In an earlier book, *What I believe*, Tolstoy had argued that Christ was not merely the founder of a religion of worship and personal salvation, but that Christ's teachings constituted a philosophical, moral, and social doctrine. These views of a Christian anarchist proved an effective counterblast to the indoctrination attempted by the Quakers. Gandhi found himself unable to accept certain basic beliefs of Christianity. He could not believe in a historical Jesus. 'God did not,' he said, 'bear the Cross only 1,900 years ago but He bears it today.' Nor could he agree that Jesus by His death and by His blood redeemed the sins of the world. According to Gandhi, what the world needed was not redemption from the consequences of sin, but from sin itself. He could not concede the exclusive claim on behalf of Christianity as the only true religion; he could not 'set Jesus on a solitary throne:[1] He (Jesus) affects my life no less, because I regard him as one among the many begotton Sons of God. The adjective "begotton" has for me a deeper, possibly a grander meaning than its literal meaning. For me it means spiritual birth.'

Though he visited a renowned Indian Christian for 'enlightenment' as late as 1901, the possibilities of his conversion had already long receded. He began to study other religions, including his own, and came to the conclusion that all religions are right and every one of them is imperfect because they are 'interpreted with poor intellects, sometimes with poor hearts, and more often misinterpreted'. The essay on 'Hero As Prophet' in Carlyle's

[1] Doke, J.: *M. K. Gandhi, An Indian Patriot in South Africa*, p. 94.

Hero Worship had first introduced him to Islam. He read a translation of the Koran and the life of the Prophet Mohammed by Washington Irving, and was struck by the poverty and humility of the Prophet, and by the courage with which he and his first followers had faced the humiliations and hardships heaped upon them.

While books on Christianity and Islam were easily available in South Africa, Gandhi had to send for books on Hinduism from India. He began to correspond on religious subjects with his friend Raychandbhai, who counselled him to be patient and to seek in Hinduism 'its unique subtlety and profundity of thought, its vision of the soul and its clarity'. Raychandbhai's scholarly exposition reinforced Gandhi's sentimental bond with Hinduism and was decisive during the period when his Christian friends believed him to be on the way to baptism.

The book which was ultimately to form his strongest bond with Hinduism as well as the greatest influence in his life was the *Bhagavad Gita*. He had read it in 1890, in Sir Edwin Arnold's verse rendering *The Song Celestial*. In South Africa, he studied other translations with the original, and the book became his daily reading. He memorized one verse every morning while going through his morning toilet, until he had the entire poem by heart. The *Mahabharata* the epic of which the *Gita* forms a part, with its central story of the family feud of the Kaurvas and the Pandavas and the final carnage on the battlefield of Kurukshetra, has been a part of Hindu heritage for at least 2,500 years. From the first Gandhi felt that the epic was an allegorical and not a historical work. The real object of the *Gita*, as Gandhi understood it, was to point to the goal of self-realization and to show that 'detached activity'—without fear of consequences or desire for a reward—was the means to the achievement of the goal. Gandhi considered that this 'detached activity' was impossible without adhering to the principle of non-violence in its widest sense. He did not accept the literal interpretation of the *Gita* as the poetic presentation of Lord Krishna's exhortation to Arjuna, the warrior, to go forward and meet his cousins in combat; the battlefield of Kurukshetra was only a symbol of the battle between good and evil which rages in every human heart, Duryodhan and his party being the baser impulses in man, Arjuna and his party the higher impulses, and Krishna 'the dweller within'. To those who insisted on taking the story of *Mahabharata* literally, Gandhi pointed out that even if the story was taken at its face value, the author of *Mahabharata* had demonstrated the futility of violence in an unmistakable manner; the war had ended in a universal devastation in which the victors were no better off than the vanquished.

This view of the *Gita* was in sharp conflict with the traditional view and with the interpretations of such eminent authorities as Bal Gangadhar Tilak and Aurobindo Ghose. To deny the historical account of the battle of Kurukshetra was, according to the scholars, to fly in the face of facts; they had a shrewd suspicion that Gandhi had given a twist to the *Gita* to fit it to his doctrine of non-violence, and that his view was tinged by the study of the Bible, particularly the Sermon on the Mount.

Gandhi has acknowledged how the passage in the Sermon on the Mount—'Whosoever shall smite thee on thy right cheek, turn to him the other also'—had gripped him when he first read it as a student. But as Vincent Sheean rightly points out: 'From this to an assumption that his was a Christian interpretation of the *Gita*, is an unjustifiable step. If you grant him the initial bold leap in which Kurukshetra becomes the heart of man, all the rest of his interpretation is within the framework of the Upanishads and the text of the *Gita*. His reasons for making this bold leap were all based upon his perception of self-evident truth (i.e. self-evident to him) as shown by the long study of the *Gita* itself.'

Gandhi could spend hours dissecting a verse, but he knew he was no scholar. He did not, however, regard the *Gita* as a book for the learned; its message was meant to be lived: 'Let it be granted that according to the letter of the *Gita* it is possible to say that warfare is consistent with the renunciation of fruit (of action). But after forty years' unremitting endeavour fully to enforce the

<hr>

[1] Sheean, Vincent: *Lead Kindly Light*, p. 291.

teaching of the *Gita* in my own life, I have in all humility felt that perfect renunciation is impossible without perfect observance of *ahimsa* in every shape and form.'[1]

He refused to admit that any book, however sacred, could be limited to a single interpretation irrespective of time and place; the meanings of great writings were subject to 'a process of evolution'. If the author of the *Gita* had not seen the contradiction between the 'detached action' and violence, it did not prevent Gandhi from exercising his judgment.

The *Gita* became Gandhi's 'spiritual dictionary' and an 'infallible' guide to conduct: 'When I see not one ray of light on the horizon, I turn to the *Bhagavad Gita* and find a verse to comfort me. I immediately begin to smile in the midst of overwhelming sorrow. My life has been full of external tragedies and if they have not left any visible and indelible effect on me, I owe it to the teachings of the *Bhagavad Gita*.'[2]

The two words *aparigraha* (non-possession) and *sambhava* (equability) opened to him limitless vistas. 'Non-possession' implied that he had to jettison the material goods which cramped the life of the spirit, to shake off the bonds of money, property and sex, and to regard himself as the trustee, not the owner of what could not be shed. 'Equability' required that he must remain unruffled by pain or pleasure, victory or defeat, and work without hope of success or fear of failure, in short, 'without hankering after the fruit of action'. Only thus could he treat alike 'insulting, insolent and corrupt officials, co-workers of yesterday raising meaningless opposition and men who had always been good to him'. Years later, Gandhi confided to a group of Christian missionaries: 'Hinduism as I know it entirely satisfies my soul, fills my whole being and I find a solace in the *Bhagavad Gita* which I miss even in the Sermon on the Mount.' The Hindu belief in the oneness of all life confirmed and sustained his own faith in *ahimsa* (non-violence). He did not accept every Hindu

---

[1] Desai, M. D.: *The Gita According to Gandhi*, p. 130.
[2] Natesan: *Speeches and Writings of Mahatma Gandhi*, Madras (Fourth Edition), p. 1061.

tenet or practice. He applied the 'acid test of reason' to every formula of every religion. When scriptural sanction was cited for inhumane or unjust practices, his reaction was one of frank disbelief. The oft-quoted text, 'for women there can be no freedom', ascribed to Manu the law-giver, he regarded as an interpolation, and if not, then he could only say that in Manu's time the women did not receive the status they deserved. Similarly, he lashed out against those who supported untouchability with verses from the Vedas. His Hinduism was ultimately reduced to a few fundamental beliefs: in the supreme reality of God, the unity of all life and the value of love (*ahimsa*) as a means of realizing God. In this bedrock religion there was no scope for exclusiveness or narrowness. It was in his view a beauty of Hinduism that: 'in it there is a room for the worship of all the prophets of the world. It is not a missionary religion in the ordinary sense of the word . . . Hinduism tells every one to worship God according to his own faith or *Dharma* and so it lives at peace with all religions'.

He chided Christian missionaries for their 'irreligious gamble' for converts. It was the way a man lived, not the recital of a verse, or the form of a prayer, which made him a good Christian, a good Muslim, or a good Hindu. The missionaries' bid to save souls struck him as presumptuous. Of the aborigines and hillmen of Assam he said; 'what have I to take to (them), except to go in my nakedness to them? Rather than ask them to join my prayer, I would join their prayer'.

The study of comparative religion, the browsing on theological works, the conversations and correspondence with the learned, brought him to the conclusion that true religion was more a matter of the heart than of the intellect, and that genuine beliefs were those which were literally lived. This was something beyond the grasp of those who had acquired, in the words of Swift, enough religion to hate one another, but not enough to love one another. In his lifetime Gandhi was variously labelled a *Sanatanist* (orthodox) Hindu, a renegade Hindu, a Buddhist, a Theosophist, a Christian and 'a Christian-Mohammedan'. He was all these and more; he saw an underlying unity in the clash of doctrines and forms. 'God is not encased in a safe,' he wrote to a correspondent who had urged him to save his soul by conversion to Christianity, 'to be approached only through a little hole in it, but He is open to be approached through billions of openings by those who are humble and pure of heart.'[1]

---

[1] *The Diaries of Mahadev Desai*, Vol. I; entry dated September 4, 1932.

Chapter 9

TRANSFORMATION

WHEN Gandhi returned from England in 1891 he began, as indeed was expected of a young barrister in India, to 'modernize' his mode of living. Oatmeal porridge, cocoa, western furnishings and western attire were some of the 'reforms' which added to the mounting expense of the large Gandhi household, to the income of which he was able to contribute very little. The style of a barrister had, however, to be maintained at all costs. When he sailed for Durban in 1893, he could not secure a first-class passage but preferred squeezing himself into the captain's cabin to the indignity of travelling on deck. The humiliations he suffered in South Africa were the more galling because their victim was conscious of his western education and status as a barrister of the Inner Temple.

When his wife and two children accompanied him to Natal, they had to change into the Parsi dress which, next to the European, was considered the most 'modern'. Inured to the freedom of their Kathiawari clothes and diet, it was with some effort that they were persuaded to accept the change. Gandhi acknowledged later that it was not his arguments but his authority that had carried conviction.

Tolstoy has recorded that before his 'conversion' his philosophy of life was 'that one should live so as to have the best for oneself and one's family and not to try to be wiser than life and Nature'. Gandhi had his 'conversion', but even in the years which later seemed to him as unregenerate, he did not live only for himself and his family. In Durban, as well as in Johannesburg, he kept an open table. His clerks and junior counsel usually lodged with him and were treated as members of the family. There were, in

C*

addition, almost always guests in the house, Indians as well as Europeans. For his wife this community living was often an ordeal. There was once a scene, graphically described in the autobiography, when Kasturbai declined to clean the chamber-pot for a Christian clerk of *panchma* (untouchable) parentage. Her prejudice struck her husband as entirely irrational. He insisted that she should not only perform the distasteful task but do so cheerfully, or else leave him. His moral zeal had blinded him with anger, and he could not see how much strain it placed on his wife. Years later he recorded that he had been a 'cruelly kind husband'.

Even in those days of 'ease and comfort', as he described them later, money-making as such did not interest him. As a budding barrister he had been anxious to make good and to contribute to the family coffers, but he would not stoop to lucrative but immoral expedients. He was told that a certain lawyer with a practice of Rs. 3,000 a month was attracting briefs through touts by paying illegal commission. 'I do not need to emulate him,' he replied; 'I should be content with Rs. 300 a month. Father did not earn more.' The nadir of his fortunes was reached when he was turned down for the post of part-time teacher in a Bombay school with a paltry salary of Rs. 70 a month. It was only in South Africa that he found himself as a lawyer. From the £300 which had been promised to him in 1894 as the minimum retaining fee, his income steadily rose to the peak figure of £5,000 a year. His public life helped him in building up his practice, but it also made heavy inroads on his time. Nor did he accept every brief that came to him. He did not view it as his professional obligation to defend a client if he was in the wrong. If he was convinced during the progress of a case that his client had withheld material facts from him, he did not hesitate to repudiate him openly in the court. He had never forgotton how as a child his frank confession of a petty theft had moved his father to forgive-ness and himself to repentance. He believed that an error must be confessed and atoned for. Parsi Rustomji, a wealthy merchant of Durban and close friend of Gandhi, once found himself in trouble for evasion of customs duties and came to him for advice. Instead of preparing a defence for him Gandhi persuaded him to make a clean breast not only of this but also other dubious transactions, and to pay up the tax as well as the penalty. To cap it all, the repentant merchant recorded a confession of his misdeeds and had the document framed and hung in his house for the edification of his descendants.

The first civil suit which Gandhi handled in South Africa had convinced him that litigation usually dragged on because litigants feared the loss of face and the lawyers the loss of fees. With his own clients his relations transcended the cash nexus. His advice was sought on professional as well as personal matters, the best way of balancing a family budget or weaning a baby. Quite a few of his clients took 'water and earth treatment' under his care. One of them, Lutavan Singh, has been immortalized in the pages of *Satyagraha in South Africa* by the ruse he played on his doctor-lawyer. Over seventy, and a sufferer from asthma, he was placed by Gandhi on a course of fasting and massage during which smoking was entirely taboo. Gandhi was worried at the slow progress of his patient and one evening slept at a point from which he could see Lutavan Singh without being observed. In the middle of the night there was a little spark; Gandhi shot out his electric torch and saw Lutavan Singh furtively smoking a cigarette. Lutavan Singh apologized, promised not to smoke during the treatment and, much to the satisfaction of his doctor, quickly recovered.

There were doubtless abler and richer lawyers among Gandhi's contemporaries, but few of them could equal his human approach to the profession of law. When a client failed to pay his dues, Gandhi would not have recourse to law; it was, he said, his own error of judgment which was responsible for the loss. Again, to a colleague who protested that clients came even on Sundays, his answer was: 'a man in distress cannot have Sunday rest'.

Two conflicting trends struggled in Gandhi for expression during the decade which followed his return from England. One was the pull of convention, the desire to live up to the standard of an English-trained barrister, and the other was an inner urge towards simplicity. In London, he had met the Bohemian scholar, Narayan Hemchandra, who in his native *dhoti* and shirt, and with hardly any money on him, had hopped merrily from one continent to another. The inspiration for a simple life also came from the *Gita*, which he read and pondered over every day. The ideal of *aparigraha* (non-possession), grew upon him. Why should he encumber himself with non-essentials? True, he had a family, but surely was it not presumptuous on his part to think that he and not God would provide for them? He decided to cancel the insurance policy for Rs. 10,000 which he had taken at the instance of a loquacious insurance agent. He began to reduce his needs and to pay less and less attention to what passed for prestige in the middle class.

One day there was much amusement in the Durban courts when Gandhi appeared with the starch dripping from his shirt-collar. This was not the handiwork of a careless launderer; it was his own first experiment in washing clothes. On another occasion his fellow-lawyers held their sides with laughter when they saw his hair cropped in a crazy fashion. He explained that the white barber had declined to attend to him, and he had become his own barber. He trained himself as a dispenser in a charitable hospital, attending the indentured labourers, the poorest of the Indians in South Africa. He read diligently on nursing and obstetrics and acted as a midwife at the birth of his youngest son, when the nurse who had been engaged did not turn up in time. Barber, launderer, dispenser, nurse, he was also a schoolmaster. Since he would not accept as a favour for his children what was denied to other children as a right, his children had to stay out of European schools, and to content themselves with the scraps of instruction they could get from their father as they walked with him the ten miles to and from his office in Johannesburg. These peripatetic lessons were often interrupted by clients or colleagues, but despite their mother's protest, Gandhi refused to put his children into European schools.

The trend towards simplicity received a tremendous fillip in

1904. One evening that year, as Gandhi was taking a train from Johannesburg to Durban, his journalist friend Polak gave him a book to read. It was Ruskin's *Unto This Last*. Gandhi sat through the night and read it from cover to cover. Ruskin had denounced classical economists for not conceiving economics in terms of human welfare, and condemned the poverty and the injustice which industrialism had brought or intensified; these and other ideas were to ferment in Gandhi's mind and to colour his outlook. But what immediately impressed him most was Ruskin's reference to the ideal of a simple life in which manual work should be the joy of existence. 'The book,' records the autobiography, 'confirmed and strengthened some of my own deepest convictions.' Many years earlier, when reading the preface to Narmada Shankar's *Dharam Vichar*, Gandhi had marvelled at the revolution effected in the poet's life by his religious studies. A similar transformation now took place in him.

When the train reached Durban next morning, Gandhi was intent on reducing Ruskin's theories to practice. With Albert West, a European friend, who was at this time looking after the *Indian Opinion* press at Durban, he discussed a plan for transferring the journal to a farm where the settlers would literally live by the sweat of their brow. A 100-acre estate situated amidst sugar plantations, served by a spring, and full of fruit trees and snakes, was purchased for £1,000. The nearest station, Phoenix, was two and a half miles from the estate and fourteen miles from Durban. The first settlers included, besides Polak and West, a few cousins and nephews of Gandhi who had accompanied him to South Africa. A hall seventy-five feet long and fifty feet wide housed the press. Eight buildings of corrugated iron and thatched roofs were put up in the little colony. Mud huts would have been more becoming for peasants, as the colonists conceived themselves to be, but there was not enough money, and Gandhi was in a hurry to complete the project. A plot of three acres was allotted to each settler; it could not be sold but could be passed on to another member of the settlement. Sanitary arrangements, though primitive, were effective. There was not enough money to sink a well ınd the little colony had to store water on roof-tops during the rains.

Indian Opinion began to be published from Phoenix. The little colony was a busy hive on the day the paper had to be printed and made ready for despatch. Gandhi and Polak corrected the proofs, the printers ran off the corrected pages, the children folded and wrapped the journal.

Gandhi's cottage was the pivot of the corporate life of the settlement. Every Sunday all the residents met in his room for a community prayer in which recitations from the *Gita* and the Bible, Christian hymns and Gujerati *bhajans* mingled to lift the audience above their immediate surroundings, beyond the boundaries of race and religion. As for Gandhi, he had found a quiet corner away from the heat and the dust of towns, away from men's greed and hatred; working on the farm among people who shared his ideals, he had time to pose questions about his inner growth.

For Gandhi the 'the fulfilment of Phoenix' was not to last long. Both public and professional work made it imperative for him to return to Johannesburg. A vivid account of the Johannesburg household has been given by one of its inmates, Millie Graham Polak, in her book *Mr Gandhi: the Man*. It was community life in the miniature. Gandhi as the benevolent patriarch had no special privilege except perhaps that of looking after everybody else. He was amusing and easily amused. The house resounded with laughter as the children joined with the parents every morning in the grinding of wheat in a hand-mill. The evening meal was a pleasant hour, interspersed with light conversation and serious discussion, and occasionally enlivened by Kasturbai's ventures in the English language. After dinner Gandhi would debate religion and philosophy and recite from the *Gita*. An intimate pen-portrait of Gandhi as he was in his late thirties has been left by Joseph J. Doke, Gandhi's first biographer, and a Baptist minister of Johannesburg.[1] In December 1907 he saw Gandhi for the first time:

[1] Doke, Joseph J.: *M. K. Gandhi*, Madras, pp. 6–8.

'. . . to my surprise, a small, lithe, spare figure stood before me, and a refined earnest face looked into mine. The skin was dark, the eyes dark, but the smile which lighted up the face, and that direct fearless glance, simply took ones' heart by storm. I judged him to be some thirty-eight years of age, which proved correct. But the strain of his work showed its traces in the sprinkling of silver hair on his head. He spoke English perfectly and was evidently a man of great culture . . .

'There was a quiet assured strength about him, a greatness of heart, a transparent honesty, that attracted me at once to the Indian leader. We parted friends . . .

'Our Indian friend lives on a higher plane than most men do. His actions, like the actions of Mary of Bethany, are often counted eccentric, and not infrequently misunderstood. Those who do not know him think there is some unworthy motive behind, some Oriental 'slimness' to account for such profound unworldliness. But those who know him well are ashamed of themselves in his presence.

'Money I think has no charm for him. His compatriots are angry; they say, "He will take nothing. The money we gave him when he went as our deputy to England he brought back to us again. The presents we made him in Natal, he handed over to our public funds. He is poor because he will be poor."

'They wonder at him, grow angry at his strange unselfishness, and love him with the love of pride and·trust. He is one of those outstanding characters with whom to walk is a liberal education, whom to know is to love.'

Doke also noted that 'to hold in the flesh with a strong hand, to crucify it, to bring the needs of his own life, Thoreau and Tolstoy-like within the narrowest limits', were positive delights to him equalled only by the joy of guiding others along the same path. We may therefore now recount Gandhi's struggle for the mastery of the spirit over the flesh which powerfully influenced his personal and public life.

Chapter 10

THE FLESH AND THE SPIRIT

GANDHI had been married at the age of thirteen in accordance with 'the cruel custom of child marriage' which was then in vogue in Hindu society and is not yet quite extinct. Marriage of a child was then considered as much a parental obligation as education is considered now. It was also a rare occasion for the reunion of the clan, when second and third cousins could meet and indulge in a little festivity. Karamchand Gandhi and his brother, who were getting on in years, decided in 1882 to have 'the last best time'[1] of their lives by celebrating a triple wedding for Mohan, his elder brother and a cousin—all in their teens.

The autobiography records with extreme candour, though with a mixture of regret and remorse, the story of the boy bridegroom. One cannot, however, resist the impression that the mature Mahatma was too exacting a critic of the child Mohan. Even for his early marriage in which he had no voice, he takes the blame himself. His father had been injured in an accident on his way to Porbandar where the wedding was to be celebrated. 'I forgot,' he writes, 'my grief over my father's injuries in the childish amusement of the wedding . . . Everything on that day seemed to me right and proper and pleasing. There was also my own eagerness to get married.' He adds that he was 'passionately fond' of his child wife, that thoughts of her haunted him in the classroom, that at night he kept her awake with his 'idle talk'; that two innocent children[2] 'had all unwittingly hurled themselves into the ocean of life'.

[1] *Autobiography*, p. 19.
[2] *idem*, p. 21.

But even as he floated, he was determined not to sink. For a boy in his teens it was a painful struggle to try to be a fond husband, a dutiful son and a good student. In a sense it was a struggle for survival, as was proved by the fact that Mohan's elder brother, who was married at the same time, was unable to continue his education. Mohan won through the conflict but it left its scars on him; one of these was to charge sex with feelings of guilt. 'I was,' he writes, 'devoted to my parents. But no less was I devoted to the passions which the flesh is heir to. I had yet to learn that all happiness and pleasures should be sacrificed in devoted service to my parents.'

When one is in one's fifties, it is difficult to do justice to the emotional problems of a boy of fifteen, even if the boy is oneself. The record of his teens seemed in retrospect unedifying to the Mahatma, and the frankness of the autobiography has helped to foster an exaggerated impression that in these early years he had let himself go. Early marriage had by no means been his own choice, and if precocity is one aspect of his sex life, its evanescence is another and perhaps a more important one. As a child he had read a Gujerati pamphlet advising life-long fidelity to the wife; the monogamous ideal was henceforth indelibly imprinted on him: 'No other woman had any attraction for me in the same sense she (Kasturbai) had. I was too loyal a husband and too loyal to the vow taken before my mother to be slave to any other woman.'[1]

The autobiography takes the reader into confidence on a few escapades into which he was pitchforked in his youth. Mehtab, the little villain, responsible for most of Gandhi's early misadventures, took him to a brothel. 'I was,' he records, 'almost struck blind and dumb in this den of vice. I sat near the woman on her bed, but I was tongue-tied. She naturally lost patience with me and showed me the door with abuses and insults.'[2] Again one evening, in a seaside resort in England, he fled from a bridge party to his room, 'quaking, trembling, with beating heart like a

[1] Quoted in *Gandhiji* (Edited by Tendulkar), p. 12.
[2] *Autobiography*, p. 37.

quarry escaped from its pursuer'.[1] On his first voyage to South Africa he was taken by the Captain to an 'outing', which included a visit to negro women's quarters. He recorded later that 'I came out just as I had gone in'.

It is significant that in all these incidents, while he allowed himself to be led into the very jaws of sin, he came out unscathed. It appeared to him later that the grace of God—or good luck—had saved him. In fact, the odds were always heavy against his succumbing. As he trembled on the brink of temptation, there were powerful influences tugging at him. One was the monogamous ideal which he had cherished since his childhood; the other was the vow to avoid meat, wine and woman, which he had taken to obtain his mother's consent for his trip to England; and finally, his own shyness. 'If I did not talk,' he wrote about his life as a student in England, 'no girl would think it worth her while to enter into conversation or go out with me.'

All the sins of his boyhood and youth which filled him with remorse in later life, were thus committed within the bonds of matrimony. Here, too, the cycle of his sex life appears to have completed itself too soon. Between the age of thirteen, when he was married, and eighteen, when he left for England, his wife was with him for scarcely three years, having spent the rest of the time, as was the custom, with her parents. And when he returned after qualifying at the bar in 1891, he was continually on the move in search of a living. He had scarcely spent six months with his family before circumstances compelled him to leave in 1893 for South Africa alone. 'The call from South Africa,' he records 'found me already fairly free from the carnal appetite'[2]. He was then only twenty-four. Not until 1896 did his wife and two sons join him in Natal. Three years later, in 1899, he had already made up his mind to limit the size of his family. Since he had always been opposed to the use of contraceptives, the decision amounted to the adoption of a virtually continent life. In 1906 he took the formal vow of celibacy (*Brahmacharya*).

[1] *Autobiography*, p. 95.
[2] *idem*, p. 25.

Henceforth he and his wife were bound by many bonds but excluding the characteristic one of marriage. They were at this time a well-adjusted couple; in their thirties they had outgrown the bickerings of their teens. Kasturbai had remained illiterate, but her heart often sensed what her intellect could not understand. Like most middle-class women, she had yearned for comfort and security for herself and for her children. The day she had landed in Natal in 1897, she had become aware with a terrific jolt of the perilous prominence of her husband who was nearly lynched in the streets of Durban. His was a restless soul; he was attracted not only to politics but to all the by-ways of social service. Their house was a veritable boarding-house for political and professional colleagues; their savings were sunk in public causes, from the subsidizing of a vegetarian restaurant to the running of a political journal. The household itself was shifted across two continents in response to the calls of public duty; a cablegram could send the family voyaging down to Durban from Bombay or *vice versa*. Gandhi was experimenting with himself and his family for ideals, which Kasturbai could not always understand. When she arrived at Phoenix Farm, her husband s blue-print for an idyllic life, her surprise and irritation were obvious. She had long since reconciled herself to dispensing with gold necklaces and diamond rings, but it required some effort to give up the modicum of comfort and to turn herself overnight from the wife of a barrister into that of a peasant. Gandhi records that when in 1906 he told her that he wanted to take the vow of life-long celibacy, she did not object. She had already consented to the metamorphosis of their external surroundings; she also accepted the renunciation of the special bond between man and wife.

The occasion for the *Brahmacharya* vow was the Zulu rebellion in 1906, in which Gandhi had led an Indian volunteer ambulance unit. During the strenuous marches through the 'solemn solitudes' of the Kraals of Zululand, it was borne in upon him that if he was to repeat the service of the kind he was rendering, he would find himself unequal to the task if he were engaged in the pleasures of family life and in the propagation and rearing of children. In a word, he could not live both after the flesh and the spirit. The life of the flesh had already in fact diminished to zero. In 1899 he had decided not to have any more children—he had four already. Nineteen years later he explained that his *Brahmacharya* vow had undoubtedly a moral basis, but it originated in the desire for birth-control. 'My own case was peculiarly for that purpose. Tremendous moral consequences developed as an afterthought perfectly in a natural sequence.'[1] That a man should practise abstinence even in relation to his wife he had first heard from Raychandbhai, the Gujerati jeweller-poet-philosopher whom he acknowledged as his 'refuge in moments of spiritual crisis'. The suggestion had first grated on Gandhi's ears. Raychandbhai had, however, thrown a seed which fell on congenial soil. The early conflict in Gandhi between the demands of sex and claims of filial duty had hindered the whole-hearted acceptance of the former. 'The life of the flesh', after a torrential beginning, tended to ebb a little too soon until it was formally and finally renounced in 1906.

Of the period immediately following the vow he writes: 'I must confess that I had not then fully realized the magnitude and the immensity of the task, I undertook.' He experimented with his food, trying out saltless, pulseless, or milkless diets, to discover a combination which would keep him in good health but fend off the passions. He found fasting useful. Experience taught him that bodily control was not enough. The root of sensuality was in the mind. Nor was it enough to control the conscious mind; lust had to be chased from the unconscious. To his horror, he dreamt sometimes of pleasures once enjoyed. It was a struggle requiring eternal vigilance. Often, when the battle seemed won, the enemy made a surprise attack. For example, after nearly nine years' observance of the vow when he returned to India in 1915, fresh associations roused the devil in him again, and it required some effort to master it.[2]

[1] *Young India*, April 2, 1925.
[2] *Harijan*, June 15, 1947.

Like every one of his ideals, that of *Brahmacharya* went through a process of evolution, until it came to mean much more than abstinence and included not only freedom from desire but also from thoughts of desire. Its scope was expanded with the years until it stood for a rule of life, the object of which was to bring man into touch with *Brahman* (God) and to lead him to *Moksha* (salvation). Thus what had begun as an instrument of birth-control developed in the course of time and in the light of experience into an aid to salvation. And finally Gandhi came to the conclusion that *Brahmacharya* in the narrower sense of sexual restraint was impracticable without the *Brahmacharya* in the widest sense—the control of all the senses in deed, word and thought. It was not a question of disciplining one appetite but all appetites; it was a rule of life, a *weltanschauüng*. 'There should be a clear line,' he wrote, 'between the life of a *brahmachari* and of one who is not. The resemblance between the two is only apparent . . . Both use their eyesight, but whereas the *brahmachari* uses it to see the glories of God, the other uses it to see the frivolity around him. Both use their ears, but whereas the one hears nothing but praises of God, the other feasts his ears on ribaldry. Both often keep late hours, but whereas the one devotes them to prayer, the other fritters them away in wild and wasteful mirth. Both feed the inner man, but the one only to keep the temple of God in good repair, while the other gorges himself and makes the sacred vessel a stinking gutter.'[1]

This was an ideal of a life consecrated to the service of God and man. Its attainment was, said Gandhi, impossible without the grace of God; mere human effort could not achieve it.

To the aspirants for this life his advice was that they should not marry; those for whom the service of their fellow men was the sole joy needed no other enjoyment.[2] Gandhi agreed with the Pauline dictum that it is better to marry than to burn, but marriage was to be treated as a sacrament in which sex was the least important factor. He advised continence even to those who

[1] *Autobiography,* p. 259.
[2] Preface to *Self-Restraint versus Self-Indulgence.*

were married; and considered the sexual life physically harmful and morally sinful unless it was for the purpose of procreation. He condemned contraceptives; not only did they cheat nature but also robbed men and women of the faculty of self-restraint. He prescribed the kind of food, exercise, bathing, reading and recreation which helped to keep the lid on the animal passions. And if, in spite of all these precautions, the flesh felt weak, one was to go down on one's knees and pray to God for protection.

These views were developed at length in articles and in innumerable letters to correspondents in his weekly journals; a collection of these entitled *Self-Restraint vs. Self-Indulgence* became a best seller, due perhaps more to the curiosity they aroused than to the popularity of the views expressed in them. Gandhi was clear in his mind that he was not preaching *Brahmacharya* for the *Sannyasin* (a hermit), a title which he disclaimed for himself. He was, he said, 'no more than an average man with less than an average ability'.[1] He was sure that any man or woman could achieve what he had achieved, if he or she would make the same effort and cultivate the same hope and faith. There was the rub. How many could combine his effort, his hope and his faith? The fact is that to formulate such a discipline is one thing; to practise it is another. A famous contemporary and one of the formative influences of Gandhi's youth, Tolstoy, had preached a somewhat similar view of the place of sex in human life.

'Men survive earthquakes,' Tolstoy had declared, 'epidemics, illness and every kind of suffering, but always the most poignant tragedy was, is and will be the tragedy of the bedroom.' After the publication of *Kreutzer Sonata*, Tolstoy affirmed that the Christian ideal of love of God and one's fellow men was incompatible with sexual love or marriage, which amounted to serving oneself. Uncharitable critics said that the author of *Kreutzer Sonata*, the father of thirteen children, was getting old and that the grapes had turned sour. In fact, for many years after he had pledged himself to continence Tolstoy was torn by a

[1] *Harijan*, October 3, 1936.

struggle of which there is plenty of evidence in his diaries. Not until he was eighty-one years old—a year before his death—did he feel freed from carnal desires.

Tolstoy's struggle for continence not only strained his own moral and spiritual reserves, but also shattered the already weakened vessel of his marriage. His wife was hysterical. 'I want to kill myself, to run somewhere, to fall in love with some one,' moaned Sonya. Their life became a round of recriminations and reconciliations. The *Diaries* round off the story of one of these quarrels with the terrible judgment: 'Between us there is a struggle to the death. Either God or no God.' The Countess was totally unable to appreciate, much less to adopt, the ideals of her husband. The changes which Gandhi had brought to his life were no less radical, the ideals which he formulated for his family were no less revolutionary, than those of Tolstoy. That the Gandhi household bore the stress was due as much to the skill of the husband as to the sacrifice of the wife. Like any other middle-class woman, Kasturbai had looked forward to ease and comfort and security for her family. A woman whose husband gave away his savings to public causes, whose children were deprived of regular education in schools, who was called upon to break up her household for political reasons, and finally whose family life shaded into community life, was certainly being subjected to an abnormal strain. But Kasturbai was sustained by the faith of a Hindu wife; she followed in the 'footsteps of her husband', however much it went against the grain. To her husband's 'reforms', her reactions were successively those of bewilderment, opposition, acceptance, conversion and championship. Whether it was the removal of untouchability or the wearing of homespun 'khadi', it was not at first easy for her to adapt herself to her husband's views, but when she did it was thoroughly and she even preached them to others. Tolstoy's wife once called her husband's disciples 'dark, dark people, pharisees, cheats, dissemblers'. To Mrs Gandhi, however, her husband's disciples were her own children. The changed attitude to sex did not introduce a discordant not into the life of the

Gandhis; Gandhi himself had no doubt that it sweetened and enriched it.

This approach to sex and marriage was not part of the Hindu view of life as understood by its interpreters, writes Radha-krishnan in his *The Hindu View of Life*. 'The very gods are married. When the Hindu descends from the adoration of the Absolute and takes to the worship of a personal god, his god has always a consort . . . There is nothing unwholesome and guilty about the sex life . . .' Again, 'while some forms of Christianity and Buddhism judge the life of the world to be inferior to the life of the monk and would have loved to place the whole of mankind at one swoop in the cloister, Hinduism, while appreciating the life of the *Sannyasin*, refrained from condemning the state of the householder'. Of the four stages of life—the four *Ashramas*—that of *Brahmacharya*, the period of training, the *Garhastya*, the period of life as householder, *Vanaprasthaya*, the period of retreat, and *Sannyasa*, the period of renunciation—each stage is important in its own way and a necessary milestone in the pilgrimage of Hindu life.

Nor is the Gandhian theory of sex in line with the findings of psychologists; so far as he was concerned, Freud may not have lived. Psychologists consider there are definite limits to this reliance on 'self-restraint', and the powerful sex impulse should not be dammed but given natural and socially acceptable expression. True, the control of sex in the Gandhian scheme of life is part of a larger discipline of body and mind. The attainment of this larger discipline is, however, an uphill task for an average member of modern society.

The fact is that Gandhi's attitude to sex and marriage was a peculiarly personal phenomenon, which can only be appreciated in the context of his personal and public life. It grew out of the precocious sex life into which he was whirled by his child marriage, and was in the nature of a reaction against this precocity. It proved an asset to him in his public career by sundering those bonds of family which sometimes make cowards of men. His personality did not lose in tenderness, nor his attitude to women suffer from a perverted puritanism. He did not regard woman only as the temptress, 'a fireship continually striving to get alongside the male man-of-war and to blow him into pieces'. Women, some of the most intelligent and the noblest, were in his entourage and in the vanguard of his movements. He became the stoutest champion of the political and social emancipation of women; his voice was raised against the tyranny of the *purdah*, the iniquity of child marriage, the ban on widow remarriage, indeed against everything which cramped Indian womanhood. He roused India's women to the sense of their own dignity and power.

When he took the *Brahmacharya* vow he did not know that the Transvaal Government was soon to goad him into his first Satyagraha campaign. When 'the call' came he realized that his vow had been part of an unconscious preparation for this struggle. He had snapped the common ties which hold men back from fearlessly following the dictates of their consciences. Personal renunciation was thus an invaluable aid to him in public life. 'Persons in power,' wrote Professor Gilbert Murray in his article in *Hibbert Journal* in 1914, 'should be very careful how they deal with a man who cares nothing for sensual pleasure, nothing for riches, nothing for comfort or praise, or promotion, but is simply determined to do what he believes to be right. He is a dangerous and uncomfortable enemy because his body which you can always conquer gives you so little purchase upon his soul.'

Chapter 11

DISCOVERY OF SATYAGRAHA

NATIVE policy in South Africa, Sir Alan Burnes,[1] has pointed out, degenerated into a defence of the 'poor white', who himself is a product of the system intended to degrade only the non-white. Behind the specious pleas of cultural differences, of conflicting ways of living, has always been economic rivalry. Lionel Curtis, a British official in Transvaal who played a part in the formulation of the system of dyarchy in the Indian reforms of 1919, recalled a conversation he had with Gandhi in 1903:

'He (Mr Gandhi) started by trying to convince me of the points in the character of his countrymen, their industry, frugality, patience. I remember that after listening to him I said, "Mr Gandhi you are preaching to the converted. It is not the vices of the Indians that Europeans in this country fear, but their virtues." '[2]

The Europeans of Natal, who had imported thousands of indentured Indian labourers—semi-slaves—to work their sugar plantations and mines, were unwilling to suffer 'free Indians' as traders or farmers, in their midst, while after the Boer War the Europeans of Transvaal raised the bogey of an 'Asiatic Invasion'. In 1905 a committee appointed by the British High Commissioner found that the accusation of secret smuggling of Indians into Transvaal lacked foundation. Even though many Indian families who had left Transvaal after the outbreak of the war returned with the cessation of hostilities, the total Indian population of Transvaal in 1903 was less than what it was in 1899.

[1] Burns, Sir Alan: *Colour Prejudice*, London, 1948, p. 73.
[2] *Mahatma Gandhi: Essays and Reflections on His Life and Work*, edited by S. Radhakrishnan, London, 1939, p. 67.

Fears among Europeans that South Africa was being flooded with Indian immigrants were exaggerated. Gandhi considered them irrational, but he recognized the strength of European feeling on the subject. He was prepared to go so far to accommodate European prejudices, as to agree to a total embargo on the 'export' of Indian labour. No more indentured labourers might be admitted, but a limited number of educated Indians were required to serve as clerks and accountants of the Indian merchants. Gandhi was prepared to meet the Europeans more than half-way even on other issues between the Indian community and the Europeans, backed by the local governments. The regulation of Indian trade by licences could be continued provided the local bodies issued them subject to the supervision of the Supreme Court. The Indians were similarly prepared to submit to local and municipal regulations regarding the ownership of land and the right of residence, provided the regulations applied to Europeans and Indians alike. Gandhi did not ask for the right of vote. 'What we (Indians) want,' he told the British High Commissioner in South Africa, 'is not politicial power; but we do wish to live side by side with other British subjects in peace and amity, and with dignity and self-respect.' This was precisely what the Boer and Briton did not want. General Smuts declared later, that the Government had made up its mind to 'make this a white man's country and however difficult the task before us in this direction, we have put our foot down and would keep it there'.

A stage was soon reached when Gandhi's policy of conciliation, of 'live and let live', was to meet with a rude rebuff. Matters came to a head on the question of the registration of Indians in Transvaal. At first it had been considered sufficient to obtain the signature or (in the case of illiterate immigrants) the thumb impression. Later, a photograph was also required and Indians had to take out new permits. When Gandhi returned from the 'Zulu Rebellion', after doing his duty (as he then conceived it) as a citizen of the Empire, he found that a new measure had been devised to make the registration of Indians as irksome and humiliating a process as possible. He was stunned when he read the clauses of the bill in the *Transvaal Gazette* of August 22, 1906, which had been prepared for the Transvaal Legislature. It required every Indian—man, woman and child above eight years—to register and to give finger and thumb impressions on the registration form. If parents failed to give finger prints of minor children, the latter were required to do so on attaining the age of sixteen, or to face the penalty, which might be a fine, imprisonment or deportation. In courts, revenue offices, indeed almost at any time or place, an Indian could be challenged to produce his registration certificate; police officers could enter an Indian's house to examine permits. 'Dog's collar' was indeed an apt description of this measure. The professed object of this drastic measure was to check the illicit influx of Indians in Transvaal. Not only was there no proof of an influx on any large scale, but the existing laws were severe enough. During the years 1905-06 the Government had successfully conducted 150 prosecutions of Indians for unauthorized entry into the country. In one case a poor Indian woman had been torn away from her husband and ordered by the European magistrate to leave the country within seven hours. A boy under eleven years was arrested and sentenced to a fine of £30 or three months' imprisonment.

The object of the new registration measure was apparently to humiliate and demoralize the better educated and prosperous Indian, and to make Transvaal too hot for him. Gandhi became convinced that if this measure became law and the Indians accepted it, it would 'spell absolute ruin to them'. It was better, he felt, for Indians to die rather than submit to this law. But how were they to die? What should they dare and do, so that there would be nothing before them except a choice between victory and death? An impenetrable wall was before him; he could not see his way through it.

In the autumn of 1906, the political prospects for Indians in South Africa seemed dim. The British victory in the Boer War had brought no relief to Indians in the British colonies; in the former Boer States it had made their lot worse. The new régime in South Africa was to blossom into a partnership, but only between the Boer and the Briton. As Gandhi looked back on the twelve years he had devoted to the agitation for elementary civic rights for the Indian community in Natal and Transvaal, he could not help feeling that 'love's labour had been lost'. His hopes of securing an amelioration of the Indians' condition by educating the public opinion in South Africa, India and Britain, had been frustrated. With the exception of a few Europeans, Christian missionaries or youthful idealists, he had been unable to make a perceptible impression upon the South African Europeans who regarded the Indian question not as a matter of political ethics but one of 'bread-and-butter and of their children's bread-and-butter'. The white man had spent blood and treasure to maintain his ascendancy in that part of the world; he was determined not to admit 'the vast waiting multitudes of Asia to reap the harvest of his travail'.[1] In India there was plenty of sympathy and a rare unanimity among all shades of opinion, reflected in the resolutions on South Africa passed every year by the Indian National Congress. Indian politics were conscious of their limitations, however; the unreality of these verbal protests was brought out bluntly in Sir Pherozeshah Mehta's remark to Gandhi when they were travelling to Calcutta for the 1901 session of Indian National Congress: 'But what rights have we in our own country? I believe that so long as we have no power in our own land, you cannot fare better in the colonies.'

In England, Gandhi was on occasions able to win influential support for his struggle for Indians' rights, particularly that of the London *Times*, but the British Colonial Office, in its anxiety to humour the South African whites, continued to dwell on the 'logic of self-government' according to which the colonies were free to do what they liked—even to grind the Indian subjects of the Empire.

It was clear that to resist the latest attack upon their self-respect, namely the measure for the registration of Asiatics, the Indians had to depend upon their own resources. They had no vote and

[1] *Autobiography*, p. 84.

no representation in the legislature. On September 11, 1906, they held a meeting at the Empire Theatre in Johannesburg which was 'packed from floor to ceiling'.[1] The main resolution on the agenda drafted by Gandhi was that the Indian community was determined not to submit to the proposed measure for registration of Asiatics. When one of the speakers declared in the name of God that he would never submit to that law, Gandhi was 'startled and put on his guard'. The suggestion of a solemn oath helped him to think out 'the possible consequences in a single moment', and his 'perplexity gave way to enthusiasm'. A solemn oath meant much to Gandhi. His life had been moulded by the vows he had taken; the three-fold vow he had taken on the eve of his departure for England had a profound effect on him, and only recently he had snapped the common ties of family and property in order to give undivided allegiance to public service. The idea of a pledge of resistance to an unjust law, with God as witness, and with no fear of consequences, demolished the wall which had been obscuring his vision. He experienced the relief and exhilaration of a mathematician who suddenly discovers the solution to an intractable problem. The solution was no fluke; his whole life had been a preparation for it. Since his childhood in his personal life truth had been his guiding principle and he had tried to practise it at any cost. He had shed those smaller loyalties which make cowards of most men. The courage and the faith he evinced on this historic occasion had behind them a life-long discipline. To his fellow-Indians assembled in that Empire Theatre Hall in Johannesburg he spoke out fearlessly: 'There is only one course open to those like me, to die but not to submit to the law. It is quite unlikely, but even if everyone else flinched leaving me alone to face the music, I am confident that I would not violate my pledge.'[2]

He asked them to search their hearts. He warned them that those who resisted the government would run the risk of confiscation of property, imprisonment, starvation, flogging

---

[1] *Satyagraha in South Africa*, p. 161.
[2] Idem, p. 168.

and even death. The meeting ended with a solemn oath by
'all present standing with raised hands, with God as witness
not to submit to the (Asiatic Registration) Ordinance if it became
law'. Gandhi did not explain the mode of resistance; perhaps
he was not himself clear about it. Of one thing there was no
doubt; it was to be free from violence. Gandhi was vaguely
aware that some new principle of fighting political and social
evils had come into being. The term 'passive resistance' was at
first employed to describe the new principle, but the association
of this term with the verbal and physical violence practised by
the suffragists in England made it unsatisfactory. *Indian Opinion*,
which was to become the voice of Gandhi's movement, invited
suggestions for an appropriate name. The word 'sadagraha'
(which means firmness in good conduct) appealed to Gandhi;
he amended it to 'satyagraha' (firmness in truth). The principles
and the technique of the new movement, however, were to
evolve gradually in the ensuing months and years; its author
was a man for whom theory was the handmaid of action.

It is not surprising that the movement should have borne
the impress of his peculiar evolution. In 1908, Doke questioned
him on the genesis of Satyagraha and recorded:

'Mr Gandhi himself attributes the birth and evolution of this
principle (Passive Resistance), so far as he is concerned, to quite
other influences. "I remember," he said, "how one verse of a
Gujerati poem, which as a child I learned at school, clung to me.
In substance it was this: If a man gives you a drink of water and
you give him a drink in return, that is nothing. Real beauty
consists in doing good against evil. As a child, this verse had a
powerful influence over me, and I tried to carry it into practice.
Then came the 'Sermon on the Mount'."

'"But surely," said I, "the *Bhagavad Gita* came first?"

'"No," he replied, "of course, I knew the *Bhagavad Gita* in
Sanskrit tolerably well, but I had not made its teaching in that
particular a study. It was the New Testament which really
awakened me to the rightness and value of Passive Resistance.
When I read in the 'Sermon on the Mount', such passages as 'Resist

not him that is evil, but whosoever smiteth thee on thy right cheek turn to him the other also', and 'Love your enemies and pray for them that persecute you, that ye may be sons of your Father which is in heaven', I was simply overjoyed, and found my own opinion confirmed where I least expected it. The *Bhagavad Gita* deepened the impression, and Tolstoy's *The Kingdom of God is Within You* gave it permanent form." [1]

[1] Doke, Joseph J.: *M. K. Gandhi*, p. 88.

Chapter 12

FIRST SATYAGRAHA MOVEMENT

IN spite of the unanimous and vehement opposition of the Indian community, the Asiatic Registration Bill was carried by the Transvaal Legislature almost *in toto*. One last hope remained; the Crown could invoke its veto on a measure which discriminated against its Indian subjects. A two-man deputation consisting of Gandhi and H. O. Ali was despatched to England to agitate for the disallowance of this bill. Gandhi spent six weeks in England; he met Dadabhai Naoroji and British friends of India in Parliament and Press. He found the Colonial Secretary, Lord Elgin, sympathetic but evasive. On the return voyage Gandhi received a cable that the Asiatic Registration Bill had in fact been vetoed by the King. The news proved too good to be true. All that had happened was that Lord Elgin had saved the face of the Imperial Government without alienating the Government of Transvaal. He had assured Transvaal's representative in London that the same measure would receive royal assent if passed by the Transvaal Legislature after the grant of responsible government. Indeed one of the first acts of the Transvaal Legislature under the new constitution was to pass the Asiatic Registration Bill. The royal assent was now a foregone conclusion. It was announced that the new law would take effect from July 1, 1907.

The Indians had failed to make themselves heard. The time had come for Gandhi to fulfil the pledge of resistance to this unjust law. He formed a Passive Resistance Association to conduct his campaign. Though the oath of resistance to the hated law had been taken by Indians present at that historic meeting in the Empire Theatre in September 1906, he had it readministered

D

to give the waverers a chance to withdraw. *Indian Opinion*, which had been for many years a drain on his purse, was to prove a handy instrument for the political education of the Indian community. It played .the part in South Africa which *Young India* and *Harijan* were to play later in India; it was read not only by his colleagues and co-workers but also by his opponents, as it unreservedly indicated his plans. Its popularity is shown by its circulation, which reached a peak figure of 3,500 in a country where the total number of potential Indian readers did not exceed 20,000 and where copies were also circulated from door to door.

General Botha sent William Hosken, a liberal European and friend of Gandhi, to attend a mass meeting of Indians in Johannesburg which was to be addressed by Gandhi. 'I am here,' announced Hosken, 'at the instance of General Botha. He entertains a feeling of respect for you and understands your sentiments, but he says he is helpless. All the Europeans in Transvaal ask for such a law. The Indians know full well how powerful is the Transvaal Government. To resist the Government will be to dash your head against a wall. I wish that your community may not be ruined in fruitless opposition or invite needless suffering on their heads.' It was Gandhi's duty to translate this speech to the audience whose reaction was eloquently voiced by Muhammad Kachhalia, an Indian merchant who, although he had so far never been active in politics, was to play a great part in Gandhi's movement. 'I have heard,' said Kachhalia, 'Mr Hosken's speech. We know how powerful the Transvaal Government is. But it cannot do anything more than enact such a law. It will cast us into prison, confiscate our property, deport us or hang us. All this we will bear cheerfully but we simply cannot put up with this law.' And then, running his fingers along his throat, he thundered: 'I swear in the name of God that I will be hanged but I will not submit to this law, and I wish that everyone present here do likewise.'[1]

The Government opened permit offices in the principal towns,

[1] Gandhi: *Satyagraha in South Africa*, p. 208.

and called upon all Indian residents in Transvaal to register by July 31, 1907, or to face the penalties prescribed by law. The Passive Resistance Association advised the Indian community to boycott the permit offices. Posters appeared with the striking caption: 'Loyalty to the King demands loyalty to the King of Kings . . . Indians be Free.' Gandhi planned the picketing of the permit offices to the minutest detail. He recruited volunteers—some of them boys in their teens—and posted them outside the permit offices to dissuade Indians from taking out the registration certificates under the new law. But volunteers were forbidden to be violent or even discourteous towards those who insisted on registering themselves. And they surrendered themselves cheerfully if the police wished to arrest them. Though pressure of every kind was ruled out in this campaign, the force of public opinion was itself strong enough for the blacklegs. There were a few instances in which permits were taken out at night in collusion with the permit offices, but by and large the boycott was effective. The Government extended the date of registration, but by November 30, 1907, only 511 Indians had taken out the registration certificates.

Meanwhile another blow fell on the Indians in Transvaal. On December 26, 1907, royal assent was given to the Immigration Bill passed by the Transvaal Legislature to stop even the limited immigration of educated Indians into Transvaal. Next day, Gandhi addressed a meeting in Johannesburg. 'Lord Elgin (Colonial Secretary in the British Government) has put an undue strain on Indian loyalty. The Imperial Government must hesitate if they mean to retain their hold on the people of India, through their affection and not at the point of the bayonet. England might have to choose between India and colonies.' General Smuts, who was dealing with the Indian affairs in the Transvaal Cabinet, treated the Indian threats with disdain. The agitation was, he insinuated 'engineered by Gandhi and his henchmen'.

On December 28, 1907, Gandhi and twenty-six of his prominent colleagues attended a Johannesburg court to show cause why, through failure to register under the law, they should not be deported from Transvaal. They were ordered to leave the country within a fortnight at the latest. As they did not comply, they presented themselves again on January 10, 1908, pleaded guilty and offered to face the consequences. Gandhi, as the author of the movement, asked for the heaviest penalty. Standing as an accused in the court where he had often figured as a counsel, he asked the Court's leave to make a short statement. 'No political speeches', replied the magistrate, but he set the tone for the judgments in future trials. Whatever Mr Gandhi's place in the hearts of his people, said the magistrate, and whatever his motives, whether the law was just or unjust, all that the court had to do was to administer the law as it stood!

Gandhi received two months' simple imprisonment. If the Government had hoped to break the spirit of the rank and file by locking up the leader, they had made a serious miscalculation. There was lively competition among the Indians in courting imprisonment. The fear of imprisonment had gone; gaol came to be known as King Edward's Hotel. Johannesburg gaol began to fill until it had 155 passive resistors, where it could accommodate only fifty. They slept on the ground and the food served to them was such that only the kaffirs could relish it; their morale was high. They asked for manual labour, but since their sentences were in most cases without hard labour, those in charge of the gaol could not oblige them.

Gandhi had hardly begun to feel settled in prison when he received a visit from his friend Albert Cartright, a liberal European, whose paper *The Transvaal Leader* had often supported the Indian cause. Cartright told Gandhi that he had seen General Smuts and had brought with him the draft of a settlement, according to which Asiatic Registration Act was to be repealed provided the Indians registered voluntarily. Two days later, Gandhi still a prisoner, was received by General Smuts in his office at Pretoria. The General praised the perseverence of the Indians, pleaded his helplessness on the registration issue in view of the strong European feeling and repeated the assurance already conveyed by Cartright that the Asiatic Registration Act would be taken off the statute-book if Indians registered on their own. The General accepted some amendments which Gandhi suggested. 'Where am I to go?' asked Gandhi. The General laughed and replied: 'I am phoning the prison officials to release the other prisoners tomorrow morning.'

It was seven o'clock in the evening. Gandhi did not have a farthing with him. Borrowing the railway fare from General Smuts' secretary, he rushed to the railway station to catch the last train for Johannesburg. He called a meeting of the Indian community within a few hours of his arrival to discuss the informal agreement he had reached with Smuts. There was a good deal of criticism. Was he not playing into the hands of the Government? Why did the repeal of the Registration Act not precede rather than follow voluntary registration? What would happen if the Transvaal Government did not keep their word? Gandhi explained that it was part of the duty of a Satyagrahi to trust the word of even an adversary. If the Government went back on its word, it was open to the Indians to resume their resistance. A rugged Pathan hailing from the North-West frontier of India persistently heckled Gandhi and even accused him of having sold the Indian community to General Smuts for £15,000. 'I swear with *Allah* as my witness,' he screamed, 'that I will kill the man who takes the lead in applying for registration.'[1] Gandhi had no difficulty in disposing of the charge of bribery, and, as for the threat held out by the ferocious Pathan, his answer was: 'to die without bitterness or anger, by the hand of a brother was not a matter for sorrow'. On the morning of Febrary 10, 1908, Gandhi left his residence to take out, as he had publicly promised, the first registration certificate in accordance with the understanding he had reached with General Smuts. As he entered his office (which was also the headquarters of the Satyagraha movement), he noticed a few Pathans loitering in the street. One of them, an old client of his, was Mir Alam, 'fully six feet in height and of a large and powerful build'. Mir Alam returned Gandhi's greeting rather

[1] Gandhi: *Satyagraha in South Africa*, p. 251.

perfunctorily and followed him. In Von Brandis Street Mir Alam asked Gandhi where he was going. Before Gandhi could reply, Mir Alam and his fellow Pathans attacked the little man, who fainted with the words 'He Rama' (Oh God!) on his lips. Were it not for some companions who warded off some of the blows, and for the intervention of European passers-by, Gandhi would have been killed on the spot.

Bleeding profusely, he was carried into the nearest shop. As he regained consciousness, his first thought was for his assailant. 'Where is Mir Alam?' he asked Doke his friend, who had arrived on the scene. 'He has been arrested along with the rest,' replied Doke. 'He should be released,' said Gandhi. Doke replied: 'That is all very well but here you are in a stranger's office with your lip and cheek bandaged. The police are ready to take you to the hospital, but if you will go to my place, Mrs Doke and I will minister to your comforts as best we can.'

Gandhi preferred to go to the Dokes' house. Immediately on arrival he called for the registration papers, as he was pledged to take out the first certificate. Mr Chamney, Registrar of Asiatics, had been a frequent target in Indian Opinion; but when he came to Gandhi that day with the registration papers there were tears in his eyes. As for Mir Alam and the Pathans, Gandhi could not prevent the law from taking its course, but he was not summoned as a witness. For ten days the Dokes nursed him with loving care. Their house became a 'caravanserai' and was visited by hundreds of Indians from millionaires to the humblest hawkers and labourers who came to inquire after their leader's health. After ten days' stay with the Dokes, Gandhi shifted to Polak's residence in a suburb of Johannesburg. As soon as he was fit enough to travel, he went to see Kasturbai and the children at Phoenix, who would have travelled down to Johannesburg on hearing of the news of the assault if they could afford the railway fare.

Further attempts on his life followed. A few days later, at a meeting in Durban a Pathan rushed towards him with a big stick and the lights went out. Alexander, the Superintendent of

Police, sent a police party to escort the Indian leader to safety; eleven years earlier he had saved Gandhi from the fury of the whites, now he was shielding him from the fanaticism of Indians.

Gandhi had risked his life to fulfil his part of the compact with Smuts. But the Boer General backed out with a brazenness which left not only Gandhi but Albert Cartright, the honest broker, gasping. The Transvaal Government did not repeal the Asiatic Registration Act; it brought forth a new measure to validate the voluntary registration of the Indians. This meant that Indian immigrants who entered the country in future would still be subject to the 'Black Act'. Gandhi gave vent to his feelings in the *Indian Opinion* in an article entitled 'Foul Play'. His colleagues taunted him with gullibility; he wrote to Smuts and recalled conversations with Albert Cartright and with the General. Unfortunately the General's recollections did not coincide with Gandhi's.

Chapter 13

SECOND ROUND

THE Indians' discomfiture looked complete. They had voluntarily put on 'the dog's collar', and the law against which they had agitated nevertheless remained on the statute-book. The Government refused to return the Indians' original applications for voluntary registration. Gandhi declared that the Indians would burn their registration certificates and 'humbly take the consequences'.

The earlier campaign in the autumn of 1907 had planned itself. Now, with better knowledge of his people and a surer grasp of the technique which he was evolving, Gandhi planned the second round in the Satyagraha struggle. A huge bonfire was held at which a large number of Transvaal Indians consigned their registration certificates to the flames. The scene was compared by the Johannesburg correspondent of the *Daily Mail* with the 'Boston Tea Party'. The Indians' struggle in Transvaal may not have been as historic an event as the American War of Independence, but the burning of the certificates was certainly a bold act of defiance. General Smuts, who may have chuckled over Gandhi's discomfiture, did not have the last laugh. The highlight of the demonstration came when Mir Alam, now out of jail, stepped forward and shook hands with Gandhi, who assured him that he had never harboured any resentment against his assailant.

Meanwhile the Transvaal Legislature had passed another measure which effectively excluded new immigrants from India. Gandhi wrote to the Government that the Satyagraha movement would also be directed against the new measure. General Smuts accused Gandhi of raising new issues; he warned the Indians that their spokesman was a person 'who, when given an inch, asked for an ell'. In fact Gandhi had been straining hard to restrict the scope and area of his struggle, and had, with some difficulty, held back Indian settlers in other colonies in South Africa from launching sympathetic movements.

The Indians were prepared to fill the prisons. In August 1908 a few prominent Indians from Natal, who had an old right of domicile in Transvaal, crossed the frontier, not to settle in Transvaal but to defy the Registration Act. They were arrested. In Transvaal the easiest passport to King Edward's Hotel—as Gandhi called the gaols—was to hawk without licence. Hawkers who had the licences refused to produce them on demand and trooped into prisons. Their example was followed by well-to-do Indian merchants and barristers who turned hawkers overnight, peddled vegetables without a licence and marched into prison. The terms of imprisonment in this second Satyagraha campaign were, unlike those in the first, usually with hard labour. The treatment of Indians in gaol became harsher. Boys in their teens were made to break stones, sweep the streets and dig tanks. One of them named Nagappa, an eighteen-year-old boy who was taken to work in early winter mornings, died of pneumonia.

Gandhi himself had a taste of this severe treatment in a Transvaal prison when he landed there in October 1908. He spent the first night in the company of some kaffir criminals, 'wild-looking, murderous, vicious, lewd and uncouth'. He kept his composure by repeating verses from the *Gita*. This was the hardest term he ever had in prison. At seven in the morning he was one of a gang of prisoners, led by a relentless overseer, which dug hard ground with spades. As the day wore on, with his bent back and blistered hands Gandhi was seen cheering up his companions, many of whom all but broke under the strain. In the evenings and on Sundays he pored over the *Gita* and books by Ruskin, Thoreau and others, which he could get in gaol. The rigorous prison routine harmonized with the philosophy of life which he had been working out, the renunciation of creature comforts and the sublimation of self in the service of humanity. His personality

D*

developed and took on that steely strength which was to become a powerful force in years to come. 'Each time he returned,' writes Mrs Polak, 'one felt that some almost indefinable growth had taken place in him during his absence in gaol.'[1]

Imprisonment failed to break the spirit of the Indians, and keeping so many of them in gaol was an expensive proposition. The Transvaal Government therefore adopted a cheaper but more drastic device. One of the penalties prescribed in the Asiatic Registration Act was 'deportation'; it had been hitherto interpreted as forcible removal to the neighbouring colony of Natal or Orange Free State. Henceforth this penalty was to be compulsory repatriation to India. It was an inhuman policy which only blind racial hatred could have approved. These poor, rootless Indian labourers, who had given the best part of their lives to South Africa, were in no position to rehabilitate themselves in India. An insight into the human aspect of this repatriation was given by Gandhi in a letter to Gokhale dated April 25, 1910:[2] 'I came into constant touch with the brave wives, sisters or mothers of the deported men. I once asked them whether they would like to go with the deported to India and they indignantly remarked: "How can we? We were brought to this country as children and we do not know anybody in India. We would rather perish here than go to India which is a foreign land to us." However regrettable this attitude of mind may be, the fact remains that these men and women are rooted to South African soil.'

Gandhi did what little he could to ameliorate the hardships of these unfortunate people. He sent some of his colleagues to accompany them. He wrote to his friend Natesan of the *Indian Review* to help these repatriates, most of whom were Tamils from Madras. Meanwhile, he had the matter taken to the Supreme Court, which declared deportation to India illegal. Another ingenious mode of attack on the Indians' struggle was devised. Some of the prominent Indian merchants who were in the

[1] Polak, M.: *Mr Gandhi: The Man*, p. 94.
[2] Tendulkar: *Mahatma*, Vol. I, p. 140.

forefront of Gandhi's campaign were faced with the prospect of losing their livelihood as well as their liberty. Muhammad Kachhalia, a rich merchant, became insolvent when his European creditors made a concerted 'run' on him, to punish him for his part in Gandhi's movement.

Prosecutions, deportations and economic pressure did not crush the Satyagraha movement. Nevertheless, it could not continue at a high pitch all the time and gradually fell to a low ebb. A sort of war-weariness crept over the Indian community, particularly over its richer section. There was a stalemate; the Indians did not give up the fight though they were unable to make a spectacular impression.

Meanwhile, in 1909 Gandhi visited England, where talks on the unification of South Africa were in progress. The South African Indians were anxious about their future in the new Boer-British partnership which was being forged. There was hardly a British politician or journalist interested in India whom Gandhi did not see during this visit. He met Lord Morley, the Secretary of State for India, Lord Crewe, the Secretary of State for Colonies, Lord Ampthill, a junior peer but an ardent supporter of the Indian cause. It was plain that the South African statesmen were unwilling to make any substantial concessions in favour of Indians, and the British Government was reluctant to intervene on behalf of the Indians in the affairs of self-governing colonies. Gandhi confessed to feelings of 'boredom and fatigue' at the end of a mission which was 'thankless and fruitless'.

After his fruitless trip to England, Gandhi saw that the Indians' struggle for their rights would be a protracted affair. Repression by the Transvaal Government had told on the small Indian community. Many merchants had suffered heavy losses and had retired from politics. A small band of Satyagrahis, however, continued to court imprisonment. To the families of these Satyagrahi prisoners the Satyagraha Association had been giving subsistence allowances, but the funds of the Association were running out. Since 1906 Gandhi's political preoccupations had brought his practice at the bar to a standstill, and all his savings had been sunk in the movement. Money was needed not only to help the distressed families, but to run the offices of the movement in Johannesburg and London, and to keep the *Indian Opinion* going. In this war of attrition, time was evidently on the side of the Transvaal Government and the Indian resisters were in danger of being starved into surrender. The gift of Rs. 25,000 from Sir Ratan Tata, the Indian industrialist, arrived in 1910 not a day too soon; it was followed by further donations, including those from the Indian National Congress, the All India Muslim League and the Nizam of Hyderabad. But this largesse could not last indefinitely. Gandhi felt that if the Satyagraha struggle was to be sustained, financial commitments must be drastically cut. He came to the conclusion that the most economical arrangement was to lodge the families of Satyagrahi prisoners in a co-operative farm. The Phoenix Settlement in Durban which he had founded in 1904 was the obvious choice; but it was ruled out, owing to its distance from Johannesburg, thirty hours away by train.

Kallenbach, a German architect who had thrown in his lot with Gandhi, came to his rescue. He bought a 1,100-acre farm twenty-one miles from Johannesburg and gave it rent free for the use of the Satyagrahis. The estate, which was styled 'Tolstoy Farm', had about a thousand fruit trees and a small house. With such local labour and materials as they could muster, Gandhi and Kallenbach put up a small colony of corrugated structures. The residents of Tolstoy Farm, whose number varied between fifty and seventy-five, hailed from almost all parts of India, and included Hindus, Muslims, Parsis and Christians. They were served by a common vegetarian kitchen and led a frugal and hard life, which was in fact harder than life in jail. All residents, including children, had their quota of manual labour. The colony tried to be self-sufficient; its workshop, under the expert supervision of Kallenbach, manufactured odds and ends. Kallenbach learnt shoe-making from a monastery of German monks and taught the craft to his fellow residents, including Gandhi.

'We had all become labourers', writes Gandhi, 'and therefore put on labourers' dress, but in the European style, viz. workman's trousers and shirts which were imitated from prisoners' uniform.'[1] Those who went to the town on private errands, had to walk the forty-two miles to and back from Johannesburg. Gandhi himself, though past forty and living only on fruits, did not think much of walking forty miles a day; he once did fifty-five miles without feeling any the worse for it.

Gandhi was in high spirits; his 'faith and courage were at their highest on Tolstoy Farm'.[2] He became a firm believer in nature-cure and it was during this period that he wrote his *Guide To Health*. 'There was not,' he writes, 'a single case of illness on the farm in which we used drugs or called in a doctor.' In Kallenbach he found an enthusiastic comrade for his experiments. They tried to work out the implications of *Ahimsa* (non-violence) and to apply the principle to snakes. They ran a school for the children of the colony where Gandhi tried his ideas on education which he had so far tested only on his children. He laid emphasis on the culture of the heart, rather than on the sharpening of the intellect, and made manual work an integral part of the curriculum.

The children of Tolstoy Farm merrily dug pits, felled trees, lifted loads, learnt carpentry and shoe-making. Gandhi had a high conception of his duty as a teacher: 'It would be idle for me if I were a liar to teach the boys to tell the truth. A cowardly teacher would never succeed in making his boys valiant . . . I saw, therefore, that I must be an eternal object-lesson to the boys and girls living with me. They thus became my teachers, and I learnt I must be good, and live straight, if only for their sakes.'

The increasing discipline and self-restraint Gandhi cultivated at Tolstoy Farm was attributed by him to his awakened sense of responsibility as a teacher. Tolstoy Farm was another milestone in his growth; it also made a valuable contribution to

[1] *Satyagraha in South Africa*, p. 375.
[2] *idem*, p. 371.

the Satyagraha struggle. Not only did it offer an asylum to the
families of Satyagrahi prisoners, but the spectacle of a handful
of Indian patriots cheerfully leading a life of voluntary poverty
and austerity, rather than surrender to the organized might of
the Transvaal Government, was to prove an inspiring example
to the rest of the Indian community when Gandhi led it in
the last phase of his Satyagraha campaign. And the men, women
and children who had known the austere discipline of Tolstoy
Farm could have little fear of gaol.

The Satyagraha struggle had continued for four years. The
Indians went in and came out of gaol. The weaker and the
richer members of the community could not sustain the tempo
of the struggle, but the morale of the minority which held
out under Gandhi's leadership was high. Public opinion in
India was becoming restive. Gokhale piloted through the
Imperial Legislative Council a resolution banning the emigration
of indentured labour to South Africa. As the coronation of King
George V drew near, the Imperial Government was also anxious
to pour oil on troubled waters and appease Indian opinion.
The result was an announcement in February 1911 by the South
African Government that it would remove the racial bar; the
entry of Indians into Transvaal was to be restricted not as Asiatics,
but by means of a severe education test.

On May 27, 1911, *Indian Opinion* announced that a provisional
settlement with the Government had been reached, and that
Indians and Chinese were free to resume their occupations.
On June 1st, the Satyagrahi prisoners were released. The clouds
had lifted and an index of the change in the atmosphere was a
football match on June 5th played at Johannesburg between the
Pretoria Passive Resisters' Eleven and the Local Passive Resister
Team.

The truce lasted till the end of 1912. The Indian community
professed loyalty to the throne, but did not join in the official
celebrations of the coronation in South Africa. Gandhi explained
in *Indian Opinion* his reasons for this stand: 'It may seem somewhat anomalous to a stranger why and how British Indians

of South Africa should tender their loyalty to the throne and rejoice over the crowning of the sovereign in whose dominion they do not even enjoy the ordinary civil rights of orderly men. British sovereigns represent, in theory, purity and equality of justice. British statesmen make an honest attempt to realize the ideals. That they often fail miserably in doing so is too true, but irrelevant to the issue before us.'

The great event of 1912 was a visit from Gokhale. For fifteen years, Gokhale had been in touch with, and lent his powerful support to, Gandhi from inside and outside the Imperial Legislative Council at Calcutta. His tour of South Africa was planned with the consent of the British Government; he came as a state guest and was given a saloon for his rail journeys. Gandhi received him at Cape Town, and acted as his secretary—and valet—throughout the one-month tour. Railway stations were illuminated and red carpets rolled out for Gokhale. The Indian community showered addresses and caskets on him, and gave him a right royal welcome. In Pretoria, the capital of the Union, he had a conference with Union ministers at the end of which he told Gandhi, 'You must return to India in a year. Everything has been settled. The Black Act will be repealed. The racial bar will be removed from the emigration law. The £3 tax will be abolished.' 'I doubt it very much,' replied Gandhi, 'you do not know the ministers as I do.'

As Gokhale turned his back on South Africa, it became clear that he had been bluffed. General Smuts told the South African Parliament that, in view of the European feeling in Natal, it was not possible to abolish the £3 tax on the ex-indentured labourers, and their families.

Another 'breach of faith' gave a new lease of life to Satyagraha movement. So far Gandhi had repeatedly turned down suggestions to enlarge the scope of the Satyagraha campaign which was confined to the original grievances regarding immigration and registration. Now that the South African Government had broken its word to Gokhale, the £3 tax could legitimately form a plank in the movement. The entry of the indentured labourers on the scene meant a large accession of strength to the movement, though there were undoubted risks in handling a mass of illiterate men who had no previous experience in the political sphere. But thanks to the interest he had taken in indentured labourers during his stay in Natal, Gandhi was not only popular with them but had an insight into their problems and psychology.

While Gandhi was planning active resistance to the Government, another bombshell fell on the Indians. A judgment of the Supreme Court invalidated at a stroke all marriages which had not been celebrated according to Christian rites and registered by the Registrar of Marriages. In other words, Hindu, Muslim and Parsi marriages became illegal, and their children became illegitimate. Gandhi vainly appealed to the Government that it should either refuse to accept this fantastic interpretation or amend the law.

Even this great insult to Indians' self-respect, like the Union Government's breach of faith with Gokhale, contrived to fit into Gandhi's strategy in his last campaign in South Africa. So far women had been kept out of the Satyagraha struggle, but now that their honour was at stake, they were summoned side by side with their men-folk to the non-violent battle.

Chapter 14

FINAL PHASE

IT was evident to Gandhi that the tactics of the Government were to wear out the Indians by a process of attrition. *Indian Opinion* in its issue of September 13, 1913 announced the failure of negotiations: 'A settlement without a settlement spirit is not settlement . . . It is much better to have an open fight than a patched-up truce. The fight this time, must be for altering the spirit of the Government and the European population of South Africa. And the result can only be attained by prolonged and bitter suffering that must melt the hearts alike of the Government, and of the predominant partner.'

Gandhi decided to launch his final campaign and to throw his 'all' into it. Gokhale had written from India enquiring about the strength of 'the army of peace' which was to wage this campaign. Gandhi replied that he could count on at least sixteen and, at the most, sixty-six Satyagrahis. Gokhale, a seasoned politician, was somewhat amused at these statistics and wondered how a handful of Indians could bring the Transvaal Government to terms. But Gokhale could not foresee Gandhi's strategy which was soon to unfold itself, and to suck thousands of Indians into the movement.

Gandhi's first move was to send a party of sixteen, including Mrs Gandhi, from Phoenix settlement in Natal to Transvaal. They were arrested for entering Transvaal without a permit on September 23rd and imprisoned. A few days later, a party of eleven women from Tolstoy Farm in Transvaal crossed into Natal without a permit, and proceeded to Newcastle; before they were arrested, they had persuaded the Indian miners to go on strike.

The strike in the coal mines was a serious affair. Gandhi hastened to Newcastle to take charge of the situation, and to guard against any disorder or violence on the part of the strikers. The mine owners invited him to Durban. 'You have nothing to lose,' they taunted him, 'but will you compensate the misguided labourers for the damage you will cause them?' The workers, replied Gandhi, were aware of the risks they ran, and in any case there could be no greater loss than the loss of self-respect which they had suffered for many years in the form of the £3 poll tax. On return to Newcastle, Gandhi told the miners of the threats held out by their masters, but the miners did not flinch; their faith in 'Gandhibhai' (Brother Gandhi) was complete. Their employers began to tighten the screws on them. They cut off water and electricity from the miners' quarters so the poor Indians, with their scanty belongings left their quarters. Gandhi did not know what to do with these jobless and homeless men. The Indian traders of Newcastle were reluctant to help the miners for fear of incurring the Government's displeasure. An Indian Christian family offered to feed them, but how long could it afford to do so? There were great risks involved in allowing hundreds of illiterate and unemployed labourers to idle about. So Gandhi decided to march this 'army' to Transvaal, hoping that *en route* it would be taken out of his hands by the Government and deposited in gaol. But, if by some miracle the miners and their families escaped imprisonment, they were to support themselves by working on the Tolstoy Farm.

The labourers covered in two days—on a ration of a pound and a half of bread and an ounce of sugar—the 36 miles from Newcastle to Charlestown which was close to the Transvaal border. A week later, on November 6, 1913 began the march across the border. There were 2,037 men, 127 women and 57 children. 'The pilgrims whom Gandhi is guiding', wrote the *Sunday Post* 'are an exceedingly picturesque crew. To the eye they appear most meagre, indeed emanciated; their legs are mere sticks but the way they are marching on the starvations rations show them to be particularly hardy.' There were a few instance of indiscipline, but, on the whole, the courage, the discipline and the fortitude of these poor, illiterate labourers were amazing. They knew little of politics, but they knew their leader whose word was law to them. One of the women was marching with a baby, the baby fell down from her arms as she was crossing a stream and was drowned. 'We must not pine for the dead,' she said, 'it is the living for whom we must work,' and marched on.

Before actually crossing the Transvaal border, Gandhi wrote to the Government that the Indian miners were not entering Transvaal to settle there, but as a protest against the Government's breach of faith, and that the strike would be called off if the £3 tax was repealed. Finding no response to his letters and telegrams, Gandhi rang up General Smuts. 'General Smuts will have nothing to do with you. You may do just as you please,' was the curt reply he received from the General's secretary. Trouble was expected at Volksrust, a border village, where the European jingoes threatened to shoot the Indians like rabbits, but fortunately the procession passed through the village without any untoward incident. Gandhi was arrested and taken to Volksrust for trial. The prosecution asked for time to prepare the case; he was bailed out and rejoined the strikers. He was re-arrested, bailed out again and rejoined his caravan. He would not have asked for bail, if he had not felt that his presence was necessary to control the rabble he was leading, and the court would never have agreed to the bail if the law did not allow this privilege to all except those charged with murder. As the caravan neared Johannesburg, Gandhi was arrested—his third arrest in four days. He was tried and fined £60 or nine months' rigorous imprisonment under the Natal Indenture Law; he elected to go to the gaol.

If the Government thought that the marchers would be demoralized after Gandhi's removal from their midst, it was disappointed. At Balfour station the marchers were placed under arrest, put into three special trains which were to deport them to Natal. There was a critical moment, when the strikers refused to board the trains without orders from *Gandhibhai* (Brother

Gandhi). They were, however, persuaded to obey. On the way,
they were starved and on reaching Natal were prosecuted and
sent to gaol. The Government hit upon an ingenious device
for working the mines and at the same time punishing the
strikers. It declared the mine compounds as 'outstations' to the
Dundee and Newcastle gaols, and appointed the mine-owner's
European staff as the warders. To complete the cruel joke, work
in the mines was made part of the sentence. The labourers were
brave men and flatly refused to be forced underground, and
for this they were brutally whipped. The news of this ruthless
repression spread and led to spontaneous strikes in the north
and west of Natal, where Indian labourers came out of plantations
and mines. The Government adopted a policy of 'blood and iron'.
Racial feeling and vested economic interests combined in savage
punishment of the poor Indian labourers who were chased back
to work in the mines by mounted military police. When Gandhi
heard of these atrocities, he felt as if bullets had passed through
his heart.

In Volksrust gaol Gandhi was made to dig stones and sweep
the compound. Later he was transferred to Pretoria gaol and
lodged in a dark cell ten feet long and seven feet wide, which
was lit at night only to check up on the prisoner. He was denied
a bench, refused permission to walk in the cell and subjected to
numberless pinpricks. Summoned for evidence in a case, he
was marched to the court with handcuffs on his hands and
manacles on his feet.

The 'blood and iron' policy of the South African Government
stirred India deeply. Gokhale, who had been in touch with Gandhi
by letter and cable, toured India in a campaign to mobilize
moral and financial support for the Satyagrahis. Bishop Lefroy,
the Metropolitan of India, backed the Indians' cause in an outspoken letter to the Press. The Viceroy, Lord Hardinge, was
impressed by the strong feeling in the country; he was advised
that 'there had been no movement like it since the Mutiny'.
He has recorded how he personally was exasperated at the action
of the Government of the Union of South Africa and the inaction

of the Dominions office in London, and how 'this feeling came to boiling point', while he was on his way to Madras at the end of November 1913, when he read the official telegrams recounting the sufferings of the Indians in South Africa. In reply to the address presented to him by Srinivasa Sastri, on behalf of the Mahajan Sabha, he declared that the Indian resisters in South Africa had the sympathy of India, and 'also of those like myself who without being Indians themselves, have feelings of sympathy for the people of this country. But the most recent developments have taken a very serious turn and we have seen the widest publicity given to allegations that this movement of passive resistance has been dealt with by measures which would not for one moment be tolerated by any country that calls itself civilized'.[1]

The Viceroy went on to ask for an impartial enquiry into the charges of atrocities levelled against the South African Government. The speech raised Lord Hardinge's stock sky-high in India, but he was bitterly criticized in London and Pretoria. General Botha and General Smuts pressed for his recall, which was seriously discussed by the British Cabinet, but given up as an impracticable proposition in view of its inevitable repercussions on public opinion in India.[2]

General Smuts found himself in an unenviable position between his own bad conscience and the South African Europeans' intransigence which he himself had encouraged. 'He was in the same predicament as a snake which has made a mouthful of a rat but can neither gulp it down nor cast it out.'[3] He resorted to the time-honoured face-saving device of appointing a Commission of Inquiry. There was no Indian on it, and two of its three members had been noted for their anti-Indian bias. Gandhi felt that unless the commission was reconstituted the Indians could expect no justice from it. Gokhale sent Andrews and Pearson to assist in the mediation. Gandhi pleaded that

[1] Hardinge of Penshurst: *My Indian Years*, London, 1948, p. 91.
[2] *idem*.
[3] *Satyagraha in South Africa*, p. 485.

he was pledged to boycott the commission. The Viceroy counselled moderation and there was an exchange of cables between Gandhi and Gokhale. Gokhale felt that the boycott would harm the Indian cause. He was worn out by anxiety and his diabetes grew worse. 'Gandhi had no business,' he said, 'to take a vow and tie himself up. This is politics and compromise is its essence.' Gokhale was afraid that Gandhi's attitude would displease Lord Hardinge, but although Gandhi valued the Viceroy's support, he was not prepared to sacrifice his principles to secure it.

Meanwhile General Smuts gave hints that the Commission of Inquiry was merely to register the decisions which he had already taken, and that its predominantly anti-Indian personnel would in fact help the South African Government to carry the Legislature with it in a new policy towards the Indians. Gandhi made two fine gestures, which were part of the strategy of Satyagraha, but nevertheless made a deep impression upon his opponents. European railway workers of the South African Railways had gone on strike, but Gandhi refused to turn the difficulty of the Government into his opportunity and deferred his next move in the struggle. His second gesture was that, in spite of strong opposition in his own camp, he did not press for an inquiry into the atrocities committed against the Indian strikers by the mine owners and the troops.

Negotiations began between Gandhi and General Smuts at Pretoria. Telegrams came from Durban that Mrs Gandhi, who had just been released from gaol, was critically ill but Gandhi would not budge from Pretoria until Smuts had agreed to the inclusion of a particular phrase in the agreement. Andrews went to see Smuts on his own, told him of Mrs Gandhi's illness, and secured his assent to the disputed phrase, and at last an agreement was signed.[1] The major points on which the Satyagraha struggle had been waged were conceded to the Indians. The £3 tax on the ex-indentured labourers was abolished; marriages performed according to Indian rites were legalized, and a domicile certificate bearing the holder's thumb-imprint was to be a sufficient evidence

[1] Chaturvedi and M. Sykes: *Charles Freer Andrews,* London, 1949, p. 97.

of the right to enter the Union of South Africa. Correspondence was exchanged between Gandhi and Smuts calling for administrative (as distinct from legislative) relief, covering such items as the rights of educated Indians to enter the Cape Colony, the status of educated Indians who had arrived during the previous three years, and permission for 'existing plural wives' to join their husbands in South Africa. General Smuts gave an assurance that 'it has always been and will continue to be the desire of the Government to see that (the existing laws) are administered in a just manner and with due regard to the vested rights'.

The Satyagraha struggle which had for all its vicissitudes continued for nearly eight years was now formally called off. Not all Indian grievances had been redressed; the Gold law, the trade licensing laws, the ghetto 'locations', the restrictions on inter-provincial migration and the bar on purchase of landed property remained. Gandhi hoped that the new atmosphere would facilitate the redress of these wrongs.

General Smuts' son has recorded that 'Gandhi's outwitting by my father was complete, and it was in this sense of failure that he set out dejectedly to brood and scheme in India'.[1] This was, however, not the opinion of his father who wrote in 1939 that it had been his 'fate to be the antagonist of a man for whom even then I had the highest respect'. As for the Satyagraha movement, he recalled: 'Gandhi himself received—what no doubt he desired—a short period of rest and quiet in gaol. For him everything went according to plan. For me—the defender of law and order—there was the usual trying situation, the odium of carrying out a law which had not strong public support, and finally the discomfiture when the law had to be repealed. For him it was a successful coup.'[2]

In gaol Gandhi had prepared a pair of sandals for General Smuts, who recalled that there was no hatred and personal ill feeling, and when the fight was over 'there was the atmosphere in which decent peace could be concluded'.

[1] Smuts, J. C.: *Jan Christian Smuts,* p. 106.
[2] Radhakrishnan, S. (Ed.): *Mahatma Gandhi,* London, 1939, pp. 277–8.

The Gandhi-Smuts agreement did not provide a panacea for the many hardships from which Indians suffered and continue to suffer. In 1924, when he concluded his *History of Satyagraha in South Africa*, Gandhi realized 'the painful contrast between the happy ending of the Satyagraha struggle and the present condition of the Indians in South Africa', and wondered whether the Indians' sufferings had been in vain. The Indians in South Africa had failed to protect themselves from further onslaughts of racial discrimination, and in some ways their position had grown worse. It was not because the weapons of Satyagraha had failed them. The veterans of Gandhi's movement, Sorabji, Kachhalia, Naidoo, Parsi Rustomji and others had passed away. 'This is the law of nature,' wrote Gandhi, 'that a thing can be retained by the same means by which it has been acquired.' The victory achieved by violence could be retained only by force; and the victory achieved by non-violence in 1914 could only be retained by non-violence. But after Gandhi's departure from South Africa there was no one with enough competence and courage to generate and mobilize effective non-violence on behalf of the Indian settlers.

Chapter 15

SOUTH AFRICAN LABORATORY

GANDHI's work did not provide an enduring solution for the Indian question in South Africa; it only postponed the evil day for the Indian minority. Forces, some of which he knew and fought, and others which were to emerge in the years to come, were to forge a new racial tyranny more ruthless and shameless than the pre-1914 world could conceive. The issues on which for eight years the Satyagraha struggle was waged and won by Gandhi have indeed only an academic interest today.

What Gandhi did to South Africa was, however, less important than what South Africa did to him. He had gone to South Africa as a junior counsel of a commercial firm for £105 a year; he stayed on to command, and then voluntarily to give up, a peak practice of £5,000 a year. In Bombay, as a young lawyer, he had a nervous breakdown while cross-examining witnesses in a petty civil suit; in South Africa he had founded a new political organization with the sure touch of a seasoned politician. The hostility of the European politicians and officials and the helplessness of the Indian merchants and labourers had put him on his mettle. 'I am the only available person who can handle the question,' he had written to Dadabhai Naoroji. The Natal Indians, who had no franchise and no representation in the Legislature, had to be saved from being pushed over the precipice; Gandhi could not avoid giving them a helping hand. No glittering rewards awaited him; the perils ranged from professional pinpricks to lynching. Nevertheless, it was a piece of good fortune that he began his professional and political career in South Africa. Dwarfed as he had felt by the great lawyers and leaders of India, it is unlikely that he would have developed much initiative in his homeland. When he founded the Natal Indian Congress at the age of twenty-five he was writing on a *tabula rasa*; he could try out ideals which in an established political organization would have been laughed out of court. What had truth and vows to do with politics? It was a question which often recurred in Indian politics, and if Gandhi was not confounded by it, it was because, far back in South Africa, he had observed and confirmed the connection. For a man who was no doctrinaire, and whose theory often lagged behind practice, it was a decided advantage that the scene of his early activities should have been one where he was unfettered by political precedents or professionals. Natal and Transvaal were no bigger than some of the smallest provinces of India. The struggle for Indian independence was conducted by Gandhi on a much larger scale and on much bigger issues, but there were not a few occasions when he derived inspiration from his experience in South Africa. He had seen Hindus and Muslims co-operating in Natal and Transvaal, and therefore never lost his faith in Hindu-Muslim unity. He had seen the vicissitudes of the Satyagraha struggle against the Asiatic Registration Act, and was never dispirited by the ebb and flow of the freedom movement in India. He had seen thousands of poor, unlettered labourers, bereft of almost all worldly goods, briskly marching, oblivious to the perils of imprisonment, flogging and shooting which awaited them; no wonder that he believed in the practicability of Satyagraha for the masses.

Not only his politics, but his personality took shape in South Africa. The most formative years of his life had been spent there. His interest in moral and religious questions dated back to his early childhood, but it was only in South Africa, that he had an opportunity of studying them systematically. The Quaker friends who made a dead set at him on his arrival in Pretoria failed to convert him to Christianity but they whetted his innate appetite for religious studies. He delved deep into Christianity and other religions including his own. From the *Gita* he imbibed the ideal of 'non-possession' which set him on the road to voluntary poverty. The ideal of 'service without self' and of 'action, without attachment' broadened his vision and equipped him with extraordinary stamina and faith for his public life.

'In this world good books,' Gandhi once wrote from gaol, 'make up for good companions.' Reading was never to him what it is to most of us, a pleasant pastime. He never read; he studied. Until the age of nineteen he had never looked through a newspaper. In England, he had ventured outside the domain of his text-books but only into the twin subjects of vegetarianism and religion. These subjects he pursued further in South Africa. In the first year before he took the plunge in politics, he read 'quite eighty books', most of them on religion. One of these books was Tolstoy's *Kingdom of God is Within You*. Tolstoy became his favourite author and in the coming years he read the *Gospels in Brief, What to do? What is Art? The Slavery of Our Times, The First Step, How shall We Escape? Letters to a Hindoo*. Tolstoy's bold idealism and fearless candour gripped him, his Christian anarchism dissipated the spell of institutional religion. Tolstoy's emphasis on the necessity of an accord between moral principles and daily life confirmed his own strivings for self-improvement. Few men read so little to so much profit as Gandhi did. A book was, for Gandhi not a mere diversion for the hour, it was embodied experience which had to be accepted or rejected. Books could thus exercise an amazing impact on him. Ruskin's *Unto This Last* drove him with compelling urgency from the capital of Natal to the wilderness of Zululand to practise a life of voluntary poverty, and literally to live by the sweat of his brow. It was in Tolstoy's books that we may seek one of the strongest influences on Gandhi. He was, of course, not given to indiscriminate imitation, but in Tolstoy he found a writer whose views elaborated his own inchoate beliefs. It was not only on the organized or covert violence of the modern state and the right of the citizen to civil disobedience, that Gandhi found support in Tolstoy. There were innumerable subjects, ranging from modern civilization and industrialism to sex and schools, on which he tended to agree with Tolstoy's analysis.

There was an exchange of letters between the two which gives an impression of gratitude and reverence by the young Indian on the threshold of his career, and of delightful surprise by the aged Tolstoy, already under the shadow of domestic tragedy and death. Many of Tolstoy's ideas were to be tested and tried by his Indian admirer. Tolstoy's diaries show how, with the background of his conjugal civil war, he was unable to practise what he preached; how the intolerable contradiction weighed upon him, until he could bear it no more and fled from Yasnaya Polyana to die at a wayside railway station.

Hind Swaraj or 'Indian Home Rule', which was written in 1908 during Gandhi's return voyage from London to South Africa, bears an impress of Tolstoy and Ruskin. Directed at the 'school of violence', the young anarchists who sought the salvation of India by using against the West its own weapon of bomb and pistol, *Hind Swaraj* is a compendious political manifesto. It ranges over a wide field; it discusses 'Home Rule', the mainsprings of the British authority in India, and of the nationalist discontent, the balance sheet of British rule in India, the nature of parliamentary system of government, the curse of industrial and materialistic civilization of the West, the Hindu-Muslim problem, and the comparative efficacy of 'brute force' and passive resistance.

When Gokhale read the book in 1912 he thought it crude and predicted that Gandhi himself would destroy it after spending a year in India. Gandhi did not destroy the book. In 1921 he wrote in *Young India* that he withdrew nothing except one word, and that in deference to a lady friend! In the same article he warned the reader 'against thinking that I am today aiming at the *Swaraj* described therein. I know that India is not ripe for it . . . I am individually working for the self-rule pictured therein. But today my corporate activity is undoubtedly devoted to the attainment of Parliamentary *Swaraj* in accordance with the wishes of the people of India'.

The ideals of *Hind Swaraj* became almost exclusively the personal ideals of Gandhi and his closest associates. The railways, hospitals, schools, factories, the parliamentary institutions and the paraphernalia of Western civilization which he denounced, have come to stay, and to prosper. Even in his lifetime he continued to tolerate them as a necessary evil. 'India is not ripe for it,' he admitted. In fact this part of his philosophy struck his own followers either too far ahead, or perhaps behind the times. That the doctrines in *Hind Swaraj* were not practicable did not, in Gandhi's opinion, detract from their validity. He did not flinch from thinking fearlessly on any problem, and from facing the conclusions to which it led him. Whether it was political philosophy, religion, or sex, he formulated his thesis fearlessly; he practised it to the best of his ability; he asked others to accept his ideas in so far as they carried conviction. It was against his nature to ram his idealism down the throats of even his closest associates, and he did not mind if he found himself in a minority of one.

The Gandhi who left South Africa in 1914 was a very different person from the callow diffident youth who had arrived at Durban in 1893. South Africa had not treated him kindly; it had drawn him into the vortex of the racial problem created by the domination of the Dark Continent by the white races. The tug of war which followed had matured Gandhi, given him his own original political philosophy and also helped him forge a new technique of social and political agitation, which was destined to play a great part in Indian politics in the next thirty years.

BOOK II

EMERGENCE OF GANDHI

Chapter 16

ON PROBATION

'INDIA is a strange country to me,' said Gandhi at a farewell meeting in South Africa. Between the year 1888, when he sailed for England, and 1914, when he finally left South Africa, he had spent less than four years in India.

He was, however, no stranger to India. Gokhale had told his countrymen, after a tour of South Africa in 1912, that Gandhi 'is without doubt made of the stuff of which heroes and martyrs are made. Nay, more, he has in him the marvellous spiritual power to turn ordinary men around him into heroes and martyrs'.

A hero's welcome awaited him when he landed on January 9, 1915 at the Appollo Bunder in Bombay. Three days later he was honoured at a magnificent reception in the palatial house of Jehangir Petit. Sir Pherozeshah Mehta, 'the uncrowned king of Bombay', who had once been sceptical of Gandhi's South African movement, hailed him as 'a hero in the cause of Indian independence', and Mrs Gandhi as 'the heroine of South Africa'. In that gathering of the westernized *élite* of Bombay, the cream of the bureaucratic and business world, Gandhi in his Kathiawari turban and cloak, and Mrs Gandhi in her plain sari, felt 'absolutely out of their element'. With his characteristic candour, Gandhi confessed that he had felt more at home among the indentured labourers of Natal than in the city of Bombay. To many of his hosts he must have appeared queer and quixotic, or to quote a contemporary opinion, 'rather an eccentric specimen of an England-returned-educated-Indian'.[1] He rebuked a Parsi Press

[1] J. B. Kripalani in *Incidents of Gandhiji's Life*. (Edited by Shukla), Bombay, 1949, p. 118.

E

correspondent who addressed him in English: 'I have not forgotten my native tongue during my stay in South Africa.' At a party given by the Gujeratees of Bombay he broke all convention by expressing his thanks in Gujerati. He was modest about his achievements in South Africa. He declared it was not he who had inspired the Indians of South Africa; it was *they* who had inspired him. Somebody had referred to Kasturbai, as the wife of 'the great Gandhi'; Gandhi said he had no knowledge of the great man.

The Government of India joined with the people of India in showering honours on him. He received a Kaiser-i-Hind gold medal in the New Year's Honours list of 1915. His association with Gokhale was a guarantee enough of his being a 'safe' politician. Just before his return to India in 1915 he had organized an ambulance corps from amongst Indians in London to serve in the battlefronts of Europe. Of course, he had led an extra-constitutional movement in South Africa, defied laws and filled gaols, but the cause for which he had fought appeared as much humanitarian as political, dear to all Indians and all Englishmen whose sense of humanity had not been blunted by racial arrogance or political expediency. Lord Hardinge's open support of the Satyagraha movement had removed any stigma of 'rebellion' from South Africa's Indian movement.

Soon after his arrival in Bombay, Gandhi had, at Gokhale's request, met the Governor of Bombay. 'I ask one thing of you,' said Lord Willingdon; 'I would like you to come and see me whenever you propose to take any steps concerning the Government.' Gandhi willingly gave the promise; it was part of the technique of Satyagraha to explore every avenue of convincing and converting an opponent. But the incident shows what a shrewd British administrator thought at a time when, to many British and Indian observers, Gandhi with his peculiar views on the superiority of the Indian over the Western civilization, the abolition of child marriage and untouchability, must have appeared, another Mahatma Munshi Ram or Swami Vivekananda, a religious or social reformer whose energies were likely to be drained off in harmless channels of non-political activity.

Gandhi himself was in no hurry to plunge into politics. His political mentor on the Indian scene was Gokhale. For eighteen years Gokhale had never taken his eyes off Gandhi. 'One day you will I hope, see a man who is destined to do very great things for India';[1] this prophecy of Gokhale was also a hope long cherished and deferred by factors beyond the control of both Gandhi and Gokhale. During his tour of South Africa in 1913, Gokhale had tried to brief Gandhi on Indian politics. Gandhi seemed hopelessly out of touch with the conditions in India. Gokhale laughed at some of his ideas and said, 'After you have stayed a year in India your views will correct themselves'. One of the first things Gokhale did was to extract a promise from Gandhi on his return to India that he would not express himself upon public questions for a year, which was to be 'a year of probation'.

Gokhale was very keen that Gandhi should join the Servants of India Society. This society, founded by Gokhale, consisted of a small band of carefully selected social workers and scholars living on a subsistence wage and pledged to devote their lives to the cause of the country. Gandhi was only too willing to fall in with the wishes of Gokhale, but several members of the Society feared there was too great a gap between the ideals and methods of the Society, and those of Gandhi. His critical approach to Western civilization and modern science, and his use of religious jargon for describing everyday social and economic problems, his extra-constitutional method of political agitation (Satyagraha) jarred on the small coterie of the 'servants of India'. While the question of Gandhi's admission 'as a servant of India' was being debated, Gandhi visited his home towns of Porbandar and Rajkot and went on to Santiniketan in West Bengal, the cosmopolitan university of poet Rabindranath Tagore, who had already provided a temporary home to the

[1] Quoted by Rajkumari Amrit Kaur in *Incidents of Gandhiji's Life*. (Edited by Shukla), Bombay, 1949, p. 7.

group of close relatives and followers who had left South Africa to cast their lot in with Gandhi.

'To the outward eye no two personalities could be more unlike than Tagore and Gandhi. Their names conjure up two different worlds, as different from each other as is the valley of Kashmir from the plains of Sind . . . They felt and lived in ways that seem to challenge each other. Even in physical appearance they seemed to belong to different racial stocks. The two men were to differ later on public questions, but by and large they confirmed and upheld each other and represented a fundamental harmony in Indian civilization.'[1]

Gandhi spent a week in Santiniketan, but it was an eventful week. Among those in Santiniketan at the time were Andrews and Pearson, the fine Christian youths who had gone to South Africa at Gokhale's bidding in the last phase of the Satyagraha struggle, and Kripalani and Kalelkar, who were before long to become Gandhi's lifelong followers. During his brief stay, Gandhi inspired an experiment in self-help at Santiniketan: he persuaded the students and the teachers to run their own kitchen, and to sack the thirty Brahmin cooks who combined orthodoxy and uncleanliness in a concentrated mixture. Tagore was pleased and amused at the sight of teachers and students scrubbing floors and washing the utensils. The experiment lasted exactly forty days, after which it was abandoned. The poet, an epicurean, chuckled over Gandhi's food fads. One day when Gandhi told him that to fry in ghee or oil was to turn bread into poison, the poet replied solemnly, 'it must be a very slow poison. I have been eating *puris* the whole of my life and it has not done me any harm so far.'

The trip to Santiniketan ended abruptly with a telegram from Poona that Gokhale was dead. Gandhi was stunned. For a moment he felt lost. 'Launching on the stormy sea of Indian public life,' he wrote later, 'I was in need of a sure pilot. I had had one in Gokhale and had felt secure in his keeping.'[2] He

[1] Kripalani, K. R.: *Gandhi, Nehru and Tagore*, p. 1.
[2] Gandhi: *Autobiography*, p. 471.

mourned Gokhale by going barefoot for a year, and out of respect for the memory of his friend, philosopher and guide, he made another effort to seek admission to the Servants of India Society. Finding a sharp division of opinion in the Society on this point, he wrote to Srinivasa Sastri, who had succeeded Gokhale as the head of the Society, that he wished to withdraw his application for admission and save those opposed to him from an awkward position.

The remainder of the year of probation was spent in travelling across the country. A visit to Calcutta and a short trip to Burma, were followed by a visit to Hardwar, the scene of the mammoth Kumbh fair. Though he was not yet the familiar figure to the Indian masses he was to become a few years later, it was something of an ordeal to be pursued by hundreds of people eager for his *darshan*. The story of the Indian struggle in South Africa was evidently known not only to the white-collar class in the big presidency towns, but had percolated to the masses. At Hardwar he saw the corruption and hypocrisy practised in the name of Hinduism: the swarms of 'sadhus' who sponged on the community, and the frauds practised by the priests to extract the last copper from the pilgrims. As an atonement for the iniquity he saw around him, he vowed never to eat more than five articles of food in twenty-four hours and never to eat after dark. Here he was expiating the sins of others. This was not the first nor the last time that he was to atone in self-mortification for the sorrows and sins of his countrymen.

During 1915—the year of probation—Gandhi eschewed politics severely. In his speeches and writings during this period he confined himself to the reform of the individual and the society, and avoided the issues which dominated Indian politics. His restraint was partly due to self-imposed silence and partly to the fact that he was still studying conditions in India and making up his mind.

Chapter 17

SABARMATI ASHRAM

WHILE his political views were yet unformed, Gandhi's immediate problem was to settle the small band of relatives and associates in the South African struggle who had cast their lot in with him. A party of eighteen boys from Phoenix (in Natal), led by Maganlal, had arrived in India while Gandhi was still in England. They had enjoyed the hospitality of two great cultural and educational institutions, Gurukul Kangri and Santiniketan. At Santiniketan Tagore received them kindly and wrote to Gandhi thanking him 'for allowing your boys to be our boys as well, and thus form a living link in the *sadhana* of both of our lives'. Gandhi was, however, anxious to set up an 'Ashram' where he could lodge these boys and other co-workers to enable them to resume the life of simplicity and service in which they had been nurtured in South Africa.

Gokhale had promised to finance the Ashram, but he died in February 1915. Gandhi received invitations to found the Ashram in various parts of the country, from his home town Rajkot, from holy Hardwar, and from Calcutta, but he chose Ahmedabad. Apart from the fact that some of the local industrialists promised to find the money for the setting up and running of an Ashram, he felt that he could best serve the people of the province of his birth. Ahmedabad, a great textile centre, was also best suited for experiments in hand spinning and weaving which appeared to him the only practicable supplementary occupations for the underworked and underfed masses in the villages of India.

The Satyagraha Ashram started with a population of twenty-five men, women and children in a small bungalow which belonged to a lawyer in Kochrab, a village near Ahmedabad. The building had not been designed for the community life of an Ashram and was soon found inadequate for the increasing number of its inmates. An outbreak of plague in the village hastened the shifting of the Ashram to a more permanent site on the bank of the river Sabarmati. The jungle was cleared and a small colony grew up. Eventually the Ashram covered an area of 150 acres. It had cottages for Gandhi, the teachers and their families, a dining-room, a school, a library, spinning and weaving sheds, a dairy farm and cultivable plots on which vegetables and cotton were grown.

Gandhi had time only to plan the Ashram. With the numerous calls he received from various parts of the country, he had to leave the execution of his plans to the competent and indefatigable Maganlal Gandhi, whose loyalty, practical ability and resourcefulness had contributed to the success of the Phoenix settlement and Tolstoy Farm in South Africa. The gratitude that Gandhi felt towards Maganlal is expressed for all time in the unique epitaph: 'His death has widowed me. M. K. Gandhi.'

The Ashram had been in existence only for a few months when it faced a crisis. Gandhi had always opposed untouchability which condemned millions of Hindus to a dwarfed life. He received a letter from Amritlal Thakkar of the Servants of India Society that a humble and honest untouchable family wanted to join the Ashram. The family consisting of Dudabhai who had been a teacher in Bombay, his wife Danibehn and their baby daughter Lakshmi, agreed to abide by the rules of the Ashram and were accepted. Their admission, however, cut across irrational but deep prejudices and brought on Gandhi's head storms both inside and outside the Ashram. The wealthy merchants of Ahmedabad, who had been supporting the Ashram, were scandalized by this outrage on orthodoxy and cut off supplies. The Ashram ran out of funds and Gandhi decided to move into the untouchables' quarters in the slums of Ahmedabad, and to live by manual work. This desperate step was averted by an 'anonymous' donation of Rs. 13,000; the donor was

Ambalal Sarabhai, a magnate of Ahmedabad with whom Gandhi was to come into conflict a little later.

The financial crisis had been tided over, but another and more difficult crisis faced Gandhi within the Ashram. Some of its inmates were unhappy about the arrival of an untouchable family and among them was Kasturbai. She had given in to her husband's heterodoxy in South Africa, but in her native environment her prejudices about untouchability revived vigorously. Gandhi was deeply distressed. The Ashram code was no respecter of persons. How could he allow his wife to flout a rule irrevocable for everybody else? He screwed himself up to pose a startling choice to her. She had to give up her untouchability complex or quit the Ashram. Kasturbai was stunned; she knew her husband too well to think that this was an idle threat. With an effort of will she accepted the untouchable family as her own.

There was yet another test for Gandhi. Maganlal, his most devoted disciple, who had run his Ashram in South Africa and who was the linchpin of the new Ashram, confessed that both he and his wife felt deep down in them a fear of 'pollution' from contact with untouchables; they packed up their few belongings and came to bid goodbye. Maganlal was exceedingly unhappy and so was Gandhi. A compromise was quickly reached; Maganlal agreed to spend a few months in Madras to learn weaving and, incidentally, to unlearn his prejudices about untouchability.

In his *History of the Satyagraha Ashram*, which was begun in Yeravda gaol in 1932 but published after his death, Gandhi defined an Ashram as 'group life lived in a religious spirit'. The word 'religious' was used here in the widest sense. Gandhi's Ashram did not enforce any theology or ritual, but only a few simple rules of personal conduct. Some of the vows administered in the Ashram, such as those of truth, non-violence and chastity, were of universal application; others, such as those to eradicate untouchability, to do bodily labour and to practise fearlessness, were intended to meet the peculiar conditions of the contem-

porary Indian society, which was caste-ridden, discounted dignity
of labour, and was dominated by an alien government.

The vows were to be observed in an intelligent and creative
way. They were not intended to be mechanical formulae, but
as practical aids to moral and spiritual growth. They may appear
to be platitudes, but nevertheless they embodied ancient truths
which were none the less valid for not having been realized by
the common run of mankind in workaday life.

We may begin with the vow of truth. 'The Satyagraha
Ashram,' wrote Gandhi, 'owes its very existence to the pursuit
and the attempted practice of truth.'[1] There was no ready-made
formula for truth. He conceded that what appeared as truth
to one person might not do so to another. 'There is nothing
wrong,' he added, 'in everyone following truth according to
his lights. Indeed it is his duty to do so.'

The vow of *ahimsa* (non-violence) was not only a negative
concept of non-injury to others. Nor was it carried in daily
life to its logical but impossible conclusion that breathing and
eating of vegetables destroyed living organisms. The motive
force of *ahimsa* the love for all that lives, had to be intelligently
interpreted. Orthodoxy in India received a rude shock when
Gandhi permitted in Sabarmati Ashram the mercy-killing of
a calf suffering from an excruciating but incurable pain. Again,
though a great champion of the cow, 'poem of pity' as he called
it, he could discuss in detail the economics of cowhide because
he felt that unless every part of the carcass was used, the cow
could not survive in India in competition with other milch
animals such as the buffalo. He did not regard non-violence
simply as avoidance of physical injury to animate beings. He
knew that guns and bombs and daggers probably take a smaller
toll of human life than ill will, malice and hatred, which cramp
and kill humanity inch by inch. The Gandhian non-violence
aimed at liberating men and women from inner as well as outer
violence.

Another vow was that of *brahmacharya* (celibacy), meant for

[1] Gandhi: *From Yeravda Mandir*, p. 1.

K*

those who wished to consecrate themselves wholly to the service of their fellow men. It may appear that Gandhi was imposing a puritanical tyranny and straining human nature to the limit, but we must remember that the restraint of sexual desire was a part of a wider discipline he advocated, including an appropriate regimen of food, manual labour, social service, prayer and sleep.

The vow of non-stealing may appear a truism for an Ashram of this type, but it had a deeper social meaning. From the *Gita* Gandhi had imbibed the ideal of non-possession. Ideally, 'man should like the birds have no roof over his head, no clothing and no stock of food for the morrow'. This is evidently impossible of attainment in the world in which we live, but Gandhi wanted human wants to be reduced to the minimum. He had already stripped himself of money and property, and brought himself down to a level of material possession where he could feel a twinge of conscience even for 'usurping' the food and the shelter which might be more urgently needed by the hungry and homeless everywhere.

The story of a theft in Sabarmati Ashram is interesting for the light it sheds on the social philosophy of Mohandas Karamchand Gandhi. The thieves had taken away a box belonging to Kasturbai. Instead of reporting to the police, Gandhi observed that the thieves apparently believed that the Ashram had things worth stealing and that they had failed to imbue the people of the locality, including the potential thieves, with the spirit of the Ashram. As for Kasturbai's box, he was, he said surprised that she had possessed one! When she explained that it contained her grandchildren's clothes, she was told that it was for her children and grandchildren to mind their own clothes. From this day hers was the tiniest kit in the Gandhian entourage.

Two more vows administered in Sabarmati Ashram, one of fearlessness, and the other of anti-untouchability, had a limited but contemporary interest; the fear of British rule, and the ill-treatment of the untouchables had cramped the Indian people in different ways and the members of the Ashram had to rise above these limitations.

A mere enumeration of the vows is enough to indicate that life in the Ashram was austere. It was also busy. Everyone had to put in some manual work. There was a spinning and weaving department, a cow-shed and a large farm. Every inmate of the Ashram cleaned his own plates and washed his own clothes. There were no servants. The atmosphere was, however, not so much of a monastery but that of a large family under a kindly but exacting patriarch. Gandhi was *Bapu*, the father of this household; Kasturbai was *Ba*, the mother. It was a motley group including little children and octogenarians, graduates of American and European universities and Sanskrit scholars, devout whole-hoggers, and thinly-disguised sceptics. It was a human laboratory where Gandhi tested his moral and spiritual hypotheses. It was also to him what the family is to most people: a haven from the dust and din of the world. It was a family linked not by blood or property but by allegiance to common ideals. The patriarch was a great democrat, and once appointed a committee to select verses for morning and evening prayers. When confronted with a request or a complaint he would laugh and say, 'I am a guest in the Ashram.' He ruled the Ashram but his authority in the Ashram, as well as in the rest of the country, was moral. When things went wrong or a member of the Ashram was guilty of a serious lapse, he would take the blame upon himself, and atone for it by undertaking a fast.

Kasturba, as she came to be known, helped in the kitchen and looked after the numerous guests. There was no chore too petty or lowly for her. She was almost unconscious of her status as the wife of a great public figure. Once she received a reprimand at a prayer meeting in the presence of almost the entire population of the Ashram for being unaware of the illness of an inmate. 'If Devadas (Gandhi's youngest son) had been ill,' said her husband, 'you would have known about it.' It was a stinging rebuke but it showed the high standard that he expected from those nearest to him.

The Ashram was a laboratory in which Gandhi experimented with himself and others. It was also a military academy, if the term may be used for training men and women for a war without violence. Early in 1915, he had told C. F. Andrews that he did not anticipate an occasion for Satyagraha for five years. Nevertheless, in his Ashram a band of young men and women were being trained in the moral and emotional controls essential for a Satyagrahi, so that the grip did not give way to hatred or violence, even under provocation. The Sabarmati Ashram was to do for the Satyagraha struggles of 1920 and 1930, what the Phoenix and Tolstoy Farm had done in South Africa. It was also to provide men and women for constructive activities which, between spells of Satyagraha, built up the nation's morale.

Chapter 18

INDIAN NATIONALISM

WHEN Gandhi came on the Indian scene, the nationalist movement had already secured a foothold among the educated and professional classes in the country. In December 1885, nearly three years before he had left for England to qualify as a barrister, the Indian National Congress had held its first meeting at Bombay. Neither in England, nor after his return to India had he evinced any interest in politics. For twenty years, from 1894 onwards, he was wholly absorbed in the struggle for survival of the Indian community in South Africa. Nevertheless within a few years of his return from South Africa, the reins of the nationalist movement of which he had been only a distant spectator were to fall into his hands, and were to remain with him until his death. A brief flash-back on this movement at this stage may help us to understand the state of Indian politics in 1915 and the nature of Gandhi's impact on it.

That the British conquest of India could not be a permanent feature was foreseen by far-sighted British administrators like Thomas Munro and Mountstart Elphinstone. India had been invaded before the British from the north-west and governed by foreigners for more than seven centuries, but they had gradually been assimilated within the Indian body politic. As Thomas Munro pointed out, there had been foreign conquerors who had been more violent and more cruel, but none had treated Indians with such secret scorn as the British, by stigmatizing 'the whole people as unworthy of trust'. Sir Henry Lawrence had commented caustically on the tendency among the British administrators to talk of the 'black fellows' as if they were very much in the way (of the British administrators) in their own country, except in so far as they might be turned to the comfort and aggrandizement of the rulers. The Mutiny led to a further severing of the races. It may not have been a purely military nor a primarily Muhammadan outbreak. On the contrary it was far from being a War of Independence, though in northern and central India it fed upon anti-British feeling. Its leadership, being feudal, it was fighting for a lost cause and foredoomed to failure.

The Mutiny was a war without pity and there were crimes on both sides. The British continued to cherish the heroism and suffering of those who had fought and foiled the rebellion. The Indians cherished the memories of those who had fought and failed against the superior might of the foreigner. The victors had no doubt that Providence had tilted the scales in their favour. 'Those who had counted the English as few at the beginning of the war had forgotten to ask on which side God was to be counted.' A bitter legacy of suspicion and fear was left by the Mutiny. The Governor-General, Lord Canning, who was nicknamed 'Clemency Canning' for not being tough enough with the 'natives', wrote to Queen Victoria of 'a rabid and indiscriminating vindictiveness' which was abroad. The correspondent of the *Times* reached the melancholy conclusion that 'perhaps confidence will never be restored'. The British commanders and civilians seemed to be less worried about restoring confidence than about tightening their grip on the country to make sure that 'it will not happen again'.

The official report on the reorganization of the Indian Army after 1857 pointed out that only next to 'the grand counterpoise of a sufficient European army, comes the counterpoise of natives against natives'. The British proportion in the army of occupation was henceforth to be adequate, and the recruitment of sepoys (soldiers) to be confined to areas and communities whose loyalty had successfully stood the test of the Mutiny. The Indian States were treated with tenderness, and built up as breakwaters against a future rebellion. A new chasm, wider and deeper than any in the first half of the nineteenth century, divided the worlds of the British officials and the Indian masses; there was too much authority or arrogance on one side and excessive sensitiveness or servility on the other. Not for another sixty years was an Indian (not a prince) to meet the ordinary run of Englishmen, official or non-official, as Ram Mohun Roy had met them.

The pacification of India seemed to be complete with the disarming of the country and the strengthening of the British garrison. One can, however, do anything with bayonets except sit on them—for ever. The social, economic and political forces, against foreign rule could not be dammed for ever. The British administrators poised peacefully in their sequestered cantonments and 'civil lines' could no more hold them back than King Canute could stop the waves of the ocean.

There were seven famines in India in the first half of the nineteenth century; there were twenty-four in the second half. In the 1870's East Bengal and the Deccan seethed with agrarian discontent which led the Government to enact legislation for the protection of the tenants and to evolve a famine code. The agrarian trouble in the country-side was accompanied by rumblings of discontent in towns. The educated classes who had been nurtured on John Stuart Mill were applying the principles of British liberalism in India and noting the gap between precept and practice.

Rabindranath Tagore has recorded his early admiration of the British. As a boy, in England, the poet had opportunities of listening to John Bright in and outside Parliament, and the large-hearted liberalism of those speeches, transcending national barriers, made a deep impression on him. Madan Mohan Malaviya had asked as a young man, 'What is an Englishman without representative institutions?' and himself answered 'Why, not an Englishman at all, a mere sham, a base institution.' There was something in the scepticism of the British officials who had seen red in the introduction of Western education in India: the products of Macaulay's Western education could call upon his successors to live up to their own traditions. The British officers who governed India were not liberals or radicals, but it was with liberal politics and radical economics that the rising middle class in India associated all the best in Britain. The first demand of Western educated Indians was for a share in the administration of their country.

The question of recruitment of Indians to the civil service provoked the first organized agitation in India in 1877-78 when Surendranath Bannerjea, the great orator of Bengal, toured the country and pleaded before crowded meetings for simultaneous examinations in India and England for recruitment to the Indian Civil Service.

The middle classes were also stirred by movements of religious and social reformation, which harked back to the golden age of Indian history. Swami Dayananda, Ramakrishna Paramhansa, and Swami Vivekananda stirred Hinduism, and by emphasizing its spiritual and cultural heritage helped to compensate for the political demoralization inevitable under foreign rule. Foreigners, including theosophists like Olcott and scholars like Max Muller, raised the self-esteem of the intelligentsia by drawing upon the rich reservoir of Indian philosophy and religion.

The segregation of the races since the Mutiny and the cold aloofness of the ruling race were a source of continual humiliation to sensitive Indians. There were not a few cases where a European got away with the murder of an Indian coolie or servant on some flimsy plea; enlarged spleen of the native was the usual explanation which the courts swallowed without any qualms. The obsequiousness of the classes which flourished on official bounty was met with a mixture of contempt and patronage. An interesting example is the permission granted in 1868, by a formal resolution of the Government of India, to native gentlemen wearing boots and shoes of European fashion to appear 'thus habited' at Durbars and other ceremonial occasions, and the injunction to those who wore shoes of Indian fashion, to take them off 'within customary limits'. The clamorous agitation from European officials and businessmen against the Ilbert Bill (by which Lord Ripon attempted to do away with racial distinctions in the administration of justice) was an eye-opener to the Indian middle class; its success indicated that organized agitations alone could bring the Government to its knees.

An important ingredient was added to the nationalist ferment by the emergence of modern industry in India. The first cotton mill was established in Bombay in 1854; in the next fifty years the number of textile mills rose to nearly 200. The Government was unsympathetic to Indian industry when it competed with the industry 'at home'. When in 1882, the duties on cotton imports were withdrawn, the Indian industrialists knew that the real beneficiary was not the Indian consumer, but the British manufacturer in Lancashire and Manchester.

It is a strange irony of history that the Indian National Congress which contributed most to the liquidation of British rule in India was conceived and founded by a Briton. Allan Octavian Hume, a former Secretary to the Government of India, who had retired from the Indian Civil Service in 1882 after more than thirty years' service, believed that though England had given India peace, she had not solved her economic problems, that the Government was out of touch with the people and it was essential to leaven the administration with a representative Indian element. He thought of an organization which could act as a 'safety valve for the great and growing forces generated by our own action'. When he met the Viceroy, Lord Dufferin and unfolded his scheme of an All-India meeting every year to discuss social matters, the Viceroy suggested that it should also discuss problems of administration. Hume visited the principal towns in India to canvass support, paid a hurried visit to England and returned just in time for the projected All-India meeting. On December 28, 1885, seventy-two representatives from different parts of India met at Bombay under the chairmanship of a Calcutta barrister, W. C. Bonnerjee, who declared that Indians' 'desire to be governed according to the ideas of government prevalent in Europe, was in no way incompatible with their thorough loyalty to the British Government'. The first speech on the first resolution in 1885 spoke of 'the merciful dispensation of Providence' which had brought India under the dominion of the great British power.

This thick veneer of loyal phrases has led present-day critics to debunk the early phase of the Congress as that of 'political mendicancy'. Of the first twenty-five sessions of the Congress, five were presided over by Europeans. In 1892 there was even a serious proposal to hold a session in London, and in 1911 the Congress session would have been presided over by Ramsay MacDonald but for his wife's death. The resolutions of the Congress repeated year after year what, today, seem to be verbal exercises. To the contemporary British administrators, however, even this rhetoric was a danger signal. The official attitude to the Indian National Congress quickly changed from a benevolent patronage to a thinly-disguised antagonism. Lord Dufferin who had blessed the birth of the Congress in 1885, belittled it three years later as a 'microscopic minority'. In 1890, government officials were directed not to attend Congress sessions. In 1898 Lord Elgin declared in a speech in the United Services Club, Simla, 'India was conquered by the sword, and by the sword it shall be held'. Lord Elgin's successor Lord Curzon tried to put the educated Indian in his proper place, and assured the Secretary of State for India in 1900 that 'the Congress is tottering to its fall and one of my great ambitions while in India is to assist it to a peaceful demise'.

It was Lord Curzon's destiny to put a new life into the nationalist movement and the Indian National Congress. The partition of Bengal, whatever its administrative merits, was taken by the Bengalis as an attack on the integrity of their province and evoked a vehement agitation. There was a movement for the boycott of British goods, and stray acts of terrorisms against Europeans took place.

From 1905 onwards there was a struggle within the Congress between its moderate and extremist wings. A split was avoided in 1906 by inviting the eighty-one-year-old Dadabhai Naoroji, who came from England, to preside over the annual session held at Calcutta. Next year, the Congress met at Surat in a tense atmosphere. While the moderates were confident of their majority in the Congress session, the extremists were conscious of their popularity in the country. There was a pandemonium and the session broke up in disorder. The moderates with nearly 1,000 adherents out of the 1,600 delegates met in a conference under the protection of the police and drew up a constitution which reaffirmed their faith in a steady reform of the existing system of government 'by constitutional means'. The extremists had lost in the first round.

'What happened in the 1907 Congress session,' wrote Valentine Chirol, a shrewd observer, 'was but a pale reflection of what was happening outside . . . The cry of Swaraj was caught up and re-echoed in every province of British India.' The discontent expressed itself in sporadic violence against British officials and loyal Indians. The Indian language papers particularly B. G. Tilak's *Kesari* in Maharashtra and Aurobindo Ghose's *Bande Matram* in Bengal stirred popular feeling. Anarchist societies grew up. 'Elaborate, persistent and ingenious' was a comment on the revolutionary movement made by an official committee which later investigated its ramifications. Gandhi, then resident in South Africa and a detached observer of Indian politics, was so alarmed by the rising tide of violence that he attempted a re-education of Indian anarchists by a series of articles in his paper *Indian Opinion*.

Meanwhile the Government was trying to rally moderate public opinion by doling out measured doses of constitutional reform. Unfortunately, each dose was pitifully small, belated and grudgingly conceded; it succeeded, not so much in satisfying as in whetting the appetite for reform. The Minto-Morley Reforms increased the elected element in the legislatures but not to the point where it could outvote the government bloc. The Government was very anxious, wrote Lord Morley, 'to avoid any appearance of a parliamentary franchise . . . We didn't want a Parliament at all; we wanted councils'. And worst of all, communal electorates were introduced for Muslims, and the evolution of the democracy was thus poisoned at the source.

The general political ferment in the first decade of this century could not but suck in the Muslim middle classes. Valentine Chirol had written in his *Indian Unrest* (1910) that 'never before had the Muhammadans of India as a whole indentified their interests and their aspirations with the consolidation and permanence of the British rule'. The Muslim middle class was not so staid as Chirol made himself believe. The Muslim League since its inception in 1906 had been a mouth-piece for affirming Muslims' loyalty and demanding a greater representation for Muslims in Councils, and in the services. The younger generation in the League was, however, chafing at the strait-jacket of a loyalty which the old guard had so firmly wrapped on it. The initial discontent was not to spring from local or national grievances but from foreign sources. The Mutiny had shattered the Imperial day-dreams of the Muslim middle class which turned for inspiration to Muslim countries. The events in the Middle East had disconcerted Indian Muslims. Persia had been carved into two spheres of influence between Russia and Britain. The Balkan Wars from which Britain kept out, had stripped the Turkish Empire of some of its European provinces. The Balkan Wars may be historically viewed as a conflict between the outmoded Turkish Imperialism and forces of nationalism in South-eastern Europe, but to the Indian Muslims they looked like the hopeless struggle of Islam, against the Christian Powers. Poets such as Iqbal and Shibli, scholars and publicists such as Abul Kalam Azad and Mahomed Ali, roused the Muslim middle class to the many dangers which beset Islam in the world. The professions of Muslim loyalty began to wear thin. In 1913 the objective of the Muslim League was declared to be not only the protection of Muslim rights, but also 'the attainment of a system of self-government suitable to India'. The same year, a Muslim (Nawab Syed Mahomed) presided over the Indian National Congress, welcomed the enlarged objective of the League and expressed the hope that the two bodies would co-operate for the good of the country.

The outbreak of the world war in 1914 created a dilemma for

the Muslim middle class. The dilemma arose (in the words of a Muslim leader) from the fact that 'the Government of our Caliph (Turkey) should be at war with the Government of our King Emperor'. The political consciousness of the Muslim middle class was thus heightened by events abroad. The Hindu middle class had become politically conscious and sensitive by the acts of commission or omission of the Government at home. The two streams of discontent were to converge in 1916 into a pact signed between the National Congress and the Muslim League.

Early in 1915, however, when Gandhi landed at Bombay, Indian political life was at a low ebb. The Government had assumed vast powers under the 'Defence of India Rules'. The Congress was dominated by the moderate leaders, Pherozeshah Mehta, Sethna and Gokhale; Tilak, the great leader of Maharashtra and of the extremist group in the Congress, recently released from prison was lying low; Lala Lajpat Rai, the fiery orator from the Punjab, was in exile; Aurobindo Ghose had retired from politics to Pondicherry. Abul Kalam Azad and the Ali brothers, the critics of British policy towards Turkey, were within a few months to find themselves in gaol. The result was to be a lull in Indian politics—a welcome lull for a government preoccupied with the war.

Chapter 19

SPLENDID ISOLATION

INDIAN politics, which seemed so stagnant early in 1915, were stirred deeply the following year by the Home Rule Movement. Its founder was Mrs Annie Besant, who had carved for herself a unique position in India's public life. A leader of the Theosophist movement, and one of the foremost educationists in the country, she had completely identified herself with India. In the words of one of her great contemporaries and friends, V. Srinivas Sastri: 'She believed in her heart of hearts, that she belonged in her spirit and by her soul to this country, that its culture, religion and philosophy belonged to her and that in future she would be born in this country to learn that culture, to spread that philosophy, to teach that religion. To her it was the greatest ambition to be known as an Indian, to be recognized in every home as an Indian . . .'

A few months before the outbreak of World War I, she had told a London audience that the price of India's loyalty was India's freedom. In a series of articles in *New India* in the spring of 1915 she had foreshadowed a political campaign which she intended to conduct. She canvassed support for this campaign at the annual Congress session in December 1915, and undaunted by the opposition it evoked from the moderates in the Congress, she founded the Home Rule League in September 1916.

Mrs Besant had sought but failed to secure Gandhi's support in launching the Home Rule League. Gandhi was opposed to a political movement which was likely to embarrass the Government during the war; he felt that the time for constitutional reforms would come when the war was over. Mrs Besant was amused at Gandhi's conviction that India was bound to get self-government after the war. She told him that only a Britain hard-pressed by the exigencies of a world war could be made to give freedom to India. 'Mrs Besant,' replied Gandhi, 'you are distrustful of the British; I am not, and I will not help in any agitation against them during the war.'[1]

Self-government for India within the British Empire through law-abiding and constitutional means, the declared objective of the Home Rule League, might seem tame in the light of later history, but in 1916-17 the impact of this organization on Indian politics was swift and strong. The appeal of the movement to the educated classes was due to the fact that it answered some of their own inchoate aspirations, and offered an outlet to the ferment which the war had generated. Mrs Besant's genius for propaganda and organization helped her in raising the political barometer. George Bernard Shaw, who had known her in her youth, had once remarked that she was capable of bearing the burden of three men. A great organizer, an eloquent speaker and a forthright writer, she quickened the political consciousness of the educated classes. Her vigorous journalism may be sampled from a few extracts from New India in the first half of 1917:

'India no longer wants your boons, your concessions and those offers you make; India wants to be mistress in her own house.' (February 2, 1917)

'Men who give their blood for the Empire are subject to this disgusting and degrading punishment (i.e. flogging) and it is a disgrace that men who fight like heroes should be whipped as slaves.' (March 20, 1917)

'Autocracy is destroyed in Russia; it is tottering in Germany; only under England's flag it is rampant.' (June 4, 1917)

The Government of India watched the progress of the Home Rule Movement with growing anxiety. In a minute dated January 17, 1917 the Home Member, Reginald Craddock, pointed out that the minds of the people who read newspapers were being poisoned against the British Government, that Home

[1] Kanji Dwarkadas: Gandhi Through my Diary Leaves, p. 10.

Rule was being advocated not so much as a constitutional reform but as the only salvation from the innumerable wrongs and grievances under which India was groaning. The popular support the movement had evoked was, from the point of view of the Government, its most deplorable feature: 'The position is one of great difficulty. The moderate leaders can command no support among the vocal classes who are being led at the heels of Tilak and Besant. The greater figures among the moderates have passed away, and so far they have no successors.'

Craddock went on to ridicule Mrs Besant 'as a vain old lady' who was influenced 'by the passionate desire to be a leader of movements', and Tilak as a man who was 'impelled by a venom and hatred against everything British'. Nevertheless he did not underrate the gravity of the problems, administrative and constitutional, which these two politicians had posed to the Government: 'Sedition in India is like the tides which erode the coast line as the sea encroaches. The last high tide was in 1907-08. The tide went out but it is flowing in now rapidly and it will reach a point higher than ever before. We must have a dam in order lest it inundates sound land.'

How was the Government of India to deal with this movement? In a minute dated February 1, 1917 the Viceroy recorded that, though he was prepared to sanction a summary action against Mrs Besant, Tilak and other leaders of the Home Rule Movement, if a clear case against them was made: 'As we stand, it seems to me impossible on paper to draw a distinction between the self-government which we advocate as the ultimate goal of British rule in India and Home Rule as advocated by Mrs Besant and Tilak, though we know in fact that the two policies are poles apart. I would suggest then that our obvious course is to announce our policy with as little delay as possible and set against a visionary Home Rule scheme our sane and practical proposals.'

On May 18, 1917, Lord Chelmsford telegraphed to the Secretary of State urging an early declaration in regard to the constitutional and administrative changes, if the possibilities of dangerous unrest in India were to be avoided and support secured from 'the influential though timid, unorganized and comparatively inarticulate body of opinion which is opposed to and afraid of any sudden and violent changes in the constitution, and looks to Government for support against extremist propaganda'. That, in asking for this declaration from His Majesty's Government, the Viceroy did not envisage any radical changes in the immediate future was made clear in a subsequent telegram on June 11: 'It seems to me that once we undertake to define our goal, we can say nothing but that it is the development of free institutions with a view to ultimate self-government. If such a declaration is made, then I think it should be accompanied by a very clear declaration that this is a distant goal and that any one who pretends that it is realizable today or in the early future is no friend to Government and no friend to India herself.'

The Home Rule agitation was thus to provide a powerful impulse for the famous declaration of August 1917 that the policy of His Majesty's Government was 'that of increasing association of Indians in every branch of the administration and the gradual development of self-governing institutions with a view to the progressive realization of a responsible Government in India as an integral part of the British Empire'.

The fact that Gandhi had not taken part in the Home Rule agitation nor in the negotiations which had led to the Lucknow Pact between the Indian National Congress and the All-India Muslim League in 1916 showed that he was largely isolated from the main currents of Indian politics. It was not Gandhi, but the Besant-Tilak combination which dominated the political scene and impressed the Government. In 1917 Edwin Montagu recorded in his diary that Tilak was 'at the moment probably the most powerful man in India'. Of Gandhi, Montagu's impression was of 'a social reformer with a real desire to find grievances and to cure them not for any reasons of self-advertisement, but to improve the conditions of fellow men. He dresses like a coolie, forswears all personal advancement, lives practically on the air and is a pure visionary'.

Gandhi did not figure much in contemporary politics because

of his self-denying ordinance on participation in political agitation
during the war. There was also another reason. His ideas and
methods did not quite fit in with those of the two dominant
groups in the Indian National Congress. Gokhale, the leader
of the moderates, whom Gandhi avowed as his mentor in Indian
politics, had paid high tribute to him; he had said at the annual
session of the Indian National Congress in 1909 that in Gandhi
'Indian humanity has reached its high watermark'. But in 1915
Gokhale had found his own closest associates reluctant to admit
Gandhi into the Servants of India Society. In any case Gokhale
died soon after Gandhi's return to India. The fact that Gandhi
had been so close to Gokhale could not add to his popularity
with the extremists who may have respected him for his South
African record, but did not understand, much less appreciate,
his policy of non-embarrassment towards the British during the
war. We have already seen how Mrs Besant had failed to enlist
Gandhi's support for the Home Rule Movement. In 1917, when
she was interned in Coimbatore, some of her followers met Gandhi
and asked for his assistance in securing her release. His suggestion
that a hundred volunteers should walk the thousand miles from
Bombay to Coimbatore was not such rollicking nonsense as it
sounded to these 'radical politicians', if we recall the effect on
public opinion of the famous marches which Gandhi had led in
South Africa and was to lead in India, but the episode shows how
difficult it was for moderates and extremists alike to understand
his technique.

This technique which was to determine the timing and mode
of Gandhi's impact on Indian politics had been developed by
him in South Africa. In these early years in India (1915-18), even
though he seemed to be ploughing his own lonely furrow, his
personality and politics had been firmly cast in moulds peculiarly
his own. Explaining why he did not join the Home Rule League
he told his friends: 'that at my time of life and with views firmly
formed on several matters, I could only join an organization
to affect its policy and not be affected by it. This does not mean
that I would not now have an open mind to receive new light.

I simply wish to emphasize the fact that the new light will have to be specially dazzling in order to entrance me'.[1]

No light could be more dazzling than that of Satyagraha, the technique of non-violent action, with which, for a decade, he had sought to guide his life in personal as well as public spheres. Gandhi believed he had discovered an effective instrument for rectifying injustices, righting wrongs and ironing out conflicts. Having discovered it and wielded it with a measure of success in South Africa, he felt he could not deny it to those of his countrymen who came to him for help. The fact that he was committed to abstention from political agitation during the war did not prevent him from championing just grievances which could not brook delay.

[1] G. A. Natesan in an article entitled 'Reminiscences' in *Gandhiji*, p. 215 on Gandhi's 75th birthday in 1944.

Chapter 20

PEASANTS AND WORKERS

ONE of the first calls for help came to Gandhi from a quarter he had not thought of. Champaran in Bihar had been seething with agrarian discontent for some time. The racial factor gave additional acerbity to the relations between the European indigo factory owners and Indian cultivators. Gandhi was present at the Calcutta session of the Indian National Congress in December 1916 when the Champaran troubles came up for discussion. He was invited to take part in it, but declined for the simple reason that he knew nothing about the matter: Champaran was for him no more than a dot on the map of India. After the Congress session, Rajkumar Shukla, a peasant from Champaran, requested Gandhi to visit the district and see things for himself. Shukla's tenacity was remarkable; he followed Gandhi from one end of the country to the other, until he escorted him to Champaran and confronted him with a problem which had strained the relations between the planters and the peasants for nearly a century.

European planters had set up indigo farms and factories in Champaran district at the beginning of the nineteenth century. The 'Bettiah Raj', the biggest landowner in Bihar, had leased plots of land to Europeans; a few of these plots were cultivated with ploughs, bullocks and labour locally commandeered by the factories. However, indigo cultivation was mostly carried on under the 'tinkathia system', according to which each tenant had to reserve three-twentieths of his holding (often the best portion) for indigo under the supervision of the factory, which bought up the crop for a fixed and usually uneconomic price. This one-sided arrangement was cloaked with agreements which the cultivators had been coaxed or coerced into signing. The tenants' discontent sometimes broke into an impotent fury such as in 1867. What with the influence the planters possessed with the district officers and the Provincial Government and the expense and delays of legal remedies, the tenants found it difficult to obtain a square deal.

What the petitions and the sporadic violence of the peasants could not achieve German industry achieved in the beginning of the present century: synthetic indigo practically drove natural indigo from the market. Indigo cultivation in Champaran district fell from 91,000 acres in 1892-97 to 8,100 acres in 1914. The planters now made a virtue of necessity and released the tenants from the obligation of growing indigo in accordance with the old agreements. This they did by exacting 'compensation' or 'damages' from the peasants for not growing indigo. Rents shot up, the average increase being nearly sixty per cent. Besides inflating the rents, the planters recovered a multitude of illegal payments in cash and kind from the tenants. The tenants were taxed for drawing water from canals which did not exist; they had to contribute towards the purchase by the planter of an elephant, a house or a car; they had to pay a death duty for the recognition of a succession valid under the law. Some of these illegal exactions were levied by the Indian *zamindars* (landlords) as well, but the *zamindars* were not half so influential with the officials as the European planters and thus in practice were less able to bleed the tenant. European planters, however, commanded considerable influence with European officials; there were instances of even manhandling of tenants in the courts by the planters or their agents.

Rajkumar Shukla had given Gandhi some details of the planter-tenant conflict in Champaran. After arriving in Bihar, Gandhi learnt enough to become anxious to investigate the facts for himself. From Patna he went to Muzaffarpur and from Muzaffarpur to Motihari, the headquarters of the district of Champaran. He was served with a notice to quit the district 'by the next available train' as his presence was considered a danger to public peace. He refused to comply. He told the magistrate who tried him on April 18, 1917: 'As a law-abiding citizen, my first instinct would be, as it was, to obey the order served on me. I could not do so without doing violence to my sense of duty to those for whom I came . . . I am fully conscious of the fact that a person holding in the public life a position such as I do, has to be most careful in setting examples . . . I have disregarded the order served upon me, not for want of respect for lawful authority, but in obedience to the higher law of our being—the voice of conscience.'

The Commissioner of Tirhut Division had ordered Gandhi's arrest without consulting his superiors. As the Government of Bihar later explained (May 23, 1917) to the Government of India: 'The Lieutenant Governor-in-Council considered that the Commissioner . . . had committed a very serious mistake of judgment both in the line of action he adopted towards Mr Gandhi and in taking that action without obtaining the approval of the Local Government. It was clearly impossible at this stage to prevent a man of Mr Gandhi's experience from making his enquiries and the course adopted by the Commissioner could only excite public interest and create the suspicion that the Government wished to stifle the enquiry. Orders were, therefore, issued to the Commissioner and District Officer to abandon proceedings, and to give Mr Gandhi every reasonable facility, but to warn him that the ryots were in an excitable condition.'

Gandhi was now at liberty to continue his investigations into the peasants' grievances; he carefully sifted the evidence, cross-examined each witness searchingly and discouraged exaggeration. A portrait of Gandhi at work, which is as intimate as it is honest, is sketched in a letter (April 29, 1917) written by a young British officer, W. A. Lewis, I.C.S., Sub Divisional Officer, Bettiah to W. H. Heycock, District Magistrate, Champaran:

'Mr Gandhi arrived last Sunday and called on me on the morning of Monday. He explained to me the object of his investigation which is to secure redress for certain definite wrongs to which he claims the *raiyats* (peasants) are now subjected. I gathered that he is already in possession of a large mass of information on local problems. Mr Gandhi impressed on me that he wishes his investigation to be impartial.

'On Wednesday afternoon, I rode out to . . . one of the villages where he was then collecting information. I sat with him for a time while his enquiries were being conducted. Each witness is subjected to severe cross-questioning as Mr Gandhi is determined to get his facts on an incontrovertible basis. Mr Gandhi is accompanied by Babu Brijkishore who is working on similar lines . . . He also records depositions in writing.

'I have received your instructions that Mr Gandhi is to receive every facility. Am I to understand that this instruction extends to Babu Brijkishore? Babu Brijkishore has not yet called on to see me nor has he asked me to grant him an interview . . .

'In a sense he (Mr Gandhi) has superseded the local authority. Mr Gandhi claims that the local administration has been very largely dominated by planters' influence . . .

'By the planters Mr Gandhi is very naturally regarded as their natural enemy. The affairs of the great majority of factories, even those which we consider well managed, will not under present circumstances stand the severe critical analysis on all points of economic detail to which they are now being subjected, and Mr Gandhi will have in his hands material based on indisputable facts to form the basis of a very formidable indictment . . .

'It is with the effect of Mr Gandhi's presence on the *raiyats* that I wish especially to deal with . . . We may look on Mr Gandhi as an idealist, a fanatic, or a revolutionary according to our particular opinions. But to the *raiyats* he is their liberator, and they credit him with extraordinary powers. He moves about in the villages asking them to lay their grievances before him, and he is transfiguring the imaginations of masses of ignorant men with visions of an early millennium. I put the danger of this before Mr Gandhi, and he assured me that his utterances are so carefully guarded that they could not be construed as an incitement to revolt. I am willing to believe Mr Gandhi, whose sincerity is, I think, above suspicion: but he cannot control the tongues of all his followers . . .

'I asked Mr Gandhi if he would accept responsibility should outbreaks occur. He said he could not but that he did not think that any such outbreaks are to be expected. In this point I differ with him . . .

'I do not know Government's attitude towards Mr Gandhi beyond the instructions I have received to give him every facility . . .

'I asked Mr Gandhi if he would be prepared to go to Ranchi to place his plans before Government, accompanied by a local officer: and Mr Gandhi says he will be willing to go.

'On matters which require redress Mr Gandhi is prepared to go to any length to secure it and would willingly immolate himself in that cause: nor will he disengage himself from the district until very great changes are effected: but he is, I am sure, amenable to reason in his treatment of these difficult problems.'

The Government of India felt perturbed at Gandhi's presence in Champaran and the possibilities of a Satyagraha struggle developing in the indigo districts of Bihar. At the suggestion of Craddock, the Home Member, the Viceroy wrote to Sir Edward Gait, the Governor of Bihar, suggesting the appointment of a Commission of Inquiry on which a seat could be offered to Gandhi as well. Sir Edward at first resisted the suggestion. 'It would be a device,' he wrote to Lord Chelmsford, 'for heading off Mr Gandhi; and it is by no means certain that it would be effective.' The Champaran Agrarian Committee was thus appointed at the instance of the Government of India and not because, as Gandhi suggested in his autobiography the Governor was 'good'.

With the evidence of 8,000 tenants in his hands, there was no aspect of the agrarian problem with which Gandhi was not thoroughly acquainted. Knowledgeable, persuasive and firm he was able to make out an irresistible case for the tenants. The committee unanimously recommended the abolition of the oppressive 'tinkathia system', and of the illegal exactions under which the tenants groaned. As for the illegal recoveries, the committee recommended a twenty-five per cent refund. Many of Gandhi's colleagues wondered why he had not held out for a

100 per cent refund. Gandhi's reasons for this restraint have been recorded by Dr Rajendra Prasad: 'I remember Gandhiji told us that these planters had been able to lord it over the ryots, because of their prestige; the mere fact that they had been obliged to give up a part of the enhancement and to refund a part of the cash was enough to damage if not altogether to destroy their prestige.'[1]

A compromise on a point of detail which pleased the planters immediately could not alter the fundamental fact that the spell of fear had been lifted from the peasantry. More than the legislation which embodied the recommendations of the Inquiry Committee, it was this psychological change which was to drive the planters out of the district within a decade. The tactical surrender on the part of Gandhi thus concealed what proved to be a strategical triumph.

The Home Rule Movement was in full swing at this time. It was with some effort that Gandhi restrained some of his colleagues from joining the movement. Apart from the fact that he did not want to embarrass the Government during the war, he believed it was best to concentrate on the task already in hand. He tried to keep the limelight away from his work in Champaran; the reports he sent to prominent public men and newspapers were meant for 'information and not publication'. He sedulously avoided the racial touch. George Rainy, a fellow member on the Inquiry Committee, is quoted to have remarked: 'Mr Gandhi reminds me of St Paul.' A British missionary, the Rev. Hodge, has recorded the memories of his happy association with the Gandhi family during these days of the struggle with the European officials and planters.

The intimate knowledge of the Champaran peasantry during this enquiry convinced Gandhi that the root of the trouble lay in their ignorance, which made them an easy prey to petty oppression. Education was the obvious remedy. He began his first experiment in 'constructive work' in Champaran and among those who helped him in this experiment were Kasturbai, Devadas,

[1] Rajendra Prasad: 'Since he came to Champaran' in *Incidents of Gandhiji's Life*, edited by Shukla, Bombay, 1949, p. 270.

F

his youngest son; Mahadev Desai and Narhari Parikh, two Gujerati youths who had recently joined his entourage, and their wives; Dr Dev of the Servants of India Society and Prof. Kripalani. Primary schools were opened in villages in mud huts which were rigged up or in buildings offered by local philanthropists. The teachers were maintained by the villagers. The curriculum included, besides the rudiments of literacy, basic hygiene and sanitation. The teachers set an example in civic sense by sweeping the roads of the village and cleaning its cesspools. Unfortunately, this campaign was not sustained by local effort after the departure of Gandhi and his colleagues from Champaran.

While Gandhi was engaged in Bihar, trouble was brewing in the textile industry of Ahmedabad. Since August 1917 a 'plague bonus', equivalent in some cases to eighty per cent of the wages, was being paid to dissuade the labour from fleeing the plague-ravaged town. When the epidemic was over, the employers wanted to discontinue the 'bonus'. The workers resisted the move arguing that the cost of living had more than doubled during the war and the bonus only partially set off the loss in purchasing power.

Apprehending a showdown between the mill owners and their employees, the British Collector of Ahmedabad wrote to Gandhi to exert his influence with the mill owners for a compromise. One of the leading mill owners, Ambalal Sarabhai, was a friend of the Gandhi family; it was his anonymous charity which had saved the Sabarmati Ashram in its early days when the admission of an untouchable family had brought a storm over Gandhi's head. Gandhi had long discussions with the representatives of the mill owners and the workers, as a result of which both parties agreed to arbitration by a tribunal consisting of three representatives of the employers and three representatives of the labour with the Collector as the chairman. Before this tribunal could commence its work, the mill owners took advantage of a stray strike, declared the agreement void, backed out of arbitration and announced that the workers who declined to accept a twenty per cent bonus would be dismissed.

Gandhi waded through a mass of data on the production costs and profits of the textile industry in Ahmedabad and Bombay, the cost of living and market conditions, and came to the conclusion that a rise of thirty-five per cent was justified. The workers who had been demanding a fifty per cent increase in wages were persuaded by Gandhi to accept thirty-five per cent, but the mill owners would not hear of anything more than twenty per cent. Gandhi had been invited by the Collector of Ahmedabad to use his good offices with the mill owners, but the latter's refusal to accept arbitration now led him to champion the workers' grievances.

When the mill owners threatened 'united action' against their employees, Gandhi's comment was that they were organizing 'a union of elephants against a union of ants'. He took up the workers' cause as another experiment in Satyagraha. The crucial question was whether the just demand of textile labour at Ahmedabad could be won by a peaceful, non-violent strike. This demand had been brought down to the thirty-five per cent bonus which he adjudged to be an irreducible minimum. The strike, organized on the principles of Satyagraha, was to be different from the familiar pattern. The morale of the workers was not to be boosted by working up their passions. There was to be no violence, neither against the employers nor against blacklegs. There was no room for bitterness, for fabrication of grievances, exaggeration of claims, or competition in invective. The strikers' enforced idleness was to be utilized in constructive activities: alternative trades were to be learnt, houses were to be repaired, and roads in workers' colonies were to be swept.

Not the least interesting feature of this dispute was that Gandhi's chief lieutenant in organizing the strike was Ambalal Sarabhai's sister Anasuyabehn. She spent several hours in the workers' tenements every day, encouraging the dispirited, tending the sick and finding work for those who faced starvation. At a fixed hour every afternoon the workers met under a 'babul' tree on the bank of the Sabarmati river to listen to Gandhi. Perfect discipline prevailed at these meetings where speeches were sober in content and style, and not only abuse but even ridicule of the opponent was taboo. A news bulletin, which Gandhi wrote and Anasuyabehn published, was issued daily. Gandhi argued that the ideal relationship between master and man should be based not on self-interest but on 'mutual regard' in the spirit of Ruskin's *Unto This Last*. The employers did not subscribe to this idealism; they brought out their own news-sheets, criticizing the 'outsiders' who ventured to interfere in the private domain of the employers!

As the strike progressed, Gandhi watched it with some anxiety. The workers' morale after the first few days began to sag. It was impossible for most of them to exist without work and wages. Alternative employment was not practicable except for a handful. Financial assistance from outside to keep the strike going was contrary to the spirit of Satyagraha. The employers offered to take those who accepted a twenty per cent bonus back to work. One of Gandhi's colleagues overheard a worker remark: 'After all Gandhiji and Anasuyabehn have nothing to lose. They move about in cars and have enough to eat.' When this remark was conveyed to Gandhi, he was filled not with anger but with anguish. The meeting under the 'babul' tree that afternoon was sparsely attended and despair was writ large upon the audience. The strike was evidently testing the resistance of the workers. It was at this moment that Gandhi announced that he would undertake a fast. Had he not declared at the beginning of the strike that if it led to starvation he would be the first to starve? The object of the fast was to rally the workers. Nevertheless, it could not but affect the mill owners, some of whom respected and even loved Gandhi. The result was an unintended but definite pressure on the mill owners.[1]

It was this feeling, that the fast was exercising an element of coercion, which led Gandhi after three days' fast to accept a compromise as a result of which the pledge of the strikers was literally but not really fulfilled. The strikers went back to work

[1] Desai, M. D.: *Ek Dharam Yudh* (A Righteous Struggle), p. 45.

when they were promised a thirty-five per cent wage increase for the first day, twenty per cent for the second day, and twenty-seven per cent from the third day until a decision was given by an arbitrator. Here again a tactical defeat contained the germs of final victory. The fundamental issue on which the breach had occurred had been the refusal of the employers to accept the principle of arbitration; on this issue they now yielded. The arbitrator's award went in the workers' favour and the thirty-five per cent bonus was ultimately won.

This strike was a turning point in the labour-employer relations in Ahmedabad. 'The principle and procedure of arbitration,' writes Gulzarilal Nanda, 'which have played so large a part in making the Textile Labour Association what it is today, were thus introduced in the industrial relations in this country for the first time.' Two years later Gandhi inaugurated the first regular union of workers, which blossomed into the Ahmedabad Textile Labour Association and bore an impress of the Gandhian concept of employer-employee relations. The Association has its own libraries, reading-rooms, schools, hospitals, recreation centres, bank and newspaper. Thus the one intervention by Gandhi in an industrial dispute led to a great constructive edifice. Though other preoccupations prevented him from devoting much time to industrial relations in later years, he never ceased to take interest in the textile workers of Ahmedabad and their Association, which he considered an excellent model for trade unions in India.

The labour dispute at Ahmedabad had scarcely been settled when Gandhi was drawn into a conflict between the peasants of Kheda district in Bombay Presidency and the local administration on the remission of land revenue. A drought had blighted the crops in this district. The 'revenue code' provided for a total remission of the land revenue when the crops were less than twenty-five per cent of the normal yield. But opinion was sharply divided on the exact damage to the crops. On-the-spot inquiries by three members of the Servants of India Society and estimates by V. J. Patel, then a member of the Bombay Legislative

Assembly, and Gandhi, put the damage at more than three-fourths of a good year's yield. The officials belittled these estimates as emanating from 'outsiders'. The peasants' petitions were returned because they had not been sent 'through the proper channel'. Interviews with district officers brought no relief and when an influential deputation waited on the Governor of Bombay, he did not see any ground for intervention in a matter which was well within the competence of local officials.

Gujerat Sabha, of which Gandhi was president at this time, took a leading part in this agitation. When petitions, interviews and Press statements failed to bring relief to the peasantry, the agitation passed into Gandhi's hands. He was reluctant to embarrass the Government during the war, but he was shocked by the obstinacy of the officials in refusing to face facts and to deal humanely with a hard-hit peasantry. He asked for a Committee of Inquiry to assess the damage to the crops. This demand was turned down and the Commissioner issued threats that those who did not pay the land revenue in full would risk the confiscation of their lands. Gandhi then called on the peasants to 'fight unto death against such a spirit of vindictiveness and tyranny,' and to refuse to pay the land revenue. The war, he declared, was no excuse for injustice and oppression. The Kheda peasants by resisting injustice would, he argued, solve a problem of the first magnitude: they would show that 'it is impossible to govern men without their consent'.

This was the first real agrarian Satyagraha which Gandhi organized in India. The basic problem was to rid the peasantry of fear: the fear of officials, the fear of forfeiture of land and property. Gandhi and Vallabhbhai Patel toured the villages of Kheda to train the people in the hard school of 'Satyagraha'. The Government tightened up the tax collection. Those who refused to pay were sternly dealt with; cattle and household goods were seized and even standing crops were attached. The peasantry showed much courage and fortitude, but the repression told severely on a district already suffering from the after-effects of drought, plague and high prices. Gandhi felt that the peasantry had reached the verge of exhaustion and it was prudent to prevent it from being driven to utter ruin. When the Government issued instructions that land revenue should be recovered only from those who had the capacity to pay and that no pressure should be exercised on genuinely poor peasants, he felt justified in calling off the no-tax campaign. This may have seemed a face-saving device and a tame end to a campaign begun with high hopes. The indirect effects of the campaign were, however, significant: it awakened the peasantry of Gujerat, Gandhi's province of birth, to a consciousness of its strength and gave it a great leader in Vallabhbhai Patel. Patel gave up his practice at the Ahmedabad bar and became a trusted deputy of Gandhi in the·many struggles which lay ahead.

To put these early experiments in Satyagraha in proper perspective we must remember that during these years World War I was in progress, and that Gandhi had no intention of distracting the Government. He avoided any collision as far as possible. In Champaran and Kheda he could not altogether avoid one, but he endeavoured to localize these conflicts and sought solutions which secured a modicum of justice to the peasantry without creating a national crisis.

His attitude to the war had indeed marked him off from other prominent leaders; he cherished the hope—which few knowledgeable politicians shared—that India would receive self-government at the end of the war if she whole-heartedly supported the British war effort.

When World War I broke out Gandhi was on the high seas; he was homeward bound, though he hoped to spend a few weeks in England. On August 6, 1914 he landed on English soil and lost no time in calling a meeting of his Indian friends to raise an ambulance unit. The argument that the Empire's crisis was India's chance did not impress him: 'I knew the difference of status between an Indian and an Englishman, but I did not believe that we had been quite reduced to slavery. I felt then that it was more the fault of individual officials than of the British system, and that we could convert them by love. If we would improve our status through the help and co-operation of the British it was our duty to win their help by standing by them in their hour of need.'[1]

Were it not for a severe attack of pleurisy he may have continued to serve in the ambulance unit he had raised, and his return to India may have been indefinitely delayed.

When he arrived in India he found that nationalist opinion was opposed to unconditional support for the war effort. Only those who were politically backward or flourished on official patronage were for loyalty at all costs. Gandhi did not favour a bargain with the Government by offering co-operation at a price and he told the Gujerat Political Conference in November 1917: 'That we have been loyal at a time of stress is no test of fitness for Swaraj. Loyalty is no merit. It is a necessity of citizenship all the world over.'[2]

Early in 1918 the war was going badly for the Allies; a German thrust was expected on the western front and the Viceroy summoned prominent leaders of Indian opinion to a War Conference in Delhi. A number of nationalist leaders including Tilak, Jinnah and Khaparde, were not invited, as they had raised the question of the terms on which co-operation should be accorded to the Government. Indian political opinion had swung heavily against vague promises unbacked by any concession in the constitutional sphere. There was also a spate of speculation about secret treaties which the Allies were alleged to have concluded in spite of their professions to the contrary. Gandhi's first impulse was to boycott the conference, but he was persuaded to attend. He supported the resolution on recruitment with a single sentence in Hindi: 'With a full sense of my responsibility, I beg to support the resolution.'

After the War Conference he salved his conscience by writing a letter to the Viceroy listing the grievances of the nationalists. While at Delhi he raised with the Home Member, Sir William Vincent, the question of the release of Maulanas Mahomed Ali

[1] Gandhi: *Autobiography*, p. 425.
[2] Natesan: *Speeches and Writings of Mahatma Gandhi*, p. 409.

and Shaukat Ali. Sir William Vincent asked him how this question was connected with the conduct of the war. 'It would solve the recruiting problem,' replied Gandhi. 'Perhaps,' rejoined Sir William, 'but what have you done yourself to help the war effort? As far as I know all the help you have given is to harass local administration.' This was an unkind cut but it stung Gandhi's conscience. The solemn thirteen-word speech at the War Conference had laid on him an obligation which he now tried to fulfil.

He threw himself heart and soul into a recruiting campaign. There was something comic in this votary of non-violence touring the villages of Gujerat to secure recruits for the British Indian army to fight in the battlefronts of Europe and the Middle East. He went to Kheda district, where a few months earlier he had organized a no-tax campaign. He found that it had been easier to persuade the villagers to queue up for prison than for the army. Gandhi and Vallabhbhai Patel, who accompanied him, discovered that they were no longer the heroes they had been in this part of the country only recently. In a village which had been conspicuous for resistance to the Government no one came out even to meet them; for three days they stayed on the outskirts of the village and cooked their own food.

British officers may have been amused at the spectacle of this erstwhile leader of a no-tax campaign turn into a recruiting sergeant, but they learnt before long that they were dealing with no honeyed loyalist. At a local war conference, where the Commissioner of the Division was present, Gandhi said: 'Among the many misdeeds of the British rule in India, history will look upon the Act depriving a whole nation of arms as the blackest.' He addressed Lord Willingdon, the Governor of Bombay, on the abolition of the Arms Act. The Governor took the opportunity of thanking him 'most sincerely for the great service you are doing the Empire in the indefatigable way you are working at your recruiting campaign'.

Not infrequently, unable to get carts for their journeys, Gandhi and his colleagues had to march on foot twenty miles a day. The strain was too much for him and at last a severe attack of dysentery laid him low. Averse to taking medicines he fasted, but in vain. He did not agree to injections owing to what he described later as his 'ridiculous ignorance' about them. His friend Ambalal Sarabhai took him to his palatial house in Ahmedabad, but since he would not submit to medical treatment devoted nursing alone could not restore him to health. One day while still suffering from high fever, he insisted on being moved to Sabarmati Ashram. Dr Rajendra Prasad, who saw him next day, found him emaciated in body and resigned in spirit to the approaching end. His whole life had been, Gandhi reminisced sadly, one in which he had taken up things left them half-done, and now he was to pass away; but if that was the will of God, it could not be helped.

Gandhi believed that he was at death's door. He recited verses from the *Gita* and summoned the inmates of the Sabarmati Ashram. They trooped in silently. 'My last message to India,' he said, 'is that she will find her salvation through non-violence, and through non-violence alone India will contribute to the salvation of the world.'

While he lay in agony watching his body slowly wear away, an 'ice-doctor' came on the scene. Gandhi let him experiment with ice-therapy which infused into him a fresh energy and hope. The will to live returned; one symptom was that he was perusaded by Kasturbai to take goat's milk on the plea that the vow he had taken many years before not to take milk applied only to cow's milk. This was, of course, a mere quibble and the bluntest comment on it is in his autobiography: 'The will to live proved stronger than the devotion to truth.'

The greatest incentive for living was to be furnished to Gandhi by the Government of India. The publication of the Rowlatt Committee Report and the Rowlatt Bills stirred him to his depths. 'If I had been well,' he said, 'I would have toured the whole of India to rouse her.' Friends came to him for consultation. How was the country to fight the new legislation which attacked civil liberties? As Gandhi brooded over it all he recalled how he had pleaded for support to Britain in her hour of need in the hope of a worthy gesture at the end of the war. Once again he had received stone for bread. He had done his best to keep out of a political agitation during the war. Now he felt an irresistible call to fight a wrong perpetrated in peace.

Chapter 21

SHADOW OF AMRITSAR

THE Rowlatt Bills which had pulled Gandhi out of his sickbed were based on the recommendations of the Rowlatt Committee, which had reported on measures to combat political violence. One of the bills provided for trials without right of appeal by special courts *in camera*, for demanding 'security' from persons 'likely to commit offences', and for arrests on mere suspicion. The other bill was intended to introduce permanent changes in the ordinary criminal law and to make even the possession of a seditious document punishable with two years' imprisonment.

Nobody had been a more vehement critic of political violence than Gandhi. Ten years before the Rowlatt Bills were conceived he had, in his *Hind Swaraj*, condemned revolutionary activities on moral as well as practical grounds. He put forward Satyagraha—'soul force'—as a superior and more effective substitute for bomb and pistol. Opposed as he was to violence, he argued that it was not right to frame a drastic legislation for the whole of India because political crimes occurred in a few places. Nor did he favour the investing an executive, which was not yet responsible to the people, with wide powers.

But the Rowlatt Bills were not the first piece of repressive legislation; they had been preceded by the Criminal Law Amendment Act of 1908, the Press Act of 1910, and the Defence of India Act of 1915. The last Act was in fact still in force in 1919. The need for fresh legislation was not apparent even to those who were friendly to the Government. Again, the Rowlatt Bills could not have been more ill-timed. Indian public opinion was expecting some spectacular gesture after the war and not a curtailment of civil liberties. 'Ours is a consecration,' Gandhi had written to

Lord Chelmsford in 1918 after the Delhi War Conference, 'based on the hope of a better future.' Throughout the war he had argued, often alone among Indian nationalist leaders, that Britain would give India a square deal after the war was over. Annie Besant and Tilak had warned him that he was heading for disillusionment and that the British would never part with power unless they were hard-pressed.

There was a rare unanimity among Indian leaders on the opposition to the Rowlatt Bills. Jinnah observed that a government which enacted such a law in peace forfeited its claim to be called a civilized government. Sapru described the laws as 'wrong in principle, unsound in operation and too sweeping'. 'We think,' said V. J. Patel, 'that all our constitutional agitation for any reforms whatsoever would die if these bills are passed.'

The reaction of the Government of India to this agitation was characteristic. It discounted its strength and attributed it to a mass hysteria among Indian politicians. It insisted that special powers were absolutely essential for district officers in fighting against anarchists—'invisible and unscrupulous foes'. Lovett, a member of the Viceroy's Council, urged Indian leaders to lead and not to follow the people in seeking measures designed to combat violence. It also appears that the Government was anxious to reassure the conservative critics of the Montagu-Chelmsford Reforms in England that in spite of some constitutional concessions which were being made the British *Raj* had not weakened. The Government of India rushed the bill through the Imperial Legislative Council in March 1919 with an almost indecent haste. The council had rarely met for more than eight hours, but the debate on the first Rowlatt Bill went on from 11 a.m., with adjournments for luncheon and dinner, until after midnight. All the elected Indian leaders voted against the bill; nevertheless it became law. The passage of the first Rowlatt Bill was an eye-opener to Gandhi. He had heard the debate in the Imperial Legislative Council and seen how the eloquent logic of Indian councillors had been wasted on the official benches. 'You can wake a man,' he wrote later, 'only if he is really asleep; no effort that you may make will produce any effect upon him if he is merely pretending sleep.' The conviction grew upon him that the 'Great Civil Service Corporation' and the British commercial community had made the Government of India impervious to popular feeling. A government which really cared for public opinion would not have enacted a measure which had been opposed by every shade of Indian opinion. And a government which was hoping to introduce a substantial measure of constitutional reforms could hardly have provided a worse prelude to an instalment of self-government.

The constitutional opposition to Rowlatt Bills having proved fruitless Gandhi felt that recourse must be had to Satyagraha to secure the repeal of the Rowlatt Act. Already in February 1919, he had drafted and circulated a pledge of resistance to Rowlatt Bills: 'In the event of these bills becoming law and until they are withdrawn we shall refuse civilly to obey these laws and such other laws as a committee to be hereafter appointed may think fit, and further affirm that in this struggle we shall faithfully follow truth and refrain from violence to life, person and property.'

Now that the Government had put the first Rowlatt Bill on the statute-book, Gandhi—though he had yet not fully recovered from his recent illness—picked up the gauntlet. He toured the country to educate the people in the implications of the Satyagraha pledge and founded a new organization, the *Satyagraha Sabha*. While in Madras he woke up one morning and told his host, Rajagopalachari, that 'in the twilight condition between sleep and consciousness' it had occurred to him that the country should be called upon to observe a day of 'hartal', when all business should be suspended and people should fast and pray as a protest against the hated legislation. The date fixed for the 'hartal' was March 30th, but it was later changed to April 6th. The idea of a 'hartal' as a measure of mourning or protest was not a novel one in India, but as a one-day national strike it was a masterly stroke. In Bombay, in addition to the cessation of business a beginning was made with civil resistance by selling certain books, including Gandhi's *Hind Swaraj* and *Sarvodaya*, which had been banned as seditious by the

Government. And on April 7th appeared *Satyagraha*, a news-sheet edited by Gandhi and published in defiance of the Press Act.

The hartal in Delhi was observed owing to a misunderstanding on March 30th instead of April 6th and it was also marred by some rioting. Gandhi promptly condemned the excesses of the mob as well as those of the local officials who, he said, had used a hammer to crush a fly. Tension mounted in the Punjab, where the local leaders felt that Gandhi's presence would assist in maintaining peace, but the Government did not let Gandhi reach the Punjab. While he was on his way to Delhi he was taken out of his compartment at a small station and put in another train bound for Bombay, where he was released. He would have again left for Delhi, had he not discovered that in his absence disturbances had broken out in the city of Bombay, Ahmedabad, Nadiad and other places in his own province which was the least expected to forget his doctrine of non-violence. He came to the conclusion that he had underrated the latent forces of violence. He decided to retrace his steps, to give up the idea of seeking re-arrest, restrict and finally suspend Satyagraha. He observed a three-day fast to atone for his 'Himalayan miscalculation' in launching a mass movement without making sure that the people were ready for it.

Meanwhile, events in the Punjab had moved to a tragic climax. The Punjab had been suffering from several undercurrents of discontent. It had provided nearly half a million recruits for the World War I; it suffered from the after-effects of the influenza epidemic which had claimed a heavy toll; it suffered, like the rest of India, from a high cost of living and its predominantly Muslim population had been disturbed by ideas of Pan-Islamism. Though Gandhi had never visited the Punjab, his name was already something to conjure with in that province. His arrest near Delhi had agitated the people. On April 10, at Amritsar, following the arrest of two local leaders, a mob ran amuck, burnt down the town hall and the post office, cut telegraph wires and injured a few Europeans, including two women. Order was restored by drafting troops into the city under Brigadier-General Dyer.

The city was quiet for the next two days, but on April 13th, the day of the *Baisakhi* festival, a meeting was held in Jallian-wala Bagh, which became the scene of a holocaust. Dyer decided to break up the meeting. The entrance was too narrow to admit the armoured cars, but he marched into the garden with his troops, who fired 1,650 rounds in ten minutes. The holiday crowd of unarmed men, women and children unable to escape from the walled compound, were caught 'like rats in a trap'. The Punjab Government estimated the number of killed at 379. Sir Chimanlal Setalvad, a member of the Hunter Committee, estimated that 400 persons had been killed and 1,200 injured.[1]

Later, Dyer explained that his object was to create a 'moral effect' by resolute action. He could not have dealt a bigger blow to the Empire which he was professing to save. Amritsar became a turning point in Indo-British relations almost as important as the Mutiny.[2] The tragedy of Amritsar should not be viewed as an isolated act, but as a symptom of the 'mutiny complex' to which the British in India periodically succumbed. The Punjab Government with Sir Michael O'Dwyer at its head, had persuaded itself of the existence of a wide-spread conspiracy to overthrow the Government. That the theory of a conspiracy had no basis in fact is proved by two secret letters exchanged between M. L. Robertson, the Inspector-General of Police, Bombay, and Sir C. R. Cleveland, Director Intelligence Bureau, Government of India—the two men who should have been best-informed on the political situation from the point of view of the Government. 'It is difficult to understand the position in the Punjab fully,' wrote Robertson on May 19, 1919. 'Have you been able to trace any organized conspiracy? We have not yet succeeded in doing so in respect of Ahmedabad.'

Cleveland replied on May 23rd: '... So far no traces of organized conspiracy have been found in the Punjab. There was organized agitation, and then in particular places, the people went mad ... I am sorry to see that the *Times of India* and the *Pioneer* have

[1] Setalvad: *Recollections and Reflections*, p. 307.
[2] Thompson and Garratt: *Rise and Fulfilment of British Rule in India*, p. 609.

committed themselves to the theory of Bolshevism or Egyptian instigation for our Indian troubles. I have satisfied myself that they have no evidence worth the name to support the theory. I regret to see wrong diagnosis as it makes the remedy so very fluky.'

Sir Michael O'Dwyer's book, *The Punjab as I knew it*, has a chapter entitled 'The Punjab Rebellion of 1919'. He describes 'the unholy alliance between Hindu extremists, Pan-Islamists, and Sikh revolutionaries for the overthrow of British rule'. On April 10th, the situation at Lahore was considered so serious that European women and children were collected in the Governor's residence. On April 13th, even before General Dyer had ordered firing in Jallianwala Bagh, Sir Michael had sent a wireless message to Simla emphasizing the need for martial law in the districts of Amritsar and Lahore. He refers in his account to 'the isolation' by the unarmed crowds of more than a thousand troops under the command of General Dyer in Amritsar. General Dyer wrote in the same vein in his first report to his Divisional Commander, General Bynon: 'I realized that my force was small and to hesitate might induce attack.' In other words, General Dyer had to order his men to fire as a measure of self-defence!

The 'mutiny complex' from which the official and particularly the European community, seemed to suffer at this time is the key to the tragic events in the Punjab in the spring and early summer of 1919, when a number of military and civil officers heaped nameless indignities and harsh penalties on Indians, particularly the educated and politically-conscious classes. It is unnecessary to recount the details of this draconian régime. The most notorious order of General Dyer was the one which required Indians to crawl on their bellies in the street where a European woman had been assaulted. Indians were made to alight from vehicles if a European passed on the road and salute him. A number of villages were machine-gunned by armoured cars and aeroplanes. Motor-cars owned by Indians were requisitioned. Colonel Johnson ordered nearly a thousand students of Lahore colleges to march four times daily for three weeks—sixteen miles a day—in the scorching heat of May to answer a roll-call. When a notice pasted on the outer wall of the college building was found torn every male in the precincts of the college, including the professors, was arrested. These military officers doubtless believed that they were holding the bastions of the British Empire at a critical moment in its history. Many of them having recently returned from European or Middle Eastern battle-fields, were impatient of half-hearted methods. Rabindranath Tagore, who renounced his knighthood as a protest against the events in the Punjab, diagnosed the root of the trouble: 'What happened at Jallianwala Bagh was itself a monstrous progeny of a monstrous war.'

The Government drew a discreet veil over the Punjab tragedy. Gandhi had called off civil disobedience on April 18th and was anxious to go to the Punjab. Since he wished to avoid a clash with the Government, he sought the Viceroy's formal permission to enter the province. This permission he could not get for nearly six months. C. F. Andrews sent him disconcerting accounts of the conditions in that province. The Government appointed a Committee of Inquiry headed by Lord Hunter to enquire into the genesis of the Punjab disturbances. The Indian National Congress decided to boycott the Hunter Committee and appointed a non-official committee consisting of eminent lawyers, including Motilal Nehru, C. R. Das, Abbas Tyabji, M. R. Jayakar and Gandhi. It was as a member of this non-official committee that Gandhi learnt the truth about the martial-law régime in the Punjab. He discovered shocking instances of high-handedness based on incontrovertible evidence which he himself scrupulously sifted. The fanciful image of the British Empire as a merciful dispensation of Providence that he had cherished seemed to crumble to the ground. Nevertheless, he tried to make himself believe that the Punjab had been wronged by a few erratic officers, and that the Government would, when it knew the truth, make amends.

On December 24, 1919, King George V issued a proclamation granting his assent to the Indian Reforms Act and an amnesty to the political prisoners. The King called upon officials and the people to co-operate. 'This is a document,' wrote Gandhi, 'of which the British people have every reason to be proud and with which every Indian ought to be satisfied. The proclamation has replaced distrust with trust, but it remains to be seen whether it would filter down to the civil service.' Immediately afterwards, at the annual session of the Indian National Congress at Amritsar, Gandhi cast his influence in favour of working the constitutional reforms; he appealed to the country to settle down quietly to work so as to make the new constitution a success. He nearly walked out of the 'subjects committee' of the Congress when he saw it was reluctant to condemn the excesses of the mobs during the Punjab disturbances. 'I agree,' he said, 'that grave provocation was given by the Government, but our people went mad too. I say, do not return madness with madness, but return madness with sanity and the whole situation will be yours.'

What Gandhi believed to be the spirit of the Royal Proclamation of December 1919 did not filter down to the British administration in India. In vain did he appeal to the Central and Provincial Governments for 'a change of heart'. When in March 1920 the appeals of twenty martial-law prisoners from the Punjab against sentence of death were turned down, he wrote: 'Judgments even of the highest tribunals were not unaffected by subtle political considerations.' He noted with surprise that the officers responsible for misrule in the Punjab had not been recalled; they were being lionized by the European community. The report of the Hunter Committee, when it came out, struck him as little better than 'thinly disguised whitewash'. Was there, he asked, some secret code of conduct governing the official class in India 'before which the flower of the great British nation fell prostrate?' The Indian members of the Hunter Committee had dissented from their European colleagues. Sir C. Setalvad has recorded how, in the course of discussions on the draft of the report, Lord Hunter lost temper with him and exclaimed: 'You people want to drive the British out of the country!' After this, according to Setalvad, the Indian members and Lord Hunter, though under the same roof, almost ceased to speak to each other.[1]

[1] Setalvad, C.: *Recollections and Reflections,* p. 311.

Gandhi publicly demanded the recall of Sir Michael O'Dwyer the Governor of the Punjab and Lord Chelmsford the Viceroy, the former for his active association with the martial-law regime, and the latter for his failure to check the provincial satraps. He was disagreeably surprised by the lack of a sympathetic understanding of Indian feeling over the Punjab tragedy. Sarojini Naidu, who was in England and heard the debate in the House of Commons, described it as lamentable and tragic. 'Our friends,' she wrote, 'revealed their ignorance; our enemies their insolence.' The speeches in the House of Lords revealed the sympathy felt even in influential quarters for British officers implicated in the martial-law régime. The *Morning Post* collected, by public subscription, £30,000 for General Dyer, who had been made to resign from the army.

Reluctantly and almost painfully, Gandhi was driven to the conviction that the system of government which he had been trying to mend needed to be ended. In December 1919 he had advised the Indian National Congress to make a success of the new instalment of reforms granted by the British Government and thus prepare for a fuller measure of responsibility. In September 1920 he declared that reformed councils and governorships for Indians were 'subtle methods of emasculation'.

Besides the 'Punjab Wrong', the 'Khilafat Betrayal' had contributed to this conversion.

Chapter 22

KHILAFAT MOVEMENT

EVENTS in the Punjab had placed a great strain on Gandhi's loyalty in 1919, but his links with the British Empire would not have snapped so dramatically during the following year were it not for another strand in Indian politics represented by the Khilafat movement.

Until 1913, loyalty to the British Government and the attainment of the rights of the Muslims were the objectives of the All-India Muslim League, as defined in its constitution. Events were to prove that Muslim loyalty was not an immutable factor. The Muslim intelligentsia received a few shocks. The reversal in 1911 of the Partition of Bengal, which had created a separate Muslim-majority province in East Bengal, was taken by a section of the Muslim community as a political defeat. The more youthful and radical sections in the Muslim League had been trying to bring it into line with the Indian National Congress. The Muslim middle class, interested more in the developments in the Muslim countries of the Middle East than in the political movements in its own country, was troubled by what seemed to it a conspiracy of Christendom against Islam. British control over Egypt, the Anglo-French *entente* on Morocco, the Anglo-Russian deal for dividing spheres of influence in Persia, the Italian invasion of Tripoli and the dismemberment of the Turkish Empire were seen as manifestations of a common peril. The discontent of the Muslim middle class found eloquent expression in the poems of Iqbal and Shibli and in brilliant articles by two able journalists, Abul Kalam Azad and Mahomed Ali.

The outbreak of the world war in 1914 added to the uneasiness of the Muslim community in India; the Sultan of Turkey, their

Caliph, was allied with the Kaiser against their King-Emperor. The Indian army had a large proportion of Muslims and the Government was anxious to allay Muslim anxiety. The British Prime Minister made a declaration of policy which was intended to set Muslim fears at rest. 'Nor are we fighting,' said Lloyd George, 'to deprive Turkey of the rich and renowned lands of Asia Minor and Thrace which are predominantly Turkish in race.' The Viceroy of India also publicly pledged 'the immunity of the Muslim holy places' in Arabia, Mesopotamia and Jeddah.

During his brief sojourn in England in 1914, Gandhi had formed some idea of the conflict that tore the politically-conscious Muslims. During the years 1915-18, when he was deliberately avoiding controversial politics, his advice was often sought by Muslim leaders on the future of the Caliphate—or as it came to be known—the Khilafat. He had opportunities of addressing the Muslim League and the Muslim University of Aligarh. Always his advice to his Muslim compatriots was to exercise patience and in spite of their deep frustration to give up thoughts of violence. He remained in touch by correspondence with Mahomed Ali, one of the leaders of the Khilafat movement who had been imprisoned. During his vist to Delhi for the War Conference in 1918, Gandhi had pleaded for Mahomed Ali's release and for an assurance by the Government that the Muslim sentiments about the future of Turkey would be respected.

The end of the war in November 1918 again brought the Khilafat question to the fore. It seemed that the vanquished Turkish Empire would be stripped of the Arab provinces, Thrace, and the best portions of Asia Minor. The Sultan of Turkey could no longer function as the Caliph of the Islamic world. The British were putting up Sheikh Hussain, the Sheriff of Mecca and a protégé of T. E. Lawrence, as a Caliph. On this background, and with the release of Mahomed Ali and his brother Shaukat Ali in December 1919, a new vigour was infused into the Khilafat movement. A Muslim deputation waited on the Viceroy in January 1920, but all that Lord Chelmsford could promise was that if a deputation of Indian Muslims wished to proceed to England he would arrange for the necessary facilities.

Some Muslim leaders, including Abul Kalam Azad, the editor of the *Al Hilal*, had already ceased to set much store by petitions to the Viceroy and deputations to England. A meeting of the Khilafat leaders debated for six hours without reaching a decision; Gandhi, who was present by special invitation, suggested that a sub-committee should go further into the question. The sub-committee consisted of Abul Kalam Azad, Hakim Ajmal Khan and Gandhi. 'It was here,' wrote Azad, 'that non-co-operation was conceived.'[1] Next day, when Gandhi placed a programme of 'non-co-operation with the British Government' before the Muslim leaders, a majority of them could not conceal their consternation and wanted time to think.

In February 1920, Abul Kalam Azad presided at the Khilafat Conference in Calcutta and advocated acceptance of Gandhi's programme. Meanwhile, the publication of the treaty with Turkey had aggravated the Muslim discontent. Turkey had been denied the leniency for which Indian Muslims had been hoping and agitating. The Viceroy's advice 'to bear with patience and resignation the misfortunes of their Turkish co-religionists' was cold comfort to Indian Muslims whose frustration was complete. The Khilafat leaders were anxious to do something immediately to express their resentment. On June 9, when the Khilafat Committee met at Allahabad it unanimously approved the programme of non-co-operation which Gandhi had outlined. Gandhi was in fact authorized to launch the non-co-operation programme after giving a month's notice to the Viceroy. A fortnight later Gandhi informed Lord Chelmsford that if the peace terms offered to Turkey were not revised in accordance with the British pledges to Muslims, he would call upon Muslims to cease co-operation with the Government and invite the Hindus to join the movement.

Meanwhile, the All-India Congress Committee met in May and considered the programme of non-co-operation. Gandhi

[1] Mahadev Desai: *Maulana Azad*, Agra, 1940, p. 27.

made the Punjab atrocities, the deficiencies of the Reforms Act and the Khilafat demand the *causus belli*. The AICC decided to convene a special plenary session of the Congress in September 1920 at Calcutta, to discuss the momentous issue of non-co-operation with the Government which, for the first time, was to commit the Congress to an extra-constitutional mode of agitation. The question may well be asked why Gandhi did not wait for the verdict of the Calcutta Congress before writing to the Viceroy and launching the movement? Was he queering the pitch for the Congress, or did the circumstances give him no option to wait?

Of one fact there is little doubt. By June 1920, Gandhi's alienation from the British *Raj* was complete. The Treaty of Sevres with Turkey and the Hunter Committee Report had revealed that no change of heart in the official world was imminent. The discontent of Indian Muslims was boiling over. In accordance with the Koranic injunction (when Islam is assailed, a Muslim should leave the country or go to war), thousands of Muslims in north-western districts had already with disastrous results attempted to migrate to Afghanistan, the nearest Muslim country. The danger was that the pent-up Muslim frustration might burst the dykes and turn into violent channels. Apart from the Muslim temper, Gandhi's own approach to politics helps to explain why he did not wait for the plenary session of the Congress before declaring a non-violent rebellion. If he became convinced that a particular course was correct, he believed in adopting it even if he was alone. And perhaps non-co-operation was the more likely to commend itself to the Congress, if by the time it met, the movement manifested some vitality of its own. Satyagraha was a weapon which in spite of his great restraint during the war he had used for redressing grievances of the indigo cultivators in Bihar, the textile workers in Ahmedabad and the peasants in Gujerat. He was now offering his assistance to Indian Muslims in vindicating the honour of Islam. In doing so he also believed that he was doing the British a service by insisting that they honour their pledges with regard to Turkey; to Gandhi, whose own life had been shaped by the vows he had taken, a pledge meant much. In addition, Gandhi, with his deeply religious outlook, unlike Europeans and educated Hindus, could understand and sympathize even though he may not have entirely agreed with the Muslim sentiment underlying the Khilafat. Unfortunately, what he knew of this movement was largely derived from Muslim divines and pan-Islamic enthusiasts. He failed to see that the Khilafat was a moribund institution, that the Turks themselves were sick of it, that the Ottoman Empire could no more remain intact after the war than the Hapsburg Empire, and that the smaller nations, Arab and non-Arab, were struggling to be free from the stranglehold of Turkey.

The merits of the Khilafat controversy apart, the British policy was one of prevarication and improvisation. In Britain, it was argued that the Turks just had no case for better treatment; in India, the Viceroy privately admitted the wrong done to Turkey but pleaded helplessness as the matter was one of high policy for the Imperial Government. Gandhi's answer to the latter argument was that the Viceroy would have done his duty if he had placed himself at the head of the agitation of the Indian Muslims, just as Lord Hardinge had publicly declared his support for Indians' struggle in South Africa in 1913. But Lord Chelmsford had no intention of making the same dramatic gesture that nearly led to the dismissal of Lord Hardinge.

To the Hindus, Gandhi's appeal was that 'they must do their duty by the sister community. Their sorrows are our sorrows'. Not for a hundred years, he said, would such an opportunity recur for forging Hindu-Muslim unity. He admitted that the Khilafat was an exclusively Muslim issue, and an international one at that but so far as Indian Muslims were concerned it was also connected with the question of Indian freedom. How could an unfree India help a wronged Turkey? 'What could a paralytic do to help others except to cure himself of paralysis?'

When the Indian National Congress in its special session in September 1920 accepted the non-co-operation programme, Gandhi became the leader of both the nationalist and the Khilafat struggles. He toured the country with the Ali brothers and Hindu-Muslim cordiality touched a high tide. Gandhi was heard with reverence by Hindus as well as Muslims. He was invited to address meetings of Muslim women where no male, except Gandhi who was considered pure enough to be an exception, could be present without his eyes being bandaged. His hope of a 'heart-felt unity' between Hindus and Muslims seemed to have been realized.

He was now heading a mass struggle, the avowed purpose of which was to end alien rule. It was an open rebellion, even though a 'non-violent' one.

He had travelled far though reluctantly on the road to sedition against the Empire whose anthem he had sung and whose wars, his non-violence notwithstanding, had seemed to him his own.

Chapter 23

ROAD TO REBELLION

'LORD READING must understand,' wrote Gandhi in *Young India* of December 15, 1921 'that non-co-operators are at war with the government. They have declared rebellion against it.'

It was the same Gandhi who had said at the Madras Law Dinner in April 1915: 'It gives me the greatest pleasure this evening at this great and important gathering to redeclare my loyalty to the British Empire . . . I discovered that the British Empire had certain ideals with which I have fallen in love and one of those ideals is that every subject of the British Empire has the freest scope for his energies and honour and whatever he thinks is due to his conscience.'[1]

That there was no equality between the rulers and the ruled, white and coloured, should have been obvious to Gandhi with his twenty years' struggle in South Africa behind him. While the predominantly European colonies had been fast moving towards a position of equality with the mother country, the so-called dependencies of Britain were standing still or moving at a snail's pace towards self-government. Gandhi was not ignorant of the origins and the basis of the British rule in India. In *Hind Swaraj* he had given a merciless analysis of Indian history. The East India Company's victories he had attributed to the divisions of the Indian princes. He had criticized *Pax Brittanica*; the peace was in name only, as it had emasculated the Indian nation and made it cowardly. The railways, the law courts and the educational system had all served to tighten the stranglehold of the occupying power. This was a scathing indictment of British rule, but the moral he drew from it was novel: India was ground down not

[1] *Speeches and Writings of Mahatma Gandhi*, p. 310.

by the British rule but by Western civilization which had perpetuated that rule. The English themselves were the victims of this civilization; they deserved to be pitied rather than hated. He talked of conquering the conquerors spiritually. 'I tender my loyalty to the British Government,' he declared, 'quite selfishly. I would like to use the British race for transmitting this mighty message of *ahimsa*.' During 1915-16 his emphasis on the materialism of the West, and the ancient culture of the East, widow-remarriage, the abolition of untouchability, the promotion of handloom industry and the revival of Indian languages, seemed to mark him out as a visionary, strangely unpolitical and other-worldly.

Those who hoped that his energies would be diverted into the innocuous channels of social reform were, however, mistaken. In his scheme of life there was no sharp demarcation between the political and the non-political. When he exhorted the people to cultivate religion, he exhorted them to fear only God and to shed all fear of temporal authority. When he preached the gospel of *swadeshi*, 'in the religious spirit which restricts us to the use and service of our immediate surroundings,' he drew the important corollary that India could not live for Lancashire before she was able to live for herself. He protested against the use of a foreign language as *lingua franca* and threw a bombshell into the War Conference of 1918 by speaking in Hindustani. The Government discovered before long that this visionary was human dynamite, completely unpredictable and uncontrollable.

Speaking on the occasion of the opening of the Banaras Hindu University in 1916, he began to think audibly. He rebuked the Indian princes for their jewellery and liveries: 'Whenever I hear of a great palace rising in any great city of India, be it in British India or be it in India which is ruled by our great chiefs, I become jealous at once and I say: "Oh it is the money that has come from the agriculturists." 'If we trust and fear God,' he went on, 'we shall have to fear no one, not Maharajas, not Viceroys, not the detectives, not even King George.' Annie Besant, who was presiding at the august function, could not bear this 'audible thinking' any more and shouted to him: 'Please stop it.' A senior

British officer murmured: 'We must stop this man from talking such rot.'

But no one could stop Gandhi from saying or doing what he believed to be right. 'I have disregarded the order served upon me,' he told the magistrate in Champaran, 'not for want of respect for lawful authority, but in obedience to the higher law of our being, the voice of conscience.' Now this was a more revolutionary doctrine than the most radical politics of the day.

The experiences of these early years filled a gap in Gandhi's education which had been caused by his long self-imposed exile in South Africa. Something of the seamy side of the idolized British Empire he already knew. The vendetta of a British Political Agent had driven him at the age of twenty-four to seek a job in South Africa. The brief experience in the courts of Rajkot and Bombay in 1902 had given him a glimpse of the 'inconsiderateness and ignorance of the English official'.[1] On his return voyage to India he noticed a distance between the English and Indian passengers on the boat—the social gulf between the rulers and the ruled. He had pinned down all these experiences to the aberrations of individual Englishmen and continued to cherish the belief that the system as a whole was just and beneficial to India, but closer knowledge of the conditions in the homeland was to disillusion him.

Of the poverty of his homeland he had some idea; he had referred to it in *Hind Swaraj*, but the truth proved to be worse than his wildest imagination. In a village in Bihar he saw a woman in an untidy dress and asked Kasturbai to speak to her. The woman took Kasturbai into her hut and said, 'Look, there is no box or cupboard here containing other clothes. The *sari* I am wearing is the only one I have. How am I to wash it? Tell Mahatmaji to get me another *sari*, and I shall then promise to bathe and put on clean clothes every day.'

In December 1917 he wrote to *Indian Opinion*, the organ of the South African Indians, that they should not expect from him contributions for relief work in flood-ravaged areas in South

[1] *Autobiography*, p. 300.

Africa: 'The deep poverty I experience in this country deters me even from thinking of financial assistance to be sent for those who have been rendered helpless. Even one pie in this country counts. I am at present living in the midst of thousands who have nothing but roasted pulses or grain flour mixed with water and salt.'

And in his presidential address to the Gujerat Political Conference in November 1917, he spoke of 'deepening poverty'. The Government, he said, honestly believed that the nation's prosperity was increasing, 'that its faith in the blue books was immovable'.

The initial deference which high British dignitaries showed to him was due to their conviction that his loyalty to the British connection was beyond question. The moment he criticized particular policies or officials, he ceased to be a *persona grata*. The officers in the districts, more than their superiors in the provincial and central secretariats, were impatient of any agitation and quickly saw red. Gandhi's first collision with authority came in Bihar with the Commissioner of the Tirhut Division and his second in Bombay Presidency with the Commissioner of Ahmedabad about whom he wrote; 'The Commissioner's attitude constitutes a greater peril than the German peril, and I am serving the Empire in trying to deliver it from the peril within.' By 1917, Gandhi was being shadowed by the secret police. Civil Service rule, he declared, was one of fear; 'it was a fetish' with the British officers that it should never be said of them that they had yielded to anything like popular agitation. His irrevocable break with the Government came when he saw how rigid was the official machine, how sensitive to prestige, how slow to recognize mistakes and how reluctant to make amends. 'It is contrary to my nature,' he wrote, 'to believe in the depravity of human beings, but there is evidence of the depravity of the bureaucratic mind that it will stop at nothing to gain its ends.'[1] And it was despair with the bureaucracy which convinced him that the system needed ending and not mending.

The Viceroy seems to have realized at an early stage that, if

[1] *Young India*, October 20, 1921.

Gandhi could be a valuable ally, he could also be a dangerous opponent. During the years 1917-18 Lord Chelmsford made some efforts—for example during the Champaran crisis and the Delhi War Conference—to retain Gandhi's goodwill, but during the next two years he gravitated towards the view held by the members of the civil service that Gandhi was ever seeking occasions for trouble with the authorities and was irreconcilable. The British attitude to Gandhi in these early years had a curious ambivalence. Personal esteem for him was overlaid by strong, if vague, suspicions of his motives and policies. The official world saw in Satyagraha only a challenge to the British rule; it did not see, what was most important to Gandhi, that the challenge had a moral and non-violent basis. The British saw no particular virtue in being evicted from India non-violently, though there is little evidence to suggest that they believed in the feasibility of a mass movement remaining non-violent. They found it difficult to appreciate Gandhi's advice that on the Rowlatt Bills or the Turkish Question, the prestige of the Government could grow by stooping to conquer; his professions of loyalty and friendship did not carry conviction to them.

The process of estrangement between Gandhi and the Government may be glimpsed from contemporary records.

Gandhi to Private Secretary to the Viceroy. April 10, 1918. 'I am daily expecting your promised reply regarding brothers Ali.[1]

'You may know that I am engaged in a domestic quarrel with the local authority on Kheda crops.[2] I am hoping that the cry of the people will have its due weight, and that their opinion will be respected.

'What vexes me, however, is the case of the brothers Ali. I seem to be ever worrying the administrators in the country when as a respectable citizen of the Empire, I should be taking my share in the war. I should have felt happier being in Mesopotamia or France. I twice offered my services but they were

[1] Maulana Mahomed Ali and Shaukat Ali.
[2] Chapter 20.

not accepted. On the contrary, I seem to be making myself responsible for embarrassing situations, and I find myself in the midst of an agitation which might from its magnitude cause great anxiety to the Government. I entertain too great a regard for Lord Chelmsford to wish to add to his anxieties and yet I dare not shirk an obvious duty regarding brothers Ali. Their internment has soured the Muslim section. As a Hindu, I feel I must assist in securing the release of the brothers, if I cannot justify the Government's action by producing before the public a case against them. If, therefore, the Government have a real case against the brothers it should be produced, and the atmosphere cleared.

'If Lord Chelmsford is of opinion that they ought not to be released, the Government must prepare for facing an agitation which must result in the incarceration of the leaders of it. But I plead their discharge with all my strength. The Government can only gain in prestige by responding to public opinion, and so far as danger to the state is concerned, I can only say that I should lay down my life for it, if their release should mean any betrayal of trust.'

Gandhi to Private Secretary to the Viceroy. April 14, 1918. 'The above was drafted, as you will observe on the 10th instant. I have slept over it all these nights. I feel that I can best serve the State by being respectfully frank. During the last four days, the war has taken a graver turn. That strengthens me in my resolve to send the letter. In all humility I ask Lord Chelmsford not only to release the brothers, but to take them in his counsel as also Mr Tilak.' . . . .

Private Secretary to the Viceroy to Sir William Vincent, Home Member. April 17, 1918. ' His Excellency the Viceroy asks me to forward the enclosed copy of a letter dated 10th April from Mr Gandhi addressed to me, and to invite urgently an expression of your opinion as to whether it would or would not be a good thing to ask Mr Gandhi to come up and see the Viceroy. It seems possible that his restless activities might be diverted into a useful channel whereas if he is left to his own devices, his movements and energies always seem to make for trouble.'

Sir William Vincent to the Private Secretary to the Viceroy. 'Your demi official of the 17th April, enclosing a letter from Mr Gandhi on the subject of Muhammed Ali. I think it would be a good thing if His Excellency did ask Mr Gandhi to come to Simla, and then explained the position to him. I also venture to suggest that it might be well to point out to Mr Gandhi, that his idea of supporting an agitation over Muhammed Ali and his brother is not in accordance with his professed zeal to help the Government during the present crisis. I would suggest that H.E. might ask him to exercise his influence and activities in directions that might be of real service to the Empire, and not increase the difficulties of the Government.

'I would also explain that the cases of the two brothers will be examined by a judicial tribunal.

'I may say myself that I regard this letter as a little less than a veiled threat, and an attempt to squeeze the Government at the moment when the position of the Empire is believed to be critical. I notice that Mr Gandhi is anxious to be employed on war service in Mesopotamia or France, and if he could be sent out to Mesopotamia in any capacity, it would save a lot of trouble.

'. . . Possibly His Excellency might also indicate to Mr Gandhi the mischievous effect of his action in Khaira.'

Gandhi to Private Secretary to the Viceroy. February 20, 1919. 'As I am not still quite out of the wood regarding my health, and as, if I am to obey the doctors' orders, I must not undertake any activity requiring considerable exertion, I thought I would refrain from such activity till I was better. But the events that have recently happened impel me to submit the following:

'After the exchange of final letters between us, I entered into correspondence with Sir William Vincent. The result was that

G

a committee to advise the Government about the brothers was appointed. This committee has duly reported to the Government, but the latter's decision has not been announced.

'I must disclose one fact to Lord Chelmsford although it hurts my sense of modesty. They (Ali brothers) have, ever since the meeting of the Muslim League at Calcutta in the December of 1917, implicity accepted the advice I tendered to them, and so have the leading Mohammedans who would, but for my advice, gladly have carried on a powerful and embarrassing agitation long ere this. I advised them that if relief was not granted, Satyagraha—I abhor the expression "passive resistance", as it very incompletely expresses the great truth conveyed by the easily understood Sanskrit word Satyagraha—should be resorted to. I assured them that I was in communication with the Government about the brothers' release. As a Satyagrahi I told them that before engaging in a public agitation about it we should know the Government side of the question, and we should exhaust all milder remedies, and be able to demonstrate to the satisfaction of impartial observers before embarking on Satyagraha.

'I feel thankful to the brothers as also to the gentlemen with whom it has been a privilege to be associated, that they have abided by my advice though the delay has almost reached a dangerous point.

'I do most earnestly trust that the Government will by releasing the brothers prevent a powerful agitation in the country.'

Gandhi to Secretary Home Department. March 12, 1919. 'With reference to the Ali brothers, I should like to say just one word. . . . I do not know the art of Government, and what I have seen of it throughout the world makes me look upon it not with any favour. But it does seem curious that the Government should ignore what is patent to everybody outside it, viz. the increasing intensity of the smouldering fire which they are simply hiding under the ashes called repression. And is it good Government to imprison ability, honesty and religious convictions . . .?'

Gandhi to Private Secretary to the Viceroy. March 11, 1919. 'Even at this eleventh hour I respectfully ask His Excellency and His Government to pause and consider before passing the Rowlatt Bills. Whether justified or not, there is no mistaking the strength of public opinion on the measures. I am sure Government do not intend intensifying existing bitterness. . . . By bowing to public opinion (the Government) will smooth down feeling and enhance real prestige.'

Gandhi to Private Secretary to the Viceroy. March 11, 1919. 'Here is a copy of the telegram I have sent to you. I do not wish to add anything to it except a very personal word. All the time that Satyagraha was going on in South Africa, I had the privilege of addressing General Smuts through his Private Secretary, Mr Lane. As the struggle developed, Mr Lane veritably became the Angel of Peace between the Government as represented by General Smuts and the Indians as represented by me. Without his unfailing good nature, and courtesy, probably the satisfactory result which was arrived at, might not have been achieved as soon as it was.

'May I hope for similar services from you? For as in South Africa, so in India, I shall ever have to worry the P.S. if the struggle is unfortunately prolonged, and I shall seize every occasion to bring Government and those I may represent, closer together.

'. . . I hope Lord Chelmsford is now free from fever and that all its effects have disappeared. Such a personal note should have been written in my own hand. But my sickness has left me disabled in more ways than one. My hand shakes as I write and it soon gets fatigued. I am, therefore, obliged to fall back upon dictation except for most intimate correspondence.'

Private Secretary to the Viceroy to Gandhi. March 13, 1919. 'I duly received your telegram of the 11th instant and showed it to His Excellency . . . It is nice of you to think me capable of sustaining the part which Mr Lane played in South Africa. At the same time it is hardly logical for you so greatly to admire the plumage of an Angel of Peace while you are hastily assuming the wings of the Stormy Petrel. .... You succeeded in South Africa because you had a cause worthy of your countrymen's enthusiasm and lives. You have a magnetic personality and proportionate responsiblity rests upon you. People will follow you not because they think they are right but because they think Mr Gandhi is right.

'I should of course be sorry to see a "struggle" such as you indicate as possible but those of us who know you, even bureaucrats, will be equally sorry to see you come down from the lofty plane where you have always claimed our admiration . . .'

Private Secretary to the Viceroy to Gandhi. May 7, 1919. 'The Afghan news will surprise you. Excited by grossly exaggerated stories of disorders in India, the hot-headed, inexperienced Amanullah has decided that "the Afghan sword shall shine in India". It is a new complication. Militarily it is not a serious proposition for us and we are doing our best to act with all restraint towards this young man in his midsummer madness.

'. . . Can we look to you for help? I believe you could be of immense assistance in stabilizing Indian opinion. I am writing this of my own initiative, though I shall show it to the Viceroy. Hoping you are well.'

Gandhi to Private Secretary to Viceroy. May 11, 1919. 'Things are indeed moving fast in India. We are sitting on so many mines anyone of which may explode any moment. The Afghan news adds to the existing complications . . .

'I had before the receipt of your letter already begun to move in my own way in the direction of securing a peaceful atmosphere within our own borders. I confess that it is a delicate situation. I need hardly assure you that the whole of my weight will be thrown absolutely on the side of preserving internal peace. The Viceroy has the right to rely upon my doing nothing less. But my weight will be absolutely nothing if I received no support from the Government. The support I need is a satisfactory declaration on the Mohammedan question and the withdrawal of the Rowlatt agitation. If it is possible to give this support, I feel that you could have, without a shadow of doubt a contented India.'

Evidently the Government of India wanted to keep Gandhi on their right side, but they had no intention of following his advice. By the middle of 1920 they had written him off as a rebel, and Lord Chelmsford's view of Gandhi fell in line with those of his advisers in Delhi, and indeed of the majority of the British officers in the provincial capitals and the districts. But the Secretary of State was hard to convince:

Secretary of State for India to the Viceroy. August 12, 1919. 'Gandhi's movements. Please refer to your telegram of the 5th August. I fear I cannot agree with either you or the Local Governments. After conversation with Lloyd,[1] Gandhi has agreed to abandon Satyagraha for the time being. I have never yet heard of instance of Gandhi's appearance in any of India having anything but a tranquillizing effect. It is recognized by me that there may be a regrettable necessity to resist movements of men who avowedly are breaking the law, but that is a matter of expediency to be decided by the facts of each case. Why restrain a man who is not misbehaving?'

Viceroy to Secretary of State for India. August 14, 1919. 'Gandhi. Reference your telegram of the 12th instant. The Local Governments and I have had painful experience of Gandhi's criminal follies. I submitted to heads of Provinces the point of cancelling restrictions and they have practically all declined to accept responsibility of having him within their jurisdiction. We cannot share your view that Gandhi's appearance has a tranquillizing effect; our experience has been that it had the reverse. Gandhi has persistently threatened us with breach of law and has only announced the intention to postpone civil disobedience.'

[1] Sir George Lloyd, Governor of Bombay Presidency.

Secretary of State to Viceroy. August 15, 1919. 'Please see your
private telegram of the 14th instant. It is no use our prolonging
the discussion on this topic. I am, however, bound to tell you
that I am still in disagreement with you and the heads of Local
Governments. I have never heard of a case in which the appearance
of Gandhi has not had a tranquillizing effect. It certainly had in
Ahmedabad and Bombay during the recent riots; also in Bihar
and Orissa, and in South Africa. Moreover, attempts to keep
order in provinces by drawing ring-fences round them is strongly
disapproved by me, and I regard this policy as largely responsible
for the inflammable condition of the Punjab. Thirdly, to my
mind it is obvious that Gandhi postponed rather than abandoned
civil disobedience as a means of climbing down, and he has given
Lloyd an undertaking not to renew it without giving him notice.
Lloyd is satisfied that he does not mean to renew civil disobedience and so far as I can hear Gandhi is a man who has kept his
word.'

Yet such was the influence which the men-on-the-spot exercised
on Whitehall that, in 1922, it was the Secretary of State who was
urging Gandhi's arrest and expressing surprise at the delay in
effecting it.

It is thus obvious that to seek the explanation of Gandhi's
transition from a loyalist to a rebel only in the events of the
summer and autumn of 1920, is a superficial undertaking. Those
events only completed a process which had begun much earlier.
The depth of his disillusionment in 1920 was a measure of the
illusion he had been hugging of a new heaven and earth being
established after the war by a grateful Empire for the help rendered
to in its hour of need by a subject people. Given the Government's
intolerance of all agitators, and Gandhi's assertion of the inherent
right of non-violent opposition to political or economic injustice,
a conflict between the two was inevitable. What is surprising is
not that it came but that it was delayed so long. While the war
continued Gandhi was reluctant to embarrass the administration
and the latter was equally loth to alienate him irretrievably. No

government, and no alien government, could accept the right of a subject people to challenge its laws and administration even non-violently. Hence when he placed himself at the head of a non-violent rebellion as a protest against the official excesses in the Punjab, and the British policy towards Turkey, it was hardly to be expected that the Government would not accept the challenge.

Gandhi was deeply human and almost sentimental, even in politics. In the closing months of 1919 and early in 1920 he was scanning the horizon for a gesture which would restore his faith in the sovereignty of British justice. He was clutching at every straw. The Royal Proclamation of December 1919, which he had hailed as a harbinger of a new era, turned out to be no more than the felicitous phraseology usual on such occasions. In any case its spirit was not caught by His Majesty's Government in India. On both the Khilafat and the Punjab issues, Gandhi found the authorities said one thing and did another. Trusting by nature, he could make many allowances for the Government so long as his faith in its sincerity remained. But when that faith was shaken, he saw the British rule in an entirely new light. He had once attributed the faults of this rule to aberrations of individuals; now its virtues appeared to him accidental or incidental. 'I said to myself,' he wrote in *Young India* (December 31, 1921) 'there is no state run by Nero or Mussolini which has not good points about it, but we have to reject the whole once we decide to non-co-operate with the system ... the beneficent institutions of the British Government are like the fabled snake with a brilliant jewel on its head, but which has fangs full of poison ...'

Chapter 24

SWARAJ WITHIN A YEAR

THE programme of non-violent non-co-operation with the Government which Gandhi presented to the Khilafat Committee and the Indian National Congress, however revolutionary it seemed to the Government and the people, represented features which had for long been a part of Gandhi's personality and philosophy. 'The English have not taken India,' he had written in 1908; 'we have given it to them. They are not in India because of their strength but because we keep them.'[1] A year later he had suggested in a message to the Indian National Congress, that 'for the many ills we suffer in India, passive resistance is an infallible panacea'. Hence when he came to the conclusion that the Government did not possess in itself any capacity for self-improvement that it was 'past mending', he enunciated the right recognized 'from time immemorial of the subject to refuse to assist a ruler who misrules'.[2] His scheme of boycotting conventional schools and establishing national schools filled his eminent contemporaries —such as Rabindranath Tagore, Madan Mohan Malaviya, Srinivas Sastri, and C. R. Das—with misgivings, but Gandhi had experimented on his children. He had criticized the use of English in schools as calculated to make Indian children foreigners in their own country. He always practised what he preached. Had he not surprised the *élite* of Bombay in 1915 by replying to their welcome in Gujerati, and scandalized the Viceroy and his colleagues by speaking in Hindi at the War Conference of 1918?

As for the British courts in India, he had recorded his verdict on them in *Hind Swaraj* in 1908. 'The lawyers have enslaved

[1] Gandhi: *Hind Swaraj*, p. 27.
[2] Letter to Lord Chelmsford dated June 22, 1920.

India, have accentuated Hindu-Muhammaden dissensions and have confirmed English authority.' The law's delays and expense in India were too well known to need any elaboration. Motilal Nehru, of the most sucessful lawyers in the land quoted a proverb to illustrate the ruinous effects of litigation. '*Adalat mein jo jita so hara, jo hara, so mara.*' (Success in the court is defeat; defeat is death.)

'Swadeshi', or the use of home-made goods, was another plank in the non-co-operation movement he had been preaching since his return from South Africa. He had told a conference of Christian missionaries in February 1916 that India could not live for Lancashire before she was able to live for herself.[1] His advocacy of the boycott of foreign cloth and the use of hand-spun and hand-woven cloth (khadi) during the non-co-operation movement was taken by the Government—and by most nationalists—as a blow aimed at Britain in her tenderest spot, her commerce with India. To Gandhi, however, the boycott of foreign cloth was not at all a pressure tactic but a means of reviving the oldest cottage industry of India. With increasing pressure on land, agriculture had long ceased to give adequate employment to the peasant; hand spinning could therefore help him to eke out a living in the normal year and act as 'a ready-made insurance policy' in periods of famine and flood. To the 'masses' Gandhi recommended spinning for economic reasons, to the educated classes for spiritual reasons—for the kinship it offered with the poorest in the land. Khadi was to Gandhi also a test for the awakening of the Indian people: a nation that could save sixty crore rupees per year spent on foreign cloth and distribute this sum among its spinners and weavers in their village homes, 'will have acquired powers of organization and industry that must enable it to do everything else necessary for its organic growth'.

As for the boycott of councils, which had been and was to prove the greatest bone of contention in the Congress, Gandhi did not subscribe to the claim that legislatures were a necessary training ground for self-government. Nor was he attracted by the

[1] Natesan: *Speeches and Writings of Mahatma Gandhi,* p. 341.

G*

strategy of 'capturing' legislatures for 'wrecking from within'. As recently as December 1919, when Gandhi had some faith in the sincerity of the British, he had pleaded for working the Montagu-Chelmsford Reforms for what they were worth. When that faith had gone the councils appeared to him only a red herring in the path of Indian nationalists.

This was in a nutshell the programme that Gandhi placed before India, the boycott of British courts, schools, councils, and cloth. With some *naïveté*, Gandhi claimed that his movement was not unconstitutional:[1] evidently in his dictionary constitutional and moral were synonymous terms. The British saw that the success of this programme of non-co-operation would paralyse their administration. Lord Chelmsford at first tried to kill with ridicule 'the most foolish of all foolish schemes', which would bring ruin to those who had any stake in the Government. He was also apparently rousing the fears of the propertied classes. A number of 'moderate' leaders joined official critics in under-lining the risks inherent in mass non-co-operation. M. A. Jinnah had cried halt at the Nagpur Congress in December 1920. Srinivasa Sastri—Gokhale's political heir—warned his countrymen against the perils of the course to which they were drifting by adopting 'an impracticable programme in unreasoning opposition to the Government'. Rabindranath Tagore who had during the Rowlatt Bill agitation praised Satyagraha ' as the ideal which is both against the cowardliness of hidden revenge and the cowed submission of the terror-striken', after his return from Europe and America early in 1921 wrote an article in *Modern Review* criticizing non-co-operation as a doctrine of 'negation, exclusive-ness and despair which threatened to erect a Chinese wall between India and the West'. Gandhi replied to Tagore (whom he called, 'The Great Sentinel') in *Young India* in passages of emotion and eloquence to match those of the poet. He refuted the charge that his movement was negative or exclusive. Non-co-operation with evil, Gandhi argued, was as positive an affair as was co-operation with good. Non-co-operation was only an invitation

[1] *Speeches and Writings of Mahatma Gandhi*, p. 523.

to the British Government to co-operate with the Indian nation on its own terms, 'as is every nation's right and every good government's duty'. As for the isolation from the West which Tagore had deprecated, Gandhi wondered if India had anything to share with the West save her degradation, pauperism and plagues! The poet had also criticized the emphasis on home-spun cloth: if big machines were a menace, so were the smaller machines. 'I have found it impossible,' answered Gandhi, 'to soothe suffering patients with a song from Kabir. The hungry millions ask for one poem, invigorating food.' And the spinning wheel struck him as the only readily available supplementary industry, a virtual reviving draught for the impoverished country-side.

The chief argument against non-co-operation whether from the British Government or the 'moderate' Indian leaders was that it was likely to open the sluice gates of anarchy. In fact a book with the telltale title *Gandhi and Anarchy* by Sir Sankaran Nair, a former member of the Viceroy's Executive Council, was published in March 1922. He quoted from *Hind Swaraj* to prove that Gandhi was opposed 'to any government in any form'; that he was undermining the respect for laws and protection to persons and property; that he disliked Parliamentary Government, and had found in Khilafat and Punjab affairs only excuses to sabotage the constitutional reforms, that he was releasing forces of disorder, which he was unable to control.

Gandhi never recanted his faith in the ideals of *Hind Swaraj* but he frankly acknowledged that these ideals could not appeal to more than a handful of people. In *Young India* of January 26, 1921 he wrote: 'I am individually working for the self-rule pictured therein. But today my corporate activity is undoubtedly devoted to the attainment of Parliamentary Swaraj in accordance with the wishes of the people of India. I am not aiming at destroying railways or hospitals, though I would welcome their natural destruction. Nor am I aiming at a permanent destruction of the law courts much as I regard it as a consummation devoutly to be wished for. Still less am I trying to destroy all machinery and mills. It requires a higher simplicity and renunciation than the people are prepared for. The only part of the programme which is now being carried out in its entirety is that of non-violence. But even that is not being carried out in the spirit of the book.'

Those who denounced the movement as negative and dangerous did not appreciate the precautions which its author had taken. 'Non-co-operation' was an incomplete and in certain ways a misleading description of a movement which was intended not only to dismantle some institutions but also to replace them with others. The students and teachers who walked out of schools run or aided by the government were invited to join 'national' schools and colleges; the lawyers and the litigants who boycotted the courts were to take their briefs to the arbitration boards; those who resigned from the army and the police were to become Congress or Khilafat volunteers. The boycott of imported cloth was to be accompanied by the promotion of hand spinning and hand-woven cloth to clothe the people in villages and towns. There was thus to be no vacuum as a result of these boycotts. The movement was moreover to be carefully phased. Between the surrender of titles and honorary offices to the Government and mass civil disobedience and non-payment of taxes, there were several stages to suit the level of discipline and organization achieved by each particular district and province. From his central control, Gandhi was to permit as much electrical current of non-co-operation to be transmitted as the people could take, and he made it clear that if there was a violent spark he would switch off the mains to prevent a conflagration. The greatest safeguard for peace was the stress he laid on non-violence. Non-co-operation with the symbols and institutions of British rule, ruled out even hatred of Englishmen. Again and again Gandhi declared that he would not do to an Englishman what he would not do to a blood brother. He had, he publicly recalled, non-co-operated even with his brother on matters of principle.

Repeatedly he drew the attention of the non-co-operators to the 'purifying' part of the movement, to its introspective and moral aspects. Violence, disunity and corruptibility of the people strengthened foreign rule and so people had to make themselves proof against these weaknesses. The change of heart which he was working for he expected first among Indians and then among Englishmen. The Indian people had thus to shed fear of the Government and also rid themselves of the curse of communalism, untouchability, use of intoxicants, forced labour and other social evils.

Gandhi had told the special session of the Indian National Congress at Calcutta in September 1920 that with an adequate response to his programme of non-co-operation, Swaraj could be attained in one year. The word Swaraj he did not define precisely. 'Gandhiji was,' writes Jawaharlal Nehru, 'delightfully vague on the subject.' On one occasion he described Swaraj as the 'abandonment of fear of death'; on another occasion he described it as 'the ability to regard every inhabitant of India as our own brother or sister'; on a third occasion Swaraj was defined as 'the capacity of the people to get rid of their helplessness'. These definitions had the merit of being homely; they did not define but only gave a glimpse of the new order he wished to usher in. The nearest he got to a political definition was in *Young India* of December 29, 1920, when he defined Swaraj as 'Parliamentary Government of India in the modern sense of the term for the time being'. This may have been a concession to educated public opinion in India which was practically unanimous in its admiration of the democratic structure of England. Gandhi himself had no admiration for the English parliamentary government; in *Hind Swaraj* he had ridiculed the Mother of Parliaments as 'a sterile woman'. He was, however, more interested in the content than in the form of Swaraj. The distrust of the apparatus of government was almost as deep-rooted in him as in Tolstoy. He would have agreed with the nineteenth-century doctrine that 'that government is best which governs least'. But he was fully conscious that the majority of his colleagues and followers were not prepared to go the whole hog with him and so he let the matter rest with the proposition that the Swaraj scheme would be formulated in due course by the representatives of the people.

'The promise of Swaraj within a year,' wrote Subhas Chandra

Bose 'was not only unwise but childish.'[1] It looked on the face
of it too optimistic a proposition that Britain's Empire in India
established for more than a century could be overthrown by
non-violent agitation in a year. The time limit set by Gandhi was,
however, not a prediction, nor the promise of a political tactician.
A year was in Gandhi's opinion long enough to awaken a people,
to make it shed its fear, and stiffen its backbone. A moral transformation of the Indian people could be expected to lead to a
transformation of the British Government and people. 'Freedom,'
Gandhi wrote, 'is like a birth. Till we are fully free we are slave.
All birth takes place in a moment.' He had, he declared, laid a
practical programme before the country. A nation that could
throw away an age-long curse (of untouchability), shed the
drink habit, and utilize its spare hours to manufacture sixty
crores worth of cloth during a single year would be a transformed
nation. Such a nation would have acquired enough discipline,
courage and self-sacrifice to convince Britain that India could not
be treated on any basis other than that of equal partnership.
Swaraj was not to come as a gift from Britain. 'The Act of Parliament,' wrote Gandhi, 'would be merely a courteous ratification
of the declared wish of the people of India even as it was in the
case of Union of South Africa.'

[1] Bose, S. C.: *Indian Struggle*, Calcutta, 1948, p. 104.

Chapter 25

CONGRESS FOLLOWS THE MAHATMA

THE programme of non-violent non-co-operation with the Government under Gandhi's leadership, had been accepted by the Khilafat Committee but it could not become a national programme until the Indian National Congress adopted it. The All-India Congress Committee had considered the issue important enough to be decided by a plenary session of the Congress. The annual session was due at Nagpur in December 1920 but events were moving fast. A special session was, therefore, convened in September at Calcutta. Lala Lajpat Rai presided over it. 'The Congress is of opinion,' ran the main resolution of this session, 'that there can be no contentment in India without redress of the two wrongs (Khilafat and Punjab) and that the only effectual means to vindicate national honour and to prevent a repetition of similar wrongs in future is the establishment of *Swarajya* (self-government). The Congress is further of opinion that there is no course left open for the people of India, but to approve of and adopt the policy of progressive non-violent non-co-operation until the said wrongs are righted and *Swarajya* is established.'

Gandhi's whirlwind tours, and eloquent articles in the Press had already electrified the atmosphere in the country. The initial reaction of several Congress leaders was, however, one of doubt; they felt Gandhi was going too fast and too far. Those who were opposed to the non-co-operation programme, or certain parts of it, included Lajpat Rai the most distinguished Punjabi of his time and president of the Congress session at Calcutta; C. R. Das and B. C. Pal—the two most influential men in Bengal; Annie Besant whose Home Rule Movement had dominated Indian politics during the war; and Madan Mohan

Malaviya, Jinnah and several leaders of the 'moderate' hue.
Gandhi had attended most of the Congress sessions since his
return from South Africa. Though a respected figure and
considered an authority on the problem of Indians overseas, he
had no party or following of his own. In the Amritsar session
(December 1919), he had taken a more active part, but even there
he had let the limelight fall on Tilak, Motilal Nehru, Malaviya
and C. R. Das. Tilak died in August 1920 but most of the other
veteran leaders assembled at Calcutta in September 1920, were
sceptical of the non-co-operation programme. Politics had
hitherto meant speaking in and outside legislatures, issuing
statements, interviewing the Governors and the Viceroy, and
finally, taking a deputation to England to see His Majesty's
ministers. In fact at the Calcutta Congress there was a suggestion
from no less a person than C. R. Das that a deputation should
be sent to England to press the Congress demands. C. R. Das
headed the opposition to Gandhi's plans for boycott of councils
on the plea that the Congress would lose points of vantage in the
fight against the Government; he favoured continuous obstruction
to the Government on the Irish model on all fronts, both inside
and outside the legislature, in order to embarrass the administration
and to lower its prestige. This line of thought which was shared
by many Congress leaders had important differences from that
of Gandhi, who was seeking to convert and not merely to thwart
his opponents.

The Calcutta Congress adopted the non-co-operation programme with 1,855 votes in its favour and 873 votes against it.
In his hour of triumph Gandhi behaved with exemplary restraint
and humility. He did not alienate his critics nor cast doubts on
their motives. The result was that in a few months C. R. Das,
Lajpat Rai and other leaders were in the vanguard of the non-
co-operation movement. Gandhi was thus able to carry through
his radical programme without splitting the Congress.

That a political programme had no chance of success without
an adequate organization to implement it, Gandhi had realized
at the age of twenty-five, when he had founded the Natal Indian

Congress to fight for the rights of the Indians in Natal. The Indian National Congress had, therefore, to be refashioned, if it was to prove an efficient instrument of 'non-violent non-co-operation'. Gandhi saw that what the country needed was not a forum for an annual pageant and feast of oratory, but a militant organization in touch with the masses. The revised constitution of the Indian National Congress, largely Gandhi's own handi-work, was approved at the Nagpur session of the Congress in December 1920; it defined the creed of the Congress 'as the attainment of *Swarajya* by all legitimate and peaceful means'. Satyagraha was thus brought within the four corners of the constitution of the Congress. The smallest unit of the Congress organization was to be the village Congress committee. A number of such committees were to be grouped into a Union Congress Committee. Union Committees were to be formed into tehsil or into district committees which in turn were to elect provincial committees. The All-India Congress Committee was to consist of about 350 members representing the Provinces. The Congress became a broad-based organization: anyone who accepted its creed and paid four annas as the annual subscription could become its member. A small working committee led by the Congress President of the year constituted the highest executive of the Congress. The Congress was thus reorganized not only on a more representative basis but in such a way that it could function efficiently between its annual sessions. It ceased to be the preserve of the upper and middle classes; its doors were opened to the masses in the smaller towns and villages whose political con-sciousness Gandhi was quickening.

The annual Congress session at Nagpur in December 1920 confirmed the decisions taken by the Special Session at Calcutta three months earlier. The opposition to the non-co-operation programme died hard. The president of the Congress session Vijayaraghavchariar was critical and so were in varying degrees Kelkar, Jinnah and Annie Besant. Fortunately C. R. Das was brought round, as the boycott of councils was no longer a live issue, the elections to the councils having already been held. The enthusiasm of the rank and file of the delegates infected their leaders; non-co-operation became the official programme and Gandhi undisputed leader of the Congress. From now until his death Gandhi was to exercise a unique influence over the Indian National Congress and Indian politics. It is relevant to ask here what had brought him to this pre-eminent position.

When Gandhi had returned from South Africa via England early in 1915, he had the halo of 'victory' around him, but did not by any means count among the front rank of India's politicians. Montagu had recorded in his diary in 1917 that 'Tilak is at the moment probably the most powerful man in India and he has it in his power, if he chooses, to help materially in the war effort'. During the war Annie Besant dominated Indian politics. Gandhi had kept out of the Home Rule movement which she and Tilak had sponsored. Gandhi's anxiety not to embarrass the Government during the war and his plea for unconditional support of the war effort had isolated him from the more militant politicians. At the same time the small-scale Satyagraha campaigns which he had organized in Bihar and Bombay had cost him the goodwill of the Government. His criticisms of the 'educated classes', his lack of faith in political bargaining and his pre-occupation with problems requiring the application of the Satyagraha technique had kept him out of the inner counsels of the Congress. He had no share in framing the Congress-League scheme of constitutional reforms which the Lucknow Pact of 1916 symbolized, and which became the 'platform' of the Congress for the next two years. He had no party of his own in the Congress. The 'moderate' leaders did not like his unconstitutional weapon of Satyagraha and the extremist leaders did not like his studied moderation towards the Government.

Gandhi was to enter Indian politics on his own terms and in his own way. He lacked a party but he possessed a technique of which he was the author and the sole practitioner. For more than thirty years Indian politicians had sought redress of wrongs from the Government by resolutions, petitions and deputations, but had made little headway. A few hot-headed young men and women had tried sporadic violence against the ruling race, but violence was costly and futile against a better organized and better equipped adversary commanding the whole coercive apparatus of the modern state. And in any case, the white-collar leaders of the Congress were not the men to pull triggers or throw bombs. Before Gandhi came, the attitude of the political leaders in India resembled that of the employee who went to his boss, demanded a rise in salary, and threatened that if the demand was not conceded, 'I would continue to serve you'. Gandhi offered a practical alternative to the futility of verbal violence and the sacrificial folly of political crime.

Would Gandhi have led the country in 1920 if Gokhale or Tilak had been alive? The question is not easy to answer. In January 1921, nearly six years after Gokhale's death, Gandhi wrote that it was 'blasphemous to conjecture what would have happened if Gokhale was alive today. I know I would have been working under him'. This is a judgment which seems to have been dictated more by sentiment than by political probabilities, as Srinivasa Sastri and other political heirs of Gokhale did not join Gandhi's mass movements. As for Tilak, Gandhi had once compared him with the ocean; in spite of mutual respect the two men had basic differences in their approach to politics. 'Politics is a game of worldly people,' Tilak had once written to Gandhi, 'and not of *Sadhus*.' Tilak criticized Gandhi for his unconditional support to British war effort; he would not co-operate with the Government until it gave a *quid pro quo* to the country. He was prepared to vary his tactics for effective action. A fortnight before his death he told Gandhi that he did not disbelieve in Satyagraha, but he had his doubts as to whether the masses could be persuaded to adopt it. Unfortunately he died on August 1, 1920, but even if he had lived it is likely that the reins of the movement would have remained in Gandhi's hands.

'I can lay no claim to scholarship. I have not his powers of organization. I have no compact disciplined party to lead and having been an exile for twenty-three years. I cannot claim the knowledge that Lokamanya had of India.' This is what Gandhi wrote after Tilak's death. However, precisely because Gandhi had been free from association with political factions of the preceding two decades, he was acceptable to various groups in the Congress. The lack of a compact following saved him from a compact opposition within the Congress. And since he was the author of 'Satyagraha', he had to lead the Congress once it adopted his programme. Lajpat Rai and C. R. Das, who began as the critics of his programme, became his trusted lieutenants. It is probable therefore that Tilak, whose entire life had been spent in opposition to British rule, would have taken his place among the foremost leaders of the non-co-operation movement. To suggest that Tilak would not have played second fiddle to Gandhi is to misjudge the great leader of Maharashtra who, when asked whether under Swaraj he would be Prime Minister, replied, 'No, sir, under Swaraj I will be a professor of mathematics in a *swadeshi* college and retire from public life'.

In speculations of this kind one is likely to forget the fundamental fact that the final decision in a mass movement depends upon the people. Gandhi was swept to the top in 1919-20 because he had caught the imagination of the country. The leaders were trying hard to keep pace with the rank and file whom Gandhi's speeches and writings had filled with a new energy and enthusiasm. The President of the Nagpur Congress, which put the seal of final approval on the non-co-operation movement in December 1920, rightly summed up the session as one in which 'instead of the President and the leaders driving the people, the people drove him and the leaders'.

Gandhi was now the Mahatma, the great soul; with his voluntary poverty, simplicity, humility and saintliness he seemed a *Rishi* (sage) of old who had stepped from the pages of an ancient epic to bring about the liberation of his country. Nay, to millions he was the incarnation of God. In the course of a tour of Bihar when the tyre of his car burst, he saw an old woman standing on the roadside. She was stated to be 104 years old and had waited in rain and without food and water for the whole day. 'For whom are you waiting?' somebody asked her. 'My

son, who is Mahatma Gandhi?' she queried. 'Why do you want
to see him,' asked Gandhi who now stood next to her. 'He is an
Avtara' (incarnation of God), replied the woman. For the next
quarter of a century, it was not only for his message that people
came to him, but for the merit of seeing him. The sacred sight of
the Mahatma, his *darshan*, was almost equivalent to a pilgrimage
to holy Banaras. The unthinking adoration of the multitude sometimes made him feel sick. 'The woes of Mahatmas,' he wrote,
'are known only to Mahatmas.' But this adoration was the
mainspring from which was drawn the immense influence he
exercised over Indian public life. He inspired old and young alike.
In his autobiography, Jawaharlal Nehru has graphically narrated
the story of the boy in his teens who was arrested during the
non-co-operation movement, stripped and tied to a whipping
post and flogged; as each stripe fell on him and cut into his flesh
he shouted, 'Victory to Mahatma Gandhi' until he fainted.

Gandhi had struck some of the inner chords of Indian
humanity; his appeal for courage and sacrifice evoked a ready
response because he was himself the epitome of these qualities.
It was because he was, to use Churchill's epithet, a 'naked faqir',
because his life was one of austerity and self-sacrifice that a great
emotional bond grew between him and the Indian people. The
number of such 'fakirs' was to multiply fast. Among those who
gave up their lucrative careers and queued up for prison under
Gandhi's leadership were Motilal Nehru, Rajendra Prasad, C. R.
Das, Vallabhbhai Patel, C. Rajagopalachari. Life acquired a
new meaning for them. Abbas Tyabji, a former Chief Justice of
Baroda wrote from a village that he was feeling twenty years
younger. 'God!' he exclaimed, 'what an experience! I have so
much love and affection for the common folk to whom it is now
an honour to belong. It is the fakir's dress that has broken down
all barriers.' Motilal Nehru, who had given up his magnificent
practice at the Allahabad Bar, wrote to Gandhi from a small
health resort where he was convalescing: 'The brass cooker has
taken the place of the two kitchens, a solitary servant not over-
intelligent that of the old retinue—the three small bags containing

rice, dal and masalo, that of the mule-load of provisions . . .
The *shikar* has given place to long walks, and rifles and guns
to books, magazines and newspapers . . . What a fall my
countrymen! But really I have never enjoyed life better.'

And it is about this period that Jawaharlal Nehru has recorded
that the movement had so wholly absorbed and wrapt him up
that he 'gave up all other associations and contacts, old friends,
books, even newspapers except in so far as they dealt with the
work in hand . . . I almost forgot my family, my wife, my
daughter.'[1]

---

[1] Nehru, J. L.: *Towards Freedom* (Autobiography), London 1945, p. 77.

Chapter 26

CLIMAX

1921 was a year of awakening for India. The non-co-operation movement gathered momentum on the crest of rising enthusiasm. The prospect of 'Swaraj within a year' shattered bonds of centuries; the hypnosis of fear had been broken. Gandhi's call for courage and sacrifice lifted politics from the doldrums in which they had drifted for decades. The Government was anxious but momentarily perplexed, wondering whether the old methods of fighting violent outbreaks would suppress Satyagraha or strengthen it.

For Gandhi this was a period of incessant activity which taxed him almost to the limits of his endurance. He travelled all over the country, keeping in touch with local leaders, directing, advising and admonishing. His daily mail was enormous and received his personal attention. His secretaries were often hard put to it to locate remote villages even with the help of railway time-tables and post and telegraph guide books. Sometimes, unable to decipher the name of a correspondent, they cut out the signature from the letter and pasted it on the envelope to serve as an address. In the midst of this unremitting activity, Gandhi found time to write for *Young India* into the pages of which he poured his very soul. Many an article which inspired the country with faith and courage was scribbled in the third-class compartment of a moving train. The four or five hours' sleep which his public engagements left him, was often disturbed by the uncontrollable enthusiasm of crowds which gathered at railway stations at all hours of the day and night to see him. In Krishandas's *Seven Months with Mahatma Gandhi* there is an interesting story of the residents of an Assam village who had threatened that if the train carrying the

Mahatma did not halt at their station, they would hold it up by lying across the track. They were as good as their word and broke into his compartment at the dead of night with naked torches and shrill cries of 'Mahatma Gandhi Ki Jai'.

This hero-worship pained Gandhi. He told an audience in Barisal: 'When I hear cries of "Victory to Mahatma Gandhi" every sound of the phrase pierces my heart like an arrow. If only I thought for a moment that these shouts could win Swaraj for you, I could reconcile myself to my misery. But when I find that people's time and energy is spent in mere useless shouting, while at the same time real work is given the go-by, how I wish that they should instead of shouting my name prepare and light up a funeral pyre of me and that I might leap into it and once for all extinguish the fire that is scorching my heart.'

Harsh words, but the spectacular aspects of the moment were less important to him than silent constructive work.

The awakening of the people, to which his movement was contributing, pleased Gandhi. In the course of his tours he noted that, 'the spirit of kindness of which the poet Tulsidas sings so eloquently is gaining ground'. His message was simple: it was not British guns, but Indians' own imperfections which kept India in bondage. India could acquire a new strength by purging her corporate life of untouchability, communal strife, drink and drugs and dependence upon foreign cloth and institutions run or aided by the British Government. Swaraj was not to come as a gift from the British Parliament. 'I have had the hardihood to say,' he declared, 'that Swaraj could not be granted even by God. We would have to earn it ourselves.'

The first reactions of the Central and Provincial Governments to Gandhi's defiance of laws in April 1919 had been sharp and swift as is evident from the following 'Clear the Line' telegrams:

Governor of Bombay to the Viceroy. April 7/8, 1919. 'Yesterday's demonstrations were large. Owing, however, to the knowledge of the presence of a military force they passed off quickly. Resistance to law has just commenced and this afternoon

Gandhi has sent the following letter to the Commissioner of Police . . .

'Although a technical offence (printing of a newspaper without authorization) has been selected, it will almost certainly be necessary for me to proceed against Gandhi and others in this or any other contravention of law, but in view of the fact that such action may result in considerable disturbance here and possibly elsewhere, I consider it proper to inform you immediately and to defer taking action until I receive telegraphic intimation of the receipt of this telegram by you.'

Viceroy to Secretary Home Department. April 8, 1919. 'Please see "Clear the Line" telegram from H.E. the Governor of Bombay dated 7th April, 1919. I think it important that, in order to deal with the possible development of the passive resistance movement, a definite plan of action should be prepared at once in the Home Department so as to co-ordinate the policy to be followed in the different provinces.

'Gandhi's first move might perhaps be met by a process of confiscating printing press. It also seems to me that in every province where the passive resistance movement shows dangerous symptoms the head of the local government might issue widely a manifesto simply worded regarding the state, object, and scope of the Rowlatt Bill, sympathizing with rational opposition, condemning those who by embarrassing the Government seek notoriety, pointing to the moral of the Delhi incident, and calling upon all sober minded people, whatever their views may be on the actual question of the bill, to discourage the policy of embarrassing and intimidating the Government by threatening them, and making it clear that the Government is determined to carry out its duty of maintaining the laws of the country and dealing rigorously with all movements that endanger the peace and prosperity of great body of citizens.

'Perhaps a counter passive resistance movement might be organized and assisted where a local government thinks such a course expedient.'

*Secretary Home Department to Private Secretary to the Viceroy.
April 9, 1919.* 'Clear the line—On the question of Gandhi's entering
Delhi and Punjab, Vincent has been in telegraphic communication
with O'Dwyer, and Barron today has also consulted Hailey.

'In the opinion of O'Dwyer the situation is now serious and it
is advisable that Gandhi should under Regulation III of 1818
be deported to Burma. In 1907 similar deportation of Lajpat Rai
was very effective . . . Vincent at any rate at present does not
agree with O'Dwyer as to the expediency of deportation as
sympathy of many who do not now approve Gandhi's conduct
would be alienated by such action. In Egypt recent doings show
how deportation might cause general conflagration.

'After consulting Sir James Meston and Sir George Lownds,
the Home Member has telegraphed to the Punjab and the U.P.
Governments and the Chief Commissioner Delhi sanctioning
the issue by them of an order under Rule 3 (b) Defence of India
(Consolidated) Rules directing Gandhi to remain in Bombay
Presidency and informing them that it will be their duty to use
all reasonable means to enforce this order. All other local
governments have been informed of this . . .'

*Secretary Home Department to Chief Secretary Bombay. April 8,
1919.* 'Please refer to the telegram dated 7th April, from H.E. the
Governor of Bombay to H.E. the Viceroy. If the Government of
Bombay is satisfied that there is a clear case of breach of law, the
Government of India think that Mr Gandhi and any other leaders
should be prosecuted. Should prosecution be decided upon it is
of great importance that it should take place with least possible
delay so as to prevent Mr Gandhi moving about the country
and creating similar trouble elsewhere. Except as a last resort,
the Government of India consider it inadvisable to use Defence
of India Act. Please report what action it is proposed to take by
Clear the Line telegram . . .'

*Secretary Home Department to Chief Secretary Bombay. April 8,
1919* (repeated to other Local Governments). 'Please refer to

our telegram of 8-4-1919. Information has reached us that Gandhi left Bombay for Delhi on 8th instant. Orders have been passed by the Punjab Government and Delhi Administration under Rule 3 of Defence of India (Consolidated) Rules excluding him from their provinces . . . The effect of this will be that if he enters Punjab—as is probable—or Delhi and possibly the United Provinces, he will be sent back to Bombay Presidency, where the Bombay Government can, if they consider it desirable, issue further orders of restriction . . . In any event Gandhi should for the present not be allowed to leave the Bombay Presidency.'

As we have already seen,[1] Gandhi was in fact arrested on April 10, on his way to Delhi and put in a train for Bombay where he was released. The disturbances which broke out in his home province in his absence and the tragedy which occurred in the Punjab a few days later, led him to temporarily suspend civil disobedience.

The 'firmness' which the Governors and the Viceroy showed in the second week of April 1919 was not to be repeated for nearly three years. Perhaps in the first flush of excitement they had accepted the inevitability of Gandhi's arrest and prosecution too lightly. When they had time for second thoughts, they felt less sure of the requirements of the situation and the precise scale and timing of the force required to cope with Satyagraha. The tragic events in the spring of 1919 at least revealed the tremendous hold which Gandhi exercised over the people, and the risks inherent in his arrest. At the same time, his restraint in the summer of 1919 led them to hope that he might not, after all, take the extreme step of open and large-scale defiance of the Government, or he might not be able to carry with him other leaders and groups in the Congress.

'I think,' wrote Sir William Vincent—the Home Member—on April 26, 1919, 'that a good many people will soon be tired of Mr Gandhi and his vagaries.' The same opinion was expressed by Sir George Lloyd—the Governor of Bombay—in a letter to the Viceroy on June 11, 1919:

[1] Chapter 21.

'I am rather anxious about things here, for Gandhi is beginning to get very restless . . . He has some game on with the Punjab, but exactly what it is we have not yet succeeded in finding out. His meetings are not well attended and his followers are very disgruntled . . . The mere deportation of Gandhi will raise a considerable storm, whilst his prosecution is a course that I cannot contemplate with any degree of satisfaction. For the rest the Home Rule party is completely split up now in this Presidency. It has suffered blows in the resignations of several important leaders . . . If it were not for Gandhi, all could be extremely well here . . . but he is a real danger point. Unless he forces our hands he is less dangerous loose than bound, for he loses influence daily, but his knowledge of that fact impels him to desperate courses to recover his influence.'

It was in view of these considerations that, even after the adoption of the non-co-operation programme by the Indian National Congress in September 1920, the Government of India prescribed 'non-interference' as the 'wisest policy' in a circular dated September 4, 1920: 'The non-co-operation scheme is so intrinsically foolish that Government have every confidence that the commonsense of India will reject it . . . For the time being the policy of non-interference is the wisest policy. They (the Government of India) think that it would be a mistake at the present juncture either to adopt repressive measures of an executive nature under special or emergency laws against the leaders of the movement or even to institute immediate proceedings against them under the ordinary criminal law because any such action would only result in making martyrs of them, and gaining for them a large number of adherents who would otherwise hold aloof.

'Government have been influenced by the fact that in the opinion of their legal advisers, the Advocate-General, and the Standing Counsel, a prosecution of Messrs Gandhi and Shaukat Ali under the ordinary criminal law would have little chance of being followed by conviction until the later stages of the programme, i.e. the withdrawal of co-operation from the army and the police services and the refusal to pay taxes had been brought into operation.

'. . . (As regards local firebrands in villages and towns) they should not be free to defy the *Sirkar* (Government) with impunity. Association with Mr Gandhi, the apostle of non-violence, does not confer immunity from prosecution on even the most prominent of his co-workers if they break the law by making speeches of a violent character.'

It was a tribute to the legal tradition of the British that even in dealing with one whom they regarded as the arch rebel they consulted their legal advisers, and that these advisers had the courage to say that the law could not be stretched to hold Gandhi guilty unless certain specific offences were committed.

On April 2, 1921, Lord Reading succeeded Lord Chelmsford as the Viceroy of India. At the end of the month the new Viceroy wrote: 'When in England, I was not unduly depressed . . . by the report of serious conditions in India . . . I am reluctantly compelled since my investigations here to take a more serious view.' He adopted (records his son-biographer) 'Fabian tactics' to bide his time for a massive assault on the movement. In the latter half of May he met Gandhi. The meeting had been arranged through the efforts of Madan Mohan Malaviya, primarily to clear some misunderstanding about alleged incitement to violence by the leaders of the Khilafat movement, which was of course inextricably tied up with the non-co-operation movement. The whole trouble had arisen from some references to Afghanistan made by Maulana Mahomed Ali at a time when rumours were rife about an imminent invasion of India by the Amir of Afghanistan. There were in all six meetings between Gandhi and Reading; their discussions ranged over a wide field: the Punjab disturbances of 1919, the Khilafat movement, the meaning of *Swaraj*. In a private letter to his son, the Viceroy confessed to a feeling of excitement, almost a thrill, in meeting his unusual visitor and described his religious and moral views as admirable though he found it difficult to understand his practice of them in politics. Gandhi agreed to ask Mahomed Ali to publicly withdraw the

passages in his speeches, which were susceptible of an interpretation of incitement to violence; in doing this he wanted to leave
no doubt in the minds of his own followers as well as in that of
the Viceroy that non-violence was the basic principle of his
movement. The Viceroy viewed the episode from another angle:
'He (Mahomed Ali) is the real factor in the situation; he is the
ostensible link between the Mohammedan and Hindu. If trouble
comes between him and Gandhi it means the collapse of the
bridge over the gulf between Hindu and Mohammedan. If
Mahomed Ali does what Gandhi desires—and that no doubt will
be to make the declaration—Mahomed Ali will be lowered in
the public esteem . . .'[1]

The Secretary of State telegraphed his congratulations to the
Viceroy on his skilful treatment of Gandhi!

The breach between the Mahatma and the Ali brothers to
which the Government was looking forward did not come.
When in September 1921, the Ali brothers were arrested, and
the Government of Bombay explained in a communique that the
charge against them was that of tampering with the loyalty of
the Indian soldier, a manifesto was signed by nearly fifty leaders,
including Gandhi, calling upon every Indian soldier and civilian
to find some other means of livelihood.

If there was no breach between Gandhi and the Khilafatists,
could there be a split in the Congress? The Bombay Government,
which was considered to have an expert knowledge of Gandhi's
politics, predicted as late as October 28, 1920, that a split in the
Congress camp was imminent: '(Against Gandhi's) prosecution
is the main fact that he has done much to split up the Congress
Party, and if left to himself, will do more. The Poona nationalists
are furious with him and will try to upset him at Nagpur. He has
alienated a considerable section of the Home Rule League by
his frankly anti-British attitude.' The Government were yet to
learn that Gandhi had a rare talent for keeping together colleagues
in spite of differences of temperament and policy so long as the
goal was common. The Nagpur Congress, held in December

[1] Reading, Marquess of: *Rufus Isaacs, First Marquess of Reading*, Vol. II, p. 199.

1920, cemented instead of sundering the bonds between Gandhi and the Congress leaders; those who could not follow him lost in prestige and influence.

During the next twelve months the British officials looked anxiously for the ebbing of the nationalist tide. In September 1921, the Bombay Government reported that 'enthusiasm for the wearing of khaddar and the sporting of Gandhi caps has waned considerably during Gandhi's absence', and the daily average of foreign clothes for bonfires was 'something like six old shirts or sarees, a few coats and old hats and caps'. The Bengal Government reported on September 17, 1921 that at Chittagong, Gandhi and Mahomed Ali addressed huge crowds, but as the 'speeches were made in Hindi they were generally not understood and did not rouse much enthusiasm!' A few days later the Bengal Government wrote that there were internal dissensions in the Congress Committee and that a 'pleasing feature' was the co-operation of leading *zamindars* and landholders with the authorities in more than one district. The U.P. Government wrote on September 19, 1921, that the majority of those who heard seditious speeches were those who had lost their land and who believed that Gandhi would give it back to them. During the same month the Chief Secretary of the Punjab Government noticed the failure of the non-co-operation party in Amritsar and quoted the Commissioner of Ambala that the Moplah riots had 'offended the Hindus and shaken the faith of the people in non-co-operation'. The Bihar Government cheerfully reported that the non-co-operators' *panchayat* courts had fallen into disrepute, the volunteer organizations had lost their popularity and the national schools were disintegrating.

It is difficult to judge, how far these conclusions were based on wishful thinking. It appears, however, that the Local (provincial) Governments were generally perturbed by the popular discontent, but they tended to underrate the importance of particular leaders or demonstrations; they were as easily alarmed as they were reassured in a situation which seemed dangerous and yet in a flux all the time. In November 1921 Calcutta's Commissioner of

Police told Withinshaw, an officer of the Intelligence Bureau, that a large number of policemen had resigned and that he feared that 'the whole lot would leave the service'.

Instead of waning, the tension between the Congress and the Government steadily mounted in the winter of 1921–22. The Ali brothers were arrested in September 1921 for tampering with the loyalty of the army; their offence had been repeated by a number of leaders including Gandhi. This was a challenge which was difficult for the Government not to accept. The hope that the movement would melt away by internal differences or popular apathy had not been realized by the autumn of 1921. The clash with Gandhi looked inevitable; the only question was when it would be in the interest of the Government to time it. To arrest or not to arrest Gandhi was the question which faced Lord Reading and his advisers. A minute recorded on October 10, 1921, by Sir William Vincent, the Home Member, sums up with remarkable objectivity the case for and against Gandhi's prosecution for signing the manifesto (declaring that 'it was contrary to national dignity for any Indian to serve as a civilian, and more especially as a soldier').

Reasons in Favour of Prosecution

(*a*) The serious effect which our inaction in face of avowed seditious (speeches) is having on the administration and upon all officers of Government from Gazetted rank downwards.

(*b*) The disheartening effect on moderate opinion ... our inaction is preventing many who are against non-co-operation from coming into the open and is also driving many into the Gandhi camp.

(*c*) The impression created among Muhammadans that they alone are prosecuted and that Hindus are treated with greater consideration. The idea is generally prevalent whether it is justified or not.

(*d*) A prosecution seems inevitable sooner or later unless Gandhi gives up his programme or comes to terms and if we are certain to be forced to such a prosecution, the present is not an unsuitable time at the beginning of cold weather to initiate such a prosecution and deal with any disorder.

(*e*) The fact that Gandhi may at any time force us to prosecute when His Royal Highness (Prince of Wales) is in India at which time a prosecution might be more troublesome than now.

(*f*) The real danger of delay is that no government in the position of the Government of India can allow such open sedition or attacks on the Army and Police to continue unchecked, without running the risk of reaching a time when the poison has gone so deep that prosecution is really impossible.

Reasons Against Prosecution

(*a*) Gandhi is pledged to secure *Swaraj* by the end of December and his failure to do so may lead him to give up the movement, and will certainly and naturally discredit him.

(*b*) He is losing a number of educated supporters who are opposed to his present activities. Muhammadans are angry because their leaders have been prosecuted. Hindus are irritated because the Khilafat question is being much made of. The cloth movement is not likely to be a success in Madras owing to the Moplah movement and in the Maharashtra . . .

(*c*) The danger at this juncture of imprisoning Gandhi would be to increase his influence very greatly. He is now not only regarded as a great national hero, but by the ignorant, as semi-divine. His confinement in jail would draw many adherents to his cause, and it is probable that he knows this. He certainly wants to be made a martyr in order to secure support for his movement, thus consolidating it at a time when many of his schemes have failed. He is equally certainly not challenging us to prosecute him for the benefit of the Government but because he believes that he will secure some advantage therefrom.

(*d*) The result of prosecution would be a great increase in unrest and probably disorder just on the eve of Prince of Wales' visit.

(*e*) If we do not prosecute Gandhi at this time we must expect *hartals* and abstensions from ceremonies (in connection with the Prince of Wales' visit) . . . If on the other hand we prosecute

H

we shall certainly encourage open demonstrations against His Royal Highness and may be faced with such wide disorder as to make it necessary to postpone the visit.

(f) I do not know how far any modification of the Turkish peace terms is possible, but if we could secure some substantial modification in favour of Turkey we should go a long way to break Mr Gandhi's movement so far as Muhammadans are concerned . . .

On the whole I am inclined to the view that we would be well advised to postpone action for the present at any rate . . . If necessary we could prosecute later, say in December or January, by which time Gandhi will probably put himself more in the wrong or abandon the movement . . . I am well aware of the dangers of this course, and am really mainly influenced by the fact of His Royal Highness' approaching visit. If this is postponed I should, I think, advocate prosecution immediately and risk the other dangers.

The visit of the Prince of Wales had been planned before Lord Reading became the Viceroy, but in spite of the disturbed political conditions Lord Reading did not advise postponement. 'Postponement,' he wrote to the Secretary of State, 'would have the disadvantage of attributing power to this (the non-co-operation) movement, and above all of creating both in England and in the Dominions, and throughout the world, the impression that India was so disloyal that it was not safe for the Prince to visit it.' On November 17, 1921, when the Prince landed in Bombay, the non-co-operators abstained from the official ceremonies. Gandhi was in Bombay on this day and was present at a big meeting held in the morning to make a huge bonfire of foreign cloth; in the afternoon rioting broke out in the town in which Europeans, Parsis and others who had participated in the reception to Prince Edward, were assaulted. Personal appeals, and a fast by Gandhi, and frantic efforts by his colleagues, saved Bombay from the maze of violence and counter-violence into which it slipped. Fortunately, in other towns there were no riots, but the people left no doubt of their sullen atittude to the British *Raj*. Wherever the Prince went, parades, receptions and banquets were arranged in his honour by the authorities but (as the memoirs of the Duke of Windsor record) he did not fail to notice 'empty streets, shuttered windows, brooding silence'.

The Prince of Wales was to visit Calcutta in the last week of December 1921. The Viceroy, anxious to avoid a *hartal* and hostile demonstration at Calcutta, encouraged Madan Mohan Malaviya's efforts for mediation between the Government and the Congress. Malaviya wired to Gandhi on December 16, 1921 that he proposed to lead a deputation to the Viceroy to urge the calling of a Round Table Conference. If the Viceroy accepted the proposal and released the leaders, would Gandhi call off the boycott of the visit of the Prince of Wales and suspend the civil disobedience movement until the Conference was over? The same proposal had been simultaneously broached by Malaviya with C. R. Das, who was then serving a term in the Presidency Jail at Calcutta. C. R. Das thought and Abul Kalam Azad agreed with him that the 'offer' brought by Malaviya was worth considering; in a telegram to Gandhi they urged him to accept Malaviya's proposal. Gandhi made his acceptance conditional on two assurances: that the date and composition of the Conference were settled in advance, and that the Ali brothers should be among the political prisoners to be released. Malaviya could not give these assurances and the negotiations fell through. The reaction of C. R. Das has been recorded by Subhas Chandra Bose in *The Indian Struggle:* 'The *Deshbandhu* was beside himself with anger and disgust. The chance of a life-time, he said, had been lost.' C. R. Das was disappointed, not because he hoped that Swaraj could have emerged from the Round Table Conference which Malaviya had proposed, but because the Conference seemed to him a good tactical move. The Mahatma had promised Swaraj within a year, and if in the last fortnight of 1921 some spectacular achievement in the form of a political amnesty and a Round Table Conference could be contrived to the credit of the Congress, the organization could save its face and gain in prestige and public confidence.

It is probable that, like C. R. Das, the Viceroy was also manoeuvring for a tactical advantage. Sir William Vincent, the Home Member, recorded a minute on November 10, 1921 in which he discussed possible courses of action to cope with the threat of civil disobedience: '(One line of action is) to propose a conference with the extremists and moderates. This is a suggestion of Mr Sarma's, made I think, largely to tide over a difficult period during the Prince of Wales' visit. I do not think myself that any good result would follow from such a conference unless the Turkish peace terms were first altered.'

Gandhi had every right to know when and where the Round Table Conference would meet and who would attend it. He was the leader of both the Khilafat and the non-co-operation movements; he could not let down the leaders of the Khilafat. In spite of the interest—and the heat—these negotiations aroused at the time there is no doubt now that Malaviya and C. R. Das exaggerated their value. The Viceroy would have been only too glad to manoeuvre the Congress into a standstill, but it is doubtful if he would have granted any substantial political concessions.

Be that as it may, there was no settlement and the tension between the Government and the Congress continued to increase. The attitude of the administration stiffened. A telegram from the Viceroy dated November 24, 1921 to the Secretary of State showed the new temper of the Government of India:

'It is . . . impossible to forecast with any certainty (Gandhi's) future actions, or that of other prominent non-co-operators . . .

'. . . apart from civil disobedience other aspects of the non-co-operation movement have assumed a serious character and have convinced us that it is essential now to take action on more drastic and comprehensive scale . . .

'. . . We have not overlooked the danger of riots and affrays ensuing, but it is regarded as lesser evil than loss of authority and discouragement of force which failure to deal with obstructors

must entail. Local Governments are being assured by us of our full
support should police or military be compelled to fire in the
legitimate discharge of their duties.

'. . . We are informing them that they should not hesitate to
prosecute under section 124A or whatever other sections of
Indian Penal Code may be applicable, any persons, however
prominent, whose arrest and prosecution they consider is required
for maintenance of law and respect of authority . . .'

In December 1921 and January 1922 nearly 30,000 people
were imprisoned. Volunteer organizations were made illegal,
meetings and processions were forcibly dispersed, midnight
searches of Congress and Khilafat offices became the order of the
day, and the treatment of political prisoners became harsher.
The Indian National Congress met at Ahmedabad in December
1921 and appointed Gandhi as its sole executive authority. Within
the Congress there was a growing pressure on him to intensify
the struggle and launch mass civil disobedience. A mass struggle
was, in Gandhi's armoury of Satyagraha, the most effective as
well as the most dangerous weapon. The All-India Congress
Committee had already, in November 1921, authorized every
Provincial Congress Committee on its own responsibility to
institute civil disobedience to the point of refusal of taxes. However, the Provincial Committees were advised by Gandhi not to
launch the movement but to watch and wait while he tried it in
certain selected areas. Mass civil disobedience, he compared to
an earthquake, 'a sort of general upheaval on the political plane—
the Government ceases to function . . . the police stations, the
courts, offices etc. all cease to be Government property and shall
be taken charge of by the people'.

Gandhi's plan was to launch civil disobedience in one district;
if it succeeded in one district he proposed to extend it to the
adjacent district and so on until the whole of India was liberated.
He gave a clear warning that if violence broke out in any form in
any part of the country, the movement would lose its character
as a movement of peace, 'even as a lute would begin to emit
notes of discord the moment a single string snaps'.

The riots which had disfigured Bombay during the visit of the Prince of Wales in November 1921 had led Gandhi to postpone civil disobedience. Evidently the atmosphere did not appear too propitious for a drastic step. The wholesale arrests and prosecutions of Congress workers and volunteers in the next two months, however, made him review the position. The Government was preventing meetings and muzzling the Press. The choice, as Gandhi described it, was between 'mass civil disobedience with all its undoubted dangers and the lawless repression of the lawful activities of the people'. He decide to take the risk, and to make a beginning with mass civil disobedience under his own supervision in Bardoli *taluk* in Gujerat. While selecting Bardoli as a spearhead of the mass civil disobedience, Gandhi warned its people that for refusing payment of land revenue, their crops were liable to be auctioned, lands confiscated, cattle driven away, and that Bardoli *taluk* may even disappear from the map.

Gandhi communicated the step he contemplated, with his reasons for it, to the Viceroy. He urged the Viceroy to respect the understanding implicit in the Reading-Gandhi conversations in May 1921 (when the Ali brothers apologized for speeches in which they were alleged to have incited the people to violence) that the Government would not interfere with non-violent agitation. Finally, he warned that unless the Government issued a notification within seven days, freeing the imprisoned non-co-operators, removing the restrictions on the Press, restoring fines and forfeitures, mass civil disobedience would begin in Bardoli 'to mark the national non-violent revolt against the Government'.

The Government of India promptly issued a reply to the Mahatma's ultimatum and asserted that the issue before the country was 'no longer between this or that programme of political advance but between lawlessness with all its consequences on the one hand and the maintenance of those principles which lie at the root of all civilized governments'.

The Congress and the Government were now poised for a head-on collision.

Chapter 27

ANTICLIMAX?

THE 'open letter' to the Viceroy, which struck him as an ultimatum, but was, from Gandhi's view-point, a sacred duty peremptory on a Satyagrahi, was dated February, 1 1922. Three days later a clash occurred between a procession and the police at Chauri Chaura, a small village in Gorakhpur district in the United Provinces. The facts were clear enough. The main body of the procession had passed in front of the police station when some constables jeered at the stragglers who hit back. The constables opened fire, and, when their ammunition was exhausted, locked themselves inside the police station. The main procession then returned and, in a mad fury, set fire to the police station, hacking to pieces the hapless policemen as they rushed out of the burning building. Among the twenty-two victims of the tragedy was the young son of the sub-inspector of police.

The news of this outrage was a bolt from the blue to Gandhi. He inferred from it that the atmosphere in the country was too explosive for a mass movement and decided to revoke the plans for civil disobedience in Bardoli which he had announced only a week earlier. He consulted such members of the Congress executive as were not imprisoned. The All-India Congress Committee met at Delhi on February 24th, and at his instance passed resolutions deploring the Chauri Chaura incident, suspending mass civil disobedience, and permitting only such activities of the Congress as were not designed to invite imprisonment. With the 'aggressive' part of the movement in abeyance, the emphasis was shifted to the constructive programme.

The sudden suspension of mass civil disobedience shocked and bewildered Gandhi's closest colleages. Subhas Chandra Bose recalled many years later: 'I was with *Deshbandhu* (C. R. Das) at the time and I could see that he was beside himself with anger and sorrow at the way Mahatma Gandhi was repeatedly bungling.'[1] Motilal Nehru and Lajpat Rai wrote from gaol urging Gandhi not to halt the movement because of a stray incident. Gandhi had a feeling that many of those who had endorsed his proposals in the Congress Working Committee and the All-India Congress Committee had done so not out of real conviction, but out of deference to him. Some of his ardent followers were troubled by doubts and torn between loyalty to their leader and their own convictions. They were at a loss to see any logic in calling off the civil disobedience movement at Bardoli after an outbreak at Chauri Chaura. Was it not open to the Government to thwart the non-violent rebellion by staging such 'incidents' through *agents provocateurs* and thus turn the Satyagraha struggle into a pious futility? Was the Congress a political institution or a testing ground for the inner conflicts of a Mahatma? Were the sacrifices of the nation to go in vain, and were the non-co-operators to continue to rot indefinitely in gaol? And was not the reversal of the 'aggressive' programme an invitation to the Government to pounce upon the non-co-operators and to turn their retreat into a rout?

Such were the angry questions shot at Gandhi by a bewildered and indignant following. Few of the critics could see that Chauri Chaura was not the cause, but only the occasion for the reverse gear which he had applied. From the moment he had come out against the Rowlatt Bills and presented Satyagraha to the country as a lever for redress of political and social injustice he had stressed the paramount importance of non-violence; this was the one theme which had recurred in his speeches and articles. And yet, as the ugly violence in Ahmedabad, Viramgam and Amritsar had shown in 1919, it was not easy to prevent outbursts of mob-frenzy altogether, particularly when the local authorities were not slow to feed it with provocative acts. 'I am sorry,' he had declared on April 18, 1919 at Bombay, 'that

[1] Bose, Subhas Chandra: *The Indian Struggle*, Calcutta, 1948, p. 108.

when I embarked upon a mass movement, I underrated the forces of evil.' He was fully aware of the undercurrent of violence in the country, and one reason why he had allowed himself to be placed at the head of the Khilafat movement in 1920 was that he hoped to divert this undercurrent into non-violent channels. Conscious of the risks, he had taken extraordinary precautions to graduate his movement and condition it to the political climate. The non-co-operation programme began with the surrender of titles and honorary offices by individuals, and was to end with the suspension of taxes and mass defiance of laws. Between these two extremes there were a number of activities, which not only asserted the nationalist feeling but also disciplined the people and prepared them for a mass movement. The improvement in the condition of untouchables, the establishment of national schools, the settlement of disputes by arbitration boards outside the courts, the formation of volunteer corps, the picketing of liquor shops, the boycott of foreign cloth, and the promotion of *Khadi*, were practical methods of organizing the masses. Gandhi's programme was one of 'progressive non-co-operation' in which the defiance of authority was to be extended according to the ability of the people to resist repression without retaliation.

While organizing the forces of nationalism against foreign rule, Gandhi had taken care not to rip open the latent fissures in the Indian society. He advised the tenants to pay rents to the landlord even when payment of tax to the Government was suspended. He advised the workers to obtain leave from their employers for joining 'hartals'. 'It is a most dangerous thing,' he wrote, 'to make political use of labour until the labourers understand the political condition of the country.' He gave much time and thought to the organization of Congress volunteers, and wrote at length in *Young India* on the technique of controlling crowds and conducting public meetings. Violence on the part of the Government he did not fear, as it could strengthen the hearts and swell the ranks of non-co-operators. Violence on the part of the people, he dreaded, as it could

H•

dissolve the movement into chaos besides provoking the superior violence of the Government.

No violent outbreak in any part of the country could escape Gandhi's notice. The Malegaon riots in which policemen were victims of mob-violence, and the Malabar outbreak in which Hindus suffered at the hands of the Moplahs, elicited his instantaneous and unqualified condemnation. He was in Bombay when the Prince of Wales arrived in November 1921, and a riot broke out in which fifty-eight persons were killed and 381 injured. In a message to the people of Bombay he said that the non-violence of the non-co-operators had been worse than the violence of the co-operators, 'for with non-violence on our lips we have terrorized those who have differed from us . . . The Swaraj that I have witnessed during the last two days has stunk in my nostrils'.

An eye-witness has left a pen-picture of his agony during this outbreak: 'Thrown into a stage of utter despondency, he began to indulge in such words of grief and bitter self-reproach as would melt even the stoniest-hearted men. Weighed down by grief and remorse he went on recalling the high hopes with which he had been directing the movement. The spirit of intolerance had gone on unchecked and had culminated in this huge con-flagration at Bombay. Why had he not, from the first, the sagacity to stand up against every such exhibition of intolerance and violence?'[1]

C. F. Andrews, who saw Gandhi on return from South Africa soon after the Bombay riots, found him 'haggard and emaciated, as one who had just passed through the valley of the shadow of death'. Andrews had noticed a spirit of violence enter the move-ment from the side of the people as the violence on the part of the Government increased. The great masses of India had awakened to the sense of their own power, but they had not yet been trained to keep this power under control. Andrews criticized the 'subtle racial appeal' in public bonfires of foreign cloth. He

[1] Krishandas: *Seven Months with Mahatma Gandhi*, Ahmedabad, 1928, Vol. I, p. 410.

had seen Satyagraha in action in South Africa during the years 1913-14; when he saw the movement in 1921 in India he felt 'it was something entirely new and less spiritual'.

The Bombay riots (November 1921) appeared to Gandhi as a red signal requiring cancellation of the mass civil disobedience movement. Most of his colleagues in the Congress executive did not share his misgivings nor understand his caution. The pressure within the Congress organization for the launching of a mass struggle continued to grow during the closing months of 1921. The failure of the peace parleys which Madan Mohan Malaviya initiated between the Congress and the Government, the wholesale arrests of Congress volunteers, the embargo on public meetings, and the arrests of leading non-co-operators combined to raise the political temperature. The 'ultimatum' sent by Gandhi to Lord Reading early in February 1922 was a step which, in the opinion of most Congress and Khilafat leaders, had been long overdue. Many of them felt that Gandhi was not going far or fast enough; they wanted to see mass civil disobedience launched simultaneously in different parts of the country to bring the Government to its knees.

There is a significant record of a discussion on civil disobedience at the meeting of the Congress Working Committee at Delhi (November 3, 1921), which shows how difficult it was for some of Gandhi's senior colleagues to understand his strategy fully. According to Krishandas: 'Both Mr Kelkar and Mr Vithalbhai Patel, while accepting *in toto* Mahatmaji's plan of starting civil disobedience, held that no special preliminary training was necessary for our people to qualify for such action . . . Mahatmaji had laid down that, where an individual proposed to undertake civil disobedience for himself, he must know hand-spinning. When the clause was read and Pandit Motilal Nehru burst out laughing . . . Messrs Kelkar and Patel indulged in loud, angry protests.'[1]

So when the tragedy of Chauri Chaura occurred it was more than a stray incident in an unknown village in a remote corner

[1] Krishandas: *Seven Months with Mahatma Gandhi*, p. 369-371.

of the Indian sub-continent. It was, as Gandhi wrote to Jawaharlal Nehru on February 19, 1922, 'the last straw'. He recalled the complaints he had received that the rank and file had been getting out of hand in many places, and that indiscipline had been increasing. 'I assure you,' he wrote to Jawaharlal, 'that if the thing had not been suspended we would have been leading not a non-violent struggle but essentially a violent struggle.'[1] Jawaharlal, who had received the news of the suspension of civil disobedience in gaol 'with amazement and consternation', after discussing the pros and cons of suspension of civil disobedience, records in his autobiography that the 'decision was right; he (Gandhi) had to stop the rot and build anew'.

With the perspective which time gives, Gandhi did not repent the drastic decision of 1922. Twenty years later, in *Harijan* (April 12, 1942), he dwelt on the limitations of the non-co-operation movement of 1920-22 and the reasons for his having taken what he described as the 'maddest risk' a man can take: 'In South Africa too I introduced (Satyagraha) as an experiment. It was successful there because resisters were a small number in a compact area and, therefore, easily controlled. Here we had numberless persons scattered over a huge country. The result was that they could not be easily controlled or trained. And yet it is a marvel the way they have responded. They might have responded much better and shown far better results. But I have no sense of disappointment in me over the results obtained. If I had started with men who accepted non-violence as a creed, I might have ended with myself. Imperfect as I am, I started with imperfect men and women and sailed on an uncharted ocean. Thank God that though the boat has not reached its haven it has proved fairly storm-proof.'

Gandhi noted that many of his colleagues, and the mass of non-co-operators were burning with indignation and were anxious to deliver 'telling blows', albeit non-violent ones, against the Government. Now, this was rather an imperfect appreciation of the technique of Satyagraha which sought to

[1] Quoted in Tendulkar's *Mahatma*, Vol. II, p. 118.

prick the conscience, to melt the heart and to open the eyes of the opponent. The technique of non-violent warfare is essentially different from that of the other variety, which is almost un-inhibited as to the means for achieving its objective. The common view of war and politics is that everything is fair, and that the protagonists should muster overwhelming pressure at as many points as possible to defeat the opponent; such a strategy was inapplicable to Satyagraha in which there was no room even for excitement. Gandhi defined civil disobedience as preparation for mute suffering, 'with effects which may be marvellous, but unperceived and gentle'.

'It is dangerous to assemble,' wrote Romain Rolland, 'all the forces of a nation and to hold the nation panting before a prescribed movement, to lift one's arm to give the final command, and then at the last moment, let one's arm drop and thrice call a halt just as the formidable machinery has been set in motion. One risks ruining the brakes, and paralysing the impetus.'[1] If we may continue Rolland's metaphor, Gandhi was bringing the machinery not to a standstill but into third gear from a premature top gear. The suspension of the 'aggressive programme' did not affect the constructive programme, the positive aspect of the non-co-operation movement. The critics did not share Gandhi's faith that the non-co-operation movement, even without the last desperate step of mass civil disobedience could prove effective.

It was not only Congressmen and Khilafatists who failed to understand Gandhi's action after Chauri Chaura. The Viceroy, Lord Reading, gleefully confided to his son that Gandhi 'had pretty well run himself to the last ditch as a politician by extra-ordinary manifestations in the last month or six weeks before his arrest'.[2] Some British observers even suggested that Chauri Chaura was a pretext to call off a movement which was showing signs of fatigue. We have already seen how for several months the official hierarchy had been debating the pros and cons of

[1] Romain, Rolland: *Mahatma Gandhi*, London, 1942, p. 132.
[2] Reading, Marquess of: *Rufus Isaacs, First Marquess of Reading*, Vol. II, p. 249.

Gandhi's arrest and how matters had come to a head in the closing months of 1921. The Secretary of State telegraphed to the Viceroy in February 1922 that he was puzzled at the delay in making the arrest. After Gandhi's 'open letter' of February 1, 1922 about launching civil disobedience in Bardoli, the arrest could not have been long delayed. But after the revocation of mass civil disobedience and the confusion in Congress ranks, the risks of Gandhi's arrest perceptibly declined. Nevertheless, Lord Reading took a few more weeks in conferring with his Council and with the Governors of Bombay and Madras before giving the order.

'It is a matter of no pride or pleasure to me but of humiliation,' wrote Gandhi in *Young India* (March 9, 1922), 'that the Government refrains from arresting me for fear of an outbreak of universal violence.' The Mahatma counselled his followers to maintain absolute discipline after his arrest. No wonder, therefore, that Lord Reading was able to record with obvious relief in a letter to his son that he had had no trouble arising from Gandhi's arrest and that 'not a dog barked'.

On the evening of March 10, Gandhi was arrested. He bade farewell to the inmates of his Ashram, heard his favourite song of the true *Vaishnava*, took his seat in the waiting car and was driven to gaol. The trial was held on March 18th, before C. N. Broomfield, the District and Sessions Judge of Ahmedabad. The prosecution relied upon three articles published in *Young India* namely 'Tampering with Loyalty', 'The Puzzle and its Solution' and 'Shaking the Manes'. The other accused was Shankarlal Banker, the publisher of *Young India*. Sir J. T. Strangman, the Advocate-General, conducted the prosecution. The accused did not defend themselves. The judge behaved with exceeding courtesy, nodding respectfully to the accused in the dock before taking his seat. Gandhi made his task easy by pleading guilty. In a statement which would have been difficult to excel in dignified emotion or eloquence, he explained his transition from a staunch loyalist to a rebel:

'My public life began in 1893 in South Africa in troubled weather.

My first contact with British authority in that country was not of a happy character. I discovered that as a man and as an Indian I had no rights. On the contrary I discovered that I had no rights as a man because I was an Indian. But I was not baffled. I thought this treatment of Indians was an excrescence upon a system that was intrinsically and mainly good. I gave the Government my voluntary and hearty co-operation, criticizing it fully where I felt it was faulty, but never wishing its destruction . . .

'The first shock came in the shape of the Rowlatt Act . . . Then followed the Punjab horrors . . . I discovered too that the plighted word of the Prime Minister to the Mussulmans of India regarding the integrity of Turkey and the holy places of Islam was not likely to be fulfilled. But in spite of the foreboding and the grave warnings of friends at the Amritsar Congress in 1919, I fought for co-operation and working the Montagu-Chelmsford reforms . . .

'I came reluctantly to the conclusion that the British connection had made India more helpless than she ever was before, politically and economically . . . She has become so poor that she has little power of resisting famines . . . Little do they realize that the Government established by law in British India is carried on for this exploitation of the masses. No sophistry, no jugglery in figures can explain away the evidence the skeletons in many villages present to the naked eye. I have no doubt whatsoever that both England and the town-dwellers of India will have to answer, if there is a God above, for this crime against humanity . . . The greatest misfortune is that Englishmen and their Indian associates in the administration of the country do not know that they are engaged in the crime I have attempted to describe . . . (Many of them) honestly believe that they are administering one of the best systems devised in the world and that India is making steady though slow progress.'

He accepted responsibility for violent outbreaks which had occurred, and asked for the highest penalty that could be inflicted upon him:

'And I wish to endorse all the blame that the Advocate-General has thrown on my shoulders in connection with the Bombay occurrences, the Madras occurrences and the Chauri Chaura occurrences. Thinking over these things deeply and sleeping over them night after night and examining my heart, I have come to the conclusion that it is impossible for me to dissociate myself from the diabolical crimes of Chauri Chaura or the mad outrages of Bombay. He is quite right when he says that as a man of responsibility, a man having received a fair share of education, having had a fair share of experience of this world, I should know the consequences of every one of my acts. I knew them. I knew that I was playing with fire. I ran the risk and if I was set free I would still do the same . . . I wanted to avoid violence. Non-violence is the first article of my faith. It is the last article of my faith. But I had to make my choice. I had either to submit to a system which, I considered has done an irreparable harm to my country or incur the risk of the mad fury of my people bursting forth when they understood the truth from my lips. I know that my people have sometimes gone mad. I am deeply sorry for it; and I am, therefore, here to submit not to a light penalty but to the highest penalty. I do not ask for mercy. I do not plead any extenuating act . . .

'The only course open to you, Mr Judge is . . . either to resign your post or inflict on me the severest penalty if you believe that the system and law you are assisting to administer are good for the people.'

Judge Broomfield acknowledged that Gandhi was in a different category from any person that he had ever tried or was likely to try:

'The law is no respecter of persons. Nevertheless it would be impossible to ignore the fact that in the eyes of millions of your countrymen you are a great patriot and a great leader. Even those who differ from you in politics, look upon you as a man of high ideals and of noble and even saintly life. I have to deal with you in one character only . . . It is my duty to judge you as a man subject to the law, who has, by his own admission, broken the law . . . I do not forget that you have consistently preached against violence and that you have on many occasions, as I am willing to believe, done much to prevent violence. But having regard to the nature of political teaching and the nature of many of those to whom it was addressed how you could have continued to believe that violence would not be the inevitable consequence it passes my capacity to understand.'

Gandhi was sentenced to six-years' imprisonment. An observer noted that he was not only serene but 'festively joyful' during the 100-minute trial. 'So far as the sentence is concerned,' he told the judge, 'I certainly consider that it is as light as any judge could inflict on me; and so far as the whole proceedings are concerned, I must say that I could not have expected greater courtesy.'

When the judge left the court, the assembly, to the embarrassment of the police officers, converted itself into a family gathering. Gandhi sat in the centre and exchanged a word or two with everyone; he joked with a five-year-old child about his foreign finery, spoke words of good cheer, shook hands and then nimbly stepped into the motor-van which took him to Sabarmati gaol. His parting message was that the country must remain peaceful, as it had done during the week of his arrest and the trial. Two days later, a special train carried him and Shankarlal Banker to Kirkee, a suburb of Poona, from where they were taken to the Yeravda prison.

Gaol-going was part of non-co-operation; in his articles and speeches Gandhi had often commented on its significance for the movement. 'Freedom is to be wooed only inside prison walls and sometimes on gallows,' he had once written. Thousands of non-co-operators had been arrested during the preceding eighteen months. The ideal non-co-operator, according to Gandhi, was to seek imprisonment not to embarrass but to convert the Government by suffering for a just cause. Arrests were to be courted 'not rudely, roughly, blushingly, certainly never violently, but peacefully, quietly, courteously, humbly, prayerfully, and courageously'. The non-co-operator was to observe gaol discipline; he was neither to seek nor to accept special privileges. The hardships of gaol life were to be borne cheerfully as 'such meek behaviour springing from strength and knowledge ultimately dissolves the tyranny of the tyrant—voluntary suffering is the quickest and best remedy for the removal of abuses and injustices'.

On entering the Yeravda prison he was told that he could not use his spinning-wheel nor sleep in the open. However, these restrictions were removed later. It was with considerable difficulty that the 'higher authorities' were persuaded to allow him to keep a few books on religion, an old dictionary and an Urdu manual. He was denied a pillow, but improvised one with his books and spare clothes. He could not be trusted with a pocket knife to slice his bread; when it was allowed, he had to deposit it with a gaol official after use. Banker, his fellow-prisoner, was taken to another cell and other prisoners were not permitted to meet the Mahatma. An African prisoner was attached to him as an attendant; unable to talk to each other, they communicated by signs. Gandhi, however, knew the language of the human heart. One day, when the African was bitten by a scorpion, Gandhi washed his wound, wiped it, sucked off the poison, and treated him until he was cured. Won over by this kindness, the African became an apt pupil at hand-spinning.

When Devadas and Rajagopalachari met Gandhi in Yeravda prison he instructed them not to make his prison life a subject of discussion in the Press. He liked the enforced solitude; it gave him the quiet and the rest which he had missed during seven years of incessant activity in India. He kept up his daily routine of morning and evening prayers, and spinning. His literary and religious studies, which had been neglected in the midst of other activities, were now resumed; he read no less than 150 books, including Henry James' *The Varieties of Religious Experience*, Buckle's *History of Civilization*, Well's *Outline of History*, Bernard Shaw's *Man and Superman*, Goethe's *Faust* and Kipling's *Barrack Room Ballads*. There is no doubt that, in spite of occasional pin-pricks, prison life proved for him, as Tagore once put it, 'a rest cure'.

Gandhi had received a taste of prison life in South African gaols, which he jocularly used to describe as His Majesty's hotels. While in South African gaols, the inconsiderate and often harsh treatment could be partly attributed to racial prejudice, it is difficult to explain why his first term at Yeravda should have been marked by lack of imagination and understanding which were to be generally extended to him in subsequent imprisonments.

It is possible that Lord Reading's view on the treatment of political prisoners—'imprisonment and not a comfortable lodging at the expense of the state'[1]—was being practised on the author of the non-co-operation movement. There is, however, a simpler explanation: the local government and the prison officials had yet to accustom themselves to Mr Gandhi as a prisoner. The timely and adequate action in treating him after an attack of appendicitis in 1924 should bear out this view.

[1] Reading, Marquess of: *Rufus Isaacs, First Marquess of Reading*, Vol. II, p. 236.

BOOK III

'WAR' AND PEACE

Chapter 28

COUNCIL FRONT

THE revocation of the 'aggressive' programme in the non-co-operation campaign, whatever its justification from Gandhi's point of view, confused the Congress rank and file; it also divided its leadership. Some of the Congress leaders, including C. R. Das, Motilal Nehru and V. J. Patel, had never really favoured the boycott of the new legislatures brought into being by the Indian Reforms Act of 1919. Born lawyers and orators, they were in their element in legislatures. In 1920 they had allowed themselves to be persuaded by the Mahatma to agree to the boycott. Now that mass civil disobedience was no longer in the offing they felt that the only way of keeping up the resistance to the Government was to enter the Central and Provincial Legislatures, not to work the new constitution, but to expose its limited and irresponsible character.

The Government of India 'under the reformed constitution' was not answerable to the Central Legislature. The upper chamber, the Council of State, had a majority of official and nominated members. In the lower chamber, the Central Legislative Assembly, nearly one-third of the members were British officials or their Indian nominees. Hardly more than one-seventh of the budget was votable by the Central Legislative Assembly. The Governor-General had powers to 'certify' as law measures rejected by the legislature.

The provinces were governed under a hybrid system known as 'dyarchy', which entrusted some departments to the control of ministers responsible to the legislature, and left others, including finance, and law and order, in the charge of officials directly responsible to the Governor who possessed the power of veto.

The Swarajists (as the Congress leaders who were in favour of entering the Councils came to be known) acknowledged the limited utility of the legislatures. These legislatures were, according to them, masks put on by the British bureaucracy to deceive the world, and it was for Congressmen to tear off these masks. The legislatures could not bring real power to the people, but they could be made useful instruments in political warfare; if Congressmen could muster sufficient strength in the legislatures to reject official bills and to refuse the supplies, the Government would either have to use its special powers or give in to the verdict of the legislature. Such a situation was in any case bound to expose to the world that the constitution under which the country was governed left the ultimate authority in the hands of an irremovable executive. Some of the Swarajists were influenced by the tactics which Parnell and his party had adopted with success in the House of Commons in the agitation for Irish Home Rule.[1] 'Continuous, consistent and persistent obstruction,' was intended to turn the councils from a tool in the hands of the Government into a thorn in its side.

Soon after Gandhi's imprisonment in March 1922, signs of a serious rift appeared among his followers. In Maharashtra and Bengal several prominent leaders declared themselves in favour of lifting the boycott of the councils. While presiding over an annual session of the Bengal Provincial Congress, Mrs C. R. Das pleaded for carrying the national struggle into the councils. The All-India Congress Committee met at Lucknow in June 1922 and appointed a committee to tour the country to ascertain how far the people were ready for civil disobedience. The Civil Disobedience Enquiry Committee reported that the country was not ready for civil disobedience on a large scale, but each provincial congress committee could be authorized on its own to defy particular laws or refuse obnoxious taxes. On the boycott of councils there was a sharp difference of opinion among the members of the committee; V. J. Patel, Hakim Ajmal Khan and Motilal Nehru were for lifting the boycott, while

[1] Patel, G. I.: *Vithalbhai Patel*, Vol. II, p. 540.

Dr Ansari and Rajagopalachari were opposed to any change in the programme framed by the Mahatma before his arrest.

C. R. Das, who had been making plans for a council-entry campaign in Alipore gaol, threw himself into this campaign after his release. In his presidential address to the Gaya session of the Indian National Congress in December 1922 he proposed that the councils should either be amended in a manner suitable to the attainment of Indian freedom or ended completely. He did not consider entry into councils as inconsistent with the non-co-operation movement. Boycott was in fact being carried to the precincts of the council chambers, to the very heart of the official citadel. The argument did not convince Gandhi's faithful followers, to whom council-entry was not a change of tactics but a violation of the principles of non-violent non-co-operation; as one of them observed: 'Ours is a purity movement, and as such is above diplomacy. To enter the councils with the object of making them a failure is not only diplomacy but it is also diplomatic duplicity which every non-co-operator should disdain'.[1]

V. J. Patel had declared that entry into legislatures was like smuggling oneself into the enemy's fort with a view to conquering it. His brother Vallabhbhai Patel retorted that the fortress of the enemy was not located in the legislatures, and that so long as it lay elsewhere the Government could continue to function for a hundred years without a legislature.

Vallabhbhai Patel, Rajagopalachari and others who were opposed to changes in the non-co-operation programme came to be known as 'No Changers'. Most of them were actuated by a sentiment of loyalty to their leader who was in gaol. In spite of the support he received from Motilal Nehru, Srinivas Iyengar and V. J. Patel, C. R. Das could not secure a majority in the Gaya Congress. The policy of the boycott of legislatures remained unaltered. Immediately after the session, Das resigned the presidentship of the Congress and founded the Swaraj Party, with himself as its leader and Motilal Nehru as secretary. The

[1] Patel, G. I.: *Vithalbhai Patel*, Vol. II, p. 537.

breach between the two groups of Congressmen was now open.

During the next few months Congress politics were extremely fluid. There were a number of resignations from the Working Committee and the All-India Congress Committee; *bona fides* were questioned; 'points of order' were raised, and the constitution of the Congress discussed threadbare in a tug-of-war between the Swarajists and the No-Changers. The Gaya Congress, which had rejected council-entry, had also toyed with the idea of resuming civil disobedience by April 1923. 'A gentleman's agreement' was reached between the two groups to observe silence on council-entry, while preparations for civil disobedience were afoot. However, the response to these preparations was not very encouraging: as against a target of 50,000 volunteers hardly 8,000 enrolled themselves. The Swaraj Party seemed to offer the only effective programme for the time being. Efforts at a compromise between the Swarajists and No-Changers were made. A special session of the Indian National Congress was convened at Delhi in September 1923 to take a final decision on the Congress attitude to the elections which were scheduled to be held in November 1923. Maulana Mahomed Ali, the Khilafat leader, who had meanwhile been released from gaol, threw his weight in favour of the Swarajists; he created a stir in the Congress session by quoting a message he professed to have received from the Mahatma ('through some spiritual trick, maybe through telepathy') that the Congress was free to amend non-co-operation to suit the changed conditions in the country. The No-Changers decided to remain neutral on council-entry with the result that the Swarajists received the approval of the Congress to participate in the elections. The Swarajists had barely two months to fight the elections, but they succeeded in capturing a solid *bloc* of seats in the Central Legislative Assembly, a substantial representation in provincial legislatures and even a majority in the Central Provinces Legislative Council. Motilal Nehru led the Swaraj Party in the Central Legislative Assembly, while Das took up the leadership of the party in Bengal Legislative Council.

Meanwhile, on January 11, 1924 Gandhi had been transferred to Sassoon Hospital, Poona for an operation following an acute attack of appendicitis. He knew that if he died on the operating table there might be an explosion of popular wrath. A few minutes before the operation, and in the presence of a few friends, including Srinivas Sastri, he dictated and signed a statement which acknowledged the courteous consideration he had received from Colonel Maddock and other doctors attending upon him. Sastri later recorded how he marvelled at the 'high-mindedness, forgiveness, chivalry, and love transcending human nature', of Gandhi at a critical juncture when his life hung in the balance. At 10 p.m. on January 12th, Gandhi was placed on the operating table. When the lights failed, Surgeon Maddock took out an electric torch which also gave out half-way through. But the operation was successful and next day a telegram informed Kasturbai at Sabarmati Ashram: 'Mr Gandhi operated on for acute appendicitis last night, had a very fair night and condition this morning satisfactory.'

The news of Gandhi's illness was received with deep concern all over India. Resolutions were moved in the Central Legislative Assembly and the Bombay Legislative Council urging his immediate release. The Governor of Bombay, Sir Leslie Wilson, was opposed to an unconditional release, but the Viceroy recognized that an undertaking not to 'indulge in subversive activities' was unthinkable from Gandhi. Both the Viceroy and the Governor, however, hoped that the split between the 'No-Changers' and 'Swarajists' would keep Gandhi fully occupied for some months and thus make it difficult for him to 'embarrass' the Government. On the morning of February 5, 1924, Colonel Maddock came to Gandhi's bedside and informed him that he was a free man.

The premature release on medical grounds did not please Gandhi; the illness of a prisoner, he argued, did not afford a valid reason for his release. The hundreds of telegrams of congratulations betrayed, he said, 'hopes of results from me which stagger me'. The wish which he had once cherished of release from the gaol by the order of a 'Swaraj Parliament' had in any case been frustrated.

Lord Reading's judgment that Gandhi's energies after his release would be distracted by dissensions in the Congress was not far wrong. The Swarajists had fought the elections and secured a firm foothold in the legislatures. They were nevertheless keen to receive Gandhi's blessing. C. R. Das and Motilal Nehru paid a visit to Juhu, a sea-side resort near Bombay, where Gandhi was convalescing. They had long discussions, but were unable to convince Gandhi. In December 1919 at the Amritsar Congress, Gandhi had thrown his weight in favour of working the Montagu-Chelmsford Reforms, but within the next few months events within India and abroad had shaken his faith in the British Government and in the possibility of achieving national freedom by constitutional means. Moreover, the programme of non-co-operation which the Congress and the Khilafat had accepted in 1920 was still in force in 1924; the boycott of councils was an integral part of this programme. Gandhi argued that the five boycotts—those of councils, courts, schools, services and foreign cloth—if fully implemented, could liberate India from foreign rule. The 'obstruction from within' which the Swarajists advocated seemed to him a contradiction in terms: one could either co-operate or non-co-operate with the government; it was no use trying to sail under false colours. The councils, warned Gandhi, gave condiments not bread. Though unconvinced himself of the wisdom of council-entry, Gandhi decided not to stand in the way of the Swarajists and advised the 'No-Changers' to maintain an attitude of 'neutrality' towards legislative work.

Nehru and Das had gone to Gandhi to convince him and to get his powerful support for the Swaraj Party. In this they did not succeed. The events of the next few months, however, were to pave the way for the political stage to be dominated by the Swaraj Party. Gandhi realized that during his absence the political climate had changed. The non-co-operators were non-co-operating 'not so much with the government, but against each other'. Hindu-Muslim unity had gone to pieces.

The constructive programme did not seem to appeal to the intelligentsia. As *Khadi* occupied the central position in this programme, at the meeting of the All-India Congress Committee (June 1924) Gandhi introduced an amendment to the Congress constitution, making it compulsory for every member of the Congress to spin a prescribed quantity of yarn. The Swarajists opposed the 'Khadi franchise' and staged a walk-out from this meeting. Next day, in the course of the debate on a resolution on Gopinath Saha, Gandhi heard C. R. Das pay a tribute to the spirit of self-sacrifice of this young anarchist. The voting gave Gandhi a narrow majority of eight but he saw that the faith in non-violence of his audience and even senior colleagues was skin deep. He resisted the impulse to run away from the meeting, but he thought of withdrawing from the Congress, confining himself to the constructive programme and leaving the political stage altogether. If he had cherished any hopes of carrying the Congress with him on the original non-co-operation programme (without, of course, mass civil disobedience) they were dissipated. He began to search for the 'lowest common measure' of agreement among the opposing factions.

In a letter to Jamnalal Bajaj in September 1924, he wrote: 'The mutual bickerings have assumed such large proportions that we must give up for the time being any idea of large-scale Satyagraha. Our failure to do so will be our undoing. Not a single thing is correctly understood. Everything misrepresented; distrust all round. It is up to us under the present circumstances to adhere to our principles and be silent witnesses of the actions of others.'[1]

He was anxious to prevent a split in the Congress; he knew the damage which had been done by the Surat split of 1907. He made a gesture to the Swarajists, which to many of his followers savoured of a surrender. After a visit to Bengal, where the Provincial Government had launched an offensive against the Swaraj Party by clapping its members into prison on charges of violence, he issued, jointly with Motilal Nehru and C. R.

[1] Kaka Kalelkar (Editor): *To a Gandhian Capitalist*, p. 57.

Das, a statement recommending that the non-co-operation programme should be suspended with the exception of the boycott of foreign cloth, and that the Swaraj Party should become an integral part of the Congress organization with powers to raise and administer its own funds. The constructive programme and the spinning franchise were to continue. The new policy was, however, a definite triumph for Swarajists.

The Gandhi-Nehru-Das pact was ratified at the Belgaum Congress in December 1924. On the eve of the session over which he presided, Gandhi held informal talks with leaders of the two groups to prevent an open rift in the Congress session. He made another gesture to the Swarajists by omitting from his Working Committee 'No-Changers' such as Rajagopalachari, Vallabhbhai Patel and Banker. He was now not only for tolerating the Swarajists, but for strengthening them. To some observers, including his faithful 'No-Changers', it seemed that he had yielded too much ground to the Swarajists. The Viceroy wrote home: 'Gandhi is now attached to the tail of Das and Nehru, although they try their utmost to make him and his supporters think that he is one of the heads, if not the head.'[1]

In June 1925 C. R. Das died. About the same time, Lord Birkenhead, the Secretary of State for India, delivered a speech which was the usual mixture of bullying and bantering aimed at the Congress. The speech, wrote Gandhi, was a notice to Indians to set their house in order. He decided to take further steps towards unity in the Congress by making a further concession to the Swarajists. He agreed to waive the 'spinning franchise'.

Within a year of his release Gandhi had come to the conclusion that the constructive programme as a preparation for non-violent non-co-operation on a mass scale was impracticable. He saw that the majority of those who had flocked under his banner in 1921 had done so at the alluring prospect of Swaraj within a year, and that the programme he offered in 1924-25—Hindu-Muslim unity, boycott of foreign cloth and removal

[1] Reading, Marquess of: *Rufus Isaacs, First Marquess of Reading*, Vol. II, p. 304.

of untouchability—was devoid of the fireworks associated with a militant programme. He recognized the need for a change in the 'political' side of the movement: 'After all, those who have led an active political life in the old fashion cannot possibly be expected to sit idle, whilst dreamers like me expect to evolve an intensely active programme out of a harmless toy like the spinning-wheel.'[1]

This was, of course, not a discovery he made in 1925. In a letter to Vallabhbhai Patel in 1921 he had shrewdly summed up the political make-up of Vallabhbhai's elder brother V. J. Patel, who, in 1925, was in the forefront of the Swaraj Party: 'His sphere is essentially the Councils. He cannot settle down to work among the masses. Not that he doesn't want to serve the country, but he had trained himself for work in legislative chambers. I think these two spheres of activities call for different qualities.'[2]

[1] Tendulkar: *Mahatma*, Vol. II, p. 266.
[2] Patel, Manibehn (Editor): *Letters to Sardar Patel*, Ahmedabad, 1952, p. 4.

Chapter 29

COMMUNAL FRONT

IF the rift in the Congress ranks on council-entry was one disappointment to Gandhi after his release from gaol, the division between Hindus and Muslims was another and greater.

The Hindu-Muslim unity of the heyday of the non-co-operation movement was now a mere memory. Trust had given way to distrust. Apart from the riots which periodically disfigured several towns, there was a new bitterness in politics and in the Press. A number of Hindu leaders, such as Lajpat Rai, Madan Mohan Malaviya and Shraddhanand, felt that the Muslim masses had received a dangerous awakening through the coalescence of the Khilafat and non-co-operation movements, and that it was necessary for Hindus to adopt measures of self-defence against Muslim communalism, which was the more dangerous because it appeared to them to have the backing of the British Government. Many Muslim politicians who had been in the forefront of the Khilafat movement had also second thoughts and felt that they had too readily joined hands with the Congress, in fighting for a new order in which the position of the Muslim community was not likely to be too secure.

In an atmosphere of mutual suspicion and fear every incident was twisted and every move of one community was suspect to the other. The Moplah outbreak in 1921, in which the Muslims of Malabar had wreaked their fanaticism on their Hindu neighbours, was a painful memory to the Hindus. The *shuddhi* movement for the conversion of non-Muslims to Hindusim and the *sangathan* movement for the unity of Hindus evoked counterblasts from Muslims in the form of *tabligh* and *tanzim* movements. The new proselytizing twist to Hindusim was resented by the

Muslim intelligentsia who, paradoxically enough, saw nothing wrong in the conversion of non-Muslims to Islam. But there was no room for logic in an atmosphere clouded by hazy memories and vague misgivings. The very Muslims who, as a gesture to their Hindu neighbours, had voluntarily given up cow-slaughter during the favourable climate of 1920-22, now insisted on ostentatiously exercising it as a religious obligation. The Hindus asserted the equally provocative right to play music before mosques while conducting their religious processions. Then there were the endless wrangles about discrimination in favour of one community or the other in the distribution of official patronage. In the Punjab a Muslim Minister, Fazl-i-Husain, who later became a member of the Viceroy's Executive Council, was accused by Hindu and Sikh leaders of a deeply-laid plan to oust the minorities from positions of vantage held by them in the administration. But Fazl-i-Husain, like many other Muslim politicians, believed that a certain amount of weightage was necessary to bring his co-religionists on a par with the Hindus.

There were not a few who put down the new tension to the non-co-operation movement and its alliance with the Khilafat cause, and blamed Gandhi for having played with the masses and roused them prematurely. 'The awakening of the masses,' wrote Gandhi, 'was a necessary part of the training. I would do nothing to put the people to sleep again.' However, he wanted this awakening to be diverted into constructive channels. The two communities had to be educated out of the mental morass into which they had slipped. Through the pages of his weekly journals, he gave his own diagnosis of the communal disease; a whole issue of *Young India* was devoted to the subject. He argued that the Hindu-Muslim tension could never have taken the form it did if the country had understood his method; the doctrine of non-violence held the key not only to the political freedom of the country but also to peace between the communities. A civilized society which had given up violence as a means of settling individual disputes could also eschew violence for reconciling differences between groups. Disagreements could be resolved by mutual tolerance and compromise, private arbitration, and in the last resort by appeal to the courts. Hearts could never be united by breaking heads. To Gandhi, the points of friction between the two communities seemed a travesty of true religion. Was it religion that drove a group of Hindu worshippers to lead a procession noisily before a mosque just as the 'faithful' knelt for prayer? Was it a religious obligation laid on the Muslim to lead cows to slaughter to wound the feelings of his Hindu neighbours? And what was the use of proselytizing when the conversion was not a moral or spiritual uplift, but 'crossing from one compartment to another', with one thing on the lips and another in the heart? As for the competition for jobs, there were, after all, a limited number to go round. Gandhi was prepared to concede special educational facilities to communities which were relatively backward to qualify for higher appointments, but to make religion instead of merit the criterion of employment was to cut at the root of the administration.

By probing into the causes of antagonism, and by appealing to the good sense of the communities, Gandhi had hoped to restore sanity. But communal tension showed no signs of abatement. There were outbreaks at Sambhar, Amethi and Gulbarga. A riot in Kohat in September 1924 was particularly serious: 155 Hindus were killed and practically the whole Hindu population was driven out of the town. This carnage hurt him deeply, the more so as he felt that the awakening, which the non-co-operation movement brought about, had run into destructive channels:

'Have I not been instrumental in bringing into being the vast energy of the people? I must find the remedy, if the energy proved self-destructive . . . Have I erred, have I been impatient, have I compromised with evil? I may have done all these things or none of them . . . All I know is what I see before me. If real non-violence and truth had been practised by the people, the gory duelling that is now going on would have been impossible.'

Out of this personal anguish, Gandhi sought a way in a twenty-one day fast. The fast, which was undertaken at Delhi in Maulana Mahomed Ali's house, was intended to purify himself, 'because the strength of the soul grows in proportion as you subdue the flesh'. It was also to recover the power to react on the people: 'It is a warning to Hindus and Mussulmans who have professed to love me. If they have loved me truly and if I have been deserving of their love, they will do penance with me . . . To revile one another's religion, to make reckless statements, to utter untruth, to break the heads of innocent men, to desecrate temples or mosques is a denial of God. The world is watching, some with glee and some with sorrow, the dog-fight that is proceeding in our midst.'[1]

The country's reaction to the fast was instantaneous. A 'Unity Conference' was convened at Delhi and met within a week of the commencement of the fast. The 300 delegates included the Metropolitan of India Dr Westcott, Annie Besant, the Ali brothers, Swami Shraddhanand and Madan Mohan Malaviya. The conference affirmed the freedom of conscience and religion, but condemned the use of compulsion and violence. It passed a number of resolutions designed to generate goodwill and to dissipate mutual suspicion. On the morning of October 8, 1924, twenty-one days after he had begun it, the Mahatma broke his fast in the presence of leaders of all the communities. As the chanting of the verses from the *Koran* and the *Upanishads* mingled with Christian hymns, C. F. Andrews noted that 'hearts were drawn together'.

But this harmony was not to last long. Within a few months Gandhi had to confess that bitter experience had taught him that those who took the name of unity meant disunion, that the leaders of the two communities were fighting not for loaves and fishes, but 'fighting like the proverbial dog, not for the bone but for the shadow'. In January 1927, he told a meeting at Comilla in Bengal that the Hindu-Muslim problem had passed out of human hands into God's hands.

The appeal for religious toleration, which he had made and

[1] Tendulkar: *Mahatma*, Vol. II, p. 198.

which had been dramatized by his twenty-one-day fast, had fallen on deaf ears; his penance had only an ephemeral effect on the warring factions. Communal outbreaks continued to occur in different parts of the country. Fazl-i-Husain told the Simon Commission that between 1922 and 1927, out of 4,750 riots in the Punjab, only fourteen were communal riots and were confined to eight towns.[1] Limited though these riots were to some of the bigger towns, they nevertheless vitiated the political atmosphere giving a setback to nationalist forces. There was also the suspicion that the local officers did not always apply the right amount of force at the right time to nip the mischief in the bud.

There is no doubt, however, that communal tension had been aggravated by political factors. The Congress-Khilafat alliance in 1920–22 had pushed communal leaders into the background. As we have already seen, one of the greatest anxieties of the Government during those years was the concord between Hindu and Muslim leaders.[2] The rift between the two communities for which the Government had eagerly waited so long came after the suspension of the mass civil disobedience in 1922. The revocation of the aggressive programme was a blow to Congressmen, but it was a greater blow to the protagonists of the Khilafat. While Congressmen could wait for Swaraj for months and even years, the cause of Khilafat could not brook delay. Eventually the Khilafat was killed by the Turks themselves when, under Kemal Ataturk, they dethroned and banished the Sultan Caliph and declared Turkey a republic. The *raison d'être* of the Khilafat movement was destroyed; the movement went to pieces, and its workers and sympathizers, bewildered and without a programme, found themselves adrift. There is something in Subhas Chandra Bose's criticism in his book *Indian Struggle* that if the Khilafat organization had not functioned separately, its members would not have drifted to Muslim sectarian bodies. One wonders, however, whether Muslim participation in the nationalist move-

[1] Husain, Azim: *Fazl-i-Husain*, p. 178.
[2] Chapter 26.

ment in 1920–22 would have been achieved without the Khilafat organization. And in any case the denouement was no more foreseen by Gandhi than by the Khilafat leaders themselves.

The political vacuum in the country after Gandhi's arrest and the dissensions among Congress leaders gave a chance to forces, which had been submerged under popular pressure in 1920–21, to re-emerge. The legislatures became cockpits for the rival communal claims. These wrangles were not unwelcome to the British. 'The more it is made obvious,' wrote Lord Birkenhead to Lord Reading, 'that these antagonisms are profound and affect immense and irreconcilable sections of the population, the more conspicuously is the fact illustrated that we and we alone can play the part of composer.'[1]

The communal problem in the nineteen-twenties was thus reduced to the struggle for fruits of political power between the professional classes of the two communities. It was a scramble for crumbs which the Government offered to political India. Gandhi had advised in his presidential address at the Belgaum Congress (1924) that 'majorities must set the example of self-sacrifice'. The 'blank cheque' which he later offered to the Muslims was ridiculed by them, and resented by the Hindus, but it epitomized his approach to this squabble for seats in legislatures, and jobs under the Government. The Hindus indeed blamed the Mahatma for bartering away Hindu interests. In the course of the negotiations through successive Unity Conferences and All-Parties Conferences the Hindus tended to deal with Muslims as the British Government dealt with Nationalist India: they gave concessions but it was often a case of too little and too late.

Though in the pages of *Young India* from 1925 onwards Gandhi continued to devote occasional attention to the Hindu-Muslim problem, he had almost despaired of a solution. He saw the urban intelligentsia split into antagonistic groups but felt he could not react to it: 'Their method is not my method, I am trying to work from bottom upward.'

[1] Birkenhead; *The Last Phase*, Vol. II, pp. 245–6.

Chapter 30

FROM THE BOTTOM UP

DURING the next three years Gandhi retired from the political scene; to be precise, he retired only from the political controversies of the day to devote his time to the less spectacular but more important task of nation-building 'from the bottom up'.

He toured the country extensively from one end to the other, using every mode of transport from railway trains to bullock-carts. He walked through bush, brier, mud and water to penetrate into the interior of the Indian country-side. Everywhere he met with a welcome which is the prerogative in India of saints and prophets. To the thousands who flocked to his meetings in villages, most of whom knew little of modern civilization or Indian politics, he was an *Avatara*, an incarnation of God. He hated this deification and endeavoured to transmute it into something positive and constructive. He exhorted the people to shake off age-old social evils such as child-marriage and untouchability, and to ply the spinning-wheel. Realizing that his tours were a considerable strain on him, over-solicitous friends in Bengal in 1925 engaged a first-class saloon for his rail journeys. 'My tour cannot do much good,' was his comment, 'if I must be thus wrapped in cotton wool. I must either live or travel like the millions of poor people, or cease to travel at all in public interest. I am certain that I can no more effectively deliver my message to the millions by travelling not even double but five-fold first than the Viceroy can rule over the hearts of India's millions from his unapproachable Simla hills.' He was very unhappy when he had to travel second class for reasons of health, and it was only when he was able to resume third class travel that he felt at peace with himself. When he had a whole third-class compartment to himself, which was not infrequent, he called it 'a fraud in a way'. His journeys, however, became a problem for him, the railway authorities and the organizers of his tours. The enthusiasm of the people often outran their discretion; for example, at Gudiathan in Madras Presidency, the people invaded the house in which he was staying, blocked all light and air, and made work or rest impossible; somehow he took refuge in a car which had to be driven a few miles from the village to save him from the unwelcome attentions of his admirers.

In the later twenties it was usual for British observers to describe Gandhi as a spent force and for Indian politicians to speak of the retirement of the saint of Sabramati. It was obvious enough that the politics of the day, the debates in the Central and Provincial Legislatures, and the communal controversies in the Press did not excite Gandhi's interest. Political freedom was, in his opinion, dependent upon the social and economic regeneration of the country; this regeneration had to come through the efforts of the people themselves. 'The fact is,' he had written, 'that political emancipation means a rise of mass-consciousness. It cannot come without affecting all the branches of national activity.'

In his speeches and writings of these years two themes are recurrent: the spinning-wheel and untouchability. The spinning-wheel or rather its product, *khadi* had figured in the non-co-operation programme, but during these years of political lull Gandhi turned it into a cult. He spoke of the 'thread of destiny'; he suggested a '*khadi* franchise' for the Congress organization, and even envisaged a 'yarn currency'. Western-educated Indians, even ardent Congressmen wondered whether the *khadi* cult was not being overdone. To the Government, once the threat of civil disobedience was over, his emphasis on *khadi* seemed only a bee in his bonnet. It was not until *khadi* again became part of an active political campaign in 1930 that the Government took it seriously, and then too as an economic weapon in a political struggle.

That Gandhi's almost emotional attachment to the spinning-wheel should have baffled both the British and the Western-educated town-bred Indians, is not surprising. They were both unable, the former from the lack of will, the latter from the lack of knowledge, to grasp the incredible poverty of the Indian village. Deeply religious as Gandhi was, he wrote: 'For the starving men and women, liberty and God are merely letters put together without the slightest meaning; the deliverer of these unfortunate people would be one who brought them a crust of bread.' Not only were the landless labourers steeped in poverty, but there were millions of peasants who spent nearly six months in enforced under-employment. Their pitifully low income, argued Gandhi, could be usefully supplemented by cottage industries. And there was no cottage industry so simple and natural to the Indian village as hand-spinning; people could spin and weave cloth in their own homes just as they cooked their food. True, the spinning-wheel could make only a meagre addition to the slender resources of the peasant, but, as Gandhi explained to the Rotary Club of Calcutta in August 1925, one-tenth of the population of India, which lived on one meal a day and could not earn on the average more than three rupees a month, was bound to consider even an income of five to six rupees from the spinning-wheel as a fortune. When Tagore expressed the fear that the emphasis on the spinning-wheel would bring about a 'death-like sameness in the country'. Gandhi replied:

'I did not want the poet to forsake his music, the farmer his plough, the lawyer his brief, and the doctor his lancet. They are to spin only thirty minutes every day as a sacrifice. I have indeed asked the famishing man or woman, who is idle for work whatsoever, to spin for a living and the half-starved farmer to spin during his leisure to supplement his resources.'

Thus while the spinning-wheel had an economic significance for the farmer, the labourer, or the helpless widow in the village, to the townsman its appeal was based on moral or (as Gandhi would have put it) on spiritual grounds. India's towns had flourished at the expense of the villages, but now they had a chance to make amends for their past sins by buying cloth spun and woven in village homes, and thus to forge a link, economic as well as sentimental, between town and village. The All-India Spinners' Association, which Gandhi had founded, set out to put the production of *khadi* on a sound footing. By the end of 1926 the Association had on its rolls 42,952 spinners, 3,407 weavers and 110 carders working in 150 production centres in 1,500 villages, and nine lakhs of rupees were distributed to these workers. This was a creditable performance, though it did not yet touch more than a fringe of rural India.

The spinning-wheel gradually became the centre of rural uplift in the Gandhian scheme of Indian economics; round it were to be built up anti-malaria campaigns, improvements in sanitation, settlement of village disputes, conservation and breeding of cattle, and hundreds of other beneficent activities required for the resuscitation of the village. The economics of the spinning-wheel were thus the economics of a new village economy. Primarily advocated as a solution of chronic under-employment in the villages, the spinning-wheel became something more than a simple tool of a cottage industry. In his efforts to 'sell' the spinning-wheel to the people, Gandhi romanticized it. He put it forward, not only as a panacea for economic ills but also for national unity and freedom. It became a symbol of defiance of foreign rule, the 'livery of freedom', as Jawaharlal Nehru picturesquely described it.

There is no doubt that the spinning-wheel symbolized Gandhi's protest against industrialism and materialism. But it would not have meant so much to him if it had not become a means of his deep identification with the humblest and the poorest in the land. 'The more I penetrate the villages,' he wrote, 'the greater is the shock delivered as I perceive the blank stare in the eyes of the villagers I meet. Having nothing else to do but to work as labourers side by side with their bullocks; they have become almost like them.' These skeletons behind the bullocks haunted him day and night. When somebody suggested that

I•

the country could patiently wait for prohibition, he said, 'Ask the wife of a drunkard to be patient; see what she will think of you. I happen to be the wife of thousands of drunkards and I cannot be patient.' He was not only the wife of thousands of drunkards, but of millions of semi-starved villagers in India; with his imaginative sympathy he could enter into the thoughts and feelings of others. The consciousness of the poverty and misery of the villages of India had gone like iron into his soul. 'The moment someone asks me (about the spinning-wheel)', he said, 'a whole volcano surges up within me.' Often his words betrayed his anguish. He told a meeting at Jalpaiguri: 'India is dying . . . if you want to save India, do it by doing the little I ask for. I want you to take up the wheel betimes or perish.' And he told the fastidious students of Chittagong that 'the pauperism of India is coarser than the coarsest Chittagong *khaddar*'.

In 1925 Gandhi toured extensively. His itinerary included Kathiawar, Central India, Bengal, Malabar and Travancore. In Travancore he saw for himself the Satyagraha launched against the fantastic prohibition of the use of roads leading to temples by the so-called untouchables. He lent his support to this struggle against orthodoxy. Untouchability figured prominently in his speeches during this his tour. At one of the meetings in Saurashtra he saw that the untouchables had been cordoned off in a corner of the meeting. He turned the tables on the orthodox by crossing into the untouchables' corner to address the meeting from there. He made it known that in future it was the orthodox (like the Europeans and Anglo-Indians in trains, as he put it humorously) for whom accommodation was to be reserved in the meetings.

1926 was the year of silence. Gandhi spent it in Sabarmati Ashram, to the affairs of which he had not given much time since its establishment a decade earlier. He had already begun in November, 1925 the publication, week by week, of the chapters of his *Autobiography* or *The Story of my Experiments with Truth*. He wrote in Gujerati, and the English translation was prepared by Mahadev Desai, with the assistance of Pyarelal, Mirabehn and Srinivasa Sastri. During this year *Young India* was a good index to

Gandhi's mind and shows how he was preoccupied more with problems of *khadi*, fasting, health and non-violence, than with the political issues of the day. The two controversies of which he became the focus turned on his own concept of *ahimsa*. When Ambalal Sarabhai, a local textile magnate, had stray dogs rounded up and killed, Gandhi was criticized for having expressed approval of the deed. Equally virulent was the criticism when he had a calf killed because it was suffering from excruciating pain and an incurable disease. 'The trouble with our votaries of *ahimsa* ' he wrote, 'is that they have made a fetish of it and are mistaking non-killing for *ahimsa*.'

At the end of 1926 he went to Gauhati to attend the annual session of the Indian National Congress. A little earlier a Muslim fanatic had killed Swami Shraddhanand. Gandhi told the leaders of India assembled at Gauhati that it was not the assailant who was guilty of the murder but those 'who excited feelings of hatred against one another'.

Early in 1927 he resumed his tour. He went to Bengal, then to Bihar and to Bombay, from where he left for a tour of the Carnatic in the last week of March. For four months he had been touring incessantly, addressing sometimes as many as thirty meetings a week and six meetings a day. He was utterly exhausted; his head reeled, his vision was blurred. But he continued to travel and to address meetings according to schedule until the crash came. A telegram dated March 27, 1927, from Mahadev Desai to Mirabehn stated: '*Bapu* has narrowly escaped of apoplexy. High blood pressure still continues. Doctors ascribe it to over-work and nervous exhaustion and advise complete rest and cancellation of all programmes, hot months at any rate. Leaving for Belgaum twenty-eighth.'

His impulse was to return to the Sabarmati Ashram, but the doctors advised him to go to a cooler place. He went to Mysore, where the climate and the rest helped him to recover faster than he had dared to hope. By the beginning of May 1927, the blood pressure had declined to normal. He was feeling 'altogether better'; had resumed his walks and his articles, and 'love letters' to his numerous correspondents. He resumed his itinerary. His themes were the same—the propagation of *khadi*, the removal of untouchability and the promotion of communal harmony. He made collections for the promotion of *khadi*. The sight of old people with trembling hands untying knots which firmly held their pies, fascinated him. He was proud of the fact that while Madan Mohan Malaviya had specialized in obtaining large grants from the princes he could make the poor empty their pockets for those poorer than themselves. In one village Gandhi's speech consisted of just one sentence: 'Empty your pockets for the poor.' In another village he opened a *khadi* shop, not by delivering a speech but by sitting down with a yard measure, a pair of scissors and a cash memo book, selling the cloth and signing the receipts; for an hour he sold *khadi* at the rate of ten rupees a minute before motoring down to the next village.

He used his tours to liberate the people from an age-long inertia, fear and superstition. He frowned on gold and silver caskets in which addresses were presented to him and asked for something 'cheaper, local and artistic'. He auctioned the caskets presented to him and credited the proceeds to his *khadi* fund. He chided the people of a village for wasting money on garlands for him: 'For every rupee saved on these garlands you should give sixteen women one meal.' While in Southern India he condemned in no uncertain terms the evil of 'devadasis'. To a municipal committee in Mysore, which boasted of a project of three lakhs for water supply and prospects of electrifying the town in six months, he offered his congratulations but with the question, 'Can you assure children of the town cheap and clean milk? So long as you do not take the broom and bucket in your hands,' he added, 'you cannot make towns and cities clean.'

Chapter 31

THE RISING TEMPO

WHEN Jawaharlal Nehru returned to India in December 1927, after a twenty month absence in Europe, he sensed a change in the political atmosphere. 'Early in 1926,' he writes, 'India was still quiescent, passive, perhaps not fully recovered from the effort of 1919-22; in 1928 she seemed fresh, active and full of suppressed energy.'[1] Signs of discontent were visible in several sectors of society, particularly among industrial workers, peasants, and middle class youth. Trade unions were gaining strength and labour was restive. The All-India Trade Union Congress had become a militant and class conscious body, and among those who took interest in its affairs were Jawaharlal Nehru and Subhas Chandra Bose. A number of strikes took place in the late twenties, the most notable being those which affected the textile industry in Bombay, the jute mills in Bengal, and iron and steel works in Jamshedpur. The labour movement was not directly connected with the political movement but it was at least against the existing order of things.

Apart from the sporadic acts of political violence which gave the Government an anxious time, Youth Leagues sprang up all over the country. A number of youth conferences were held in which radical solutions for political, social and economic ills were put forth.

Agrarian discontent was brewing in several provinces, but it was in Gujerat, in Bombay Presidency, that it came to a head. Bardoli *taluk* had been selected by Gandhi as the spearhead of the no-tax campaign which was to climax the non-co-operation movement early in 1922. The Chauri Chaura tragedy had robbed

[1] Nehru: *Autobiography*, p. 170.

Bardoli of that distinction, but six years later the revenue department of the Bombay Government brought Bardoli to the forefront. A periodical assessment was due, and the task was entrusted to Jayakar, a duputy collector of Surat, who made a survey and recommended a thirty per cent increase. The premises of Jayakar's report were questioned by the Settlement Commissioner, but the Government of Bombay sanctioned a twenty-two per cent increase in land revenue. The peasants of Bardoli lodged a protest through their representatives in the Bombay Legislative Council. Failing to get redress through petitions, they approached Vallabhbhai Patel to take up their cause. Vallabhbhai, once a prosperous lawyer, had thrown up his practice to join the non-co-operation movement; he had distinguished himself as the chairman of the Ahmedabad Municipality, but it was in Bardoli that his organizing ability was to flower fully. He studied the facts and told Gandhi that the peasants had a just grievance. 'Go forward,' said the Mahatma, 'and victory to Gujerat!'

Thus began an amazing and, what seemed at first, an unequal struggle between the peasants of Bardoli and the Bombay Government. The Government turned down Patel's appeal for the review of the assessment and declared that it would not be responsible for losses which the peasants might suffer by listening to 'outsiders'. There was an unconscious irony in the British officers describing Vallabhbhai Patel, a leader of Gujerat, as an outsider in Bardoli *taluk*. The peasants' answer was a pledge not to pay the 'arbitrary, unjust and oppressive assessment' until the Government either reverted to the old rate or agreed to a new assessment. Vallabhbhai's task was not easy. The peasants of Bardoli were considered gentle; it was said that even their dogs did not bark at strangers.[1] Among them was a fair sprinkling of well-to-do peasants and rich merchants who had made their pile abroad, and were thus the more vulnerable to official pressure. Vallabhbhai set out to educate the people of Bardoli into the technique of Satyagraha. He called upon them to be prepared

[1] Parikh, Narhari: *Sardar Vallabhbhai Patel*, Vol. I, p. 313.

for utter ruin in the fight against the Government. Their response was fine; even their children sang: 'If we are cut to pieces, we shall keep our pledge. Wake up brave fighters, the battle-drums have sounded. Wake up the brave, run away the coward.'

The Government tried to break the peasants' resistance. It offered concessions to those who would pay up; it tried to wean the richer or the weaker peasants; it sold crops for a song, and forfeited, in lieu of the tax, land, household goods, and cattle. Since no one from the villages would either carry or buy the confiscated property, Pathans were imported to do the dirty work. The peasants' weapon against weaker brethren or high-handed officials was boycott, and this weapon they used with deadly effect.

Gandhi was deeply interested in this large-scale experiment in Satyagraha to which he gave his support in public and private, but Vallabhbhai Patel urged him to defer the departure for Bardoli. The struggle threatened to develop from a local into a national issue. V. J. Patel appealed to Lord Irwin for intervention. The Congress Working Committee debated the implications of the campaign and independent observers, including H. N. Kunzru, made fact-finding surveys. There were resignations by some members of the Bombay Legislature. The Indian Press and even the British-owned *Statesman* and *Pioneer* backed up the demand for an enquiry. Reluctantly, the Government bowed to the storm and agreed to an independent review of the assessment by a committee of two British officers. This committee reported that there was justification for a five per cent increase in land revenue as against the twenty-two per cent which had actually been levied. The peasants of Bardoli conferred the title of *Sardar* (the leader) on Vallabhbhai Patel. A successful struggle after years of inertia was an uplifting experience for lovers of Indian freedom; the campaign was an index to the latent energy which was waiting to be harnessed to the national cause.

Meanwhile, Indian politics had been emerging out of the doldrums of the mid-twenties. The Swaraj Party had held the political stage since 1923. It had set out to create an atmosphere of resistance to the bureaucracy and to wreck the constitution. Founded by Pandit Motilal Nehru and C. R. Das, it had counted amongst its members such outstanding men as Lajpat Rai and Madan Mohan Malaviya. It had started well. In 1923 and 1924, in two provinces, it had made the system of dyarchical provincial government unworkable. In the Central Legislative Assembly it had delivered calculated blows at the prestige of the Government in spite of the communal franchise and the solid *bloc* of official and nominated members; it had thrown out budgets and demanded a round table conference for a new constitution. The early official impression of the Swaraj Party may be gleaned from a letter which the Viceroy wrote to the Secretary of State in London: 'For the present, the Swarajist has it all his own way; there is none to compare with him; there is none to attack him . . . The Moderate presents a very dull and dreary appearance as compared with the Swarajists.'[1]

Sir Michael O'Dwyer, the Governor of the Punjab, thought that the 'Swarajist sabotage' was more difficult to deal with than open rebellion. There may have been more than humour in the reported remark of Sir Malcolm Hailey, the Home Member of the Viceroy's Executive Council and the leader of the official group in the Central Legislative Assembly, on his appointment as Governor of U.P. He was, he said, glad to go to a place where 'Pandits and Patels' would cease to trouble him.

The high discipline of the Swaraj Party did not last long. The lack of an absolute majority in the legislatures made co-operation with other parties necessary, and this co-operation had sometimes to be purchased at a high price in terms of principles. The Government could lure the weaker members of the party by throwing crumbs of official patronage in their way —a provincial ministership or a visit to Geneva. Some of those who had been elected on the communal franchise could not escape the virus of communalism which was rampant in the country. The Muslim members gradually fell off, and the Swarajists from Maharashtra picked up the slogan of 'responsive

[1] Reading, Marquess of: *Rufus Isaacs, First Marquess of Reading*, Vol. II, p. 283.

co-operation'. The crowning blow came with the defection of Lajpat Rai, the Deputy-Leader of the party. The general elections in 1926 reduced the strength of the Swarajists both at the centre and in the provinces. Except in Madras they lost seats everywhere. In the United Provinces Motilal Nehru was the only Swarajist elected to the Central Legislative Assembly. 'It was a fight,' observed Nehru, 'between the forces of nationalism and a low order of communalism and the latter won.'

The Government now found it less difficult to have its way in the legislatures. In February 1926, before the general elections, Motilal Nehru had declared, 'We have no further use for these sham institutions.' His son records how he became more and more disillusioned and was driven to the painful conclusion that constitutional methods were ineffective and futile in India in the conditions which were then prevailing. There was no Central Parliamentary Board to keep Congress legislators under discipline. It was a heart-breaking job to wage a battle of wits year after year with an irremovable executive, which was backed by an official *bloc* in a legislature elected on a communal franchise, and to lead a not-too-highly-disciplined party in co-operation with groups, each of which had some personal or communal axe to grind. There was a good deal of truth in Vallabhbhai Patel's jibe (a 'No-Changer' since 1922) at the Swarajists that 'those who had set out to smash the Government had themselves been smashed'.[1] The Swarajists' disillusionment with parliamentary methods was to prove an important factor in their return to the Gandhian fold.

In spite of the many undercurrents of discontent, Indian politics nevertheless seemed placid on the surface in 1927. Lord Reading had prophesied that his successor would have an easy interlude of eighteen months, which would be only a lull before the storm. The prophesy turned out to be true, but the storm was brought on by the British Government itself. On November 2, 1927, a number of Indian leaders including Gandhi, Motilal Nehru, Ansari and Jinnah, were summoned to the Viceregal

[1] Parikh, Narhari: *Sardar Vallabhbhai Patel*, Vol. I, p. 386.

Lodge at Delhi and handed a document which announced the appointment of a Royal Commission. This was the only business transacted at this meeting: Gandhi, who had travelled a thousand miles, wondered why a postcard had not been used to convey the information. The document handed to the Indian leaders was not even news, as its contents had been correctly forecast by the Press. 'Never had Indian leadership felt itself to be so affronted,' writes the Viceroy's biographer.[1] The Indian Reforms Act of 1919, under which India was being governed, contained a clause for a review of the constitutional position after ten years. This provision had been regarded as a safeguard by the British Conservatives and as a lever for further advance by Indian nationalists. The appointment of a Royal Commission in 1927, two years ahead of the schedule, raised a spate of speculation. It was suggested that the Conservative Government in England were anxious to handle the Indian question itself rather than leave it to a Labour Government which might come into power after the general elections. Support to this view is lent by the observation in Birkenhead's *The Last Phase* that 'we could not afford to run the slightest risk that the nomination of the 1928 Commission should be in the hands of our successors'.

There was an additional reason for hastening the appointment of the commission. The Swaraj Party had been pressing for greater autonomy in provinces and responsibility at the centre, and had declined to be satisfied with minor modifications within the four corners of the Indian Reforms Act 1919. It is probable, therefore, that Lord Birkenhead and the Conservative Government were throwing a sop to Indian political opinion and providing a focus for political activity for some time. In this connection it is interesting to recall the advice Lord Reading gave to Lord Birkenhead in December 1925 to appoint a commission 'to create a favourable atmosphere' and to spike the Swarajists' guns.[2]

Whatever may have been the motive behind Lord Birkenhead's

---

[1] Johnson, Alan Campbell: *Viscount Halifax*, p. 190.
[2] Reading, Marquess of: *Rufus Isaacs, First Marquess of Reading*, Vol. II, p. 342.

move, it completely misfired. The members of the commission, with the exception of its chairman, Sir John Simon, were all 'second flight men'; the junior member of the commission (as Viscount Simon describes him in his *Retrospect*) was Clement Attlee, the future Premier of Britain, then a back-bencher in the House of Commons. What hurt Indian feeling most was that no Indian had been included in this 'all-white commission'. The argument that a Royal Commission answerable to the British Parliament could not draw its personnel from outside may been sound constitutional practice, but it was a political blunder of the first magnitude. The commission came to be looked upon in India as an inquisition by foreigners into India's fitness for self-government; the Indian National Congress decided to boycott the commission 'at every stage and in every form'. Even moderate and Muslim politicians, whose co-operation Birkenhead had almost taken for granted, were unanimous in denouncing the commission, the boycott of which provided a common platform for parties which were otherwise poles apart. This united front was facilitated by periodical outbursts from Lord Birkenhead, who seemed to take a pleasure in baiting nationalist feeling with the shafts of his own brand of political wit. On the very day the Central Legislative Assembly began to debate Lajpat Rai's famous resolution on the boycott of the Simon Commission, Birkenhead declared that the policy of boycott would merely persuade Parliament that India had gone too far on the road to self-government! The Viceroy tried to pour oil on troubled waters; he appealed to the 'verdict of history', and called upon those who had the power to help not to hinder; privately he tried to wean Muslims from the 'boycott party', but Birkenhead's arrogance had alienated Jinnah, and the boycott resolution passed through the Central Legislative Assembly by sixty-eight votes to sixty-two.

As a belated concession to Indian public opinion, committees of the Central and Provincial Legislatures were appointed to assist the Simon Commission. These committees had, however, only an advisory status and did not satisfy the wounded pride of Indian nationalism. Black-flag demonstrations and shuttered shop-windows greeted the 'Simon Seven' in most of the towns they visited. The demonstrations were broken up by the police and in one of them, at Lahore, Lala Lajpat Rai, the pre-eminent leader of the Punjab, was assaulted by a young British officer. Lajpat Rai's injuries hastened his death a few days later. This tragedy fanned public indignation and added to the vigour of the boycott. The attitude of the authorities also hardened, and the beating up of processions became a routine.

The boycott of the Simon Commission had raised the political barometer and brought together a number of parties which had otherwise little in common. A challenge from Birkenhead stung Indian leaders to seek an agreed solution of the constitutional problem. 'I have twice in three years,' declared Birkenhead, 'during which I have been Secretary of State, invited our critics in India to put forward their own suggestions for a constitution to indicate to us the form in which in their judgment any reforms of constitution may take place'. 'That offer,' he added, 'is still open.' As an answer to this challenge, a series of All-Parties Conferences took place and a constitutional scheme was drafted. The *Nehru Report*, as it came to be known, envisaged a parliamentary system of government, joint electorates and some complicated formulae for the protection of minorities. When it came up for approval before the last meeting of the All-Parties Conference in August 1928, the controversy on 'dominion status' vs. 'complete independence' flared up. The *Nehru Report* had adopted dominion status as the basis of its recommendations to secure the lowest common measure of agreement among the Congress, the moderates and other political groups. The younger wing of the Congress did not like Indian freedom to be hedged in by any limitations. But Motilal Nehru was keen on carrying through the report, which bore his name, *in toto*. Jawaharlal Nehru and Subhas Chandra Bose threatened to resign from the Congress; their resignations were not accepted, but they founded an Independence League to promote among Congressmen the ideology of complete independence. The annual session of the Congress was due in December 1928, in Calcutta, and it looked as if a head-on collision between the old guard and the younger group in the Congress was inevitable.

Gandhi had played little part in the All-Parties Conference or in the drafting of the *Nehru Report*. Nevertheless, he had commended the report for satisfying 'all reasonable aspirations'. He had taken little active interest in the Congress session at Gauhati in 1926 or at Madras in 1927. It is doubtful if he would have taken any more interest in the Calcutta session in December 1928 were it not for urgent summons from Pandit Motilal Nehru. The Pandit, anticipating a crisis at Calcutta, had urged the Mahatma to attend the Congress session: 'You have made me sit in the Presidential chair and put upon my head a crown of thorns; but at least do not look at my difficulties from a distance.'

A rift at the Calcutta Congress was avoided by a compromise formula framed by Gandhi. The Congress passed a resolution accepting the *Nehru Report* on the condition that, if by December 31, 1929, it was not accepted by the Government, the Congress would demand complete independence and fight for it, if necessary, by resorting to non-violent non-co-operation. Gandhi would have preferred to give the Government two years to make up its mind and for the Congress to set its house in order. To those who talked glibly of independence, he said, 'you may take the name of independence on your lips as the Muslims utter the name of *Allah* or the pious Hindu utters the name of Krishna or Rama'. The British Government, he warned the Congress, was going to concede neither dominion status nor independence until the nation was ready to assert its rights, until 'the necessary sanctions had been forged'. If the Congress were to give a non-violent battle to the Government, it had first to close its ranks. The Congress roll was, he said, a 'bogus show'; what the Congress needed was a living register of members; if Congressmen were serious about the resolution they had passed, hard work lay ahead of them.

The Calcutta Congress opened the way for Gandhi's return to politics. If the British Government did not concede the demand

of the Congress—and there was little prospect of their doing so—
the Congress was committed to a non-co-operation movement
and it was obvious to all that Gandhi alone could conduct such
a movement. In March 1922 he had been sentenced to six years'
imprisonment and premature release in 1924 for reasons of health
had not pleased him. Not until March 1928 had he felt 'morally'
freed from his term of imprisonment. Political as well as personal
reasons were thus dictating an end of his retirement from active
politics.

Chapter 32

YEAR OF GRACE

THE Calcutta session of the Congress (December 1928) had given to the British Government, to use the words of Jawaharlal Nehru, 'an offer of a year's grace and a polite ultimatum'. If dominion status was not conceded by the end of 1929, the Congress was to launch a struggle with the Government. Gandhi had been toying with the idea of visiting Europe in 1929, but having piloted the main resolution of the Congress session, he felt it would be 'an act of desertion' to leave India. By giving a year's ultimatum, the Congress had thrown the ball into the opponent's court and the next move lay with the Government. He knew that freedom was not likely to descend as a gift from the British. When speculation started on the significance of a tea party at New Delhi given by Speaker Patel, where the Viceroy and the Mahatma were among the guests, Gandhi's comment was: 'There cannot be much breaking of ice at a private, informal tea party. In my opinion it cannot lead to any real advance or action unless both are ready. We know that we are not ready. England will never make any advance so as to satisfy Indians' aspirations, till she is forced to it.'

When he thought of 'preparation', he did not think of any political moves. It was not part of the strategy of Satyagraha to plan moves months and years ahead. Meanwhile, the country had to be educated and disciplined. Gandhi toured the country, calling upon the people to spin and weave in their homes, and to boycott foreign cloth. He evolved a scheme whereby Congress organizations were to enrol volunteers to sell *khadi*, and to collect foreign cloth from door to door. Foreign cloth was to be publicly burnt and the foreign cloth shops picketed. Early in

March 1929 he was at Calcutta when a huge pyramid of foreign finery was ceremoniously consigned to the flames. The Bengal Provincial Congress Committee received a notice that it was an offence to burn foreign cloth in or near a public place. Gandhi had as yet no intention of breaking the law. 'I am capable,' he observed, 'of breaking all the regulations that hurt my moral sense, but that time is not for me yet.' He had, however, been advised that Shraddhanand Park at Calcutta, where the meeting was held, was not a public thoroughfare. As the bonfire was lighted he was placed under arrest. He refused to sign the bond requiring him to appear before the Chief Presidency Magistrate on March 5. However, the case was postponed to enable him to fulfil his engagements in Burma, which he was visiting after fourteen years.

On his return from Burma, three weeks later, he presented himself for trial and was fined one rupee. Someone paid the fine without his knowledge. The inevitable result of this prosecution was to give a fillip to the boycott of foreign cloth. The day of Gandhi's trial was celebrated by bonfires of foreign cloth all over the country.

The Government saw the growing signs of unrest. Apart from the ultimatum which the Congress had given, and the possibility of a clash early in 1930, there were other disquieting symptoms. Industrial labour was seething with discontent. There had been strikes in Bombay and Jamshedpur. In April 1929, when Speaker Patel rose in the Central Legislative Assembly to give his ruling on the Public Safety Bill (which sought more powers for the executive to curb the 'extremists'), bombs were thrown from the visitors' gallery. Two young men, Bhagat Singh and B. K. Datt, were arrested; their intention, they deposed later, was not to kill anybody but 'to make the deaf hear'. Terrorist outrages occurred in several parts of the country, and groups of young men were rounded up and prosecuted for political violence in what came to be known as a series of 'conspiracy cases'. These anarchists became popular heroes; even those who deplored their method applauded their motive. Public

feeling reached a peak when a number of them went on hunger
strike as a protest against treatment of political prisoners; one
of them, Jatin Dass, died in gaol and was honoured as a
martyr.

The official reaction to this heightened tension was to arm
the executive with still greater authority. The Public Safety
Bill, which Speaker Patel had ruled out of order, was nevertheless,
made law under the Viceroy's special powers. In March 1929 a
number of trade union leaders, 'some of them communists,
some near-communists and some trade unionists', were brought
up for trial in what came to be known as the 'Meerut Conspiracy
Case'. 'It seems to me,' wrote Gandhi, 'that the motive behind
these prosecutions is not to kill communism but to strike
terror.' He added that 'The Government were giving the usual
periodical exhibition of its red claws which usually remain under
cover'.

However, the Viceroy, Lord Irwin, had no intention of trying
strong-arm methods only. He had advised Lord Birkenhead
against the inclusion of an Indian in the Royal Commission
but experience had made him wiser. Sir John Simon and his
colleagues were busy touring the country, collecting and sifting
evidence. The Commission's report was not to be published
until May 1930, but Lord Irwin was aware of the trend of these
recommendations and could see that they were not likely to
cut much ice with Indian public opinion. In the summer of
1929 he visited England and conferred with British statesmen.
Some light is thrown on the way Irwin's mind was working by
his correspondence with V. J. Patel during the summer of 1929.
Patel had urged him to find a formula which would make it
worth the Congress leaders' while to agree to take part in a
Round Table Conference in London. 'You may rely on me,' the
Viceroy had written, 'to do my best to find a way of peace
out of our present difficulties, and I hope that, on your side, you
will use whatever influence you have, if anything is done at
this end, to get Congress leaders to meet it half-way.'[1]

[1] Patel, G. I.: *Vithalbhai Patel*, Vol. II, p. 1053.

Lord Irwin's mission was facilitated by a change of government in England. Wedgwood Benn, Secretary of State in the Labour Government, shared Irwin's anxiety to reverse the process of estrangement of Indian opinion which had gone on since the appointment of the Simon Commission. Benn approved of Irwin's proposal for a Round Table Conference in London between the representatives of India and Britain to discuss the constitutional problem. He also approved of Irwin's idea of heralding the announcement of the conference by a declaration reaffirming that the goal of British policy in India continued to be dominion status. Neither Lloyd George nor Lord Reading —the two stalwarts of the Liberal Party—gave much encouragement to Lord Irwin. The Labour Government depended for its majority upon the support of the Liberals, but the Secretary of State was prepared to take the risk.

Lord Irwin returned to India on October 25, 1929. On October 31st, was issued a 'Gazette Extraordinary' of the Government of India containing an announcement of a conference in which His Majesty's Government were to meet representatives of both British India and the Indian States for the purpose of seeking the greatest possible measure of agreement for the final proposals which were to be presented to Parliament. The statement continued: 'In view of the doubts which have been expressed both in Great Britain and India regarding the intentions of the British Government in enacting the Statute of 1919, I am authorized to state clearly that in their judgment it is implied in the declaration of 1917 that the natural issue of India's constitutional progress, as there contemplated, is the attainment of dominion status.'

The Viceroy's announcement was an ingeniously worded document which could mean much or little, but it had a favourable reception in India. The moderate leaders, to quote Lord Irwin's biographer, saw the conference 'as their supreme oportunity for the full exercise of their intellectual power and were henceforth Irwin's faithful allies'. The Congress leaders, scanning the horizon for a gesture which may lead to progress in self-government and prevent a clash with the Government, saw signs of 'a change of heart'. A 'joint manifesto' issued under the signatures of Gandhi, Motilal Nehru, Patel, Tej Bahadur Sapru, Annie Besant, Jawaharlal Nehru and others, after expressing their appreciation of the sincerity underlying the declaration, indicated the conditions necessary for the success of the conference. These included a policy of conciliation, the release of political prisoners, and a predominant representation for the Indian National Congress in the Round Table Conference. The 'manifesto' interpreted the paragraph about dominion status to mean that the conference would meet, not to discuss when dominion status was to be established, but to frame a dominion constitution for India.

Lord Irwin's announcement was thus well received in India, but a storm broke over him and the Labour Government in England. The British Press and Parliament subjected the announcement to a protracted *post mortem*. Lord Reading, whose opinion as a former Viceroy carried some weight, said that the declaration was calculated to undermine the prestige and authority of the Simon Commission. Lloyd George, the leader of the Liberal party, poured scorn on Wedgwood Benn, whom he called the 'pocket edition of Moses'. Baldwin, the leader of the Conservative party, whose protégé Irwin was believed to be, did not really rally to the support of the Viceroy's policy. Sir John Simon and his colleagues felt that they had been shabbily treated by the Labour Government, which did not consult them; after the announcement of a round table conference, their report was likely to have only an academic interest.[1] The Labour Government, which did not have a clear majority in the House of Commons, was on the defensive. Wedgwood Benn explained the declaration as a 're-statement' and an interpretation of Montagu's declaration of August 1917 and thus made out that no radical departure had been made in British policy towards India.

The debate in the British Parliament disillusioned Indian

[1] Simon, Viscount: *Retrospect*, p. 151.

leaders. The temporary bridge which the Viceroy's declaration had thrown between the Government and the nationalists had been knocked off. Jawaharlal Nehru had been with some difficulty persuaded to sign the 'joint manifesto' which had hailed the Viceroy's announcement. A fortnight later his father was sharing his doubts. Within a few weeks the Indian National Congress was due to meet at Lahore. If no understanding was reached with the Government in the meantime, the Congress was committeed to a declaration of complete independence and a non-violent rebellion.

A last-minute effort, in which V. J. Patel and Tej Bahadur Sapru were the prime movers, was made for a reconciliation between the Congress and the Government. 'We must continue our efforts to put pressure on the Viceroy on the one hand and Congress leaders on the other,'[1] wrote Patel to Sapru on November 13, 1929. An interview between the Congress leaders and the Viceroy was arranged. Motilal Nehru, who had for months hoped against hope for a sincere gesture from the Government, was now pessimistic. In a letter to V. J. Patel he wrote on December 9: 'Do you expect Jinnah, Sapru, Gandhi, myself and yourself to be of one mind when we meet the Viceroy . . . With the Wilsonian attitude of Mr Jinnah who insists on the fourteen points of the Delhi Conference, with his want of faith even in dominion status and willingness to accept anything that comes his way . . . do you expect Gandhi and myself who are willing to concede dominion status for the sake of peace in the country to be of the same mind with Mr Jinnah? I expect no results from our interview, but I have to redeem my promise. . . . At present all roads lead to Lahore.'

The interview took place on December 23. That morning Lord Irwin had returned from a tour of South India, and as he had approached the capital a bomb had exploded under the Viceregal train. Gandhi congratulated the Viceroy on his miraculous escape. There was, however, not much progress on the political plane. The Viceroy, chastened by the recent

[1] Patel, G. I.: *Vithalbhai Patel,* Vol. II, Bombay, 1950, p. 1071.

debate in the British Parliament, was unable to given an assurance
that the Round Table Conference would definitely discuss a
scheme of reforms on the basis of dominion status.

The interview ended abruptly. V. J. Patel, who had arranged
it, and Sapru and Jinnah, who had set much store by it, were
surprised at what appeared to them a new rigidity in the attitude
of Gandhi and Motilal Nehru since the signing of the 'joint
manifesto' only six weeks before. The Viceroy felt almost
personally betrayed; the edifice he had been constructing laboriously since the summer crumbled to pieces before his eyes.
It must be admitted that the mood of the Mahatma and Motilal
Nehru was definitely not the same in the last week of December
as it had been in the first week of November. There were good
reasons for it, which even V. J. Patel failed to appreciate at the
time. The debate on the Viceroy's declaration in the British
Parliament had been an eye-opener for the Congress leaders;
circumstances had compelled the Secretary of State to belittle
in Britain what the Viceroy had tried to boost in India. Indian
leaders could therefore scarcely be blamed for not taking the
declaration at its face value.

A week after the abortive interview at Delhi, the Indian
National Congress was to meet for its annual session at Lahore.
The year of grace which the Calcutta Congress had offered to
the British Government in December 1928 was drawing to a
close; the Congress was pledged to a declaration for complete
independence if dominion status was not conceded by Britain.
The Congress leaders sought from the Viceroy something more
than a vague indication of the direction of the British policy
to convince their party that India was assured of a sizable advance
towards self-government. It was all very well for Lord Irwin
to say 'that the assertion of a goal is of necessity a different thing
from the goal's attainment', but such an approach could hardly
help Gandhi and Motilal Nehru in carrying the rank and file
with them at the ensuing Congress session. And the argument
that it was impossible to prejudice the issue or encroach upon
the constitutional responsibility of British Parliament did not

carry conviction to them. Had not the British Cabinet on several occasions committed itself to particular policies in anticipation of the Parliamentary verdict? The bland fact remained that the Labour Government had neither the courage, nor perhaps the conviction, to dismantle the imperial structure in India and to instal a self-governing dominion instead.

'All roads lead to Lahore,' Motilal Nehru had aptly summed up the political situation at the end of 1929 in his letter to V. J. Patel. The Lahore session was going to be a momentous one, as it was likely to declare a struggle which only Gandhi could lead. The choice of the Mahatma as President of the Congress seemed almost inevitable, but he declined the honour on the plea that he could not devote the necessary time to the day-to-day work of the presidency, and that in any case he could continue to serve the Congress without holding office. At his instance the All-India Congress Committee elected Jawaharlal Nehru, who thus entered this high office, to use his own words, 'not by a main entrance or even a side entrance but by a trap-door'.

Politically, the election of Jawaharlal Nehru was a master-stroke of the Mahatma. Only a year before there had been a clash between crabbed age and youth at the Calcutta Congress. Youth had looked askance at the outmoded shibboleths of the old guard. A compromise ingeniously devised by Gandhi had prevented a split. The Congress, instinct with new hope and energy, needed a young man at the helm. The forty-year-old Jawaharlal whom Gandhi described as 'pure as crystal . . . truthful beyond suspicion . . . a knight *sans peur et sans reproche* ' was to be in fullness of time the Mahatma's political heir. There was a bond of deep affection between the two men in spite of the twenty years and widely differing intellectual backgrounds which separated them. Gandhi had been unhappy with some of the activities of Jawaharlal since the latter's return from Europe at the end of 1927. 'You are going too fast,' he wrote to him early in 1928. 'You should have taken time to think and become acclimatised.' A few days later he confessed: 'the differences between you and me appear to be so vast and so radical that there seems to be no meeting ground between us.' This intellectual gulf widened or narrowed from time to time; it was rarely bridged, but it did not affect their emotional affinity or their mutual loyalty.

In December 1929 events were on the march, there was a promise of a struggle and Jawaharlal was in his element.

Chapter 33

CIVIL DISOBEDIENCE

THE Indian National Congress was meeting in the Punjab after exactly ten years. The Amritsar Congress was held in December 1919; the non-co-operation movement had followed in 1920. Was history going to repeat itself? There was little doubt that the Lahore Congress was going to be a momentous one. 'The year of grace', which the Calcutta Congress had granted, was over. Dominion status had not been conceded; the offer of the 'minimum national demand' embodied in the *Nehru Report* would lapse; henceforth Swaraj would mean complete independence. At midnight on December 31, 1929, as the new year dawned, the Indian National Congress unfurled the flag of independence on the bank of the Ravi. The Congress called upon its members in the central and provincial legislatures to resign their seats and authorized the All-India Congress Committee to launch civil disobedience.

The significance of the Congress session was not lost upon the Government. According to Alan Campbell Johnson, Lord Irwin's biographer, the Viceroy seriously considered the banning of this session. Early in January, the Punjab Government advised the Government of India that, in the opinion of its legal advisers, Jawaharlal Nehru and S. D. Kitchlew should be prosecuted for speeches delivered by them as President-designate and Chairman of the Reception Committee of the Lahore Congress. The advice was not accepted, as events had already moved fast.

In an appraisement of the Congress position immediately after the Lahore Congress, the Viceroy reported to the Secretary of State 'the striking effect on the political situation made by the recent meeting at Lahore'. It had seemed clear, wrote the

Viceroy, that the Lahore Congress would be the scene of a struggle between the two wings of the Congress which had clashed but compromised at Calcutta a year earlier; a split was avoided at Lahore by the 'capitulation' of Gandhi and Motilal Nehru to the left-wing Congressmen, consisting of 'revolutionaries' and 'irreconcilables' who were expected henceforth to provide the driving force to the Congress. Though the decision to boycott legislatures could still cause a split, the Congress as a whole, by passing the independence resolution, had, in the Viceroy's opinion, declared itself as a body which intended to pursue 'an illegitimate aim by illegal and unconstitutional means'. Wedgwood Benn acknowledged the gravity of the situation and promised his support for 'firm executive action', even though it was likely to 'evoke criticism in some quarters', with which he was prepared to deal. However, he expressed a desire to be consulted in advance if extraordinary powers were to be invoked, though, in an emergency, the Viceroy could act first and inform him later.

There was little doubt that in executing the decisions of the Lahore session, the Congress would be guided by Gandhi. His writings and speeches acquired the forthright frankness which had marked them ten years earlier. The people had the right, he wrote, to alter or abolish an unjust government. If the atmosphere remained non-violent, he promised to lead a civil disobedience campaign. He was conscious of the risks inherent in a mass movement. The lesson of Chauri Chaura, however, had not been lost on Congressmen. At the same time, Gandhi made it known that there was to be no easy reversal of the movement once it was launched; while every possible effort was to be made to restrain the forces of violence, civil disobedience would continue 'so long as there is a single resister left free or alive'. In 1920-22 Gandhi had proceeded cautiously, spent months in preparing the country, graduated the programme of non-co-operation and shown an obvious reluctance in embarking upon mass civil disobedience. In 1930 he proceeded with swifter and surer steps; it was as if his labours in the previous decade had not been wasted and he was picking up the thread where

K

he had left it off in 1922. 'The call of 1920,' he wrote, 'was a call for preparation. The call in 1930 is for engaging in final conflict.'

Gandhi was not spoiling for a fight: in Satyagraha a struggle is the last step, when all other avenues have been tried. In *Young India* of January 30, 1930, he made an offer to the Viceroy: if the British Government would accept 'Eleven Points', he would not press on with civil disobedience. These 'Eleven Points' (which included reduction in land revenue, abolition of salt tax, scaling down of military and civil expenditure, release of political prisoners, and levy of duties on foreign cloth) seemed to the official world a conveniently wide net to win to his movement peasants as well as industrial workers, professional classes as well as business interests. To Gandhi's own colleagues, a month after the declaration of independence, the proposal was something of an anti-climax. Gandhi knew fully well that the 'Eleven Points' did not add up to political independence, but by listing them he was setting up a tangible test for the willingness of the Government to part with power. The Eleven Points were of course too high-pitched and unrealistic for the Government, which took scarcely any notice of them.

A struggle between the Congress and the Government was now inevitable. In January 1930, Gandhi told Tagore that he was furiously thinking 'night and day'. The first step he took was to call for the celebration of 'Independence Day' on January 26. On that day, in the towns and villages of India, hundreds of thousands of people took a pledge that 'it was a crime against man and God to submit to British rule', and undertook to join a campaign of civil disobedience and non-payment of taxes if the Congress launched it. Independence Day revealed the latent enthusiasm in the country; Gandhi felt the country was ripe for a mass movement. He suggested the inauguration of the movement with the breach of the Salt Laws. The Salt Tax, though relatively light in incidence, hit the poorest in the land, but salt did not quite seem to fit into the plan of a national struggle for liberation. Salt manufacture was confined to the sea-coast or salt mines, and even if a strike could be organized among the politically backward labourers engaged in the industry, the prospect of launching a successful Satyagraha struggle did not appear to be bright. These and other doubts assailed Gandhi's closest adherents even as they followed his lead.

Gandhi announced that he would himself perform the first act of civil disobedience by leading a group of Satyagrahis to the sea-shore for the breach of the Salt Laws. He communicated his plans to the Viceroy in a letter, which was an indictment of British rule as well as an appeal for restoring to India what was her due:

'Dear Friend—Before embarking on civil disobedience and taking the risk I have dreaded to take all these years, I would fain approach you and find a way out. My personal faith is absolutely clear. I cannot intentionally hurt anything that lives, much less fellow-human beings even though they may do the greatest wrong to me and mine. Whilst, therefore, I hold British rule to be a curse, I do not intend to harm a single Englishman or any legitimate interest he may have in India . . .

'I must not be misunderstood. Though I hold the British rule in India to be a curse, I do not, therefore, consider Englishmen in general to be worse than any other people on earth. I have the privilege of claiming many Englishmen as dearest friends. Indeed much that I have learnt of the evil of British rule is due to the writings of frank and courageous Englishmen who have not hestitated to tell the unpalatable truth about that rule . . .

'In common with many of my countrymen, I had hugged the fond hope that the proposed Round Table Conference might furnish a solution (of Indian freedom) . . . But when you said plainly that you could not give any assurance that you or the British Cabinet would pledge yourselves to support a scheme of full dominion status, the Round Table Conference could not possibly furnish the solution for which vocal India is consciously, and dumb millions unconsciously, thirsting.

'. . . if India is to survive as a nation, if the slow death by starvation of her people is to stop, some remedy must be found for immediate relief. The proposed conference is certainly not the remedy. It is not a matter of carrying conviction by argument. The matter resolves itself into one of matching forces. Conviction or no conviction, Great Britain would defend her Indian commerce and interests by all the forces at her command. India must consequently evolve (non-violent) force enough to free herself from that embrace of death . . .

'I know that in embarking on non-violence, I shall be running what might be fairly termed a mad risk, but the victories of truth have never been won without risks, often of the gravest character. Conversion of a nation that has consciously or unconsciously preyed upon another far more numerous, far more ancient and no less cultured than itself, is worth any amount of risk.

'I have deliberately used the word conversion. For my ambition is no less than to convert the British people through non-violence and thus make them see the wrong they have done to India. I do not seek to harm your people. I want to serve them even as I want to serve my own. I believe that I have always served them. I served them up to 1919 blindly. But when my eyes were opened, and I conceived non-co-operation, the object still was to serve them. I employed the same weapon that I have in all humility successfully used against the dearest members of my family. If I have equal love for your people with mine, it will not long remain hidden. It will be acknowledged by them even as members of my family acknowledged it after they had tried me for several years. If people join me, as I expect they will, the sufferings they will undergo, unless the British nation sooner retraces its steps, will be enough to melt the stoniest hearts.'

The Viceroy's reply was brief: it expressed his regret 'at Mr Gandhi's contemplating a course of action which was clearly bound to involve the violation of the law and danger to public peace'.

Gandhi decided to lead the first band of Satyagrahis from Ahmedabad to Dandi on the sea-shore. The Satyagrahis were elected from Sabarmati Ashram which had according to the testimony of one of its inmates, reached 'its zenith in physical energy and moral strength'.[1] Sabarmati was now assuming the role which Phoenix and Tolstoy Ashrams had done in South Africa; it became the recruiting ground for the vanguard of freedom and a hub of political activities. There was nothing secret about these activities. Richard Gregg has recorded how a correspondent of a British-owned paper, who had been sent to Ahmedabad to report what was going on in 'the enemy's camp', instead of being turned away was, at Gandhi's instance, accommodated in the Sabramati Ashram, treated as a guest, and allowed to see things for himself.

The prayer meeting on the evening of March 11, had a record attendance. 'Our cause is strong,' said Gandhi, 'our means the purest, and God is with us. There is no defeat for Satyagrahis till they give up truth. I pray for the battle which begins tomorrow.' That night perhaps the only person in the Ashram who slept was the Mahatma himself. Next morning, at 6-30, he began the 241 mile march to Dandi on the sea-shore. The seventy-nine Satyagrahis included scholars, newspaper editors, untouchables, weavers. The oldest was the sixty-one-year-old leader, the youngest a boy of sixteen. The people of Ahmedabad turned out in their thousands to cheer them. The roads were strewn with green leaves. Gandhi, the oldest member of his volunteer band, walked so fast that younger men found it difficult to keep pace with him. He felt all the better for the exercise; he rose as usual at 4 a.m., conducted the morning prayers, addressed meetings in villages through which he passed, did his daily quota of spinning, wrote articles for his journals and letters to his correspondents. He announced that he would not return to Sabarmati Ashram until the Salt Tax was repealed.

Meanwhile, the authorities had been watching the movement with mingled anxiety and bewilderment. The British had no intention to liquidate their Indian Empire. Earl Russell, the Under-Secretary of State for India, had commented on the Congress demand for complete independence: 'None knows

[1] Mirabehn: *Bapu's letters to Mira*, p. 101.

better than the Indians themselves how foolish it is to talk of complete independence. Dominion status is not possible at the moment and would not be for a long time.'

The same opinion had been expressed by Lord Irwin when he said that the assertion of a goal was not the same thing as its attainment. Ever since the conclusion of the Lahore session of the Congress the Government had been deliberating on the policy they should adopt towards the Congress. Early in January, the Government of India explained its dilemma to the provincial governments. If it prohibited meetings or processions the result might be physical clashes which would further embitter public feeling; such prohibitory orders were also likely to give the Congress what it wanted, opportunities for defying orders. If, on the other hand, the Government took no action, the Congress was likely to gain in prestige, and constitutionalists and loyalists would face greater demoralization. As a happy mean between these two extremes, the Government decided that there should be no 'dramatic departure' in the policy towards the Congress, and that the restraining action of the Government 'should not exceed the immediate requirements'. This studied moderation largely explains the restraint in dealing with the Independence Day celebrations on January 26, 1930, and with the early phases of the Salt Satyagraha.

The first impulse of the Government, as of the Congress intellectual, was to ridicule 'the kindergarten stage of political revolution', and to laugh away the idea that the King-Emperor could be unseated by boiling sea-water in a kettle. The experts of the Government of India did not take the breach of the Salt Tax seriously. Tottenham, a member of the Central Board of Revenue (the department which dealt with Salt Tax), described the breach of Salt Laws 'as Mr Gandhi's somewhat fantastic project'. A committee of two senior officers reported early in February that salt did not appear to be a promising field for initiating a no-tax campaign; that the most that could happen was that small quantities of inferior salt would be sporadically produced in certain areas and consumed locally; that neither government revenues, nor the price of salt were likely to be affected.

The Collector of Kaira, one of the districts through which Gandhi's itinerary lay, was so apprehensive of the political effects of Gandhi's march that he recommended to the Bombay Government that the march should be prohibited. 'So long as it is conducted peacefully,' wrote the Government of Bombay to the Government of India, 'there is no provision of law which permits prohibition of the march.' The Government of India concurred in the view and added that the time for arrest would come when the matter had passed from the 'sphere of words to that of action'. Section 117 of the Indian Penal Code, under which the arrest was proposed, being bailable, there was nothing to prevent Gandhi from continuing the march if he chose to be bailed out. Moreover, neither the Bombay Government nor the Government of India could rule out the possibility that Gandhi's march might end in a fiasco: if the 'salt earth' collected by Gandhi's party, after it reached the sea-shore were confiscated and no one was prosecuted, would not Gandhi 'look ridiculous'? The Government of India therefore saw the wisdom of 'waiting on events' and taking action only when the results of the march became clear. The district magistrates through whose districts Gandhi was to march were therefore directed to telegraph daily reports simultaneously to New Delhi and Bombay to enable the policy-makers of the provincial and central governments to adjust the official policy to the exigencies of the political situation.

At first there was an understandable tendency on the part of the local officials to belittle the effects of the march. The report of the District Magistrate of Ahmedabad for the first three days stated that, though Gandhi excited deep veneration, the crowds were 'not large except in Ahmedabad City', that in one village the reception was poor and that the welcome extended to the Satyagrahis depended upon the attitude and influence exercised by village headmen. The Bombay Government reported that those who attended meetings in Broach district did so out of curiosity rather than out of real interest, that the effects of the march were expected to be transient. Later, reporting on Gandhi's stay in Surat, the Bombay Government cheerfully noted 'the complete absence of Muslims', who formed a considerable portion of the population.

The Government of India suggested to the Bombay Government that district officials should tour the villages through which Gandhi had passed to repair the damage and to improve the morale of the loyalists. While some embarrassment to authority in Gujerat by non-interference with Gandhi's march was inevitable, from an all-India point of view, it seemed most expedient not to arrest him. The Governor of the Punjab assured the Viceroy that the march had aroused little enthusiasm in his province, that the Congress Press was making much of it and that 'in reality it is rather a frost'. There is no doubt, he added, that Gandhi was 'dreadfully anxious' to get himself arrested, as his arrest was likely to whip up popular enthusiasm. Similar views were held by the Governor of the United Provinces. Till the last week of March, and indeed until the middle of April, there was almost a consensus of opinion in the Viceroy's Executive Council, as also among the Governors, that the delay in making Gandhi's arrest had a 'disconcerting effect' on his movement and that it had 'upset' his plans. As late as April 10th, in a telegram to the Private Secretary to the Viceroy, Haig expressed the unanimous opinion of the Executive Councillors that the situation had developed 'satisfactorily and exactly as we had anticipated'.

In the last week of March, the Government of India issued instructions 'based on past experience in handling such movements' to the local (Provincial) Governments, advising them to avoid situations in which they would have to make wholesale arrests or enter into a test of endurance with the Congress; it was preferable to arrest only the leaders, whose imprisonment was likely to discourage or disorganize the movement. If it became necessary to arrest large numbers of Satyagrahis, it was advisable to use the minimum possible force: the use of force against those who were not violent tended to alienate public sympathy. The Local Governments were exhorted to exercise special care in avoiding congestion in gaols and in treating young boys and women. This was sound advice, but unfortunately, as the tempo of the movement grew, the temper of the authorities also rose. Vallabhbhai Patel had already been arrested on March 7th under the orders of local officials who had acted without consulting even the Provincial Government. Early in April Jawaharlal Nehru was arrested in Allahabad. From Dandi, where he had made the first symbolic breach of the Salt Laws, Gandhi sent a message that 'at present Indian self-respect is symbolized, as it were, in a handful of salt in the Satyagrahi's hand. Let the fist be broken, but let there be no surrender of salt'. No less than 60,000 Indians were gaoled. Among those convicted for the breach of the Salt Laws were Rajagopalachari, Madan Mohan Malaviya, J. M. Sen Gupta, B. G. Kher, K. M. Munshi, Devadas Gandhi, Mahadev Desai, Vithalbhai Patel. Women from aristocratic and middle-class homes picketed liquor and foreign cloth shops.

There were stray cases of violence, such as in Chittagong, where some terrorists raided the arsenal to seize arms. But on the whole India remained non-violent. Those who had scoffed at Salt Satyagraha and failed to see any connection between salt and Swaraj had underrated Gandhi's knack for organizing the Indian masses for corporate action. The Government also at last did what it had been planning for so long and at the same time dreading. It decided to arrest Gandhi.

The arrest took place on May 5, 1930 at Karadi, a village near Dandi, under Bombay Regulation XXV of 1827, which was resurrected from the dusty covers of the state archives to detain him without trial. Just before his arrest Gandhi had planned a more aggressive phase of his 'non-violent rebellion' by 'raiding' and taking possession of the salt depots at Dharsana. The raid, which was led by the aged Imam Sahib, an inmate of the Sabarmati Ashram, took place on May 21st. The leaders were arrested and the rank and file beaten up; an account of this raid was given in the *New Freeman* by an American correspondent Webb Miller:

K•

'In eighteen years of reporting in twenty-two countries I have never witnessed such harrowing scenes as at Dharsana. Sometimes the scenes were so painful that I had to turn away momentarily. One surprising feature was the discipline of volunteers. It seemed they were thoroughly imbued with Gandhi's non-violent creed.'

Meanwhile, the All-India Congress Committee had extended the scope of civil disobedience to include the breach (besides the Salt Tax) of forest laws, the non-payment of taxes in ryotwari areas, and the boycott of foreign cloth, banks, shipping and insurance companies. A series of 'ordinances' issued by the Viceroy conferred extraordinary powers on the executive to enable it to crush the Congress, or to use the official jargon, 'to cope with the emergency'. The Congress Committees were unable to function normally; their responsibilities were taken over by individuals called 'dictators'—an appellation which evoked much righteous indignation in official quarters. In fact, the only prerogative of these functionaries was to dictate themselves to prison; their nomination as 'dictators' was invariably and immediately followed by arrest and imprisonment.

Gandhi's arrest stimulated rather than slackened resistance to the Government. Though at the time official propaganda belittled it, the Government were aware of the hold Congress had acquired over the people. In his *Rebel India,* Brailsford has borne testimony to the influence of the Congress in several parts of India, and particularly in Bombay. A similar testimony is available in official records; for example, in a report given by the Director of the Intelligence Bureau to the Home Member, after a visit to Bombay in August 1930. The Congress, he wrote, was able to command whatever support it wanted in that town; its volunteers and picketers were fed free by the people; its 'stranglehold' on business of every sort was complete; many businessmen were prepared to continue in the movement, even though ruin stared them in the face; in short, the Congress was 'completely in command', with the initiative entirely in its hands.

Chapter 34

TRUCE

SINCE his arrest in early May Gandhi had been making up arrears of rest in the Yeravda gaol in Poona, which he picturesequely described as 'Yeravda Mandir' (Yeravda Temple). In prison he maintained his routine of prayer, spinning and studies, and ceased to worry about the political situation in the country and the fate of the movement he had launched. He knew he had done his duty; he hoped the people would do theirs.

A week after his arrest, Lord Irwin published his correspondence with the British Premier and indicated that the civil disobedience movement had not deflected His Majesty's Government from its policy of constitutional reforms and the decision to hold a Round Table Conference in London. 'Those who were responsible for executing his orders testify,' writes Alan Campbell Johnson, 'that his religious convictions seemed to reinforce the very ruthlessness of his policy of suppression.' The Viceroy was at this time directing the sternest repression which nationalism had known in India, but he did not really relish the role. 'You know,' he had written to V. J. Patel as late as in April 1930, 'that no one wishes more fervently than I, that the affairs of India may speedily be again guided into smoother waters.' In July 1930, in his address to the Simla session of the Central Legislature, he expressed the hope that it was perhaps not too late for 'wiser counsels to prevail'. He did not discourage the efforts at conciliation made by George Slocombe, the correspondent of the *Daily Herald,* and the two moderate leaders, Sapru and Jayakar.

George Slocombe, who had been distressed by the turn which

events had taken in India, had gathered from an interview with Motilal Nehru that under certain conditions the Congress was prepared to call off civil disobedience. A little later, Motilal Nehru was arrested and lodged in Naini prison, where his son Jawaharlal had preceded him. The Nehrus were interviewed by Sapru and Jayakar on the possibility of a truce; since they would not commit themselves without consulting Gandhi, they were carried in a special train to Poona. The discussions, which were attended, besides Gandhi and the Nehrus, by Vallabhbhai Patel, Sarojini Naidu, Jairamdas Daulatram, and Syed Mahmud, revealed that there was little common ground between the Congress and the Government. In a letter dated August 15, 1930, the Congress leaders explained to the peacemakers that mere declarations of good intentions, however well-meant, could not satisfy the Congress; that India must be allowed to determine her own future; that self-government without the control of defence and economic policy and the right of secession from the Empire was hardly worth having; that the Congress was prepared to call off civil disobedience if its basic assumptions in constitution-making were accepted and amends made for the policy of repression by releasing political prisoners, returning confiscated property, and reinstating officials dismissed for participation in civil disobedience.

The Congress reaction to the peace feelers threw into sharp relief the gulf between the Congress and the British. In Britain, Winston Churchill was carrying on a crusade against handing over the people of India to 'an oligarchy of lawyers, politicians, fanatics and greedy merchants'. 'We ought to make it perfectly clear,' he said, 'that we intend to remain rulers of India for a very long and indefinite period and though we welcome co-operation from loyal Indians, we will have no truck with lawlessness and treason'. Ramsay MacDonald's Labour Government continued in office with the support of the Liberals; it was in no position, even if it had the intention, to make a radical concession to India. Thanks to the 'voluntary censorship' of the British Press, the British public was almost entirely in the dark about the real state of affairs in India and unable to appreciate Gandhi's methods or motives. The boycott of foreign cloth, which reduced British exports of cloth to India to nearly one-third, was probably the only part of the movement which made an impact on British public opinion. In India, Lord Irwin's advisers were confident of crushing Gandhi's rebellion and carrying on the administration with the help of the moderates and the Muslims. The majority in the Viceroy's Executive Council and almost all the Governors and senior civil servants were for further tightening of the screws on the Congress.

Meanwhile the constitutional caravan had moved on. The report of the Simon Commission, published during the summer, made an elaborate survey of the Indian constitutional problem and meticulously catalogued the difficulties which hampered a substantial advance. Its recommendations were so low-pitched that they did not evoke the enthusiasm of even conservative opinion in India. The first Round Table Conference met in London in 1930. The Congress was not represented on it but some of the delegates, who had left their country in turmoil, were anxious to return with some tangible result and pleaded for a conciliatory policy towards the Congress. In his farewell address (January 19, 1931) Ramsay MacDonald expressed the hope that the Congress would participate in the next session of the conference. A little earlier, Lord Irwin's speech in the Central Legislature had included a surprisingly chivalrous reference to the 'spiritual force which impels Mr Gandhi to count no sacrifice too great in the cause, as he believes, of the India he loves'. About the same time, Wedgwood Benn wrote to Irwin about a dinner party to which he had invited Sapru, Jayakar, Sastri and some members of the Cabinet, and how the Indian leaders, though satisfied with the results of the Round Table Conference, had urged some 'spectacular action'. Acknowledging that it was impossible to expect 'anything like submission, or recantation' from the Congress, Benn wondered whether the Viceroy could help to create a 'bilateral situation' which would lead to an amnesty and to the abandonment by the Congress of civil disobedience in favour of co-operation with the Round Table Conference.

Irwin had already decided not to interfere with a meeting of the Congress leaders in Allahabad. He released Gandhi and the members of the Congress Working Committee on January 25, 1931—the eve of the Independence Day—to the accompaniment of a conciliatory statement. Almost immediately, the Government of India confidentially sounded the local (Provincial) Governments as to the next step they should take with regard to the Congress to create an atmosphere in which 'mutual difficulties' could be understood, 'irritating conditions avoided by one side and 'unreasonable demands' on the other. To this peace feeler from New Delhi almost all the local (Provincial) Governments reacted sharply. They reminded the Government of India that it was not the British Government but the Congress which was in the position of 'the conquered party', that while a peace move could be useful for publicity in Britain and America, it would be interpreted in India as a climb-down. As the Chief Commissioner of Delhi put it, the view of the man-in-the-street would be that the Government had been defeated (*sarkar har gai*). H. W. Emerson, the Home Secretary, and James Crerar, the Home Member—the two men who were the Viceroy's top advisers in political matters —pointedly drew his attention to the misgivings of the provincial governments and urged caution in making further concessions to the Congress. They stressed the dangers of a stampede among the supporters of the Government—the moderates, the Muslims, the services, the army, the police—and of creating an impression that the future lay with the Congress. The next step, they argued, had to be judged by its probable effects not so much on the Congress as on the friends and supporters of the Government. 'A false move,' wrote Emerson, 'may have very grave consequences.'

As the events were to show, the Viceroy was not discouraged by the unfavourable reactions of his principal advisers in New Delhi and the provincial capitals, but it became almost impossible for him, in view of this domestic opposition, to make any substantial concessions to Gandhi in the parleys which followed.

The unconditional release of the members of the Congress Working Committee had not by itself brought the Congress any nearer to the Government. The members of the Congress Working Committee, as they congregated in Allahabad—where Motilal Nehru lay on his death-bed—saw no warrant to call off civil disobedience, but they withheld this decision from the Press on the receipt of a telegram from Sapru and Sastri who were on their way back home and were anxious to give the Congress leaders first-hand impressions of the Round Table Conference. Gandhi was not impressed by the achievements of the conference; nor did he feel optimistic on the possibilities of an understanding with the Government. Nevertheless he wrote to Lord Irwin and asked for an interview. His argument was that, as a Satyagrahi, he had a moral obligation to make a response to the Viceroy's gesture in releasing the Congress Working Committee.

The Gandhi-Irwin parleys began on the afternoon of February 17, 1930. They lasted for a total of twenty-four hours, spread over eight meetings. There were long intervals during which hopes of a settlement alternately receded and revived, but finally, on the morning of March 4th, an agreement was reached. The Delhi Pact, or (to give it its popular name) the Gandhi-Irwin Pact, provided for discontinuance of the civil disobedience on the part of the Congress, and the revocation of the ordinances and the release of civil disobedience prisoners on the part of the Government. The amnesty did not cover political prisoners detained without trial or convicted for covert or open violence; nor did it cover the Garhwali soldiers, who had declined to fire at an unarmed crowd in Peshawar. The restitution of lands sold to third parties and reinstatement of those who had lost their jobs during the non-co-operation movement were also not included in the agreement. There was a concession in a small way to poor people on the sea-coast to manufacture salt, and the recognition of picketing of foreign cloth. There was to be no inquiry into the allegations of excesses by the police; this was a crucial point on which both the Congress and the Government were very sensitive, and negotiations nearly broke down on it. Gandhi did not insist on the inquiry when Irwin told him that, though he (Gandhi) had the right to ask for an inquiry, it was wise to let bygones be bygones and not to rake up bitterness afresh.

On the constitutional issue the Delhi Pact accepted safeguards 'in the interest of India' for such matters as defence, external affairs, minorities and finance. This was the clause which dealt Jawaharlal Nehru a 'tremendous shock', and which seemed so obviously at variance with 'complete independence' to which the Congress was pledged. The agreement did not even guarantee dominion status; its terms fell manifestly short of those which the Congress leaders had considered as the minimum for a truce in August 1930 during the negotiations initiated by Sapru and Jayakar. There was no reference to the Eleven Points which Gandhi had enunciated only a year before as a test of the sincerity of the British Government. Critical observers wondered if there was anything in the Delhi Pact which could not have been obtained from the Government in December 1929, without putting the country through the crucible of a severe repression.

Alan Campbell Johnson was not wrong in reaching the conclusion that in the Delhi Pact Gandhi's gains were consolation prizes, and Irwin's only surrender was in agreeing to enter into negotiations.

Later, nationalist observers argued that the Gandhi-Irwin Pact was part of a deep strategy on the part of the British Government; that the Congress had been tricked into calling off the struggle when it was on a rising tide of popular enthusiasm; and that Gandhi was persuaded to attend the Round Table Conference, the failure of which was certain, to prove to world opinion (and particularly American opinion) that it was not British reluctance but Indian disunity which impeded India's progress to self-government. However plausible, and even attractive, this view might be from a nationalist angle, there is little evidence to support it. George Schuster, Finance Member of the Viceroy's

Executive Council, recorded a minute, soon after the release of Congress leaders at the end of January 1931, in 'which he wondered whether, in the event of the civil disobedience being abandoned even for a short time, it would at all be possible for the Congress to get the movement going again. But in holding this opinion Schuster seems to have been in a minority of one; the consensus of opinion among British experts in the centre and in the Provinces was that the Congress would use a truce to reorganize and recuperate its forces, collect the sinews of war, walk out of the Round Table Conference on some pretext and launch a revolt which would be the more difficult to combat because, in the meantime, the friends and allies of the Government would have been demoralized by negotiations with the Congress.

Lord Irwin had thus to work for a truce with the Congress against heavy odds. He had, of course, the support of the Secretary of State, but in the later stages of the negotiations even Wedgwood Benn, anticipating criticisms in the British Press and Parliament, began to raise doubts. What would happen if the agreement signed by Gandhi was not accepted by his followers in some Provinces? The clauses in the agreement were numbered; did it not create the impression of a contract between the Congress and Government? How could 'safeguards' be described as being in 'the interest of India'; was it not more honest to describe them in the interest of both India and Britain? Could not the references to the police and picketing be reworded? The Viceroy telegraphed back to say that the agreement had already been reached, and to reopen any major question was to risk a failure. It is interesting to note that some of the changes in phraseology which had troubled Benn so much, when communicated to Gandhi, were described by the latter as 'inconsequential' and accepted without cavil.

Lord Irwin's stock with Indian nationalists fluctuated from time to time. It was at its highest immediately after the Gandhi-Irwin Pact, and touched its nadir a year later when the Pact had gone to pieces and the Congress was in opposition and outlawed. The impression among Congressmen was that the Gandhi-

Irwin Pact had been a clever manoeuvre, and that Irwin had led the Mahatma up the garden path of the Viceroy's House. A fellow-prisoner read to Gandhi, in July 1932, B. G. Horniman's description of Lord Irwin as 'an agile opportunist who endeavoured to cover his inconsistencies and change of principle and policy with a thick veneer of unctuous rectitude and hypocritical professions of sincerity'.[1] Gandhi's comment was that the description did less than justice to the Viceroy, who, though loyal to the British Empire, had meant well by India. Indeed it was his belief in Lord Irwin's sincerity which had made Gandhi give way during the negotiations on several points of detail. He saw in Irwin a kindred spirit. 'The two Mahatmas', Sarojini Naidu's epithet for the two negotiators, was apt in so far as it emphasized their religious make-up.

So far as Gandhi was concerned, there is little doubt that he took the Delhi Pact as the beginning of a new chapter in the Congress-Government relations. In a letter dated March 6, 1931 from the house of his host at Delhi, Dr Ansari, to the Private Secretary to the Viceroy, he wrote:

'I must ask for one favour. I told you that it would be a point of honour with the Working Committee to see that there was a cent per cent fulfilment of the conditions obligatory on the Congress. You will help me to implement this obligation if you will draw my prompt attention by wire, where necessary, to any irregularity on our part, that may come under your notice . . .

'I pray to God that the friendship at which the settlement is an attempt will become a permanent fact.'

The attitude of Lord Irwin or—to give him his later and more familiar title—Lord Halifax to Indian nationalism represented by the Congress seemed to alternate strangely between opposition and conciliation. He had advised against the inclusion of an Indian in the Simon Commission, but took great pains to push through the proposal of a Round Table Conference and the dominion status declaration of October 1929. He

[1] Mahadev Desai: *Diaries* (entry dated July 19, 1932).

directed a severe repression against the Congress, but did not rudely or irrevocably bang the door against its leaders, with the result that he signed a truce with Gandhi before leaving India. In subsequent years his utterances were more often than not critical of Gandhi and the Congress. But in 1947, when Mr Attlee's momentous declaration of February 20th, fixing a date for British withdrawal from India, was under fire in the House of Lords, it was Halifax whose defence of the Labour Government's policy tilted the scales in its favour.

It is arguable that, by initiating the negotiations at the very end of his term, Irwin was risking his own political future. Though his advisers were confident that the Congress could be crushed by further doses of 'ordinance rule', Irwin saw that repression itself could lead nowhere and he seems to have acted on the assumption that the Congress, once it was convinced of British sincerity, might switch on to constitutional methods and give its powerful co-operation to the forging and working of a new constitution.

This policy had immeasurably fewer chances of success in 1931-32 than it had in 1930-31. The fact that Irwin was to leave India shortly afterwards was itself unfortunate, the more so as senior officers at the centre and in the provinces were not at all happy about the *modus vivendi* with the Congress. Moreover, after the Lahore Congress the Government had written off the Congress, enlarged the size of the Round Table Conference and packed it with elements with which the Congress had nothing in common. Such a conference could hardly frame a progressive constitution for India. That Gandhi should have agreed to the conference without any definite commitment from the Government (on which he and Motilal Nehru had insisted in December 1929) was itself surprising. Gandhi's reasons for signing the pact should, however, be sought not in its clauses, but in the logic of Satyagraha. His speech at the Karachi session of the Indian National Congress gave a peep into the working of his mind:

'I have often wondered myself what we are going to do at

the conference when we know that there is such a gulf between what we want, and what has been as yet offered at the conference. But considerations of a Satyagrahi decided me. There comes a stage when he may no longer refuse to negotiate with his opponent. His object is always to convert his opponent by love. The stage of negotiation arrived when the Working Committee (of the Congress) was released after the Premier's declaration. The Viceroy also made an appeal to us to lay down arms and to indicate what we want.'

To the suggestion that there was no need for a truce with the Government when the Congress was in a position to continue civil disobedience for at least another year, Gandhi's answer was: 'Well, for that matter, we might be capable of carrying on the struggle for twenty years, and a true Satyagrahi fights to the last, even if the rest are tired into submission. But the truce was made not because we were tired out, but because it was imperative. He who will fight on, because he can fight on is no Satyagrahi but a conceited person guilty before God.'[1]

The obvious inconsistencies in Gandhi's position can thus be explained only in terms of his own technique. The Satyagraha movements were commonly described as 'struggles', 'rebellions', and 'wars without violence'. Owing, however, to the common connotation of these words, they seemed to lay a disproportionate emphasis on the negative aspect of the movements, namely opposition and conflict. The object of Satyagraha was, however, not to achieve the physical elimination or moral breakdown of an adversary but, through suffering at his hands, to initiate those psychological processes which could make it possible for minds and hearts to meet. In such a struggle a compromise with the opponent was neither heresy nor treason, but a natural and a necessary step. And if it turned out that the compromise was premature and the adversary was unrepentant, there was nothing to prevent the Satyagrahi from returning to non-violent battle. It is true that national feeling could not be made to reach a high watermark at will, but Gandhi did not set much store

[1] Tendulkar: *Mahatma*, Vol. III, p. 109.

by political freedom on the crest of a passing wave of emotion; he believed that India would be independent when she came of age, and then no Power would be able to keep her in bondage.

When Gandhi arrived to attend the Karachi Congress in March 1931, a few days after the Delhi Pact, the atmosphere was surcharged on account of the execution of Bhagat Singh and his companions. Gandhi drafted a resolution, which Jawaharlal Nehru sponsored, admiring Bhagat Singh's bravery and sacrifice, and at the same time deploring political violence as a method for the attainment of freedom. A few months later, when terrorist outrages recurred in Bengal and Bombay, Gandhi regretted this resolution and felt that the 'Bhagat Singh cult' had been overdone. He asked political anarchists to desist from the way of violence: 'If you must kill English officials, why not kill me instead?'

The Karachi Congress approved of the Delhi Pact, though it put an interpretation on it which seemed more consistent with the ideals of the Congress than with the clauses of the Pact.

In April, Gandhi was in Bombay and bade farewell to Lord Irwin. The new Viceroy, Lord Willingdon, was already in Bombay but did not send for Gandhi. The hard-headed officials at Delhi and in the provincial capitals, to whom the Delhi Pact had been a bitter pill, had now a sympathetic chief. The friction began within a few days of the signing of the Pact. The Congress received complaints that in Bardoli and Borsad all the prisoners had not been released, forfeited lands had not been restored nor village officials reinstated. Tension mounted in Bengal, where the agreement did not in any case cover thousands of young men who had been detained without trial. The United Provinces were suffering from agrarian discontent. In the North-West Frontier Province the repression against the Red Shirts was not relaxed and permission was refused even to Gandhi to enter that province.

Young India of July 9, 1931, came out with an editorial listing breaches of the Pact with the startling title: 'Is it crumbling?'

On July 18th, Gandhi met the Viceroy at Simla and demanded a judicial inquiry into the complaints on the working of the Pact. On August 14th, he wrote to the Viceroy: 'The sum total of all the circumstances betrays a fundamental difference of outlook between us.' The Government accused the Congress of having acted in a spirit contrary to the Delhi Pact, which thus verged on repudiation by both sides. Negotiations were resumed, however, and a compromise ('the second settlement') was patched up. It was agreed that the Congress complaints regarding the working of the Gandhi-Irwin agreement in Bardoli would be looked into by a Collector under precise terms of reference, that the Congress would participate in the Round Table Conference and that its sole representative would be Gandhi.

A special train was arranged from Simla to Kalka, and other trains were held up to enable Gandhi to reach Bombay in time to sail on August 29th, in the ss *Rajputana*. Mahadev Desai, Pyarelal, Devadas and Mirabehn accompanied him. Also with him on the ship were Sarojini Naidu and Madan Mohan Malaviya. As he sailed, his mood was one of despair leavened only with a little hope: 'When I think of the prospects in London, when I know all is not well in India . . . there is nothing wanting to fill me with utter despair. The horizon is as black as it possibly could be. There is every chance of my returning empty-handed. But believing as I do that God has made the way to London clear for me through the "second settlement", I approach the visit with hope.'

Chapter 35

THE ROUND TABLE CONFERENCE

'HE is perhaps the best sailor on board the ss *Rajputana*,' wrote Mahadev Desai, the Mahatma's secretary. Gandhi, who travelled second—the lowest—class on the ship spent most of the day and the whole of the night on the deck, rose and retired at his usual hours, and followed the Ashram routine of prayers, spinning and studies. Little boys and girls of the home-going English passengers became his friends; they watched him ply the spinning-wheel, and when they peeped into his cabin in the morning or in the evening they were rewarded with armfuls of grapes and dates. At Aden the Indian community presented him an address. Messages of good wishes came from Madame Zagloul Pasha, the widow of the Egyptian patriot, and from leaders of the Wafd Party. At Marseilles he was greeted by Madeleine Rolland, the sister of the French savant, and was given a warm welcome by French students, who hailed him as the 'spiritual ambassador of India'.

On September 12, 1931, he arrived in London. He had accepted Muriel Lester's invitation to stay in Kingsley Hall in the East End in order to be 'among the same sort of people to whom I have given my life'. Friends had pleaded with him that his residence was inconvenient for his fellow delegates and colleagues attending the Conference. He agreed to have an office at 88 Knightsbridge, but every evening late though it was, he returned to sleep in Bow. Sometimes he returned from committee meetings after midnight, but the light still appeared in his room at 4 a.m. for the morning prayer. He had his morning walk in the mean streets of East End; he visited his neighbours in Bow; he made friends with the children. 'Here I am,' he would say, 'doing the real round table work, getting to know the people of England.'

Gandhi was the sole representative of the Congress at the Round Table Conference. As the Gandhi-Irwin Pact had not been working very well and the political situation remained fluid in certain parts of the country, the Working Committee of the Indian National Congress had been reluctant to spare other front-rank leaders for the Round Table discussions in England. It was understood, however, that if Gandhi was able to reach an agreement on the fundamentals of a treaty between India and Britain, he could summon to London his colleagues and, indeed, the entire Congress Working Committee to assist in hammering out the details. Unfortunately, the Round Table Conference never got near a treaty of this kind and the Mahatma had to fight single-handed against elements—Indian and British— who were brakes on real progress in constitution-making. The British Press and politicians made out that Gandhi, however eminent as an individual, was only one of the Indian delegates and the Congress was just one of the numerous parties of which a cross section had been brought together at the Conference. All the delegates were nominees of the Government; they had a sprinkling of able individuals, but the majority of them were drawn from the Princely order, the landlords, the titled gentry and the leaders of communal groups and vested interests, big and small. Many delegates were only too willing to become pawns in the political intrigues, the jockeying for position, the scramble for jobs and seats in legislatures and in services, to which the Conference gradually reduced itself.

What with its composition and what with its procedure, which the British Government controlled, the Conference sidetracked its energies into secondary issues and particularly the communal problem. Gandhi saw through this game and did some plain speaking in public as well as in private. Surely, he asked, the British Government had not invited the Indian delegates from six thousand miles to London to settle the communal question. He pointed out that the various communities had been led to place an undue emphasis on the communal question as a condition precedent to constitutional advance; this had turned them virtually into hungry wolves prowling about for the prey under the new constitution. The problem had been presented to the Conference in an inverted way; it had been called upon to divide a cake, the size of which was not known. 'Let us know what we are going to get,' he demanded, 'so that on that basis I might endeavour to bring about unity even in the present ill-assorted group. I could tell them they are dashing a precious thing to pieces.'

G. D. Birla, a fellow delegate to the Conference, had suggested to the Mahatma to prepare his first speech, as it was to be a momentous occasion. As they sat in the car on their way to the St James's Palace for the Conference, Gandhi told Birla that he had not been able to find time to write the speech, adding, 'God will help me in collecting my thoughts at the proper time. After all we have to talk like simple men. I have no desire to look extra intelligent. Like a simple villager, all that I have to say is "we want independence".'[1] His extempore speech, delivered 'in the spirit of a simple villager', was nevertheless a brilliant exposition of the Congress stand and the Indian case for self-government. The Congress, said Gandhi, was the oldest and the most representative political organization in India; it represented all communities, but above all the poor semi-starved dumb millions. 'If you examine the records of the prisons of India,' he added, 'you would find that the Congress represents a large number of Muslims.' As for the untouchables, he claimed to represent them in his own person; if there was a referendum he would, he said, top the poll.

He pleaded for an honourable and equal partnership between Britain and India, held not by force but 'by the silken cord of love'. The Congress had accepted the principle of Federation, as also the principle that there should be 'safeguards', but the safeguards had to be devised in the interest of India and not to reduce self-government to a mockery. If all the safeguards which

[1] *Incidents of Gandhiji's Life*, edited by Shukla, p. 24.

were being proposed were incorporated in the new constitution, the responsible government which India would enjoy could be no better than 'the responsible government prisoners have in their cells; the prisoners too have complete independence immediately after the cell door is locked up'. He admitted that the British had more organizing ability, but Indians knew their country better. He was against any special treatment for European business interests, but he assured them that there would be no discrimination against them either. He advocated adult suffrage, a single-chamber legislature and indirect elections. He even envisaged the possibility of British troops remaining in India for some time after the grant of independence; he explained that it was for the British to initiate Indians into the mysteries of defence. 'Having clipped our wings it is their duty to give us wings wherewith we can fly.'

All this homely eloquence was wasted on the Conference. There was a financial crisis and a change of Government in Britain; in the new Government the Conservatives were heavily weighted. The British public was preoccupied with domestic issues; the financial crisis was for it a more urgent issue than the niceties of an Indian Constitution. Inevitably, even if imperceptibly, there was a change in emphasis. Sir Samuel Hoare, the new Secretary of State, told Gandhi that he sincerely believed that Indians were unfit for complete self-government. The Conservative Press was outspoken. The *Daily Mail* declared that 'without India, the British Commonwealth would fall to pieces. Commercially, economically, politically and geographically it is our greatest imperial asset. To imperil our hold on it would be the worst treason any Briton could commit.'

Meanwhile, the Round Table delegates were busy with the bargains and counter-bargains of the communal problem. In these squabbles they were encouraged by the vested interests from India and the 'die-hard' elements from Britain to expose to the world that it was Indian disunity and not British reluctance which barred the path to Indian self-government. Gandhi was prepared to give a 'blank cheque' to Muslims and other minorities to remove all their legitimate fears, provided they were willing to press the national demand for freedom. The Hindu delegates were not ready for this generous gesture, and the Muslim nationalists were not represented at the Conference. The delegates of the minority groups, Muslims, Anglo-Indians, Indian Christians and Scheduled Castes then joined hands in a 'Minorities Pact', combining separate electorates with weighted representation for each of the several minorities. Ramsay MacDonald's comment that this pact covered 115 million people or about forty-six per cent of India's population brought a crushing rejoinder from Gandhi. 'You had,' said the Mahatma, 'a striking demonstration of the accuracy of this figure; you have had on behalf of the women of India a complete repudiation of special representation, and as they happen to be one half of the population of India, this forty-six per cent is somewhat reduced.' The Minorities Pact, without the support of the Congress, was still-born, but it advertised to the world, as perhaps it was intended to do, that the Indian parties were irreconcilable and that the British Government would have to impose a solution of the communal question to make further advance possible.

Gandhi had to drink many a bitter cup of humiliation to the dregs during these days. The interminable bargaining, the controversies on the secondary issues, the tactical manoeuvres, the behind-the-scene alignments disgusted and disillusioned him. He had anticipated difficulties on the communal issue, and had indeed suggested to the Congress Working Committee that he should go to London only after securing a communal settlement in India. He had been overruled by his colleagues; but he had not been prepared for the demonstration he witnessed in London. The insincerity of some of the delegates was patent; most of the others seemed unable to appreciate that the central question was that of constitution building and not of scrambling for the spoils of freedom even before it had been won. Within a fortnight of his arrival in England, Gandhi confessed to a feeling of isolation in the Conference. He had a frank exchange of views with Sir Samuel Hoare and they had agreed to differ.

Gandhi realized that he had underrated the forces arrayed against him and the Congress. It was almost with a sense of relief that he saw the Conference trail off to a formal conclusion. The British Premier, Ramsay MacDonald, in his concluding address promised to impose a solution of the communal problem and to appoint a committee to go to India for further investigation so that an 'all-embracing statute' could be framed.

Meanwhile, the news from India had been disconcerting. The 'truce' had been working less and less satisfactorily. A new ordinance had been issued for Bengal, and Congress workers had been arrested in North-West Frontier and the United Provinces. To his colleagues in India it was already obvious that the Mahatma's political mission had been a failure. C. F. Andrews called it a 'magnificent failure', but to many observers there was hardly any magnificence in it. They could not help feeling that the Mahatma had miscalculated and underrated the forces arrayed against the nationalist elements. V. J. Patel, who had been sceptical about the wisdom of the Gandhi-Irwin Pact, was in London during the Conference and had urged the Mahatma to appeal to the League of Nations and not to pin hopes on the Conference. Shrewd politician as he was, it infuriated him to think that the Mahatma would not even attempt to take tactical advantages over his adversaries and use militant propaganda to influence world opinion.

In London's East End, among the poor of London, 'uncle Gandhi' had become a popular figure with the children. He answered their innocent and often penetrating questions. He told them stories of his childhood. He explained to them why he had chosen to stay in the East End and why he wore his meagre dress. He advised them to return good for evil. There was an interesting sequel to this advice, when the father of a four-year-old girl told the Mahatma that he had a bone to pick with him. 'And what is it?' asked Gandhi. 'Well my little Jane comes every morning to me, hits me and wakes me up and says, "Now, don't you hit back, for Gandhi told us not to hit back".' On October 2nd, his birthday, the children presented him with 'two woolly dogs, three pink birthday candles, a tin plate, a blue pencil and some jelly sweets'—gifts which he especially treasured and took to India. 'Thousands and thousands of children in England will have seen Gandhiji,' wrote Mahadev Desai, 'before he leaves the English shores. And who knows it may be this generation with whom we may have to settle accounts?'

One of the most pleasant surprises of the tour was the courtesy and even affection Gandhi received from the cotton operatives of Lancashire, which had been hit the hardest by the Congress boycott of British goods. He listened with obvious attention and sympathy to the tale of woe of those who were jobless. Many of them saw the background of the boycott which he had sponsored when he told them: 'You have three million unemployed, but we have nearly 300 million unemployed for half the year. Your average unemployment dole is seventy shillings. Our average income is 7s 6d a month.'

Some of his English friends felt that by staying in the East End he was ignoring the middle and upper classes of England, who really determined the political future of India. So they arranged for him to meet the best minds of Britain in politics, religion, science and literature. He met George Bernard Shaw, who found in him 'a kindred spirit'. He addressed the Members of Parliament in committee rooms. He met the Bishops and the Church dignitaries. He spoke to the boys at Eton and to the students of the London School of Economics. At Oxford, where Dr Lindsay, the Master of Balliol, had invited him, he had talks with Dr Gilbert Murray, Gilbert Salter, Professor Coupland, Edward Thompson and others and spoke at a meeting organized by the Indian students. He went to see Lloyd George; Charlie Chaplin, of whom he had never heard before, came to see him.

It is difficult to assess the results of these informal contacts. The Englishman's courtesy for the distinguished guest often concealed the real impact of his personality. It was apparent that the gulf between the Congress aims and the prevalent British view was almost unbridgeable; only a tiny minority was prepared to go the whole hog with the Mahatma in his claim for an equal partnership between India and Britain. Immediately, he was unable to carry conviction; it appeared to most British statesmen and thinkers that he wanted India to travel too far and too fast on the difficult road to self-government. Nevertheless, the homely logic and the transparent sincerity of the man left an indelible impression on some of those whom he met. They formed clearer impressions of him than the loin cloth and goat's milk version with which the popular Press regaled them. While his opinions might appear utopian or revolutionary, he could no longer be dismissed as 'humbug', the appellation with which *Truth* had heralded his arrival in England.

C. F. Andrews, though a partial observer, was perhaps not far wrong in estimating the long-term effects of Gandhi's visit, when he summed up the value of these contacts outside the Round Table Conference: 'His unique personality gripped the best Englishmen and his originality of thought set those whom he met thinking as they had never done before. They were not always in agreement with him, but they all unanimously respected the greatness of his soul, which they found in him. England is a very small country and impressions like these go round very fast indeed. No serious-minded man or woman could any longer take the view, which had been very widely held before, that Mahatma Gandhi was only an impossible fanatic after all.'[1]

The news from India was far from reassuring. The compromise which had been patched up between the Congress and Government, just before his departure for England, had virtually broken down. The Mahatma was anxious to return home; he declined invitations to prolong his itinerary in Europe and to visit America, but he decided to spend a few days with Romain Rolland in Switzerland on his way back to India.

Accompanied by Mahadev Desai and Pyarelal (his secretaries), Mirabehn (Miss Slade) and Devadas (his son), Gandhi arrived at Villeneuve on December 6th. In his book *Mahatma Gandhi*, published soon after the first non-co-operation movement in

[1] Chaturvedi, B. and Sykes, M.: *Charles Freer Andrews*, London, 1949, p. 254.

the early nineteen twenties, Rolland had interpreted Gandhi's life and message with remarkable insight and expressed the hope that the message of non-violence and self-sacrifice might yet save the violence-ridden Europe from self-destruction: 'One thing is certain; either Gandhi's spirit will triumph or it will manifest itself again, as were manifested, centuries before, the Messiah and Buddha, till there finally is manifested in a mortal half-god the perfect incarnation of the principle of life which will lead a new humanity on to a new path.'

Gandhi and Rolland were closeted together for hours daily. A glimpse into their conversations, which ranged over a wide field, has been given by Rolland's sister:

'My brother describes for Gandhi the tragic situation of Europe; the sufferings of the people oppressed by dictators: the drama of the proletariat who in their desperate effort to break the shackles of an anonymous ruthless capitalism and pushed forward by their legitimate aspiration for justice and freedom see only one way out, that of rebellion and violence. For man in the West is by education, by tradition and by temperament unprepared for the religion of *ahimsa*.

'. . . Gandhi listens; reflects. He reaffirms his unshakable faith in non-violence. Yet he understands that to convince sceptical Europe the concrete example of a successful experiment in non-violence would be necessary. Will India furnish it? He hopes so.'[1]

Gandhi's visit to Switzerland evoked a good deal of local enthusiasm. The Syndicate of the Milkmen of Lemen telephoned Gandhi's host that they would like to supply milk to the 'King of India'; a Japanese artist hurried from Paris to make sketches of the Indian leader; a young musician played a violin under his window. Correspondents from Italy asked the Indian saint to indicate the ten lucky numbers for the next drawing of the national lottery; school children brought him flowers. He addressed private gatherings of pacifists. At Lausanne and Geneva he addressed public meetings and answered questions. What should

[1] Shukla (Editor): *Incidents of Gandhiji's Life*, p. 294.

Switzerland do in the event of an invasion? Should she rely upon her army? 'An army is useless,' replied Gandhi; 'it would be enough to have all citizens, men, women and children making of their bodies a wall against the enemy.' On the class struggle his comment was; 'Labour does not know its power. Did it know it, it would only have to rise to have capitalism crumble away. For Labour is the only power in the world.' Gandhi received a good deal of heckling at the public meetings, but the hecklers were, as Romain Rolland wrote later, 'silenced and suffocated' by these rude truths, and left the meeting quivering with rage. The Swiss bourgeois was shocked by the plain speaking of the Mahatma; his pacifism seemed too militant, his economics too radical. The Press became frankly hostile and his hosts feared that, were it not for the fact that he was leaving Switzerland the next day, his expulsion as an undesirable was quite on the cards.

Gandhi had planned to spend a day in Rome on his way back. Romain Rolland warned him to be on his guard against the wiles of the Fascists and arranged for his stay with a friend whose integrity was beyond doubt. In Rome he walked through the Vatican galleries; in the Sistine Chapel he was spell-bound: 'I saw a figure of Christ there. It was wonderful. I could not tear myself away. The tears sprang to my eyes as I gazed.'

The Pope did not grant him an audience but Mussolini did. Of the latter a prison official said in Yeravda gaol, five months later, that he was an attractive personality. 'Yes,' said the Mahatma, 'but he looks like the executioner. How long will a rule based on bayonets last?'[1]

After he had boarded the Italian liner *Pilsna* for Brindisi, Gandhi learnt that *Giornale d'Italia* had published an interview with him in which he was supposed to have announced that he was returning to India to resume the civil disobedience movement. He had given no interview in Rome and cabled to London that the report was a complete fabrication. In spite of this denial several British papers and politicians persisted in the insinuation

[1] *Diaries of Mahadev Desai.* (Entry 26th May, 1932.)

that Mr Gandhi was lying. It seemed as if *Giornale d'Italia* provided just the excuse for which diehard politicians in England and British bureaucrats in India were looking to revert to the time-honoured policy of 'no truck with the Congress', of which the Gandhi-Irwin Pact had been a temporary aberration.

Chapter 36

END OF THE TRUCE

GANDHI landed at Bombay on December 28, 1931. Within a week he was in gaol and civil disobedience was resumed; the Indian National Congress was practically outlawed and the Gandhi-Irwin Pact had gone to pieces. The explanation for this swift and somewhat unexpected turn in the political scene is to be sought not only in the incidents of that crucial week which spanned Gandhi's return and rearrest, but in the undercurrent of antagonism between the Congress and the Government which the Gandhi-Irwin Pact had failed to eradicate.

We have already seen that the Gandhi-Irwin Pact had conceded very little to the Congress so far as its fundamental demand for independence was concerned. Gandhi believed, however, that the Pact had opened up a chink, however small, in the barrier of suspicion between nationalist India and the British Government. Lord Irwin derived much satisfaction from the fact that the Congress had, at least for the time being, diverged from the path of non-co-operation and agreed to take part in the discussions for a new constitution for India. Unfortunately, Lord Irwin laid down his office soon after the Pact had been concluded and his policy of conciliating the Congress had not only critics among diehards in Britain, but also sceptics among many of his colleagues and senior officials in India. Between March 5, 1931, the date of the signing of the agreement, and August 29, 1931, when Gandhi sailed for England, Indian politics were rocked by a series of crises which brought the Congress and the Government to the verge of a conflict.

As early as June 16, 1931 the Government of India, while forwarding the draft of a comprehensive ordinance for dealing with the renewal of civil disobedience, drew the attention of the Secretary of State for India to 'certain elements of instability' in the political situation. They did not fear an immediate resumption of civil disobedience, as in their view even militant Congressmen wanted 'a reasonable period for organization and consolidation'. It was this consideration which was 'the cause of anxiety to the Government of India; for there can be no doubt that one effect of the settlement has been to increase the prestige of the Congress and to lower that of the Government. Assisted greatly by economic conditions, the Congress have been able to extend their influence in rural areas, and to pursue, what is reason to believe, a deliberate policy of obtaining mass support in villages in the event of the resumption of civil disobedience'.

The Government of India went on to express the apprehensions of the Provincial Governments, 'lest in prosecuting the policy of the settlement, the Government should permit the situation to deteriorate to an extent which would involve extremely grave risks'. In August 1931, when Congress non-participation in the Round Table Conference seemed a certainty, the Provincial Governments were advised that if civil disobedience was renewed the Congress Working Committee would be declared an un-lawful body, Gandhi, and possibly other important leaders, would be put under arrest within the first ten days and a series of ordinances would be promulgated.

Gandhi's departure for London seemed at first to clear the atmosphere and to ease tension. The 'second settlement', which enabled him to leave for London at the end of August 1932, after prolonged and precarious parleys in Simla, was a patched-up affair and barely touched the fringe of the problems which were pressing for a solution.

There were three storm-centres in Indian politics during the summer and autumn of 1931: Bengal, North-West Frontier and the United Provinces. The Gandhi-Irwin Pact had brought little relief to Bengal. The political amnesty did not cover thousands of young men who had been 'detained' in gaol without a trial. Secret terrorist activity directed against European officials and non-officials complicated the problem for the Congress, which found itself between the Scylla of the revolutionaries' terrorism and the Charybdis of the Government's counter-terrorism. For the latter it was difficult to believe that there was no connection between the revolutionaries and the Congress, particularly when both drew most of their members from the Hindu middle class. Congressmen thus often found themselves subject to laws and ordinances specifically framed for anarchists. While Gandhi was in London the spotlight had fallen on Bengal on at least three occasions. The police fired upon political prisoners in Hijli gaol and (as it turned out later, after a judicial enquiry) somewhat ruthlessly. There was a communal riot at Chittagong in which Europeans and Anglo-Indians were alleged to have taken a somewhat mysterious role. Worst of all was a drastic ordinance as a result of which the entire Hindu population in certain areas was virtually treated as hostile; identity cards were made obligatory for every one between twelve and twenty-five years; dress was regulated; schools were controlled or closed; the use of cycles banned; a curfew imposed; and collective fines inflicted on a whole village or town for the crimes of a few.

In December 1932, George Lansbury, the leader of the Labour Opposition in Parliament, had written to Sir Samuel Hoare, the Secretary of State: 'I had several discussions with Sir Tej Bahadur Sapru and his colleagues during their stay in this country, as well as Gandhi and his friends. On leaving, they one and all impressed on me the fact that in their judgment—that is the judgment of men connected with every section of opinion in India, they were convinced that if the Bengal Ordinance remains as it is, there is bound to be a period of very great difficulty for the Government, and of course trouble and difficulty for the Indians.' In his reply, Sir Samuel was all courtesy to Lansbury, but could promise little relief to Bengal.

Almost as intractable was the problem of the North-West Frontier. In this backwater of the Indian sub-continent the local officials had been inured to no opposition except in the form of sporadic risings in the tribal belt, which could often be put down by a show of force. The growth of the Red-Shirt movement under Khan Abdul Ghaffar Khan and its close alliance with the Congress had posed a difficult problem for the semi-military administration of this province. That Abdul Ghaffar Khan preached nationalism with non-violence did not seem to make any difference to those who believed that the Pathans' partiality for the gun was incurable. The Government of the N.W.F.P. continued to urge on the Viceroy the dangers of delay in arresting Abdul Ghaffar Khan. Abdul Ghaffar Khan was, on the other hand, sure that he was more sinned against than sinning. When Gandhi was in London, Abdul Ghaffar Khan wrote to him (November 16, 1931) begging that he acquaint the people of Britain with the tale of woe of which the latter's agents in India were the authors: 'The Government have started a severe repression against *Khudai Khidmatgars* (Red Shirts). They raid their offices and beat them there. Khudai Khidmatgars are being clapped into gaols, are refused interviews and caned into the bargain.'

The homely eloquence of the Red-Shirt leader was too much for the local administration; the Viceroy yielded to the pressure from Peshawar and permitted the Governor to arrest Abdul Ghaffar and to assume emergency powers four days before Gandhi landed at Bombay.

The third storm-centre was the United Provinces. Here the problem was basically economic. The peasantry had been hit hard by a steep fall in prices. The Government had afforded some relief by granting remissions in land revenue, but the landlords did not scale down the rents. The Government appeared loth to do anything which would alienate the sympathies of the landlords, who as a class were loyal to the British *Raj*. Gandhi had tried in vain to secure some further relief for the distressed peasantry of the U.P. by discussions with the Governor of the province at Nainital, and later with the Viceroy at Simla. After Gandhi's departure for London, Jawaharlal Nehru continued to apprise him of the developments in the situation. It seemed to Nehru that the provincial government were trying 'to restrain its District Officers, but not wholly with success'. The crux of the

problem from the point of view of the Congress was the pre-
vention of ejectment of tenants for non-payment of rent and
revenue. During the previous season, many of them had sold
their scanty belongings and cattle—to pay the full demand from
the State and the landlord; they were faced again with demands
which were beyond their means or alternatively, with the
prospect of eviction from lands which they and their ancestors
had tilled for many generations. The Allahabad District Congress
Committee, under the direction of Jawaharlal Nehru, decided
upon a Satyagraha campaign; it was, as Nehru put it, not a 'no-
rent campaign' but a 'fair-rent campaign', to secure for the poor
peasant remissions of revenue and rent commensurate with the
fall in prices. He sent a long cable to London explaining to Gandhi
the mounting crisis in the agrarian situation in the United
Provinces.

Gandhi replied briefly: 'Your cable. You should unhesitatingly
take necessary steps meet every situation expect nothing here.'
Gandhi was aware of the distress of the peasantry in U.P. and he
had faith in the judgment of Jawaharlal Nehru. Moreover, he
could reasonably argue that he was sanctioning a local Satyagraha
campaign to deal with a primarily economic issue. To the Viceroy
and his advisers, however, Gandhi's cable to Nehru confirmed
their suspicion that Gandhi was irreconcilable. With the Round
Table Conference bogged on the communal and constitutional
issues, and Gandhi's unconcealed disappointment, a recrudescence
of civil disobedience seemed to them not only possible but
probable.

As we have already seen, the Government had perfected its
plans for an offensive against the Congress. For months the
Government of India and the Provincial Governments had been
working out the details of the special powers with which executive
officers were to be armed to deal a knock-out blow to the Congress
if civil disobedience was resumed. The ordinances had been
drafted and circulated to Provincial Governments; civil disobedience 'manuals' had been drawn up. On November 6, 1931,
while the Round Table Conference was still in session, the Home

Department of the Government of India informed the Provincial Governments that the Secretary of State had accorded his general approval to the measures for dealing with civil disobedience: 'On the understanding that the final decision to put it into force must rest with His Majesty's Government on receipt of information from the Government of India showing that as a result of the revival of civil disobedience a state of emergency had arisen which justifies such action. The Government of India anticipate that in the event of a decision to revive civil disobedience in more than local areas, they should be able at once to furnish the information which would enable His Majesty's Government to grant the sanction.'

On December 19, 1931, when Gandhi was on the high seas, the Government of India by a circular letter alerted the Provincial Governments regarding the anticipated struggle with the Congress as a result of the meeting of the All-India Congress Committee, which was to meet at Bombay soon after Gandhi's return. The *casus belli* included a general revival of the civil disobedience movement, the support of the no-tax campaign in U.P., or the boycott of British goods or institutions; if the Congress voted for any of these policies, it was to be considered a declaration of war against constituted authority.

The temper of the official world may be gauged from a letter which the Bombay Government addressed to their superiors in Delhi on December 21st, pointing out the inconvenience of lodging Mr Gandhi in gaol in Bombay Presidency: 'If the Government of India still consider it essential that the place selected should on the mainland of India . . . Coimbatore might be a suitable place. I am, however, to say that the Governor-in-Council considers that the moral effect of Mr Gandhi's internment would be far greater and that it would have a more valuable effect in showing the determination and power of Government to crush the civil disobedience movement, if Mr Gandhi were removed to Andamans, or possibly Aden might be considered in order to place him beyond reach of political exploitation.'

The proposal was not considered a practical proposition by the Government of India, but Gandhi's arrest under the Bombay Regulation XXV of 1827 was a foregone conclusion. Lord Willingdon had evidently decided not to repeat that hesitation which his three predecessors, Lords Chelmsford, Reading and Irwin, had exhibited in arresting the author of civil disobedience. Many senior officers in the Central and Provincial Secretariats believed that Gandhi's movements of defiance of authority had thriven on the initial indecision or leniency of the Government and that a more resolute policy could have nipped the evil in the bud. For many of them the Gandhi-Irwin Pact had been a bitter pill; the Pact did not alter the basic fact that the Congress was pledged to liquidate the Indian Empire, which the servants of the Crown had sworn to serve and defend. The fact that the Congress, under Gandhi's leadership, eschewed the use of force did not seem to make much difference to those who considered non-violence a mere mask. Those British officials who did not doubt Gandhi's *bona fides* questioned his ability to control the popular feeling once it had been worked up.

When Gandhi landed at Bombay on December 28, 1931, after four months' absence from India, he was far from being optimistic, but he certainly did not expect to be confronted with a first-class political crisis. The arrests of Jawaharlal Nehru and Abdul Ghaffar Khan and the promulgation of ordinances in the United Provinces and the North-West Frontier had brought matters to a head. 'I take it,' Gandhi told a mass meeting of the citizens of Bombay, 'that these (ordinances) are Christmas gifts from Lord Willingdon, our Christian Viceroy.' The Congress Working Committee came to the conclusion that the Government had decided on a showdown and that the only answer to the Government was a revival of civil disobedience.

Gandhi was anxious, however, to ascertain the Government's point of view and to seek a peaceful solution so long as there was a single ray of hope; he could not lightly plunge the country into another ordeal. On December 29th, he sent a wire to Lord Willingdon: 'I was unprepared on landing yesterday to find

Frontier and United Provinces ordinances, shootings in Frontier, and arrests of my valued comrades in both, on the top of the Bengal ordinance awaiting me. I do not know whether I am to regard these as an indication that friendly relations between us are closed, or whether you expect me still to see you and receive guidance from you as to the course I am to pursue in advising the Congress. I would esteem a wire in reply.'

Two days later the Viceroy's reply arrived: he was prepared to concede that Gandhi was not responsible for the 'misdeeds' of his colleagues in the U.P. and N.W.F.P. and offered to grant an interview to the Mahatma if he would undertake not to discuss events in these two provinces. It was a curious condition to impose, for there was hardly any point in Gandhi seeking an interview if the main issues between the Congress and the Government were barred from discussion. Willingdon must have been exceedingly naïve if by this stipulation he hoped to drive a wedge between Gandhi on the one hand and Jawaharlal Nehru and Abdul Ghaffar Khan on the other. In his reply Gandhi affirmed: 'I may not repudiate moral liability for the actions of my colleagues whilst I was absent from India, and it was because it was necessary for me to advise the Working Committee of the Congress and in order to complete my knowledge I sought with an open mind and with the best of intentions an interview with His Excellency . . .'

Gandhi once again appealed to the Viceroy to reconsider his decision and to see him 'as a friend without imposing any conditions as to the scope or subject of discussion'. He offered to go to these two provinces to study both the official and the popular versions of recent events, and (if the enquiries proved the Congress to have been in the wrong) to correct his colleagues and co-workers. It is true that the Congress Working Committee had already sketched a plan of civil disobedience; but this plan was not to be enforced until Gandhi had explored with the Viceroy all avenues of maintaining peace. The Viceroy's reaction to the Mahatma's second telegram was sharp: he accused Gandhi of holding out threats of civil disobedience and warned him that

L*

he and the Congress would be responsible 'for all the consequences which may follow from the action which the Congress have proclaimed as their intention of taking'.

This exchange of telegrams caused much political excitement at the time; politicians and columnists fiercely debated whether the conflict could have been prevented if Lord Willingdon had agreed to see Gandhi. But the conflict was not caused by the refusal of an interview; its causes lay deeper in the inherent antagonism between the Congress and the Government.

It is difficult to resist the impression that by December 1931 many British officers felt that the truce with the Congress had been a mistake. A former member of the Indian Civil Service gives a peep into the mind of the British officers in the districts in such situations: 'In some ways, and certainly to many of the service, those periods when the fight was on were preferable to those which would follow when the leaders of the Congress would be released, and the district officer must make uneasy friends with those he had been fighting.'[1]

Throughout the period of the truce it seemed to most executive officers that the Congress was using the breathing space to consolidate its position and to prepare for another 'rebellion'. A wave of apprehension, almost of panic, appears during these ten months to have percolated from the bottom to the top. The District Officers warned the Provincial Governments of the 'deepening crisis' and sought assurances that they would be supported in taking appropriate action against Congressmen at the right time. The Provincial Governments asked the Government of India for assurances that they would be backed if they dealt firmly with what they viewed as 'a deteriorating situation'. The Government of India conveyed something of this apprehension to His Majesty's Government and sought permission to arm itself with an omnibus emergency powers ordinance and to act vigorously when the zero hour arrived.

Such being the temper of the Central and Provincial Governments and of local officers, only the intervention of His Majesty's

1 Woodruff, Philip: *The Guardians*, p. 248.

Government could possibly have staved off the crisis. Sir Samuel Hoare, the Secretary of State, had impressed Gandhi during the Round Table Conference with his extreme frankness; he had warned Gandhi that if the Congress tried to force the pace by 'direct action' the Government would crush it with all the force at its command. Gandhi had begged him to reconsider his position: 'It would be such a tremendous strain on both the communities, yours and ours, if you set yourselves to do it . . . But Sir Samuel what do you mean by a rebellion like this? Rebellion is not so terrible when it is completely peaceful.'[1]

Sir Samuel knew how unhappy Gandhi had been with the results of the Round Table Conference; Gandhi had assured him, however, that after his return to India he would strain every nerve to avoid a breach with the Government. The fabricated interview with Gandhi which Signor Gayada of *Giornale d'Italia* had broadcast from Rome had surprised Sir Samuel, but he had sought and obtained a repudiation from Gandhi while he was still on the high seas. Sir Samuel may have preferred peace to hostilities with Gandhi, but he had neither the will nor perhaps the strength to oppose the combined weight of official opinion in India; already he had approved plans of offensive against the Congress; now he gave permission to press the button which was to unleash a *blitzkreig* against the Congress.

[1] Lester, Muriel: *Entertaining Gandhi*, p. 134.

Chapter 37

TOTAL WAR

'IN the last fight,' Gandhi warned a mass meeting in Bombay soon after his return from England, 'the people had to face *lathis*, but this time they would have to face bullets.' He had sensed the mood of the Government, even though he did not know the thoroughness of its preparations to crush the Congress. Lord Willingdon had the reputation of a firm and hard-headed administrator, and had every intention of living up to it. The Governors in the Provinces shared his resolution to put trouble-makers in their proper places; many of them were ready, even impatient, to teach a lesson to an organization which, they believed, had flourished on half-hearted measures of the Government. Sir Frederick Sykes, the Governor of Bombay, had complained to Lord Willingdon soon after the latter's arrival in India in April 1931, of the 'disabilities' under which his Government had to fight the Congress campaign in 1930. In a letter to the Viceroy dated November 12, 1931, he urged 'a really rapid, organized and weighty handling' of civil disobedience when it was renewed. He wrote:

'The last thing I can conceive is that we should be justified in going slow until the movement gained strength. Above all we must select our weapons to fight the Congress and not fall into the mistake of doing what our opponents expect. I cannot do better than quote the views which the Commissioner of Police Bombay has recently expressed on the subject: "They (the Congress) rely on the traditional humanity of the British combined with their fear of international criticism to protect them from any really drastic action and they thus persuade us to fight this rebellion on their terms, and with methods chosen by them . . .

We cannot possibly embark on another campaign of this kind of warfare. It prolongs the agony and is undignified. Instead of fear which is the root of all decent government it begets contempt . . . It is in my opinion essential that the fact that the Government intends to treat a renewal of civil disobedience movement with the severity which a rebellion demands should be clearly demonstrated".'

It was Sir Frederick's Government which suggested that Gandhi should after arrest be deported to the Andamans or Aden; it was his Government which produced the first 'Civil Disobedience Manual' for the guidance of its officers in dealing with the movement. The introduction to this Manual contained a significant reference to public opinion: in the 1930-31 movement care had been taken not to alienate public opinion 'more than was absolutely necessary in the hope of inducing the more sober elements of the community to unite in opposition to the movement'. That hope had not been realized, and in the event of a renewal of the movement the District Officers were henceforth to assume that 'a large section of the public opinion will be antipathetic to the Government and primary attention should be given to crushing the movement before it gets fully under way'. Some of the instructions in this Manual reveal the determined mood of the administration. It laid down for example, that civil disobedience prisoners were as a rule to receive rigorous and not simple imprisonment; the directive applied to women 'unless they are of good birth and convicted of non-violent offences only'. Fines were to be imposed in all cases, except where recovery was doubtful. The maximum sentences were to be invoked for second offences for civil disobedience and action against children was to be taken under the Whipping Act or Reformatory Schools Act.

The Government of India and the Provincial Governments were thus resolved to give short shrift to the Congress. The plans for dealing with civil disobedience were pulled out of the 'top secret' pigeon-holes of the Secretariat and put into execution with lightning speed. Within a few hours of the arrest of Gandhi and the members of the Congress Working Committee on January 4, 1932, a series of ordinances were promulgated. Not only the Working Committee, but the Provincial Committees and innumerable local committees were declared illegal; a number of organizations allied with or sympathetic to the Congress, such as Youth Leagues, National Schools, Congress Libraries and Hospitals were also outlawed. Congress funds were confiscated; Congress buildings were occupied and almost every possible measure was taken to prevent the Congress from functioning. That the Ordinances were drastic and severe and covered almost every activity of Indian life was admitted in so many words by the Secretary of State in the House of Commons in March 1932.

By skimming off its leadership and freezing its funds, the Government hoped to demoralize the Congress. The powers acquired through the Ordinances included those which permitted the administration to control or forfeit any funds 'which were suspected of being held or used for the purposes of an unlawful association'; officials were authorized to examine account books, make inquiries or order searches. Even associations not directly connected with the Congress, but suspected of sympathy with it, such as the Gujerat Sabha and the Madras Mahajan Sabha, had their funds frozen. The Government went so far as to seek the intervention of the Secretary of State for India to stop the payment of royalties from Columbia Gramophone Company to the All-India Spinners Association for the sales of a record of a talk given by Gandhi during his stay in England.

A new prison policy was devised with the double purpose of deterring Congressmen from courting imprisonment and easing pressure on gaols. In a circular letter dated January 21, 1932, the Provincial Governments were advised by the Home Department of the Government of India to impose fines in lieu of imprisonment or, in addition to short terms of imprisonment, to prefer collective fines to prosecution of individuals, and to offer release (before trial and even after conviction) to those civil disobedience prisoners who undertook not to take any part in the movement. Gaol administration hardened perceptibly. The first Congress campaign (in 1930–31) had received a great impetus from the participation of women. In the second campaign (1932–34) treatment in gaols seemed to have been almost designed to scare away women. Mirabehn, Gandhi's disciple and the daughter of a former Admiral of the British Fleet, gave an account of the conditions in Arthur Road gaol which was a severe indictment of conditions in women's prisons. She noticed that women political prisoners were allowed to interview their children through iron bars. Her neighbours in this gaol were three criminals, two thieves and a prostitute; these criminals were not locked up for the night, while the political prisoners were.

One of the greatest anxieties of the Government during the truce period had been the penetration of the Congress influence in the country-side; difficult as it was to fight the middle-class nationalism in towns, the possibility of disaffection spreading in the peasantry seemed to the Government a more sinister threat. This is the most plausible explanation of the severity with which 'no-tax campaigns' in the rural areas were handled. These campaigns were conspicuous in Allahabad and Rae-Bareilly districts of the United Provinces and a few districts of Bombay, Bengal and Bihar and North-West Frontier Province. The India League Delegation which toured the country in 1932 recorded that in one tehsil in the U.P. 209 summonses had been issued, 298 attachments made and forty-four auctions effected. In Bombay Presidency, some of the movable property of Gandhi's Ashram at Sabarmati was attached; in Ras village the Delegation found that sixteen encampments containing armed police pickets encircled the whole cultivated area, and out of a total of 2,600 acres, 500 acres had been confiscated and sold and 900 acres had been seized but were waiting to be sold. Punitive police were stationed in refractory villages at the cost of their population; non-payment of taxes was punished with seizure and sale at nominal prices of animals and implements of peasants.

On reading a newspaper report about the expected irrevocable sales of confiscated lands by the Bombay Government, Gandhi addressed a letter to Emerson, who was Lord Irwin's Private Secretary and was now Secretary of the Home Department. Gandhi protested against the sales of land beyond recall. He added: 'I would like the legacies of bitterness to be left either by government officials or Congressmen to be reduced to the minimum if they cannot be avoided altogether.' Gandhi did not receive a reply, but the Home Member of the Viceroy's Council recorded his views in this file which give a good glimpse of the official attitude: 'The irrevocable sale of certain lands has probably had a greater effect than anything else in producing a return to normal conditions in Gujerat. It has made people realize that in the end it is the Government and not the Congress that controls the situation.'

A similar firmness guided the Government in its dealings with the Press. The initial success of the Salt Satyagraha campaign in 1930 was partly attributed in official circles to the publicity it had received. In 1932, by a series of drastic measures the freedom of the Press was curtailed. Apart from the prosecution of press correspondents, the forfeitures of securities from newspapers were used as deterrents. On July 4, 1932, just six months after the resumption of civil disobedience, the Secretary of State for India stated in the House of Commons that action had been taken under the Press Laws against 109 journalists and ninety-eight printing presses. In November 1932 the *Free Press Journal* of Bombay had its security of Rs. 10,000 forfeited and had to deposit a fresh security of Rs. 20,000: its offence was the reprinting of an article on untouchability from a 1930 issue of *Young India*. In Bengal even the proceedings of the Provincial Legislative Council could not be published if they contained criticism of the Government. A number of Provincial Governments made it an offence for a newspaper to publish photographs of Gandhi and other Congress leaders; the Madras Government went so far as to authorize certain magistrates to destroy the portraits of Congress leaders. Confronted with the risk of financial ruin and extinction on the one hand, and sullen acceptance of the stringent regulations on the other, it is not surprising that most newspapers chose the safer course.

Gandhi had meanwhile been lodged in the Yeravda Prison in Poona. The Bombay Government had not been able to persuade the Government of India to deport him from the Indian mainland nor to transfer him to some other province. Two of his closest colleagues, Vallabhbhai Patel and Mahadev Desai were lodged with him. The latter's diaries are a very full and lively record of Gandhi's life in gaol. The Mahatma knew enough to gauge the scale of the official offensive against his movement. Repression, he wrote to Sir Samuel Hoare, 'was crossing all legitimate limits'. Suffering was, however, an essential part of Satyagraha to purify those who invited it and to convert those who inflicted it. If the ordeal through which the country was passing was fiery enough, Gandhi hoped it would only burn out the dross. If people remained true to their pledge of resistance, no repression, however severe, could possibly crush them. From the new constitution which was being forged in England by British experts and Indian observers, Gandhi did not expect much. 'Why don't you accept half the loaf today?' asked Thomas, the Home Secretary to the Government of Bombay, who came to see him in gaol. 'I would,' replied the Mahatma, 'if it was bread and not stone.'

Gandhi was as busy in gaol as he had been outside. Prayers and spinning figured in the daily routine. He washed his clothes, dictated or wrote his heavy mail (one day he wrote as many as forty-nine letters), most of it to his 'family' in the Ashram. He warned his correspondents not to give publicity to his letters from gaol, which were treated as private. He read copiously, developed a keen interest in astronomy, and often gazed into the sky to decipher the 'Mysterious Universe'. He had his moments of relaxation, particularly when he exchanged sallies with the irrepressible Vallabhbhai Patel, whose barbed wit made him a delightful companion. Before long, however, a shadow came over this little group in Yeravda Prison—the shadow of a fast. The possibility of the untouchables being granted separate electorates in the new constitution had been weighing upon Gandhi's mind. On March 11, 1932 he wrote a letter to the Secretary of State for India in which he informed him that if his fears proved true, he would fast unto death.

Meanwhile, the Government of India and the Provincial Governments had reasons for satisfaction with the success which seemed to have attended the measures adopted by them to crush civil disobedience. The Congress had been in (what came be known later) a *blitzkreig* fashion suddenly deprived of its leaders, organization and resources. In January 1932 the Congress had been virtually caught napping. Except in the U.P. and N.W.F.P., where the sense of a crisis had persisted throughout the period of truce, the Congress rank and file expected that the political emergency would somehow be averted and the Mahatma would pull off a compromise to avoid a final breach with the Government. As Jawaharlal Nehru says in his *Autobiography,* it looked as if Congressmen 'entered unwillingly to battle'. The Government had acted with lightning speed not only in applying its carefully planned repression but in blocking publicity which alone could sustain popular morale and boost a nationalist movement.

In spite of this initial handicap, no less than 61,551 convictions for civil disobedience took place in the first nine months of the movement in 1932; this figure was a little higher than that of the campaign in 1930-31. Judged by convictions the movement was strongest in the U.P., Bombay, Bengal and Bihar (each of which contributed more than 10,000 prisoners), and the weakest in the Punjab. In the small N.W.F.P. there were 5,557 convictions, just half of those in Bombay Presidency. For the first four months the movement functioned with vigour; after that the number of convictions declined and except occasionally (such as in April 1932, when the Congress attempted to hold an annual session with Pt. Malaviya as President) the stream of civil resisters became a mere trickle.

By the end of 1932 the Provincial Governments and the Government of India were exchanging mutual felicitations on having attained a victory over the Congress; they would not, however, shed the special powers assumed under the ordinances earlier in the year. Through the Provincial Legislatures, which without the Congress Party were fairly obsequious bodies, the Government was able to pilot legislation the result of which was to adorn the ordinance with a constitutional stamp. The approval of the Ottawa Pact by the Central Legislative Assembly was another triumph for the Government, not only because it furthered Imperial commerce, but also because it was a slap in the face of the Congress which had called for non-co-operation with the Government.

There was to be no drawn battle this time, and for years to come Lord Willingdon was resolved not to accept from Gandhi and the Congress anything less than an unconditional surrender. He had decided to keep the Mahatma under a political quarantine. At the end of 1932, when Tej Bahadur Sapru and M. R. Jayakar were returning from the constitutional discussions in London, the Secretary of State suggested to the Viceroy that they should be allowed to see Gandhi in gaol. In a long cable dated January 4, 1933, the Viceroy opposed the suggestion:

'We (Governors and the Executive Council) recognize that the chief object of such an interview would be to show that we are not unreasonable and that we are giving Gandhi and the Congress every opportunity of co-operating in the new constitution; but we are of the opinion that such an interview could not fail to have very embarrassing results and would tend to destroy the favourable position achieved partly by the consistent policy followed during the last year and partly by the success of last Round Table Conference.

'. . . . The Congress is in a definitely less favourable position than in 1930, and has lost its hold on the public. If Congress recovers its position or even if any action such as the proposed interview is taken which conveys the impression that Government are trying to win over Congress to co-operate, it will have a most disheartening effect on the more moderate elements who under present conditions will, it is hoped, be able to assert themselves at the first election, and to give the new constitution a fair start. Already in at least two provinces, U.P. and Bihar and Orissa, such parties are being formed but they are not yet stable, and if Congress is restored to credit these newly formed parties would fail, Congress would again become predominant and would be back in a position to neutralize the safeguards so elaborately worked out at the Round Table Conference and wreck the new constitution . . .'

The Secretary of State, always anxious not to press his views on the Viceroy to the point of disagreement, could not, however, conceal his misgivings about the ultimate object of the policy outlined by the Viceroy. In a personal letter dated January 12, 1933 Sir Samuel accepted Lord Willingdon's views on the dangers of a 'spectacular amnesty' and particularly of Gandhi's release. 'At the same time,' he added: 'We would urgently ask you to send us your views as to what you contemplate is eventually going to happen. Rightly or wrongly, we feel that Gandhi is not in the least likely to make a formal retraction of civil disobedience. This view was confirmed by every one of the Round Table Conference delegates who talked to me about him. This being so, do you desire to keep him in prison for an indefinite time? We feel that if this is your view, it will be extremely difficult to maintain the position here during many months and perhaps years.'

The Viceroy and his advisers were fully able to visualize the Indian political scene without Gandhi and the Congress. Civil disobedience had been crushed; the Congress was demoralized and divided; the more moderate Congressmen might be expected to coalesce with other groups to work the new constitution to form a party which might be strong but not overwhelmingly so in the legislatures, thus causing no serious inconvenience to the Government. And the Congress weakened by defection of its right wing, and with Gandhi's prestige damaged, the risks of the revival of civil disobedience were reduced to the minimum. This was as satisfactory a prospect as the Viceroy and his advisers could contemplate in 1933. And it seemed to Lord Willingdon that this prospect could become a political reality by an inflexible attitude towards Gandhi.

The Viceroy's view of Gandhi's personality and politics did not err on the side of generosity. In a letter dated July 1, 1933 to the Secretary of State, he wrote: 'The leadership of Gandhi is being openly attacked both from the left and from the right, as having led Congress after fourteen years of constant struggle to a position perilously near failure. There are profound differences in Congress ranks as to the policy to be pursued and a general sense of despondency. The only man who might pull the Congress together is Gandhi. He realizes very clearly that his influence depends virtually on his relations with the Government. If he could produce the impression that the Government are prepared to treat with him, his influence will rise at once one hundred per cent.'

Passages like these make one doubt whether the Viceroy had the slightest understanding of Gandhi's make-up or philosophy of life. Eighteen years earlier, soon after Gandhi's return from South Africa, Lord Willingdon as Governor of Bombay had granted him an interview in the course of which he had asked him to come and see him whenever he contemplated any agitation against the Government.[1] That Gandhi had nothing to hide and had the courage to function in the open may have been Willingdon's view in 1915; as Viceroy in 1933 he had a different opinion. In the letter quoted in the preceding paragraph, he told the Secretary of State: 'It is very necessary throughout to view Gandhi as what he really is and not what he poses being, Gandhi is the most astute politician in India and the acknowledged leader of the party whose aim is independence, or at least a constitution with no effective safeguards, and which will place all real power in the hands of the Congress. The Congress may change its tactics, but they will never change their objects. It is vital that these considerations should be borne firmly in mind whatever may be the twists and turns of Congress manoeuvre.'

[1] Gandhi: *Autobiography*, p. 457.

The idea of Gandhi as a Machiavellian politician with the Congress as his pliable tool, extending his influence over the ignorant Indian public by contriving an interview with the Viceroy, was an incredible misreading of the Mahatma and the millions who obeyed his slightest nod. In his *Nine Troubled Years*, Sir Samuel Hoare (later Lord Templewood) rightly observes, 'If I made any criticism, it would be that Lord Willingdon did not, like Irwin, understand Gandhi's personality and on that score underrated his power.' Lord Willingdon's past experience as an administrator seems to have been more of a liability than an asset to him in his role as the Viceroy. The Indian problem struck him primarily as an administrative one, requiring timely and judicious use of coercion to crush trouble-makers. He was almost incapable of understanding the deep intellectual and emotional roots of the movement for political liberation: the enthusiasm it evoked, struck him as a variant of ignorant fanaticism. Little as he understood the springs of Indian nationalism, he understood Gandhi even less. Civil disobedience was a part of the Gandhian technique of Satyagraha, which sought to achieve changes in political as well as social spheres by organizing the masses non-violently, by offering resistance without retaliation, and non-co-operation without hatred. To Gandhi the non-violent basis of the movement was its most significant one; to Willingdon not only was the conscious moral superiority of Gandhi and his followers irritating, but a non-violent movement was the more insidious for the odium it brought on those who had the responsibility for keeping law and order.

In a speech to the Central Legislative Assembly on September 5, 1932 the Viceroy declared: 'The leaders of the Congress believe in what is generally known as direct action, which is an example of the application of force to the problems of politics . . . The fact that the force applied is as a rule not physical force in no way alters the essential characteristic of the attitude which at the present moment inspires Congress policy.'

Those who had spent a lifetime in governing India were

not to be taken in by the language of non-violence, however much it was flavoured with morality and religion. The fact that the British were being made to abdicate their authority in India by non-violent methods did not please those whose position was challenged. And in fairness to them, it must be admitted that many of them sincerely believed that India, with its welter of races and languages and internal divisions and defencelessness against foreign invasion, was not ripe for self-government.

Gandhi was often driven to the verge of despair by the wall of prejudice behind which British statesmen entrenched themselves. When he criticized their actions he was denounced as a demagogue; when he claimed to be their friend he was accused of hypocrisy. When he applied for an interview he was suspected of out-manoeuvring the Government; when he launched a campaign he was irreconcilable; when he circumscribed its scope or withdrew it he was alleged to have lost credit with his followers.

It was the object of Satyagraha—of which civil disobedience was one form—to penetrate this wall of prejudice. When reasoning failed voluntary suffering at the hands of the opponent was intended to melt his heart and to release the springs which hindered understanding. In practice this method of 'attack' on the opponent was not always easy nor quick in producing results. With their moral defences exposed, the British officials answered the challenge to their position with increased assertion and self-complacency. The successive civil disobedience movements, however, furthered the cause of Indian nationalism at least in two ways. They lifted the spell of fear which had enveloped Indian masses for nearly a century and a half, and they wore out, however slowly, British rigidity into scepticism and scepticism into fatigue. Administering a sub-continent in the best of conditions was for many civil servants an arduous enough task; in the face of tenacious opposition from vocal sections of the population, the task ultimately became almost an impossible one. In his preface to the report of the India League Delegation on the condition of India during 1932,

Bertrand Russell recalled the bitter legacy of Ireland: 'Who now attempts to justify the period of black-and-tan tyranny in Ireland? Who fifty years hence will have a good word to say for the present tyranny in India? No one. It is in our power to cause much misery, perhaps much moral deterioration; it is not in our power permanently to hold India by force.'

But we are anticipating events. By August 1932 Lord Willingdon and his advisers felt that under the hammer-blows of the Government civil disobedience had wilted. The number of convictions in a single month had come down from a peak figure of 17,818 in February 1932 to 3,047 in August 1932. The movement seemed to be at a low ebb; it was to receive a further setback from its author. The announcement of a fast by Gandhi, as a protest against the grant of separate electorates to untouchables, was to stir public opinion powerfully, but it was to divert it into non-political channels.

Chapter 38

HARIJANS

ON September 13, 1932, newspapers all over India carried a sensational announcement: Gandhi, still a prisoner in Yeravda Gaol, had decided to fast to death from September 20th, as a protest against the grant of separate electorates to the depressed (untouchable) classes in the new constitution. The correspondence between Gandhi on the one hand and British ministers on the other revealed that, unknown to the public, the crisis had been brewing for several months.

In March 1932, two months after his imprisonment, Gandhi had addressed the Secretary of State on the 'Communal Award' which was to lay down the quantum and mode of representation under the new constitution. He had argued that separate electorates would divide the Hindu community without doing any good to the depressed classes. He recalled, what he had said at the second Round Table Conference, that he would resist with his life the grant of separate electorates to the depressed classes. 'This was not said,' he assured Sir Samuel, 'in the heat of the moment or by way of rhetoric.'

When the Communal Award was published on August 17, 1932, it confirmed Gandhi's worst fears. In spite of the double vote given to the depressed classes, for their own separate constituencies as well as for the general (Hindu) constituencies, the fact remained that separate electorates were to be set up for these classes. Gandhi immediately wrote to the British Premier that he would embark on 'a perpetual fast unto death', which could only end 'if during its progress the British Government, of its motion or under pressure of public opinion, revised their decision and withdrew their scheme of communal (separate) electorates for the depressed classes'. The fast was to continue even if he was released. Three weeks later Ramsay MacDonald acknowledged Gandhi's letter 'with much surprise' and 'very sincere regret'. The Government's award, was, he explained, only an effort to weigh justly conflicting claims; only an agreement of the communities could supersede it with another electoral arrangement. Not content to question the justification of the fast, the British Premier went on to question Gandhi's motives: 'As I understand your attitude, you propose to adopt the extreme course of starving yourself to death not in order to secure that the depressed classes should have joint electorates with other Hindus, because that is already provided, nor to maintain the unity of Hindus, which is also provided, but solely to prevent the depressed classes, who admittedly suffer from terrible disabilities today, from being able to secure a limited number of representatives of their own choosing to speak on their behalf in the legislatures which will have a dominating influence over their future.'

This was an unkind cut, but it only revealed the lack of understanding on the part of the British Premier and his advisers of Gandhi's deeply emotional and religious approach to the problem. Their first impulse was to scent a political motive in the fast: Gandhi was trying a stunt to recover the prestige he had lost through the decline of civil disobedience. But Gandhi's interest in the depressed classes was neither a recent nor a temporary phase; it was rooted in his deep humanitarianism and dated back to his childhood. He came face to face with the evil of untouchability in his home; his beloved mother was devout but not devoid of the prejudices common among the *Vaishnava* Hindus. The children had orders not to 'defile' themselves by touching the family sweeper Uka, or by playing with 'untouchable' class-mates. Gandhi was an obedient child but he visibly chafed at these restraints; even at this early age he perceived the inconsistency between untouchability and the beautiful anecdotes of the sacred *Ramayana,* in which he had heard of the hero Rama being ferried across the Ganges by a 'low caste' boatman. As he grew this fellow-feeling with the lowliest of the low grew. In South Africa his associates belonged to all castes and communities. To the first Ashram he founded after his return to India he welcomed an untouchable family; this had outraged the wealthy merchants of Ahmedabad who had been contributing to the upkeep of the Ashram. Starved of funds, Gandhi and his companions had decided to move into the slums of Ahmedabad, but an anonymous donor had rendered this course unnecessary. The abolition of untouchability was included in the constructive side of the programme of non-co-operation. Untouchability was a recurrent theme in his speeches during his cross-country tours of the later twenties. During the discussions at the Round Table Conference, it hurt him to see the representatives of the untouchables play into the hands of communal and politically reactionary elements. How strongly he felt on this subject was revealed in his speech at the meeting of the Minorities Committee on November 13, 1931: 'I claim myself in my own person to represent the vast mass of the untouchables. Here I speak not merely on behalf of the Congress, but I speak on my own behalf, and I claim that I would get, if there was a referendum of the untouchables, their vote and that I would top the poll.

'We do not want on our register and on our census "untouchables" classified as a separate class. Sikhs may remain as such in perpetuity, so may Muslims, so may Europeans. Would untouchables remain untouchables in perpetuity?'

If the British ministers failed to fathom the depth of Gandhi's feeling on this subject they were even less able to see the ethics of fasting for the solution of what was to them a political problem. Fasting struck them as a thinly-disguised method of coercion. The British reaction to Gandhi's fasts was well exemplified in Low's cartoon as a 'Prophecy for 1933', in which Lord Willingdon was shown going on hunger strike at the instance of 10 Downing Street 'to force Mr Gandhi to admit the new constitution as touchable'. There was no Englishmen more willing or able to understand Gandhi than C. F. Andrews, but even he wrote to him (March 12, 1933) from Birmingham: 'I hardly think you realize how very strong here is the moral repulsion against fasting unto death. I confess as a Christian I should do it and it is only with the greatest difficulty that I find myself able to justify it under any circumstances.'

Gandhi, however, did not have to justify his fast to anybody except to his own conscience, or, as he put it, to his Maker. Fasting had a definite place in his discipline of life. A fast was sometimes the only way out for the agony of his soul. It could not be used without the deepest searching of the heart; not until 'the still small voice' had spoken in clear, unmistakable accents. But was it not possible that he could be mistaken? Could not his own conceit masquerade as an inner voice? Gandhi did not deny that he might be mistaken, but if he was, his death from voluntary starvation would be, he argued, a good riddance for those who had fallen under his false spell.

Was not the fast a form of coercion? Gandhi was aware that his fast did exercise a moral pressure, but the pressure was directed not against those who disagreed with him but against those who loved him and believed in him; he sought to prick the conscience of the latter and to convey to them something of his own inner anguish at a monstrous tyranny. He did not expect his critics to react in the same way as his friends and co-workers, but if his self-crucifixion could demonstrate his sincerity to them, the battle would be more than half-won. The fast dramatized the issues at stake; ostensibly it suppressed reason, but in fact it was designed to free reason from that mixture of inertia and prejudice which had permitted gross social iniquities to exist for centuries.

The news that Gandhi was about to fast shook India from one end to the other. September 20, when the fast began, was observed all over India as a day of fasting and prayer. At Santiniketan, Rabindranath Tagore, dressed in black, spoke to a large gathering on the significance of the fast and the urgency of fighting an age-old evil. There was a spontaneous upsurge of feeling; temples, wells and public places were thrown open to the depressed classes. A conference of leaders of caste Hindus and depressed classes was summoned to devise alternative electoral arrangements to replace those provisions of the British Award which had provoked Gandhi to offer the supreme sacrifice.

Meanwhile, the sands of time were running out. The Government were willing to remove Gandhi to a private residence in Poona under certain restrictions; but Gandhi preferred to fast in gaol. He took his last meal of lemon juice and honey with hot water at 11 a.m. on September 20; an hour later the fast began. The same evening he told Press correspondents that his fast was based on faith in his cause, faith in the Hindu community, faith in human nature itself, and faith even in the official world. 'My cry,' he added, 'will rise to the throne of the Almighty God.' Next morning he was taken to a segregated yard in the prison, where under the thick shade of a low mango tree he spent the day. Vallabhbhai Patel and Mahadev Desai were already with him; they were joined by Sarojini Naidu, who had been lodged in the women's gaol. The Government made a fine gesture by transferring Kasturba from Sabramati, where she was serving her term of imprisonment, to Poona to join her husband.

The Hindu Leaders' Conference met at Bombay. The leaders, who included Madan Mohan Malaviya, Tej Bahadur Sapru, M. R. Jayakar, Rajagopalachari, N. C. Kelkar, Rajendra Prasad and Moonje, were anxious for a quick solution. They had, however, to carry with them the leaders of the depressed classes, particularly Ambedkar, who was not only a stubborn advocate of separate electorates but fully conscious of his pivotal position: no solution to which he did not agree was likely to commend itself to the Government. Gandhi was the last person to allow the conference to be stampeded into a wrong decision. He sent a message to the assembled leaders through his son Devadas that he (Devadas) 'as his father's son was prepared to forfeit his father's life rather than see any injury being done to the suppressed classes in mad haste'. The conference considered a number of proposals; some of its members paid visits to Poona to discuss them with the Mahatma.

What with the progress of the fast and what with the strain of the negotiations, Gandhi's strength began to ebb quickly.

Ambedkar bargained hard; he was reluctant to give up separate electorates, which the Communal Award gave to his community, unless he received some counter-balancing advantages. Eventually, an agreement, popularly known as the Poona Pact, was reached; it doubled the representation for the depressed classes in the provincial legislatures but revised the electoral system. Voters from the depressed classes were to hold a primary election and to choose a panel of four candidates for each seat; these four candidates were to submit for election to a joint electorate of caste Hindus and untouchables. Reservation of seats was to continue until it was ended by mutual agreement, but the method of primary election was to lapse after ten years.

The agreement was reached none too soon. 'We are definitely of the opinion,' declared a board of doctors who examined Gandhi, 'that his condition portended entry into the danger zone.' Gandhi would not, however, break his fast until the Government set its seal of approval on the Poona Pact. Premier MacDonald hurried to London from Sussex, where he was attending the funeral of his aunt, and was joined by Sir Samuel Hoare, the Secretary of State, and Lord Lothian, the Chairman of the Franchise Committee. The British Cabinet accepted the Poona Pact and Gandhi broke the fast.

India could breathe again, but the saving of his own life was from Gandhi's viewpoint the least important aspect of his self-imposed ordeal. He made it known that he would fast again if the reform of untouchability was not relentlessly pursued and achieved within a measurable period. 'Regarding the agreement,' he declared, 'I assure my *Harijan* friends, as I would henceforth like to name them, that they may hold my life as a hostage for its due fulfilment.'[1]

The Poona Pact substituted one scheme of electoral representation of the depressed classes for another. The paradox, however, was that the new constitution, of which these electoral arrangements were a part, was not acceptable to Gandhi and the Congress. Critics also pointed to the extra weightage which the

[1] Pyarelal: *The Epic Fast*, p. 145.

revised arrangements granted to the depressed classes in the provincial legislatures; as against the seventy-one seats which the British Award had given, the Poona Pact conceded 148. Before long the Poona Pact was to evoke opposition in Bengal where the caste Hindu representation had been nibbled at one end by the Europeans and at the other end by the depressed classes. Gandhi, however, disliked this constitutional arithmetic; he felt that for all the wrongs they had done to their weaker brethren, the caste Hindus could never be too generous to them. The fast had at least one good result; it did away with separate electorates for the depressed classes. The insidious influence of this mode of representation as a wedge in Indian politics was to become fully visible in the next decade, and it was well that at least one crack in national life was closed in time.

More important, however, than these constitutional arrangements, which incidentally did not come into force for nearly four and a half years, was the emotional catharsis through which the Hindu community had passed. The fast had been intended, as Gandhi had avowed, 'to sting the conscience of the Hindu community into right religious action'. The scrapping of separate electorates was only the beginning of the end of untouchability.

Meanwhile, on September 29 the Government withdrew the special facilities which had been provided to Gandhi in prison for interviews and correspondence in connection with the anti-untouchability work. These facilities were, however, restored in November, partly because the Government feared that Gandhi might begin another fast, and partly because they sensed that Gandhi was in dead earnest and his concentration on social reform was likely to ease the pressure in the political sphere.

One of the greatest campaigns of social reform in history was thus launched by a state prisoner. Nobody knew better than Gandhi that an ancient tyranny could not be blasted overnight and that the results of the fast had to be followed up by work in the field and by propaganda. Under his inspiration an all-India organization was established with G. D. Birla as President and the indefatigable A. V. Thakkar as Secretary. From his prison cell Gandhi issued a series of Press statements and a stream of letters to his numerous correspondents to educate the public on the evils of untouchability. He arranged for the publication of a weekly paper, *Harijan*, to promote this campaign. *Harijan* means 'Children of God'; it was Gandhi's name for the untouchables: 'All the religions of the world describe God pre-eminently the Friend of the friendless, and Help of the helpless, and the Protector of the weak. Who can be more friendless or helpless or weaker than the forty million or more Hindus of India, classified as untouchables?'

A good chunk of the *Harijan*, as of *Young India*, was written by Gandhi himself. 'I was delighted,' Jawaharlal Nehru wrote to Gandhi from Dehra Dun Gaol after reading the first two copies of *Harijan*, 'to see the old rapier touch of overmuch kindness and inexhaustible patience which extinguishes, or as you say, neutralizes the opponent. I pity the poor *Sanatanists*. With their anger and abuses and frantic cursing they are no match for this kind of subtle attack.' The *Sanatanists* (orthodox Hindus) relied upon the texts of Hindu scriptures. Gandhi doubted whether there was any support in them for untouchability. As he wrote to Rajagopalachari: 'It is not our position that there is no untouchability at all in the *Shastras* . . . They (the orthodox) are expected to prove that untouchability as at present practised has sanctions in the *Shastras*. It is an impossible task to perform honestly.'

But even if it were possible to prove a sanction for this tyranny from some ancient manuscript, Gandhi would not have felt bound by it. Eternal truth could not, he asserted, be confined within the covers of a book, however sacred. Every scripture, he argued, had certain permanent elements—certain universal truths —but it also contained injunctions relevant to the contemporary society; the latter, if they did violence to human dignity, could be ignored.

Harijan took the lead in pulling out this skeleton in the Hindu cupboard. Even Miss Mayo, the author of *Mother India* (a book which Gandhi once picturesquely described as a 'drain inspector's chronicle') could not have been more assiduous in exposing this plague-spot of Hinduism. *Harijan* published graphic pen-pictures of 'the denizens of hell', the miserable habitations in which these outcasts lived. Their disabilities were listed at length. In some parts of the country they were denied access to village wells, water-taps, schools and post offices, and prevented from using umbrellas and wearing sandals. The menfolk could not wear a *dhoti* below their knee, and the womenfolk were forbidden to put on clean clothes or jewellery. They could not ride a horse or a cycle. If a caste Hindu passed in front of their house they had to bow in respect. In Southern India certain communities were condemned to remain invisible as well as untouchable. Some of these disabilities were rare; none of them was universal, but in sum they constituted a damning indictment.

Gandhi believed in conversion and not compulsion, 'so that the opponents of today might become the reformers of tomorrow'. He did not as a rule favour legal aids to fight social evils. His encouragement, at the beginning of 1933, to the introduction of temple-entry bills in the Central Legislature therefore looked some-what incongruous. He was still a prisoner; the Congress was an outlawed body and had withdrawn its representatives from legislatures. But such was his preoccupation with this reform and so impressed was he with its urgency that he was not averse to help from any quarter for a cause which was humanitarian in essence and above politics. The temple-entry bills were not, moreover, intended to enforce temple entry, but only to remove the legal bars which decisions of British courts, based not on statutory law but on religious usage, had created in certain parts of the country. Gandhi took the advice of constitutional experts like Jayakar and wrote to the Viceroy, but the official attitude was one of indifference if not positive obstruction. The Government of India did not want to alienate orthodox Hindu opinion to oblige the leader of the rebellion against the British *Raj*.

As Gandhi threw himself into the movement, he discovered that the evil was of a much greater magnitude than he had thought at first. The task of the reformer was stupendous. How was he to fight this age-old evil? How was he to convince his co-workers

M

that he was in dead earnest? How was he to acquire greater application and dedication for this great mission? Gandhi's anguish was brought to an end by 'a call from within' to embark on a twenty-one day fast from May 8, 1933: 'I had gone to sleep the night before without the slightest idea of having to declare a fast next morning. At about twelve o'clock in the night something wakes me up suddenly, and then some voice—within or without—I cannot say, whispers, "Thou must go on a fast." "How many days?" I ask. The voice again says, "Twenty-one days." "When does it begin?" I ask. It says, "You begin tomorrow." I went off to sleep after making the decision.'

Friends and physicians asked him if, by risking his life, he was not risking the cause which was so dear to him. His answer was characteristic: if God required more service from his body, even the fast would not dissolve it, and if the Harijans' cause was His own, he would throw up men and women to carry on the good work. On May 8, 1933, the first day of the fast, he was released and taken to 'Parnakuti', Lady Thackersy's house in Poona, where he went through the twenty-one day ordeal.

The civil disobedience movement had been suspended for six weeks immediately after Gandhi's release and on his advice. As soon as he recovered some strength, he telegraphed to the Viceroy a request for an interview 'to explore the possibilities of peace'. Lord Willingdon's reply was a polite rebuff. Gandhi was again arrested on August 1, and sent back to Yeravda prison. He was released three days later but confined within the limits of Poona City. He defied the order, was rearrested and sentenced to a year's imprisonment. Back in gaol, he commenced a fast on August 16, to protest against the denial of the facilities for the promotion of the campaign against untouchability which he had been receiving during his earlier incarceration. His condition deteriorated rapidly and he was released.

He was now faced with a curious dilemma. If he went back to gaol, the Government was likely to refuse him facilities for Harijan work; if he undertook a fast the Government might release him. This was a 'cat and mouse' game, to which he decided not to be a party. He announced his intention not to offer civil disobedience during the unexpired portion of his sentence of a year's imprisonment.

With this self-denying ordinance on his political activities, his energies were directed exclusively towards abolition of untouchability. In September 1933 he moved to Wardha and announced a gift of the Sabarmati Ashram to the Harijan Sevak Sangh. On November 7th he set out on a country-wide tour to promote the Harijan cause. During the next nine months he covered 12,500 miles, penetrating into some of the remotest parts of the country, which were off the beaten track of national leaders. He called on caste Hindus to purge themselves of prejudice against the Harijans, and he urged the Harijans to shake off the vices (drugs and drink) which hindered their absorption into Hindu society. He pleaded for the opening of temples to Harijans: 'temples are for sinners, not for saints; but who is to judge where no man is without sin?' He ridiculed the superstition that anybody could be unclean by birth, or the shadow or touch of one human being could defile another human being. Bathing was all very well, he told a village audience, but even buffaloes had long daily baths.

He wore himself out in making his collections for the Harijan Fund. In ten months he received eight lakhs of rupees. He could, if he had wished, have obtained this amount as a gift from a Maharaja or a millionaire, but he did not set much store by money as such. The millions of men, women and children who contributed to his begging-bowl became fellow-soldiers in the campaign against untouchability. He used every occasion and every situation for the education of the unsophisticated masses. When a girl in Malabar, which he described as the blackest spot on the untouchability map of India, took off her gold ornaments and presented them to the Harijan Fund he told her, 'Your renunciation is truer ornament than the jewellery you have discarded. A bangle for an autograph', he would bargain with women. 'Andhras are no Scotsmen,' he chaffed a Telgu audience to persuade the unwilling to untie their purse-strings. 'I am a

Harijan worker, my time is precious,' he scolded a palmist who offered to read his hand. 'Is there a cure for untouchability?' he asked a village doctor. In another village a woman barber was brought in to shave him. As she set about her job in a business-like way, Gandhi noticed she was loaded with gold and silver ornaments. 'What are these wretched things?' he said, 'they don't make you beautiful. Indeed they are ugly and harbour dirt.' The poor woman was visibly disappointed. 'I borrowed them especially for this occasion,' she replied. 'I could not come before you without good ornament.' Before leaving she had contributed her wages to the Harijan Fund.

The Harijan tour was by no means a triumphal progress. Gandhi was attacking an age-old tyranny and long-established vested interests, which did not stick at anything to preserve themselves. The *Sanatanists* accused him of a dangerous heresy; they organized black-flag demonstrations; they tried to heckle him and disrupt the meetings he addressed. This was no mere rowdyism but a deliberate strategy calculated to discredit the apostle of non-violence; if his followers retaliated in kind or summoned the police, Gandhi's embarrassment would have been completed. In May 1934, while he was at Puri in Orissa, he decided to cover the remaining itinerary in that province on foot. Though he was able to visit fewer villages, he felt he knew them better; he escaped the hustle and the terrific noises which were inseparable from his train and car journeys; moreover, by thus exposing himself to his opponents he hoped to disarm them.

On June 25th, while he was on his way to the municipal hall in Poona, a bomb was thrown at his party; seven persons, including the chief officer of the municipal committee, were injured, but Gandhi was unhurt. He expressed his 'deep pity' for the unknown thrower of the bomb. 'I am not aching for martyrdom,' he said, 'but if it comes in my way in the prosecution of what I consider to be the supreme duty in defence of the faith I hold in common with millions of Hindus, I shall have well earned it.'

In March 1934 he suspended his Harijan tour to visit Bihar,

which had been stricken by a terrible earthquake. Agatha Harrison, who accompanied Gandhi, recorded that the sights she saw were grimmer than those she had seen in Japan after the 1923 earthquake. On the victims of the earthquake, his presence seemed to act as a soothing balm. They gathered in their thousands to flank the roads on which his car sped past or to fill the railway stations through which his train passed. As they caught a fleeting glimpse of him they seemed to forget, for the moment, their own distress; they decorated their villages with bamboo arches and green foliage to welcome him. He asked them to bear the calamity with fortitude. 'I want no beggars,' he said; 'it would be deplorable if this earthquake turned us into mendicants.'

Gandhi drew his own lesson from the earthquake: it was a retribution for the sin of untouchability. Tagore protested against this interpretation, the unscientific explanation of physical phenomenon which encouraged elements of unreason. If the Mahatma could ascribe the earthquake to the sin of untouchability, could not his opponents maintain with equal force that the earthquake was God's vengeance for the heresy which he was preaching?

Gandhi was unrepentant. There was, he observed, an indissoluble marriage between matter and spirit. His reasoning, if it could be called reasoning, was that of a man of faith: 'To me the earthquake was no caprice of God, nor a result of the meeting of mere blind forces. We do not know the laws of God nor their working. Knowledge of the tallest scientist or the spiritualist is like a particle of dust. If God is not a personal being for me like my earthly father, He is infinitely more. He rules me in the tiniest detail of my life. I believe literally that not a leaf moves but by His will. Every breath I take depends upon His sufferance.'

In the course of this tour in Bihar, someone asked him, 'Is the God who sent the earthquake a heartless and revengeful deity?' 'No,' replied Gandhi, 'He is neither. Only His ways are not our ways.'

Tagore's protest articulated the misgivings of the urban-educated *élite,* which respected the Mahatma but was often baffled by his allusions to the inner voice and divine intervention. 'What can I say about matters I do not understand,' Jawaharlal Nehru had wired to Gandhi in May 1933, when the twenty-one day fast for self-purification was about to begin, 'I feel lost in a strange country where you are the only familiar landmark.' Srinivasa Sastri, with his customary frankness, remonstrated with Gandhi in a letter dated November 16, 1932: 'The expressions inner voice, and God's call and such like are becoming commoner than ever in your writing. As expressing your state of mind, they are quite proper. But these exalted phrases have been over-worked in the past. He who uses them incurs a risk. An old saying warns us not to take the name of God in vain. Neither may we take it too often.'

Summing up his impressions of the Harijan tour, Gandhi declared early in August, 1934, that 'untouchability is on its last legs'. He had quickened the conscience of the Hindus to the wrongs they were inflicting on the Harijans, and he had roused the Harijans to the consciousness of their rights. But the battle was by no means over. Not only were the orthodox, the *Sanatanists,* to be reckoned with, but a section of the Harijans, led by Ambedkar, impugned Gandhi's *bona fides.* Ambedkar had been a prominent figure at the Leaders' Conference which had framed the Poona Pact in September 1932, but before long he had second thoughts and denounced the new electoral arrangement and Gandhi's anti-untouchability campaign. It looked as if Ambedkar could not forget nor forgive the humiliations he had suffered in his village school where he had been made to sit outside the class-room. He was unsparing in his criticism of Gandhi, Hindus and Hinduism. 'If the Hindus wish to be one,' he wrote 'they will have to discard Hinduism.'[1] He viewed untouchability as a political and not as a social problem; he even argued against political freedom which, he feared, was likely to make caste Hindus more powerful and untouchables weaker. Ambedkar held out threats that Harijans would abandon Hinduism. Religion,

[1] Ambedkar: *What Congress and Gandhi Have Done To The Untouchables,* p. 187.

retorted Gandhi, was not a matter of barter; it would be odd if the souls of fifty million people were set up for auction.

Even though the opposition of the *Sanatanists* died hard, and even though militant Harijan leaders were critical, Gandhi had succeeded in piercing an ancient sore. In an article entitled 'The Revolution Is Over', Rajagopalachari wrote: 'Untouchability is not yet gone. But the revolution is really over and what remains is but the removal of the debris.' This was probably an optimistic verdict, but there is no doubt that the reformists had made a good beginning. The Congress Ministries in 1937-39 removed some of the legal disabilities of the Harijans, and untouchability itself became illegal in the constitution of free India. A social tyranny which had deep roots needed a continuous war on all fronts, legal, social and economic, and for many years to come.

Chapter 39

RETIREMENT FROM POLITICS

'EIGHTEEN months ago,' observed Lord Willingdon on October 13, 1932 in an interview, 'things were in a mess. I will guarantee that conditions are today 100 per cent better than they were then, and I go further and guarantee that the people of India are 100 per cent happier.' The Viceroy had apparently good reasons for this self-congratulation. The civil disobedience movement, after the first flush, had begun to decline: the number of convictions, according to official records, was 14,803 in January 1932, 17,818 in February, 6,909 in March and 5,254 in April. From 3,818 in May the figure had come down to 2,791 in September. Gandhi's fast against the grant of separate electorates to depressed classes diverted public attention from political to social issues, but it also broke the forced isolation of the Mahatma from the Indian people. For nearly eight months the Government had, by rigorous checks on interviews and correspondence, virtually sealed him off from his adherents; simultaneously it had set out to crush the contagion he had left behind. Newspapers had been forbidden to publish news about his movements; in certain provinces even his photograph could not be published or displayed. As the number of convictions for civil resistance fell, and the Congress, as an illegal body, functioned less effectively, it did not appear impossible to the optimists in the Government of India that in the course of a few years, perhaps months, Gandhi's name would be erased from the political map of India.

The emotional convulsion, particularly among the Hindu masses, which followed his fast in September 1932 revealed once again that Gandhi's personal prestige was beyond any damage which any temporal authority could hope to inflict. The

Government found it expedient not to deny facilities for interviews and Press statements to their distinguished prisoner; it was
not prepared to incur the odium of obstructing a settlement which
alone could save his life. During the tense week of the fast, when
the untouchability issue was dominant, there was hardly the
time or the urgency to discuss political issues. Nevertheless, after
he had broken the fast, Gandhi made a significant statement:
'No one would be more delighted than I would be to endorse
any worthy suggestion for co-operation by the Congress with
the Government, and with the Round Table Conference. I would
only emphasize and underline the adjective worthy. In spite of
my repeated declarations it is not generally recognized that by
instinct I am a co-operator.'

Lord Willingdon was determined not to parley with the
'naked fakir'; the back of the Congress was bent, but not yet
broken. Total war required total victory. Neither Shaukat Ali, who
had wired to 'his old chief', nor Sapru and Jayakar were allowed
to interview Gandhi; there was to be no repetition of the Gandhi-
Irwin Pact. Gandhi's hints on the possibilities of peace were
spurned, and the special facilities for carrying on from within the
gaol the campaign against untouchability were withdrawn during
the fast.

Gandhi demanded that these facilities should continue. After
an initial hesitation, the Government yielded; it was not only the
threat of a fast which made it yield. The Viceroy telegraphed to
the Secretary of State on November 9, 1932: 'It seems clear that
Gandhi himself intends to concentrate all his attention and
activities on the untouchability problem, and the question of his
making any advance in connection with civil disobedience will
presumably recede into the background. This development suits
us and I would certainly do nothing to disturb it. Gandhi himself
would probably prefer that the civil disobedience issue should for
the present be allowed to sleep and the fact that we are giving such
very full facilities in regard to the untouchability question, may
perhaps, by diverting attention, lessen the pressure you have in
mind.'

M*

That Gandhi's preoccupation with the campaign against un-touchability was complete was proved by the announcement in May 1933 of a three weeks' fast for 'self-purification'; his expla-nation for the fast baffled his friends no less than the Government. C. Rajagopalachari wired to Vallabhbhai Patel, Gandhi's con-science-keeper and fellow-prisoner in Yeravda gaol, that 'it was stupid to hope that *Bapu* may survive the ordeal, and that the tragedy would put back the clock for Harijans and the country'. 'I agree,' telegraphed Vallabhbhai Patel, 'that it is stupid to hope that he will survive this ordeal, but I am not one of the stupid lot. It is much more stupid, however, to try to persuade him to alter or abandon this resolve with any hope of success.'

Eight months earlier, Gandhi had been at death's door within a week of the commencement of his fast; the Government therefore took no risks and released him on May 8th, the first day of the fast. The same day he dictated a long statement on civil disobedience, advising suspension of the movement for six weeks: 'I can only say that my views about civil disobedience have undergone no change whatsoever. I have nothing but praise for the bravery and self-sacrifice of the numerous civil resisters, but having said that I cannot help saying that the secrecy that has attended the movement is fatal to its success . . .

'There can be no doubt that fear has seized the common mass. The ordinances have cowed them down . . .

'Now I would make an appeal to the Government. If they want real peace in the land, they should take advantage of this suspension and unconditionally discharge all the civil resisters . . . If there is will on the part of the Government, a *modus vivendi* can be found.'

Gandhi went through the three weeks' ordeal in a friend's house at Poona; he belied the fears of the Government, his associates and doctors, and survived the fast. While he was convalescing, leading Congressmen who were not in gaol assembled at his bedside in Poona to take stock of the political situation. The discussions showed that many Congressmen felt that the time had come to withdraw civil disobedience, though opinions differed on the manner and terms of the withdrawal.

However, Gandhi was authorized to explore possibilities of peace and to contact Lord Willingdon. Once again he was rebuffed: the reply from the Private Secretary to the Viceroy read: 'In reply to your telegram asking for an interview His Excellency has directed me to say that if the circumstances were different he would gladly have seen you. But it would seem that you are opposed to withdrawing civil disobedience except on conditions and that the interview you seek is for the purpose of initiating negotiations.'

After this rebuff events moved rapidly. Gandhi decided to resume civil disobedience, but to confine it to select individuals. He announced his intention to march from his Ashram at Ahmedabad to Ras a village in Gujerat, which had suffered much during the civil disobedience movement. On August 1st he was arrested, taken to Poona released and ordered to reside within the limits of Poona City. He defied the order, was rearrested and sentenced to a year's imprisonment. Back in gaol he began a fast on August 16th, because the Government declined to give him as a convict the same facilities for carrying on Harijan work which he had enjoyed as *détenu* during his last term in Yeravda gaol. The Government refused to be 'dictated' to. On the sixth day of the fast he was removed to the hospital, but when his condition became critical he was set at liberty. 'This discharge,' he declared, 'is a matter of no joy to me. It is a matter of shame that I took my comrades to prison and came out of it by fasting.'

As he lay in bed convalescing he brooded on his future course of action. If he courted imprisonment again, the Government might again refuse to grant him facilities for Harijan work. He could go on a fast and the Government might again release him rather than let him die in gaol. As as way out of this dilemma he announced that, for the unexpired portion of his one year's sentence, he would abstain from civil disobedience. It was a paradoxical, if not an altogether fantastic, situation in which the author of civil disobedience found himself; though out of the gaol for the next eleven months he was committed, of his own volition, not to defy the Government.

This sequence of events may have baffled the Government, but it drove some of Gandhi's closest colleagues to despair. Already in September 1932, by undertaking a fast on what seemed to many of them a side-issue, he had dealt a severe blow to civil disobedience; while the major political battle was still in progress, he had opened a second front on a social problem. His twenty-one day fast in May 1933 was entirely unconnected with politics, but on release he had suspended mass civil disobedience. The suspension was for six weeks, but the appeal to the Government for a reciprocal gesture sounded like overtures for peace. Two militant Congressmen, Subhas Chandra Bose and V. J. Patel, who were in Europe, openly declared that Gandhi as a political leader had failed, and that the time had come 'for a radical reorganization of the Congress on a new principle with a new method for which a new leader is essential'. The token revival of civil disobedience, confined to individuals, made little visible difference; the movement was henceforth alive more in theory than in practice. The final suspension of even individual civil resistance (except in Gandhi's person) should therefore have been no surprise, but Jawaharlal Nehru has recorded in his *Autobiography* how the news came to him in gaol with 'a stab of pain', and how he felt that the chords of allegiance that had bound him to Gandhi for many years had snapped. As time was to show, the chords between Nehru and Gandhi were strong enough for strains of this kind. The statement which Gandhi issued, while suspending the movement, had been avowedly drafted in answer to 'intense introspection, searching of heart and waiting upon God':

'This statement owes its inspiration to a personal chat with the inmates and associates of Satyagraha Ashram. More especially is it due to a revealing information I got in the course of conversation about a valued companion of long standing who was found reluctant to perform the full prison task preferring his private studies to the allotted task. This was undoubtedly contrary to the rules of Satyagraha. More than the imperfection of the friend, whom I love more than ever, it brought home to me my own imperfection. The friend said that he had thought that I was aware of his weakness. I was blind. Blindness in a leader is unpardonable. I saw at once that I must for the time being remain the sole representative of civil resistance in action.'

Satyagraha, he went on, was a 'spiritual weapon'; it was henceforth to be confined to one qualified person—himself. The statement was (to use Nehru's words) 'an amazing performance for a leader of a political movement'. Nevertheless the fact remained that the decision to suspend mass civil disobedience was inevitable; indeed it was overdue. The movement was at a low ebb even in the autumn of 1932 when Gandhi's fast on untouchability diverted attention from it. The Harijan work opened safer channels for activity, which not a few Congressmen were glad to use. The temporary suspension of mass civil disobedience in May 1933 nearly killed it; the revival of individual civil disobedience was to the Government, little more than a minor nuisance. It is, therefore, neither the fact of the withdrawal nor its timing which fully accounts for the anger or sorrow expressed by prominent Congressmen at the time. The harsh repression by the Government had temporarily numbed the country, but many Congressmen felt that if their leader's strategy had been determined less by moral and more by political considerations, the Government could have been embarrassed to a greater extent. Congressmen had accepted non-violence as a policy for wresting self-government from the British; they had agreed to eschew the use of physical force, but they chafed at the innumerable limitations with which the Mahatma encumbered himself. In May 1933 he had unambiguously condemned secrecy as inconsistent with Satyagraha. Yet so pervasive was the repressive apparatus of the Government that the alternative to functioning secretly was not to function at all.

The rank and file had been anxious for quick results. In 1920 the prospect of 'Swaraj within a year' had contributed to the popular upsurge behind non-co-operation; in 1930 and again in 1932 people expected civil resistance to be a short and swift affair. The popular conception of civil disobedience differed in essentials from that of Gandhi. For him civil disobedience was part of Satyagraha, and Satyagraha was a way of life applicable equally to personal, social and political problems. Though he described Satyagraha as a science, he also called it 'a science in the making'. There were no cut-and-dried solutions. The Satyagrahi had to seek the truth, stand by it, incessantly work for it and, if necessary, suffer for it. There were various forms of Satyagraha in application to politics, ranging from a token protest in the form of a one-day strike to a mass disobedience of iniquitous laws. The latter was a drastic course to which Gandhi resorted in 1920, 1930 and 1932 and 1942. But in the pharmacopoeia of Satyagraha there were other remedies, which might take more time but were equally efficacious. These modest remedies were grouped together as 'constructive programme' and included such activities as spinning, removal of untouchability and Hindu-Muslim unity. Thus, when Gandhi suspended mass civil disobedience, he did not suspend Satyagraha in its widest sense. To the intelligentsia, however, the constructive programme, as a substitute for civil disobedience, looked too anaemic. Curiously enough, the Government's view was the same as that of most Congressmen. It was the defiance of laws *en masse* or the non-payment of taxes which struck the Government as a real challenge; when Gandhi suspended civil disobedience and concentrated on his constructive programme, the political crisis seemed to be over.

A revolutionary movement, even when it was non-violent, could hardly be sustained indefinitely at a high pitch. Nearly 78,000 Congressmen had gone to gaol: thousands had sacrificed their personal fortunes and wrecked their health and homes for the cause. If the will to be free had been even stronger, the queue to the gaol would have been endless, and even the harshest repression would not have stopped the flow of Satyagrahis to gaol. Paradoxically, Gandhi's regret was not that more people had not gone to prison; numbers did not matter to him. His complaint was that even though the people had, on the whole, been non-violent, they had not inwardly ceased to harbour hatred against the British; even if a fraction of those who had opposed British rule had purged themselves completely of hatred, they would have induced a change of heart in their rulers. Four years after he had launched civil disobedience, the British had, if anything, become more bitter and suspicious of the Congress; and political terrorism was still alive. Gandhi came to the conclusion that his message of non-violence had not gone home and that the country needed further discipline in non-violence through the suspension of civil disobedience and its substitution by the constructive programme.

This reasoning was no more than specious obscurity to those Congressmen who believed that the failure of civil disobedience was not due to a qualitative defect in non-violence, but to the fact that, great as the response of the people was, the flow of civil resisters had dried up under official repression. Thoughtful Congressmen were sure that the sacrifices of the people had not gone in vain. In a note to Gandhi dated July 5, 1933, Dr Ansari answered the question whether the movement had failed:

'It used to be said of non-co-operation of 1920-21 that it had failed. How far it had failed was revealed when without any preparation the country was called upon to embark once more on the civil disobedience movement in 1930. The tremendous response that the Congress received from the people is the measure of success of non-co-operation. It is again said that the present civil disobedience movement has failed. But has it failed . . .? The marvellous spirit that the mass movement had at its inception cannot in the very nature of things sustain itself except for a short time.

'. . . Abandonment of the movement will not mean abandonment of methods as such . . . It would only mean that having fought long enough we prepare to rest.'

It was this feeling that the country, as represented by the Congress, needed a respite which made Gandhi's statement of April 1934 almost inevitable. The individual civil disobedience which had been in force since July 1933 had now been further restricted to Gandhi's person. Though there was no formal or final suspension of civil disobedience, the popular view was that the movement was over. The fact that Gandhi reserved for himself the right to offer civil disobedience was taken more as a verbal distinction than as an immediate political possibility. Discussions with Congress leaders convinced Gandhi that the country was fatigued and in no mood to continue civil disobedience, and that a section of Congressmen was keen on the revival of the Swaraj Party and on re-entering legislatures.

Gandhi had once been opposed to Congress participation in legislatures, but experience had revealed to him that a number of able Congressmen, who had no faith in the constructive programme, found the councils useful for self-expression when there was no mass movement. During 1924-25, Gandhi had tried to convert the council-wing, the Swarajists; in 1934-35, he encouraged the revival of this wing. The resolution on council-entry at the All-India Congress Committee meeting at Patna (May 1934) was moved by Gandhi himself. This generous appreciation of the Swarajist view-point spared the Congress the feuds which in 1924 had brought it to the verge of a schism; it laid the foundations of the electoral victory of the Congress in 1937. It required much courage and magnanimity on Gandhi's part to give full scope within the Congress organization to a group whose outlook he did not personally share.

Among those who doubted the wisdom of this step was Vallabhbhai Patel, to whom Gandhi explained the reasons for supporting the parliamentary group: 'The revival of the Swaraj Party was badly needed. The group which has stood so many vicissitudes does need a niche in the Congress. May be there is an element of inexperience and self-interest among those who are in favour of revival of this group. But we have to accept the facts. We can reform this group; we can control it; we can do nothing more and nothing less. I have helped the Swarajist Party to stand on its feet. They had the desire to contest elections, and to return to legislatures but did not have the courage to do so.'[1]

On June 6, 1934 the Government of India announced that, since civil disobedience had been formally discontinued and as a

[1] Letter to Sardar Patel, dated 23rd April, 1934, in collection edited by Manibehn Patel, Ahmedabad, 1952.

practical policy it could be regarded as having already ceased to exist, the notifications declaring the constituent parts of the Congress organization illegal were being withdrawn.

This announcement certainly breathed the air of triumph which the Government felt at the voluntary withdrawal of civil disobedience. The suspension of the movement and the revival of the Swaraj Party were measures which made many Congressmen feel unhappy; they seemed to them a poor reward for the sacrifices which they had undergone and almost a recognition of defeat. Gandhi was aware of this feeling of frustration of which perhaps the strongest expression came in a letter from Jawaharlal Nehru, who wrote of his 'spiritual isolation' and complained of the toning down of Congress ideals. Gandhi's answer was that the ideals had not changed: 'I am the same as you knew me in 1917 and after. I have the same passion that you know me to possess for the common good. I want complete independence for the country in the full English sense of the term. And every resolution that has pained you has been framed with that end in view . . . But I fancy that I have a knack for knowing the need of the time. And the resolutions are response thereto . . .[1]

When such explanations were necessary to his closest colleagues, it is not surprising that Gandhi was misunderstood by the rank and file. The conviction grew upon him that some of his followers had tired of his methods and views and that they pretended to accept policies with which they really differed; that his personality was unfairly dominating the Congress and interfering with its democratic spirit. He felt that he owed it to himself and to his followers not to strain their loyalty unduly. The suspension of civil disobedience and the revival of the Swaraj Party were not the only issues. There were other differences of outlook which were glossed over or bridged temporarily during the mass struggle against the Government. His renewed emphasis on the spinning-wheel as 'the second lung of the nation' seemed misplaced to many as was his moral and religious approach to the removal of untouchability. He himself viewed with misgivings the nascent

[1] Letter dated August 17, 1934, quoted in Tendulkar's *Mahatma*, Vol. III.

Socialist group which he described as a body of 'men in a hurry'.

It was on the crucial issue of non-violence, however, that he felt most deeply the differences between himself and the intelligentsia in the Congress. After fifteen years of preaching and practising non-violence, it almost hurt him to see how little it was understood by those who professed to follow him. Mass civil disobedience had struck the imagination of Congressmen but this was only one aspect of his non-violent technique. There was another aspect, the constructive programme, which he now stressed, and which seemed strangely unpolitical to many Congressmen.

It was this divergence in outlook that drove Gandhi to retire from the Congress in October 1934. 'I do not leave the Congress in anger or in huff nor yet in disappointment,' he wrote to Vallabhbhai Patel. He was restoring freedom to the Congress; he was also regaining freedom of action for himself. Henceforth, at least for the next three years, not politics but village economics were to be his dominant interest.

Chapter 40

RURAL ECONOMICS

THE Bombay session of the Indian National Congress in October 1934, which formally registered Gandhi's retirement from that organization, also authorized the formation, under his guidance, of the All-India Village Industries Association. This Association, 'unaffected by and independent of the political activities of the Congress', was to work for the revival and encouragement of the village industries and the moral and physical advancement of the village. The resolution was an index of the new orientation that Gandhi was giving to his own activities and those of the Congress.

Ever since Gandhi entered Indian public life in 1915, he had been pleading for a new deal for the village. The acute pressure on land and the absence of supplementary industries had caused chronic unemployment and under-employment among the peasants whose appalling poverty never ceased to weigh upon Gandhi's mind. His advocacy of the spinning-wheel derived from its immediate practical value as a palliative. The All-India Spinners Association, to which he had given a good deal of his time during the years of political quiescence, had in a period of ten years extended its activities to 5,300 villages, and provided employment to 220,000 spinners, 20,000 weavers and 20,000 carders, and disbursed more than two crores of rupees in Indian villages. These figures may not seem impressive today in the context of large-scale state-sponsored planning, but they represented solid work on the part of an organization often against heavy odds.

Nobody knew better than Gandhi that the All-India Spinners Association had only scratched the surface of the problem of rural poverty, but he began to think and plan for the revival of the village economy as a whole. His Harijan tour had revealed to him how, with the decay of village industries, Harijans had sunk deeper and deeper into poverty; the reform of untouchability was thus linked with the economic amelioration of these unfortunate people. The revival of village industries thus acquired a new urgency. The *Swadeshi* cult, which insisted on the use of articles made in India and had swayed the country during periods of intense political excitement, received a new twist in the nineteen-thirties. It was not enough, argued Gandhi, that an article should be of Indian origin; it was equally important that it should be made in a village. He appealed to town-dwellers to examine each article of daily consumption which was manufactured in India or abroad, and to find a substitute for it from the village. The broom could do duty for a brush; a 'kikar' tooth-stick for a tooth brush; hand-pounded rice for factory-polished rice; 'gur' for factory sugar, and hand-made paper for the products of the paper mills. Village products might sometimes cost more, but they distributed wages and profits among those whose need was the direst. For nearly 150 years, the cities had drained villages of wealth and talent. 'For the city dweller,' wrote Gandhi, 'the villages have become untouchable. He does not know them; he will not live in them, and if he finds himself in a village he will want to reproduce city life there. This would be tolerable, if we could bring into being cities which would accommodate thirty crores of human beings.'[1]

Since eighty-five per cent of the population of India lived in villages, their economic and social resuscitation was a *sine qua non* for freedom from foreign rule. Gandhi described the exploitation of the village in the interest of the town as a species of violence. The growing gap in economic standards and social amenities between the village and the town had to be bridged. This could best be done by volunteers from the towns who spread themselves in the countryside to help revive dead or dying rural industries and to improve standards of nutrition, education and sanitation. Gandhi expected these public-spirited men and women to

[1] Gandhi, M. K.: *Cent Per Cent Swadeshi*, p. 18.

support themselves on 'a village scale'; if they put on their work a price which villages could not sustain, village economy would face bankruptcy. Voluntary work alone could overcome the financial hurdle which made official programmes of rural uplift a snail-pace affair. A striking example was quoted by Mahadev Desai in *Harijan* of September 11, 1937: Chandranath, a man innocent of higher education, but fired with zeal of constructive work, enlisted the voluntary labour of 15,000 villagers and completed a canal three miles long and a roadway of equal length. The official estimate for this project, added Mahadev Desai, was Rs.50,000.

It was not Gandhi's habit to preach what he did not practise; he decided to settle in a village. He could have gone to his native Gujerat, but he had a number of devoted workers in that province. Maganwadi, near Wardha, was suggested, but it was a large village and did not present the difficulties which workers would face in small and undeveloped villages. His choice eventually fell upon Segaon, which was also situated near Wardha but had only a population of 600 and lacked such bare amenities as a *pucca* road, a shop and a post office. Here, on land owned by his friend and disciple Jamnalal Bajaj, Gandhi occupied a one-room hut. Those who came to see him during the rains had to wade through ankle-deep mud. The climate was inhospitable; there was not an inhabitant of this village who had not suffered from dysentery or malaria. Gandhi himself fell sick but was resolved not to leave Segaon. He had come alone; he would not allow even his wife to join him. He hoped he would draw his team for village uplift from Segaon itself, but he could not prevent his disciples, old and new, from collecting round him. When Dr John Mott interviewed him in 1937, Gandhi's was the solitary hut; before long a colony of mud and bamboo houses grew up. Among its residents were Prof. Bhansali, who had roamed in forests naked and with sealed lips, subsisting on *neem* leaves; Maurice Frydman, a Pole, who became a convert to the Gandhian conception of a handicraft civilization based on non-violence; a Sanskrit scholar who was a leper and was housed next to Gandhi's hut so that he could tend him; a Japanese monk who (in Mahadev Desai's words) worked like a horse and lived like a hermit. No wonder that Vallabhbhai Patel called Segaon a 'menagerie'. Gandhi referred to it as the 'Home For Invalids'.

Sevagram (as Segaon was 'renamed) was not planned as an Ashram; Gandhi never conceived it as such and did not impose any formal discipline upon it. This motley group consisting of men and women of vastly dissimilar temperaments and attainments, bound to him by varying degrees of respect or affection and by the common ideal of service to the village, constituted a human laboratory which gave him, in the words of Mahadev Desai, 'enough exercise in the practice of ahimsa (non-violence) in the domestic field. Its successful practice would mean its automatic extension to the political field. That is why he always longs to get back to his laboratory in order to be free for more self-examination and more experimentation. The difficult instruments make his immediate task more difficult is true, but it is also true that they make him all the fitter for the larger task'.

Before long, Sevagram became a centre of the Gandhian scheme of village welfare. A number of institutions grew up in and around it to take up the various strands of economic and social uplift. The All-India Village Industries Association, with its headquarters at Maganwadi, supported and developed such industries as could easily be fostered in the villages, required little capital and did not require help from outside the village. The Association set up a school for training village workers and published its own periodical, the *Gram Udyog Patrika*. There were other organizations such as the Goseva Sangh, which sought to improve the condition and breed of cows, and the Hindustani Talimi Sangh, which experimented in Gandhi's ideas on education.

To rid India's seven hundred thousand villages of poverty, disease and ignorance was a colossal task and required a multi-sided effort. Fostering village industries could create employment and pump purchasing power into the villages; it could also shake the villagers out of their lethargy. 'The 400 adults of Segaon,' wrote Gandhi, 'can easily put ten thousand rupees annually into their pockets if only they would work as I ask them. But they won't. They lack co-operation; they do not know the art of intelligent labour, they refuse to learn anything new.'

Gandhi felt that the villagers could be educated out of this inertia by bands of selfless workers 'infiltrating' into the villages, helping the villagers to revive village industries, running village schools, improving sanitation and popularizing a balanced diet. Labour and material were available in the village; they had only to be harnessed in its service.

'How to turn waste into wealth', was how Gandhi summed up the objects of the All-India Village Industries Association to Lord Farringdon who visited him. Gandhi explained that his programme did not cover rural indebtedness, because 'it requires state effort. I am just now discovering things people can do without state aid. Not that I do not want state aid. But I know I cannot get it on my terms'.

Among the things which villagers could do, but often failed to do, was to keep their villages clean. Gandhi attributed this to the untouchability complex, 'to the fear of touching our own dirt and, therefore, of cleaning it'. He exhorted everyone to be his own 'scavenger', to join in a campaign to keep village tanks and wells and streets clean, and to remove the cause for that reproach of Lionel Curtis that Indian villages were 'dung heaps'.

Nutrition was another problem on which Gandhi wrote and spoke frequently. Ever since his student days he had experimented on himself with foods and fasting. Nutrition took on a new urgency as a problem of the Indian masses, when he realized with something of a shock that apart from their poverty their food habits were responsible for their undernourishment. The deficiency in vitamins was inexcusable, when green leaves were available for the picking. He appealed to Indian scientists to pursue research into Indian diets in the context of Indian conditions: 'It is for you to make these biological experiments. Don't say off-hand that Bengalis need half a pound of rice every day and must digest half a pound. Devise a scientifically perfect diet for them. Determine the quality of starch required for an average human constitution.

I would not be satisfied until I have been able to add some milk and milk fat and greens to the diet of our common village folk. I want chemists who would starve in order to find an ideal diet for their poor countrymen. Unfortunately our doctors have never approached the question from the humanitarian standpoint at any rate from the poor man's standpoint.'[1]

'As a practised cook,' he wrote on the modes of cooking which did not destroy the nutritive value of foods and on the superiority of hand-ground wheat and hand-polished rice to the factory products. 'The textile mills,' he explained, 'had brought un-employment in their wake, but rice and flour mills have also brought in undernourishment and disease.'

It was obvious to Gandhi that rural India could not be trans-formed without the help of the urban intelligentsia. To make the country village-conscious he advised the Congress to hold its annual sessions in villages. The Faizpur Congress was the first to be held in a village; Gandhi noted that the session was free from the scramble and hustle inevitable in big towns, that village hedges could do duty for barbed wire, and exhibitions of village handicrafts could entertain as well as instruct.

He interpreted every problem in terms of the needs of the village. The educational system had always struck him as inadequate and wasteful. The vast majority of the people had been denied the rudiments of education; but even those who went to village primary schools soon unlearnt what was taught them because it had little to do with their daily lives and environ-ment.

The medium of a foreign language at the high school standard had created a barrier between the millions in the villages and the few thousands of the upper crust of the society. It was to evolve a system of education which suited the real needs of the people that Gandhi summoned a meeting of educationists and the education ministers from the Congress-governed provinces. The system of 'Basic Education' which evolved from these discussions was to evoke much controversy, but it definitely provided a corrective

[1] *Harijan*, March 22, 1935.

to the stereotyped ideas along which education departments were working in India.[1]

Work in the villages was an arduous and slow affair; it was 'plodder's work', as Gandhi put it. It did not earn banner headlines in the Press and did not seem to embarrass the Government. Many of Gandhi's colleagues did not see how this innocuous activity could help India in advancing to the real goal—that of political freedom. Gandhi was accused of sidetracking the main political issue; his answer was: 'I do not see how thinking of these necessary problems (of village uplift) and finding a solution for them was of no political significance and how any examination of the financial policy of the Government has necessarily a political bearing. What I am asking the masses to do is such as can be done by millions of people, whereas the work of examining the policy of our rulers will be beyond them. Let those few who are qualified do so. But until these leaders can bring great changes into being why should not millions like me use the gifts that God has given them to the best advantage. Why should they not clean their doors and make of their bodies fitter instruments?'[2]

It is interesting to reflect that the first reaction of the Government to Gandhi's village uplift work was to consider it a well-laid plan to revive civil disobedience on an unprecedented scale with the support of the rural masses; a circular was in fact issued to the Provincial Governments by the Government of India in 1934 to be on their guard and to carry on counter-propaganda in the villages.

A more serious criticism of Gandhi's village work was that he was turning his back on science and industry and advocating a primitive economy which would perpetuate poverty. In *Hind Swaraj*, Gandhi had mercilessly criticized machinery, mills and industrial civilization, but during the next forty years of his life he further elaborated his ideas on machinery, relating them to his fundamental doctrine of non-violence. His principal objection to mechanization was that it tended to concentrate the production

---

[1] For details of Basic Education, see the following chapter: 'Congress in Office'.

[2] *Harijan,* January 11, 1936.

of wealth in a few hands. In a country where the hands were too many and the work too little, machinery could only add to unemployment and poverty. 'I would favour,' he had written in 1921, 'the use of the most elaborate machinery if thereby India's pauperism and resulting idleness could be avoided.' There was a distinction in his mind, however, between mass production and production for the masses; the former under free enterprise often made the rich richer and the poor poorer. He was not opposed to machinery as such. Even his beloved spinning-wheel was machinery, but it was 'machinery reduced to the terms of the masses'. He welcomed simple tools and instruments which 'lightened the burden of the millions of cottages' without atrophying the limbs of man. He also recognized that some of these comparatively simple machines, such as sewing machines required factories for their manufacture. 'I am socialist enough to say,' he added, 'that such factories should be nationalized or state-controlled. They ought only to be working under the most attractive and ideal conditions, not for profit but for the benefit of humanity, love taking the place of greed as motive.'

Mahadev Desai has recorded an interesting discussion which Charlie Chaplin had with Gandhi in London in 1931. 'Supposing you had in India the independence of Russia, and you could find other work for your unemployed and ensure equitable distribution of wealth, you would not then despise machinery?' asked Chaplin. 'You would subscribe to shorter hours of work and more leisure for the worker?' 'Certainly,' replied Gandhi.[1] It is true that Gandhi's opposition to industrialization was based to a large extent on the evils it brought in its train—displacement of labour and concentration of wealth—but an equally important consideration in his mind was the effect such an economic organization had on the social structure. Decentralization of production in thousands of villages was closely linked with the decentralization of political power which was basic to Gandhi's ideal of a non-violent society. Only in small communities, producing for their local needs and

[1] *The Nation's Voice,* edited by C. Rajagopalachari and J. C. Kumarappa, p. 129.

free from glaring inequalities, could there be a genuine democracy based on human rather than material relationships. Exploitation of the many by the few within a country, and of the backward peoples by colonial powers, had been accelerated by the industrial revolution in the West. In a highly industrialized society, the economic and political structures seemed to take increasingly the pyramidal shape and militarism became a greater menace than ever before. A non-violent society had to be so organized as to reduce the inequalities and tensions within it and to remove the temptations for an assault from without. Such a society had to be based on a decentralized economy. 'You cannot build non-violence on a factory civilization,' wrote Gandhi, 'but it can be built on self-contained villages. Even if Hitler was so minded he could not devastate seven hundred thousand non-violent villages. He would become non-violent in the process. Rural economy, as I have conceived it, eschews exploitation altogether and exploitation is the essence of violence. You have, therefore, to be rural minded before you can be non-violent.'

Gandhi's picture of the ideal Indian village was of a 'republic', independent of its neighbours for its vital wants, yet inter-dependent in other ways, growing its own food and cotton and (if surplus land was available) money crops. As many as possible of its activities were to be on a co-operative basis; it was to have its own theatre, school and public hall; elementary education was to be free and compulsory; an elected 'panchayat' was to decide disputes; guards selected by rotation from a register were to police the village.

The image of this 'perfect democracy based on individual freedom' could be dismissed as utopian, but to Gandhi it was the only form a non-violent society could take. He did not care what label was applied to his ideas. Indian socialists, who by 1935 were a strong wing within the Congress, sometimes criticized him. Gandhi claimed that he was a socialist long before many Indian socialists had avowed the creed. 'But my socialism,' he wrote, 'was natural to me, and not adopted from any books. It came out of my unshakable belief in non-violence. No man could be actively non-violent and not rise against social injustice wherever it occurred.'

He did not accept the inevitability of class war or of violence; he believed his non-violent technique could end social injustice no less than foreign rule. By eschewing force, his socialism did not become a pious futility; in spite of its humanitarian and ostensibly gentle methods, it had revolutionary implications. Unlike capitalists and socialists, he considered property as an evil; he saw the unreality of the debate about ownership of property which had little relevance for millions of people who were no more than at a subsistence level, if not below it. Addressing the women of India he said: 'Let them remember that millions of men have no property to transmit to posterity. Let us learn from them that it is better for the few to have no ancestral property at all. The real property that a parent can transmit to all equally is his or her character and educational facilities.'

If he tolerated the institution of property, it was not because he loved it or considered it essential for the progress of humanity, but because he wished to abolish it with the non-violent technique. Gandhi would have vested the ownership of property neither in the individual nor in the state but in God. Those who had the possession of property were thus to consider themselves as trustees; but they were not to be its primary, let alone exclusive, beneficiaries. No one was to keep more to himself than he needed; everyone was to work according to his capacity and to receive according to his real need. This theory of trusteeship might seem a rationalization of the privileged position of the princes, landlords and business magnates. In fact, it was a radical theory which called for voluntary sacrifices from the 'haves' in the interest of 'have-nots'.

A model landlord of Gandhi's conception: 'would at once reduce much of the burden the ryot is now bearing. He . . . will reduce himself to poverty in order that the ryot may have the necessaries of the life. He will study the economic conditions of the ryots under his care, establish schools in which he will educate his children side by side with those of the ryots. He will purify the village well and the village tank. He will teach the ryot to sweep his roads and clean his latrines by himself doing this necessary labour. He will throw open without reserve his own gardens for the unrestricted use of the ryot. He will use as hospital, school or the like, most of the unnecessary buildings which he keeps for his pleasure.'[1]

How were the propertied few to be persuaded to subordinate their own greed to the good of the community as a whole? The first step was to reason with the rich; if argument failed non-violent non-co-operation was to be invoked. Just as no government could survive for long without the co-operation, willing or forced, of the people, economic exploitation was impossible without the active or passive acquiescence of the exploited.

Gandhi did not seek refuge from hard realities into the safety of a rigid doctrine. His ideas were evolved in response to the social and economic conditions around him. He had once criticized Indian socialists, but as years passed the latter saw that their ideas were present in the Gandhian programmes, though sometimes under a guise which they did not readily recognize. Gandhi was not a theorist, but a practical man, dealing with practical problems. In pre-independent India he had to function without the help of the Government and often in the face of its opposition. The problems of poverty, disease, ignorance and inertia did not admit of being postponed to a distant date when the millennium would come into being.

It was all a question of perspective; those who had learnt to think of India in terms of the economics they learnt at the university or in the seminars of political parties were not always able to appreciate the real problems of India. As early as 1911, Keynes, while reviewing the *Economic Transition in India,* wrote: 'Sir Theodore Morrison [the author of the book] argues too lightly from the West to the East without a full enough consideration of the deep underlying factors upon which depends the most advantageous direction of the resources of the nation ... The mills of Bombay and Calcutta figure too much in the public eye.'

[1] *Young India,* December 5, 1929.

Keynes went on to say that these mills hardly influenced the general well-being of India which could be improved only by applying the brains and the capital of new India to her fields and villages. The central idea in Gandhi's mind was to relieve the grinding poverty which stalked the village; he shrank from the idea of further pauperizing the village for the greater prosperity of a few big towns. Rather than turn the wheels of a few gigantic plants, he wished the hundreds of thousands of cottages in the country-side to hum with activity, to cater to their own needs, as well as to send their wares to the towns. If in Switzerland and Japan work and wages could be carried to thousands of cottages, why could it not be done in India?

In one important respect conditions in India differed from those in other countries; an alien government had neither the incentive nor the organization to undertake radical changes in the country's economy. When Gandhi had torn himself away from politics to work in the villages, the Government even suspected him of an astute and deeply-laid plan to prepare the rural masses for a country-wide civil disobedience campaign.

Two and a half years later, the wheel was to come full circle; the new constitution was scheduled to come into force from April 1, 1937. Gandhi had seen the new constitution being beaten into shape and had never had a high opinion of it. But as the elections drew near, he wondered whether this constitution, its limitations notwithstanding, could be used to improve the lot of the people.

Chapter 41

CONGRESS IN OFFICE

IN 1937, with the coming into force in the provinces of the new constitution, a new field opened for constructive work for the Indian National Congress under Gandhi's inspiration.

The new constitution which was enacted by the British Parliament in 1935 and came into force in 1937 embodied the policy of self-government for India by measured stages. The Indian Reforms Act of 1919 had contained a provision for a review of the constitutional field after ten years. Though discussions were initiated two years earlier than scheduled with the appointment of the Simon Commission in 1927, nearly a decade was to lapse before the next instalment of reforms was actually granted. For ten years Indian politics were rocked by nationalist discontent and witnessed two major civil disobedience campaigns while a series of official conferences and commissions hammered out the details of a constitution.

In Britain the 'Indian Question' aroused a fierce political controversy. Winston Churchill led the opposition to Indian self-government, which he denounced not only as a betrayal of the British Empire but of the Indian peoples whose future was, in his view, safer in the hands of British officials than those of Indian politicians. He had poured scorn on Lord Irwin for parleying with Gandhi. Lord Willingdon's strong-arm policy pleased him but he wanted the Government to consolidate its 'victory' over the nationalists by refusing to relax the Imperial authority in India. Sir Samuel Hoare who, as Secretary of State for India in the British Cabinet, had to pilot the new constitution through Parliament and to bear the brunt of Churchill's opposition, has analysed its springs: 'The splendid memories gathered round the

Indian Empire blinded him to the changes that had come about since the days of Clive, Wellington, Lawrence and Kipling. The India that he had served in the Fourth Hussars was the India of polo and pigsticking, of dashing frontier expeditions, of paternal government freely accepted and the great white Empress revered as a mysterious goddess.'[1]

The India of nineteen-thirties was not the same as the India of eighteen-nineties, not only because of the passage of time but because of the imprint of Gandhi's personality on Indian politics. This was something that Churchill with all his sense of history could not understand. The reasons are not far to seek. Gandhi's religious make-up and doctrines of truth and non-violence sounded only hypocritical nonsense to Churchill, the military strategist and politician, while Gandhi's challenge to Britain's moral right to govern India touched him in a particularly tender spot.

Faced with a solid *bloc* of opposition in the Press and Parliament, spokesmen of the British Government had in England to defend the very features of the new constitution which were most repugnant to Indian opinion: the 'safeguards' or the overriding powers retained in the hands of the Viceroy and the Governors to prevent Indian democracy from running amuck. The British dilemma was aptly summed up in a comment by the *Manchester Guardian* that, since the British could neither govern nor get out of India, it was necessary 'to devise a constitution that seems like self-government in India and at Westminster like British *Raj*'.

The new constitution, as it finally emerged, was as impressive for the powers it conferred on the elected representatives of the people as for those it withheld. It was as if a motor vehicle had been set in motion in low gear with the brakes on. The Indian Federation, when it came into being, was to incorporate Provinces as well as Princely States. The latter were allotted nearly one-third of the total seats in the federal legislature, and since their representatives, because of the absence of elective bodies, were likely to be the nominees of the princes (who in turn were

[1] Templewood, Lord (Sir Samuel Hoare): *Nine Troubled Years*, p. 98.

dependant for their very existence on the British Government) Indian nationalists viewed the new constitution with a feeling bordering on dismay. The powers of the federal legislature were circumscribed; a substantial part of the budget, that relating for instance to the military, the services, the interest charges etc. was outside its purview. In the Provinces a wider field was permitted to ministers responsible to elected legislatures, but even here their powers had been restricted in financial and other matters on which the Governors had been invested with overriding and preventive authority.

These limitations led Jawaharlal Nehru to describe the Indian Reforms Act of 1935 as 'a Charter of Slavery'. At the Lucknow session of the Indian National Congress he declared that the new constitution offered Indians responsibility without power. The Congress decided, however, to contest the elections under the new constitution. The Congress election manifesto reaffirmed the rejection 'in entirety' of the new constitution, and demanded its replacement by another constitution based on political freedom for India and framed by a constituent assembly. 'The Congress realizes,' went on the manifesto, that 'independence cannot be achieved through the legislatures nor can the problems of poverty and unemployment be effectively tackled by them.' However, the decision to contest the elections was taken partly because it was considered unwise to leave the field clear to anti-national elements, and partly because there was a powerful wing within the Congress which saw possibilities of constructive work in the Provinces even within the limited framework of the new constitution.

The results of the general election were known in February 1937. The Congress won clear majorities in U.P., Bihar, Orissa, C.P., and Madras. In Bombay it won nearly half the seats and with allied groups could form a government. It was the largest party in the N.W.F.P. and Assam.

The Congress Manifesto had not given any clear lead as to what the Congress was to do if it won majorities in the provincial legislatures. The subject was one on which opinion was sharply

N

divided. Those who opposed the formation of ministries felt that nothing could be got out of the new constitution, that the Congress would have to bear all the odium for the apparatus of imperialism without securing a real relief to the people, and (worst of all) the Congress would go the way of 'moderate' parties by ceasing to be a militant organization and getting out of touch with the masses from whom it derived its real strength. Those who favoured the assumption of responsibility for administering the provinces recognized the limitations of the new constitution, but were unwilling to yield any vantage point to the Government or to the political parties subservient to it; many of them were also convinced that the new constitution could be used for the service of the masses. As a compromise between these two opposing views, it was decided by a convention of Congress members of provincial legislatures, and of the All-India Congress Committee in March 1937, that the Congress would agree to form ministries, provided the leader of the Congress party in the provincial legislature was satisfied and was able to state publicly that the Governor would not use his special powers of interference or set aside the advice of the ministers 'in regard to their constitutional activities'.

The Government of India had been anxiously watching the attitude of the Congress after the results of the elections were known. At the instance of the Viceroy, an 'appreciation' of the Congress position was prepared on March 17, 1937 by the Home Secretary, Reginald Maxwell, which throws some light on the official approach to this crucial question. In his opening paragraphs Maxwell played down the Congress success at the elections: 'The statement that the result of the elections indicates that electorate has set its seal on the policy and programme of the Congress in regard to the new Act is of course on the face of it absurd. There is probably not one in 10,000 of the electors who ever read the new Act and the Congress resolution itself shows that their leaders do not understand its provisions.'

The decision in favour of office acceptance appeared to Maxwell as a concession to the right wing of the Congress; and the condition as to the exercise of the Governors' powers as a concession to the left wing. The fact that the assurances were to be given publicly, not by the Governors but by the leaders of the Congress parties in the provincial legislatures, was taken as a hint that the Congress was willing to accept office. Nevertheless, Maxwell saw a number of traps in the decision of the Congress, and he believed they had been contrived cunningly by Gandhi, about whom he wrote: 'In exercising his influence on the situation and trying to find a *via media* between the opposing views, Gandhi has probably tried to include something in the resolution to placate Nehru, and no doubt at the same time he is influenced by his usual desire to set up a negotiating point on which he would either be called upon to arbitrate in future between the Governors and their ministries or at any rate which would make it appear that the Government had to some extent yielded to Congress stipulations.'

The suspicion that Gandhi was manoeuvring in a political battle of wits did less than justice to him. Temperamentally, he was not suited to the parliamentary or the ministerial role. His faith in the possibility of attaining Indian freedom through legislatures had been irrevocably shaken in 1920; after his release from gaol in 1924 he had differences with C. R. Das and Motilal Nehru, who were in favour of lifting the boycott of councils. Ten years later, in 1934, Gandhi had encouraged the revival of the parliamentary wing of the Congress, as he felt that work within the legislatures was the best outlet for the energies of some Congressmen. Gandhi's attitude to legislatures and to office acceptance was ultimately to prove crucial. In 1937, when the controversy on office acceptance was at its height, he wrote: 'The boycott of legislatures, let me tell you, is not an eternal principle like that of truth and non-violence. My opposition to them has lessened but that does not mean that I am going back on my former position. The question is of strategy and I can only say what is most needed at a particular moment.'[1]

The need of the moment was constructive work. Since the suspension of civil disobedience, Gandhi had been preoccupied

[1] *Harijan*, May 1, 1937.

with activities, which though non-political in common parlance, were nevertheless important such as a clean water supply, a cheap and nutritious diet, a sound educational system and a healthy and self-sufficient economy for Indian villages. He wondered whether, with all its deficiencies, the new constitution could further this programme of village uplift. There was no reason why Congress ministries in the provinces could not encourage village industries, introduce prohibition, reduce the burdens on the peasantry, promote the use of home-spun cloth, extend education and combat untouchability.

Another consideration seems also to have influenced him. During the last two decades he had launched three major civil disobedience campaigns. He had seen the country vibrate to a new political consciousness under their impact, but he had also seen that the spirit of non-violence had been slow in permeating the people, and that even his closest colleagues had sometimes chafed at the self-imposed restraints of Satyagraha. And violence seemed not only latent, but near the surface, erupting unexpectedly; 'he atmosphere requisite for launching of a Satyagraha campaign was not easy to create. At the same time the discontent in the country continued to grow. The new constitution was far from offering political freedom to India, but it had created an electorate of thirty millions; these millions and the many millions who had still to win the vote could all be affected by provincial governments. The new constitution could be construed, wrote Gandhi, as an attempt, however feeble and limited, to replace the rule of the sword by the rule of the majority. 'If the Congress worked the new constitution,' he suggested, 'to achieve its goal of independence, it would avoid a bloody revolution and a mass civil disobedience movement.'

The Congress offer of March 1937 to accept office, provided the Governors gave assurances of non-interference in day-to-day administration, was thus influenced by Gandhi's desire to glean something constructive out of the new constitution and not to lay traps for the Government. Official spokesmen at first took the line that any such assurance, or 'gentleman's agreement' would do violence to the constitution, and that the Governors could not contract themselves out of the terms of an Act of Parliament or Instruments of Instructions issued to them. Nevertheless it became apparent to the Government that a section among Congressmen was anxious to accept office, and that without some sort of assurance it would not be possible for them to form ministries. The *interim* ministries formed in the Congress-majority provinces were sure to be voted out of office on the day the new legislatures met. The alternative of suspending the constitution was always open to the Government, but this would have been a false start for a constitution on which British statesmen and Parliament had laboured so long and so hard.

Lord Linlithgow had told an Indian visitor in August 1936 that he could not change even a comma of the Government of India Act.[1] This was true so far as it went, but it was not a catastrophic limitation; the constitution by which the British themselves were governed flowed not from a legal document but from a series of conventions developed in the actual working of their constitution. Gandhi's approach to the new constitution was not that of a constitutional lawyer, not even that of a political strategist. He wrote in *Harijan* of September 4, 1937: 'I had not studied the Act (The Government of India Act 1935) when I advised office acceptance. I have since been studying *Provincial Autonomy* by Prof. K. T. Shah . . . I see nothing in the Act to prevent Congress ministries from carrying out the programme suggested by me. The special powers and safeguards come into play only when there is violence in the country or a clash between the minorities and the so-called majority community, which is another word for violence.'

The debate on the assurances from the Governors was brought to an end by a long statement issued by the Viceroy, which was so phrased as to allay the fears of the Congress without surrendering any constitutional ground. Lord Linlithgow gave an assurance that the Governors would be anxious not only not to provoke conflicts but to avoid them. This statement did not change the

[1] Birla, G. D.: *In the Shadow of the Mahatma*, p. 207.

legal position, but the controversy had made it clear to the Government that, with solid majorities in the legislatures at their back, the Congress ministries would not lightly brook interference from the Governors. The Viceroy's statement, though vague, was conciliatory in tone and the Congress decided to form ministries.

The formation of the Congress ministries in six provinces— Bombay, United Provinces, Bihar, Central Provinces, Orissa and Madras—was a significant event; a political party which was committed to the liquidation of the British Empire had agreed to run the administration in these provinces. The experiment was not as explosive as it was feared. The Congress ministers were preoccupied most of the time not with the best means of precipitating crises, but with those of fulfilling the social and economic programme enunciated in the Congress Election Manifesto. It was in this programme that Gandhi was interested and by which he judged the work of Congress ministers. He advised them to set an example of simplicity and frugality in their personal lives in line with the poverty of the people whom they governed; he urged them to cultivate 'industry, ability, integrity, impartiality, and an infinite capacity for mastering details'.

Two items in the legislative programme of the Congress ministries appeared particularly important to Gandhi; these were prohibition and education. Himself a total abstainer, Gandhi's advocacy of prohibition derived not only from his own puritanism, but from solicitude for the half-starved peasants and industrial workers who dissipated part of their meagre earnings on drink which would have been better spent on milk for their children. When the Congress ministry of Bombay introduced prohibition Gandhi congratulated it in *Harijan* and appealed to Bombay's 'fashionable citizens who think that they need spirituous drinks as they need water' to think of their poor brethren, if they did not appreciate abstinence for themselves.

On education, Gandhi had ideas based on his own experience. At Phoenix and Tolstoy Farm in South Africa, he had helped run schools for children. The conviction grew upon him that the value of academic instruction had been overrated and that character-building and the acquisition of practical skills had not been given due recognition. For his own children he had considered general knowledge and the dignity of labour sufficient and in spite of their protests, had given them little regular academic training. Handicrafts had always seemed to him a valuable medium of training the hands as well as the head. He observed, however, that children easily tired of manual work. He came to the conclusion that what was needed was not a vocational-cum-literary training, but literary training through vocational instruction. Vocational training would thus cease to be a drudgery and literary training would have a new content and usefulness.

In October 1937, Gandhi placed his ideas before an educational conference which met at Wardha and included, besides the Congress ministers, a number of prominent educationists. He suggested that education suited to the Indian village could best be imparted through a handicraft centre; that the medium of instruction should be the mother tongue; that a seven-year course of elementary education should be devised and the sale of the handicrafts produced in the schools should make education at least partially self-supporting. A detailed scheme of elementary education based on these ideas was prepared by a committee of educationists headed by Dr Zakir Husain. The committee outlined a curriculum for teaching children through concrete life situations relating to a craft or the social and physical environment of the child. It recognized the importance of pre-school education, but for financial reasons ruled it out. The school-going age was fixed from seven to fourteen years. Literary training was to be enough to prevent relapse into illiteracy, and the skill in the crafts through which education was imparted was to be such as to enable the student to practise it as a vocation if he adopted it after leaving the school.

The Wardha Scheme of Education, as these proposals came to be known, stirred the stagnant pools of Indian education and stimulated administrators and educationists to think along new and progressive lines. The scheme had its critics. Did it not sacrifice academic training to manual work? Were teachers in schools to be turned into slave-drivers? Gandhi explained that the object of the scheme was not primarily to produce craftsmen but to exploit for educative purposes the resources implicit in craftwork. Nor was the mass-production of shoddy articles in schools intended; a certain degree of skill was, however, inevitable, and it was enough if the sale of handicrafts covered the teachers' salaries. The idea was to substitute a co-ordinated training in the use of the hand and the eye for a notoriously bookish and volatile learning which most village children unlearnt after leaving school or found of little use in their daily lives.

If Gandhi confined his attention to child education, it was not because he was indifferent to higher education. He had not forgotten his own struggles in high school and college with the arbitrary spellings and grammar of the English language; how he had to spend three years in digesting in English what he had already learnt in Gujerati. The English language had created an impassable barrier between the small educated minority in towns and the mass of the population. 'High Schools are,' wrote Gandhi, 'schools for cultural conquest by the English.' He did not deny that the English language had vast literary treasures, but he added that: 'the nobility of (English) literature cannot avail the Indian nation any more than the temperate climate or scenery of England can avail her. India has to flourish in her own climate, and her scenery and her own literature, even though all the three may be inferior to the English climate, scenery and literature. We and our children must build on our own heritage. We can never grow on foreign victuals.'[1] And why was it assumed that without the knowledge of English they would cease to have access to its literature? Indians did not learn Russian to be able to read Tolstoy, nor did the Japanese learn English to read Shakespeare.

While it is possible to differ with Gandhi on the degree of emphasis which he placed on handicrafts in child education or on the details of the curriculum drawn up for 'basic education', the re-orientation which he wished to impart to India's educational

[1] *Harijan,* July 9, 1938.

system was long overdue. The adoption of the mother tongue as a medium of instruction, the vocational bias to correct learning by rote common in Indian schools, and the modification of the curriculum so as to relate it to the environment of the child were beneficent reforms to which his powerful advocacy gave a new impetus.

Education was one of the many spheres in which the Congress ministries attempted to effect improvements. Substantial agrarian reforms were carried out to protect the interest of the tenant against landlords, and to mitigate the problem of rural indebtedness. 'The Agrarian legislation of the Congress ministries,' writes Prof. Coupland, 'boldly conceived and swiftly carried through, was a notable achievement.'[1] As he explains, the old official governments had been handicapped in this work by the fact that the bulk of their supporters belonged to the landlord class.

For a political party which had remained many long years in opposition to get into the seat of power was a novel and even a hazardous experience. The left wing in the Congress, which opposed formation of ministries, had in fact stressed the risks of internal dissensions and scramble for loaves and fishes among Congressmen. Gandhi found himself inundated with requests for jobs and ministerships; he expressed his surprise and distress at this trend, because to him the legislatures and ministerships were only one and a limited medium of service to the country. He felt that for the majority of Congressmen the work lay in the villages in the numerous fields of social and economic uplift. The caucus system, the struggle for power and pressure politics, which are accepted as part of political democracy, appeared to him as unhealthy practices. In the pages of *Harijan* he lashed out against the corruption in Congress ranks. The Congress Working Committee passed resolutions to discourage interference by party members in day-to-day administration. 'I would go,' he wrote, 'the length of giving the whole Congress organization a decent burial rather than put up with the corruption that is rampant.' Mere numbers did not matter; ten million Congressmen

[1] Coupland, Reginald: *India, a Restatement*, p. 159.

N•

with 'violence and untruth in their hearts' could not bring political freedom; but ten thousand Congressmen without the burden of having to carry doubtful companions could achieve the goal. As an 'experienced servant and general', he deprecated the struggle for the 'spoils of office', and the dissipation of energy in factional rivalries.

The existence of a Central Parliamentary Board composed of some of the top leaders of the Congress, to some extent provided an antidote to indiscipline, but even then there were crises which threatened to split Congress parties in the provinces. One such crisis was caused by the reshuffling of the Congress ministry without the permission of the Congress High Command by the Premier of the Central Provinces, Dr N. B. Khare. He had to resign. The Congress High Command was accused by its critics of cutting the thread which bound the provincial ministers through the legislatures with the electorate. But were it not for some such central control the ministries in the Congress-majority provinces would have been exposed to the instability and intrigue which often characterized some non-Congress ministries, such as those in Sind and Assam. The Congress leaders had good reasons for exercising a central control over their ministries. For the struggle for political freedom was not yet over. A non-violent struggle did not make discipline the less necessary, and unless the Congress ministries were subject to some control from the top they ran risks of compromise with vested interests.

The opponents of the Congress regarded such direction of Congress ministries by the Congress High Command as authoritarianism. Gandhi answered the charge: 'They say this is fascism, pure and simple. But they forget that fascism is the naked sword. Under it Dr Khare should lose his head. The Congress is the very antithesis of fascism, because it is based on non-violence pure and undefiled. Its authority is not derived from the control of panoplied blackshirts.'[1]

There could be nothing further from Gandhi's scheme of things than fascism. His whole life had been a struggle against

[1] *Harijan*, August 6, 1938.

violence in every guise. To substitute love for hate, and 'soul force' for 'brute force', he had attempted one experiment after another with himself, with small groups, and finally on a national scale. Throughout British rule it had been the practice to summon the police or the military to suppress communal riots; but when Congress ministries did so, Gandhi could not conceal his surprise and dismay. For seventeen years he had been preaching non-violence to the Congress, and most Congressmen accepted it as a policy, a few as an article of faith. If the millions who professed to obey the Congress had imbibed his message there would have been no riots. Were there not enough Congressmen, he asked, to form themselves into 'peace brigades' and to lay down their lives in an endeavour to still the frenzy of fanatical mobs? These 'peace brigades', on which Gandhi dwelt at length, were not forth-coming; they called for a degree of discipline and sacrifice which was rare. Moreover, communal riots were no longer an outcome of local disputes but symptoms of a political communalism which was to engulf the country during the next decade. The Muslim League, frustrated by the results of 1937 elections, and nettled by the decision of the Congress not to form coalition ministries, was launching during these years countrywide propaganda campaigns, the inevitable result of which was to widen the gulf between Hindus and Muslims. In the prevalent tension riots flared up frequently with or without sufficient provocation. The Congress ministers, preoccupied with their legislative programmes and harassed by the cares of office, had neither the time nor perhaps the faith to form peace brigades and fell back upon the police and the military to curb the law-breakers.

When the Congress ministries accepted office, neither the Congress leaders nor the Government knew exactly how the new partnership in the provinces would actually work out. It was not easy for either side to leave the history of its long conflict behind but association in day-to-day problems seemed to break some barriers. 'Fancy,' wrote Mahadev Desai (Gandhi's secretary) to G. D. Birla, 'Garret, the Commissioner of Ahmedabad, now going to the station to receive Minister Morarji and travelling a

fair distance with him in third class.'[1] Of the I.C.S. officers serving
in the provinces nearly half were Europeans. Though their
salaries were a charge on the revenues of the provinces, and their
careers were protected by the constitution, many of them tried to
adapt themselves to provincial autonomy and to their new bosses.
The tempo seemed to have quickened all round; in the provincial
secretariats, the new ministers insisted on drafting new measures
of social and economic reforms with unwonted speed; in the
districts the new democratic structure made increasing demands
upon the time of the executive officers. There was some meddling
in day-to-day administration by local politicians. The British
officers had been able to adapt themselves to dyarchy during the
twenties; in the thirties they tried to adjust their step with
provincial autonomy, even if it required visibly greater effort.
The regime of the benevolent despots in the districts, conferring
titles and lands and jobs for loyalty to the British *Raj,* was no
longer unquestioned. Here was something that was not easy to
accept by those who had been reared in the Imperial tradition.
As Philip Mason, a former member of the I.C.S., sums it up, 'it
is hard to serve where you have ruled'.[2]

'The partial democracy of 1937-9,' wrote Jawaharlal Nehru in
his book *The Discovery of India,* 'was always on the verge of
conflict.' There were the crises in U.P. and Bihar on the release of
political prisoners, and there was a crisis in Orissa on the selection
of an officiating Governor. There was the perpetual near-crisis on
the policy of the Government towards the Indian States and the
declared opposition of the Congress to Federation. The inherent
contradiction between popular governments in the provinces and
a completely authoritarian government at the centre remained.
This contradiction could lead to curious anomalies; the U.P.
Government had, for example, to draw the attention of the Home
Department of the Government of India to the complaint that
the Central Intelligence Department was censoring the correspondence of Jawaharlal Nehru, whom the Premier of U.P. and his

[1] Birla, G. D.: *In the Shadow of the Mahatma,* p. 243.
[2] Woodruff, Philip: *The Guardians,* London 1955, p. 244.

colleagues held in high esteem. In spite of these points of actual or potential conflict, the relations between the Congress ministries and the Governors became stabilized on the whole at a satisfactory level. The Governors found their ministers earnest, and sometimes extremely competent; the ministers often found the Governors helpful. Equations varied from province to province; if excessive cordiality was rare, overt conflict was also usually absent. 'Taken as a whole' sums up Prof. Coupland, 'the record of its ministries was one in which the Congress could take reasonable pride. Its leaders had shown that they could act as well as talk, administer as well as agitate.'

'Between Indian nationalism,' to quote Jawaharlal Nehru again, 'and an alien imperialism, there could be no final peace.' In the spring of 1939, however, a rupture between the Congress and the Government appeared by no means inevitable. As late as on June 20, 1939, Jawaharlal Nehru, as Chairman of the non-official National Planning Committee, wrote to Sir Jagdish Prasad, a member of the Viceroy's Executive Council, seeking the co-operation of the Government of India in collecting the data for various sub-committees of the National Planning Committee. In July 1939, the Government of Indian nominated their Economic Adviser Dr Gregory to attend the meetings of the National Planning Committee, and agreed to supply information required by the Committee subject to the usual proviso that it should be such as could be disclosed in the public interest.

A breach between the Congress and the Government may have been inevitable in the long run, but it might have been postponed, if not averted, in the Congress ardour for social and economic reform and the Government's anxiety not to disturb stable administrations in the provinces in a period of acute international uncertainty.

The outbreak of the war precipitated the crisis and brought the brief partnership between the Congress and the Government to a sudden end. It would be well at this stage to refer to the communal problem, which was in a sense to dominate and even distort Indian politics during the war and post-war years.

Chapter 42

THE GENESIS OF PAKISTAN

'THAT eternal problem' is how Gandhi had described the Hindu-Muslim question in the nineteen-twenties, when he had almost despaired of a solution. The communal controversy was stilled by the civil disobedience movement, but the Round Table Conference had again revived it. From the year 1937, when the new constitution was inaugurated in the provinces, communal antagonism was to reach a new crescendo, to give an unexpected twist to Indian politics, to undo the work of Indian nationalists over half a century, to frustrate Gandhi's cherished hopes, and to put his belief in non-violence to the severest test in the last years of his life.

The Hindu-Muslim problem was not new to India. The Muslims, who constituted nearly one-fourth of the total population, differed from the Hindus in their religious tenets, usage, laws and customs; however, these differences were accepted and taken for granted by the two communities. During the Muslim rule, non-Muslims may have suffered at the hands of a whimsical or a fanatical ruler, but on the whole the masses had learnt to live in a spirit of 'live and let live'. The evolution of a common language, dress and ceremonial in different parts of the country had assisted the process of adjustment. In fact, cultural and social life of the two communities differed not along communal but regional lines; a Bengali Hindu was nearer a Bengali Muslim than a Punjabi Hindu and a Gujerati Muslim had more in common with a Gujerati Hindu than with a Madrasi Muslim.

The British conquest of India placed the two communities on a level—of common subjection—but as the process of conquest had proceeded from the sea-coast inwards, it affected the Muslim

majority provinces of north-western India last of all. This accident
of history gave a start to the Hindus in acquiring Western education
and taking to modern commerce and thus contributing to the
emergence of a Hindu middle class subsisting on government
service, 'the professions' and trade. The growth of the Muslim
middle class was unfortunately impeded by the Mutiny, which
some British observers tended to regard as a Muslim revolt.
Muslim theologians, by throwing their weight against Western
education, further handicapped Muslim youth in competing for
jobs under the Government.

In the closing decades of the nineteenth century the attitude of
the Government to the Muslim community began to change. The
demand of the middle class, then necessarily Hindu in composition,
through the Indian National Congress for a larger share in the
government of the country brought about a new orientation in
the policy of the Government. Muslims were henceforth seen not
as potential rebels but as probable allies. To this re-orientation,
the Muslim leader who made the greatest contribution was Syed
Ahmad Khan. He corrected the view of the Mutiny as a Muslim
revolt by recording the services of Muslim nobles who had served
the British Government faithfully and well. He founded the
Aligarh College and the Muhammadan Educational Conference,
and exhorted Muslims to take advantage of Western education.
There were occasions when he criticized the Government, but his
criticisms were discreet and came from one whose loyalty was
above suspicion and whose services were well rewarded by the
Government. Syed Ahmad Khan was nominated to the Imperial
Legislature Council and the Public Service Commission and
granted a knighthood.

Sir Syed Ahmad Khan's main concern was the raising of his
community in the social and economic spheres. He did not want
Indian Muslims to be caught in the maelstrom of politics; this was
not only because he wished to cultivate British goodwill but
because he was afraid that a democratic system would place
Muslims at a permanent disadvantage. He exhorted Muslims to
keep away from the Indian National Congress. Thus he threw

his powerful influence in favour of the isolation of his community
from the nationalist movement just when this movement started
on its career. He also raised the great question mark which was
to shadow Indian politics for the next sixty years: what would
be the position of the Muslim community in a free India? If
British autocracy were to be replaced by an Indian democracy,
would it give a permanent advantage to the Hindus, who heavily
outnumbered the Muslims? Was it (as Sir Syed Ahmad put it)
a game of dice in which one man had four dice and the other
only one? Had Muslims anything to gain from the withdrawal of
the British rule?

Nawab Viqar-ul-Mulk, another eminent Muslim educationist
and politician, in opposing the setting up of elective institutions
drew the stark moral for his co-religionists: 'We are numerically
one-fifth of the other community. If at any time, the British
Government ceases to exist in India we shall have to live as
subjects of the Hindus . . . If there is any device by which we can
escape this, it is by the continuance of the British *Raj* and our
interests can be safeguarded only if we ensure the continuance of
the British Government.'[1]

There was only one possible answer which nationalists could
give to the question as to how Muslims would fare in a free India:
they would fare no better or no worse than the other communities.
There was no reason to assume that in a free India political parties
would follow communal affiliations, and social or economic issues
would not cut across religious divisions. A democratic system
could embody the fullest guarantees of religious liberty, cultural
autonomy and equal opportunities for all. Unfortunately, this
line of thought could not be appreciated by those who were
unable to visualize India of the future in any terms except those
of the sordid present.

When, under the impact of the growing nationalist ferment in
the country, the adoption of the elective principle seemed
inevitable, a deputation of Muslim leaders, led by the Aga Khan,
waited on the Viceroy in 1906 and pleaded that Muslim represen-

[1] Albiruni, A. H.: *Makers of Pakistan*, p. 109.

tatives to legislatures should be elected by Muslim voters only. It is difficult to say whether the deputation was (as Maulana Mahomed Ali once described it) 'a command performance', but there is no doubt that Principal Archbold of the Aligarh College actively assisted in arranging the interview and Lord Minto was readier than is customary on such occasions to give assurances on an important constitutional matter.

That the grant of separate electorates could be a source of mischief was recognized by Lord Chelmsford and Edwin Montagu, the authors of the joint report which formed the basis of the Government of India (Reforms) Act of 1919: 'Division by creeds and classes means the creation of political camps organized against each other, and teaches men to think as partisans and not as citizens; it is difficult to see how the change from this system to national representation is ever to occur. The British Government is often accused of dividing men to govern them. But if it unnecessarily divides them at the very moment when it proposes to start them on the road to governing themselves, it will find it difficult to meet the charge of being hypocritical or short-sighted.'

It was not a mere coincidence that the All-India Muslim League, which ultimately became the mouthpiece of Muslim separatism, was founded in 1906, and that among its founders were the Aga Khan and some of the leading lights of the deputation which had waited on the Viceroy. Separate electorates were thus to contribute further to the isolation of the Muslim community from the main stream of Indian national life.

This isolation was temporarily broken in the years immediately preceding the world war of 1914-18. Unfortunately, it was not so much national feeling as the travail of Turkey and other Muslim states in the Middle East which provided the impulse for a *modus vivendi* with the Hindus. The resultant unity was symbolized by the Congress-League Pact in 1916. Later, it found a concrete expression under Gandhi's leadership in the non-co-operation movement. A common leadership could not, however, make up for the essential divergence of ideals; while the Hindus thought mostly in political terms of achieving self-government for India, the Khilafatists were preoccupied with the fate of Turkey. Muslim leaders denounced the British Government but based their denunciations on edicts issued by their religious leaders (Ulema). The appeal to religious emotion was fraught with risks; it could also be invoked against other communities. Moreover, this emotion was harnessed to a romantic concept which was brought to an inglorious end by the Turks themselves. Thus the one important and successful experiment in bringing the Muslims into the heart of the nationalist movement failed to break the psychological isolation of the Muslim middle class and indeed confirmed its tendency to view political problems from a religious angle.

When Gandhi came out of gaol in 1924 he was shocked to see that the fabric of Hindu-Muslim unity, at which he had laboured so hard, had gone to pieces. There was an exceptional bitterness in communal controversies. Gandhi's movements in 1919-23 had swept the lower middle class into the political vortex and the politicians of nineteen-twenties were pandering to this new audience; it was as if the controversy had extended from the parlour to the street corner. In this vulgarization of politics a section of the Press, particularly the Indian language Press, took a notorious part. It was during this period that Gandhi described the newspaperman as 'a walking plague who spreads contagion of lies and calumnies'.

Gandhi denounced this madness; he appealed for human decency and tolerance; he fasted; he prayed. But it was all in vain. His voice, once so powerful, was drowned in a din of communal recriminations by bigots on both sides who blamed him for partiality to their opponents.

A favourite solution in the nineteen-twenties was a communal pact through an All-Parties Conference. There had been a precedent in the Lucknow Pact of 1916. The argument was that communal amity, once attained by the leaders, would percolate to the masses. The sequence which the Unity Conferences and All-Parties Conferences followed had a dreary uniformity and

partook of the nature of a comic opera. Leaders of a number of
political parties and religious organizations would meet to the
accompaniment of sentimental effusions of goodwill. As they
sat down to allocate jobs and seats in legislature—the spoils of
Swaraj, as it were—they found it difficult to reconcile their
antagonistic claims, and after debates which seemed to emit
more heat than light they dispersed among blazing fireworks
of mutual recrimination. That such heterogeneous groups should
have been able to agree on anything was inconceivable, but there
was a basic unreality about these discussions. All the patronage
and power which these leaders set out to share was in fact controlled by the British Government. Gandhi disliked this petti-
fogging politics, but he would have liked to disarm Muslim
fears by generosity on the part of the Hindus. Unfortunately,
Hindu politicians, especially from the Punjab and Bengal, seemed
to be as incapable of generosity as the Muslim politicians were
of trust. Moreover, what was a mere insurance against future
risk to the Muslim was seen as the thin end of the wedge by the
Hindu.

The pattern of the unity conferences was nearly repeated
at the Round Table Conference when the second session, attended
by Gandhi, failed to bring off a solution acceptable to the motley
group of delegates whom the Government had assembled in
London. Since constitution-making seemed to founder on the
lack of an agreement, the Government decided to impose a
solution. The British Premier issued a Communal Award to
determine the quantum and mode of representation in legislatures,
and the new constitution based on this Award came into force
in April 1937. The Award had conceded the principal demands
of Muslim spokesmen. The perpetuation of the communal
franchise (separate electorates) in the Award was repugnant
to the Indian National Congress, but the Congress decided
not to reject it until some better solution, acceptable to all the
communities, could emerge. Whatever the shortcomings of
the Communal Award as a 'package solution' of the communal
problem, it might have been expected to end the communal

controversy and to release the energies of the people for more constructive work.

Events were to show that the communal controversy, far from being suppressed, was to rage like a hurricane during the next ten years and to pull down many familiar landmarks. The history of this decade can not be understood without reference to the personality and politics of Mr M. A. Jinnah. That communal antagonisms should have reached a new peak in the closing years of the British rule was perhaps natural: it was, in political terms, a war of succession. However, it is doubtful if the communal problem would have dominated Indian politics in the way it did without Jinnah's impact on it.

Six years younger than Gandhi, Jinnah had also studied law in England, but unlike Gandhi his main interest outside legal studies had been in politics and not in religion. Jinnah had in his youth come under the influence of Dadabhai Naoroji; he was a friend of Gokhale and took to law and politics in Bombay. In his early forties he was a front-rank politician and took a prominent part in the conclusion of the Lucknow Pact in 1916, which brought the National Congress and the Muslim League on to a common platform. These were the years when he was described as the 'ambassador of Hindu-Muslim unity'. 'A new spirit is abroad,' he said in 1916 and added, 'but for a real new India to arise all petty and small things must be given up. She is now India *irredenta* and to be redeemed all Indians must offer to sacrifice not only their good things but all those evil things they cling to blindly—their hates and their divisions, their pride in what they should be thoroughly ashamed of, their quarrels and misunderstandings.'[1]

Whether in the Imperial Legislative Council of which he was an elected member, or outside, Jinnah's stand on most political problems reflected a spirit of nationalism. He joined the Home Rule movement and supported the demand for Indian self-government as a condition precedent to wholehearted Indian support to the British Government in the war against Germany.

[1] Bolitho, Hector: *Jinnah*, p. 65.

In 1919 Jinnah condemned the Rowlatt Bills which hastened Gandhi's conversion from a loyalist into a rebel. He criticized the Government for its policy in the Punjab and towards Turkey, but he did not join Gandhi's movements; in fact he left the Indian National Congress just as Gandhi began to dominate its counsels. Like many another 'moderate' leader, Jinnah would have liked the Congress to remain an unofficial parliament of the Indian intelligentsia in which well-educated (and well-dressed) gentlemen debated current affairs in the King's English and passed resolutions for the information of the Indian Press and the British Government. Jinnah had once (December 1918) led a demonstration to foil a farewell function in honour of the retiring Governor of Bombay, Lord Willingdon. But this was perhaps the solitary lapse from that lofty, almost Olympian, dignity with which Jinnah loved to play the game of politics in those years. When Gandhi broadened the scope of his movement to embrace the illiterate millions in towns and villages, Jinnah feared that the march to disaster had begun. 'What the consequences of this may be,' he wrote, 'I shudder to contemplate.'

It was not only Gandhi's politics which jarred upon Jinnah. Gandhi's religious frame of mind, his habit of self-analysis, his emphasis on such abstractions as truth and non-violence, his conscious humility, his voluntary poverty—all these were alien to Jinnah's own make-up and struck him either as a political irrelevance or as downright hypocrisy. There are indications that Jinnah even suffered from a feeling that he had been unfairly edged out of the forefront of the political stage by Gandhi. Louis Fischer records that Jinnah told him: 'Nehru worked under me in the Home Rule Society. Gandhi worked under me at the time of the Lucknow Pact.' It is doubtless true that in 1916 Jinnah was in the limelight and in 1920 he had almost ceased to be a political force. Several other leaders had a similar experience, which is to be attributed to the intensity with which Gandhi's personality and doctrines appealed to millions of Indians who had so far been little affected by politics.

In the nineteen-twenties, Jinnah headed an independent group

in the Central Legislative Assembly, where he held the balance
between the Government and the Congress. This was a role
which he could play with masterly skill. He did not align himself
with the Government or the Congress, and though he pleaded
for communal unity his price for co-operation continued to
rise. His opposition to the solution of the communal problem
in the Nehru Report went a long way to kill it in 1928. To
Gandhi's civil disobedience movements in the early thirties he
took no more kindly than he had done ten years earlier to the
non-co-operation movement. At the Round Table Conference
he ploughed a lonely furrow; as Sir Samuel Hoare puts it, 'he
never seemed to wish to work with anyone'. After the Conference
he almost bade good-bye to Indian politics and settled down
in England. But as the time came for the general elections under
the new constitution, he returned to India and led the Muslim
League to the polls. The League did not get more than five per cent
of the Muslim votes, but within four years of this disastrous
defeat Jinnah was able to build up his position so skilfully that
he was accused of placing a veto on India's constitutional
progress.

We have already seen that the Congress had agreed with
Gandhi's blessing to form governments in the summer of 1937
in provinces where its adherents commanded majorities in
the legislatures. The Congress decided not to form coalition
ministries; it had comfortable majorities and did not require
the support of other parties to remain in office. The Congress
leaders were also influenced by the fear that coalition cabinets
might lead to compromise and conflict and thus weaken the
Congress, which had yet to win political freedom for the country.
As against these considerations was the fact that out of the 450
Muslim seats in the provincial legislatures, the Congress had
contested only fifty-eight and won twenty-six. The Congress
did take Muslim legislators in the cabinets, but after they signed
the Congress pledge. Whatever the justification for this decision,
which was taken against Gandhi's advice, it cut the leaders of
the Muslim League, particularly Jinnah, to the quick. The

separate electorates on which they had banked all these years had only helped to keep Muslims out of the Congress and failed to bring the Muslims an effective share in political power.

From 1937 onwards a new exacerbation enters Jinnah's speeches and writings; a new desperation leads him from one tactical position to the other until he reaches the end of the abyss. The Congress ministries, without the representatives of the Muslim League, offered him the handiest pegs on which he could deposit all the grievances of Muslims, real or fancied. 'The fact is,' he declared, 'the Congress wants domination of India under shelter of British bayonets.' The Congress was, he alleged, 'encircling' the Muslim League and trying to 'break up its solidarity'. He ridiculed the Congress proposal for a Constituent Assembly which Gandhi had endorsed as a solution of the political and communal problems: 'It is puerile to ask the British Government in the first instance to call a Constituent Assembly of another nation and afterwards have the honour and privilege of placing the constitution framed by this supreme assembly of India on the statute-book of British Parliament.'[1] Gandhi was Jinnah's chosen target. He was the 'sole dictator and interpreter of the Congress'. Light had 'not yet dawned within the territories of Segaon'; Gandhi was trying 'to subjugate and vassalize the Muslims under a Hindu Raj and annihilate the Muslims'.

Jinnah dealt summarily with Muslim politicians. This bullying of followers and opponents was not a mere freak of temperament. A certain conceit had always characterized him and allowance has also to be made for his frustration during these years. It is difficult, however, to resist the impression that a good deal of this bullying was deliberate; it was a new technique, influenced by the propaganda methods followed with seeming success in contemporary Europe.

In September 1938, just after the Munich Pact, when the free world was torn between a sense of relief at the war having been averted and a feeling of anguish at the sacrifice of the

[1] Ahmad, Jamiluddin: *Recent Speeches and Writings of Mr. Jinnah,* Lahore, 1946, p. 126.

Czechoslovak Republic, Jinnah delivered a curious speech at Karachi. He compared the Indian Muslims to Sudeten Germans: 'Only those succeed with the British people who possess force and power and who are in a position to bully them . . . I would draw their (of the British) attention—and here also of the Congress High Command—and ask them to mark, learn and inwardly digest the recent upheaval and its consequent developments . . . It was because the Sudeten Germans were forced under the heels of the majority of Czechoslovakia, who oppressed them, suppressed them, maltreated them, and showed a brutal and callous disregard for their rights and interests for two decades —hence the inevitable result that the Republic of Czechoslovakia is now broken up and a new map will have to be drawn up.'[1] It was a strange verdict for anyone outside Nazi Germany to pass on the tragedy of Czechoslovakia. While Jinnah's opponents might or might not 'mark, learn and inwardly digest' the lessons of that unhappy episode, he had done so. He had seen the success of Nazi propaganda in working up popular feeling at home, and wearing down opposition abroad.

Jinnah's campaign against the Congress steadily rose in tempo. In the spring of 1939 he declared that the provincial part of the new constitution had utterly failed to safeguard Muslim rights. A few months later he questioned the suitability of a democratic system of government 'in such a vast country with differing nationalities'. He blamed the Governors and the Viceroy for not exercising their special powers to protect the interests of the Muslims in Congress-governed provinces. When the Congress ministries resigned in November 1939, as a protest against India's participation in the war without her consent, Jinnah announced the celebration of 'a day of deliverance' of Muslims 'from tyranny, oppression and injustice' during two and a half years of Congress rule in which Muslim opinion was alleged to have been flouted, Muslim culture destroyed, Muslim religious and social life attacked, and Muslim economic and political rights trampled upon.

[1] Quoted by Hector Bolitho in *Jinnah*, p. 118.

What was this tyranny against the Muslims which the Congress ministries were alleged to have plotted? The Muslim League had published in 1938-9 two reports (Pirpur Committee and Shareef Reports) to list the grievances of Muslims in Congress-governed provinces. Most of the allegations related to isolated incidents in villages and towns, in which Muslims, or for that matter Hindus, may have suffered; such incidents were common in all provinces and at all times and responsibility for them usually rested on a petty official, who had been guilty of negligence or abuse of power. Some of the grievances were of a more general character, such as the singing of the national anthem and the hoisting of the national flag on public buildings. One of the charges was that excessive reverence was paid to Gandhi and that his birthday had been declared a holiday. 'To declare my birthday as a holiday,' commented Gandhi, 'should be classified as a cognisable offence.' As for the national anthem and the national flag, his advice to Congressmen (through the pages of *Harijan*) had been to respect the susceptibilities of Muslims and not to sing the song or hoist the flag if a single Muslim objected. So far as the Wardha Scheme of Education was concerned, the complaint that it did not provide for religious instruction of Muslim children had little meaning because the curriculum did not include such instruction for any community.

Under the constitution, the Governors had special responsibilities for the protection of the minorities. One of them, Sir Harry Haig (Governor of the United Provinces), wrote after his retirement: 'In dealing with communal issues, the Ministers in my judgment normally acted with impartiality and a desire to do what was fair. Indeed towards the end of their time they were seriously criticized by the Hindu Mahasabha on the ground that they were not being fair to the Hindus, though there was in fact no justification for such a criticism.'[1]

Early in 1940, the Congress President Dr Rajendra Prasad wrote to Jinnah suggesting that the charges against the Congress ministries should be investigated by a judge of the Federal

[1] *Asiatic Review,* July 1940.

Court. Jinnah turned down the suggestion and called for a Royal Commission. A Royal Commission in wartime and for raking up such a controversy was hardly likely to be appointed, but it looked as if Jinnah wanted to keep the controversy alive as long as he could. His propaganda was directed not so much at the Congress or the British Government as at his own community; it was, to use a contemporary phrase, 'for home consumption'. Anything which widened the gulf between Hindus and Muslims and indicated that the differences between the two communities were irreconcilable proved his thesis that a democratic set-up was impossible for India.

Jinnah began to develop his two-nation theory; the differences between Hindus and Muslims were not only confined to religion, but covered the whole range of their social, cultural and economic life. In March 1940, the two-nation theory was officially accepted by the All-India Muslim League, which declared that no constitutional plan for India would be workable or acceptable to Muslims unless it was based on a demarcation of Muslim majority areas in the north-west and the east as independent states. Pakistan, which Muslim spokesmen had dismissed during the Round Table Conference as a 'students' scheme', had now become the goal of the Muslim League.

Gandhi's first reaction to the two-nation theory and the demand for Pakistan was one of bewilderment, almost of incredulity. Was it the function of religion to separate men or to unite them? He described the two-nation theory as an untruth; in his dictionary there was no stronger word. He discussed the attributes of nationality. A change of religion did not change nationality; the religious divisions did not coincide with cultural differences. A Bengali Muslim, he wrote: 'speaks the same tongue that a Bengali Hindu does, eats the same food, has the same amusements as his Hindu neighbour. They dress alike. His (Jinnah's) name could be that of any Hindu. When I first met him, I did not know he was a Muslim'.

To divide India was to undo the centuries of work done by Hindus and Muslims; Gandhi's soul rebelled against the idea that Hinduism and Islam represented antagonistic cultures and doctrines, and that eighty million of Muslims had really nothing in common with their Hindu neighbours. And even if there were religious and cultural differences, what clash of interests could there be on such matters as revenue, industry, sanitation or justice? The differences could only be in religious usage and observances with which a secular state should have no concern.

'Vivisect me before you vivisect India,' was Gandhi's anguished comment, but however strongly he felt on Pakistan, he was the last man to force his views down the throat of a single individual. 'I know,' he confessed, in *Harijan*, April 6, 1940: 'no non-violent method of compelling the obedience of eight crores of Muslims to the will of the rest of India, however powerful the majority the rest may represent. The Muslims must have the same rights of self-determination that the rest of India has. We are at present a joint family. Any member may claim a division.'

This was the only possible attitude for a man of non-violence, though it may have encouraged Jinnah in the belief that if the Muslim League persisted in its demand and could carry Muslim public opinion, Pakistan would become a reality. Until almost the last stage, Jinnah did not define the boundaries nor fill the outlines of his Pakistan proposal; each of his followers was thus free to see Pakistan in his own image. The orthodox dreamed of a state reproducing the purity of pristine Islam, a community living in conformity with the teachings of the holy Prophet. Those with a secular outlook hoped for tangible benefits from their 'own' state.

Though it came like a bolt from the blue to Indian nationalists, the Pakistan idea sold fast with the Muslim community, particularly with its middle class. There were several reasons for this development. The Muslim middle class, which for historical reasons had been left behind in the race for the plums of government service, trade, and industry, was attracted by the idea of a Muslim state. In a competitive society anything which promised a short-cut to success was welcome. Muslim landlords in Bengal and Punjab saw the prospect of deliverance from the 'progressive

politicians' who indulged in dangerous talk of abolishing *zamindari*.
Muslim officials were glad of the new vistas which were expected
to open to them in a new state, without the Hindu seniors
hovering over their heads. Muslim traders and industrialists
began to cherish visions of free fields for prosperous ventures
without the intrusion of the Hindu competitors.

Of these 'material' advantages of Pakistan, its advocates may
not have always been conscious, but these advantages seemed to
reinforce the appeal the proposal made to them. Ever since
the days of Sir Syed Ahmad Khan the Muslim community had
been exhorted by some of its prominent leaders to keep away
from the anti-British movement; however specious the arguments,
those who gave and those who followed this advice had a guilty
feeling in the deeper recesses of their hearts. The Pakistan idea
for the first time seemed to satisfy the religious emotions as
well as the political instincts of the Muslim middle class. The
vision of a sovereign Muslim State in India was reminiscent of
the past glories of Muslim rule; it was too fascinating a prospect
not to catch the popular imagination. The Muslim intellectual
felt a new exhilaration for a programme which promised
independence from both the British and the Hindus; the fact
that it brought his community into collision with the majority
community and not with the British only made the movement
somewhat less hazardous.

Pakistan seemed to fulfil a psychological need of the Indian
Muslims. As W. C. Smith explained in 1946.

The Muslim League, then, has been becoming the organ of
a surging nationalism; at its centre a hard core of business interests
intent on power, but beginning to be supported also by an
awakening peasantry and surrounded by a nationalism's complete
paraphernalia, of poetry, and a whole cultural renascence of youthful
idealism and open-hearted devotion.'[1]

The outbreak of the world war helped the propagation of the
separatist ideology. The resignation of the Congress ministries
allowed the League to occupy the political stage. If the Congress

[1] Smith, Wilfred Cantwell: *Modern Islam in India*, London, 1946, p. 275.

.ministries had remained in office, the atrocity stories against them could not have been repeated without being challenged. As it was, the Governors could hardly be expected to give a 'clearance certificate' to those who had now become their political opponents. The war itself was an important consideration for not alienating the Muslim League. The Viceroy and his advisers were anxious not to do anything which would offend Jinnah. The demand for Pakistan probably surprised the British Government as much as it surprised the Congress. Initially, its significance in British eyes was that it confirmed their stock thesis that constitutional progress of India was barred not by British hesitation but by Indian discord. The declaration in August 1940 that 'it goes without saying that they (the British Government) could not contemplate transfer of their present responsibilities for the peace and welfare of India to any system of government whose authority is directly denied by large and powerful elements in India's national life' was the first tacit recognition that the British Government were prepared to consider even such drastic solutions as Jinnah had propounded. The Pakistan resolution of the All-India Muslim League had only been passed in March 1940. But for the war, it is doubtful if even an indirect endorsement of the Pakistan proposal would have been publicly made so soon. The war was, however, dictating the pace of events, which neither the British Government nor the Indian leaders could entirely foresee or control.

Chapter 43

RAJKOT

IN the late thirties, if the rising communal feeling seemed a red signal to Gandhi, the growing discontent in the Princely States was another.

The States posed a complex problem; there were 562 of them, some as big and populous as the larger provinces of 'British' India, and many hardly distinguishable from small estates. In the Chamber of Princes, an advisory body constituted under the Government of India Act 1919, only 109 States were represented directly; 127 States were allotted twelve seats and 326 States were not considered fit for any representation at all. Varying widely in size, resources and the level of administration, the majority of the States had been recognized as political entities in the course of the British conquest of India. The relations of the rulers of these States with the Government were governed by treaties or 'sanads', which were concluded with the East India Company and dated back to the eighteenth and nineteenth centuries; in truth, the princes were subject to supervision and intervention by the Paramount Power (as the British Government came to be described). The princes could not deal directly with foreign powers or with other princes. In internal administration, they had a greater latitude but the British 'Resident' could always, if he chose, have his way.

Thanks to the role played by them in the suppression of the Mutiny (1857) the States had come to be regarded as a valuable bulwark of the Empire. They constituted, to quote Prof. Rushbrook Williams, 'a network of friendly fortresses in debatable territory'. So long as a prince remained loyal to the British *Raj* and did not commit acts of outrageous folly or tyranny, he was usually left alone. The protection which the Paramount Power afforded to the regimes in the States gave a sense of security to the princes, but made the States political, social and economic backwaters.

Gandhi had a first-hand knowledge of the conditions in the States. His father and grandfather had been ministers in Porbandar and Rajkot. As a young lawyer, he had found the atmosphere of these States suffocating. Their feudal structure, however natural to the eighteenth century, had become an anachronism in the twentieth. The smaller States lacked the framework of a good government. In the larger States, even in the better governed ones, administration was highly autocratic. The ruler had unfettered powers over the life and property of his subjects; there was little distinction between the State exchequer and his privy purse; he could squander the revenues of the State on personal luxury while the people were starved of essential services. Above all, with a few exceptions, these States lacked the rule of law, the freedom of speech and association, indeed the very elements of civil liberties. There were hardly any representative institutions in the true sense of the term. The larger States had legislatures, but many of them were packed with nominees of the ruler and had little power; they were, to use Prof. Coupland's picturesque expression, 'durbars in a new costume'.

'Hopes and aspirations,' the Montagu–Chelmsford Report had warned, 'may overlap frontier lines like sparks across a street.' It was impossible for the Princely States to remain insulated from developments in the rest of India. There had been a tremendous awakening in the Provinces under direct British rule from 1920 onwards, when the Congress followed Gandhi into the non-co-operation movement. Gandhi had resisted suggestions for bringing the people of the States into the struggle for Indian freedom. Though the right of the people of the States to self-governing institutions was recognized, and the rulers were exhorted to do their duty to their people, the latter were expected to fight for their rights without any 'external aid' from political parties outside the States.

In July 1938, Gandhi reviewed this policy and described it as: 'the aseptic method in which the physician allows the poison to work itself out by setting in motion all the natural forces and letting them have full play. . . . by its resolution of non-interference the Congress put the States people on their mettle, in other words set in motion the natural forces, i.e. powers latent in the people themselves.'

There were also other reasons for this restraint. Gandhi had found the conduct of the civil disobedience movement in British India a difficult enough task; its extension to the States in the early twenties or thirties would have made this task a stupendous one. The people in the States had hardly any opportunities for self-expression and if they had been brought into the non-violent mass campaigns, it may have been difficult to keep them under control or to train them in resisting the repression by the autocratic administration the authority of which they challenged.

From 1937 onwards, there were two factors which quickened the pace of events in the States. The formation of popular governments in the provinces raised hopes and turned the passive resignation of the people into active discontent. The prospect of an All-India Federation, as envisaged by the Government of India Act (1935), also reacted on the Princes and the people in different ways but brought a conflict nearer. The representatives of the Princes had subscribed to an All-India Federation at the Round Table Conference, but as it became evident to them that federation presupposed surrender of some of the powers and prerogatives of the constituent units, their enthusiasm for a federal structure visibly cooled off. To the Indian nationalist, however, the danger of a federal solution was that it left too much power in the hands of the Princes.

The only way in which the States could properly fit into the free India of the future was by acquiring a democratic basis themselves. Responsible government in the States was thus important not only for people of the States, but also from the larger considerations of Indian freedom and unity.

With this background, it is not surprising that in 1938-9 a number of States witnessed an agitation for civil liberties and for the introduction of democratic institutions. Hyderabad, Travancore, Jaipur, the Orissa States were all convulsed with local campaigns, but the spotlight was to fall on Rajkot, a small principality in Western India, where Gandhi's intervention turned a local issue into a national one, and brought into sharp focus not only the problem of the Indian States, but his technique of non-violent action.

Rajkot had been a second home to Gandhi. He had received his early education in Rajkot, where his father had been the *Diwan* (Chief Minister); his wife, Kasturbai, had been brought up here. The people of Rajkot had been agitating for responsible government, and Vallabhbhai Patel, Gandhi's friend and colleague, had taken a hand in this movement. In December 1938, an agreement was reached beween Patel and the Thakore (ruler) of Rajkot. The latter agreed to grant an amnesty to political prisoners and to appoint a committee of ten (of whom seven were to be the nominees of Patel) to frame a scheme of political reforms for Rajkot. The Thakore, however, backed out of the agreement; it was alleged that he was influenced in this *volte face* by Sir Patrick Cadell, the President of the Thakore's Council, and Mr Gibson, the Political Agent. Gandhi, while denouncing this 'cold-blooded breach of a solemn covenant entered into between the Rajkot ruler and his people', criticized these officers and appealed to the people of Rajkot 'to set Thakore Saheb free'. Events were to reveal that, guided by Durbar Virawala, a minister who had nothing to learn in cunning and intrigue even in Indian States, the Thakore hardly needed any promptings from other quarters for his tortuous policies.

To Gandhi the point at issue was not so much the measure of constitutional reform for Rajkot but the fact that its ruler had committed a breach of faith with his people. If solemn agreements could be flouted, how was a peaceful transition from an autocratic to a democratic system ever to be effected in Indian States? In spite of his indifferent health, he proceeded

o

to Rajkot to persuade the Thakore not to break his word of honour; his wife had preceded him. The endless discussions with the shifty ruler and his elusive minister produced little result, and in desperation Gandhi went on a fast. What had started as a minor controversy in a remote corner of India thus developed into a first-class political crisis. The Viceroy, responding to Gandhi's appeal for 'the right approach' by the Paramount Power, called upon the Chief Justice of India, Sir Maurice Gwyer, to adjudicate upon the terms of the agreement. Sir Maurice's verdict went in favour of the people's interpretation and the right of Patel to nominate a majority of the members of the committee which was to draw up a scheme of political reforms for Rajkot.

Gandhi broke his fast and the dispute seemed to have ended happily. However, he had not reckoned with the ingenuity of the Thakore and his minister. The composition of the Reforms Committee got involved in endless polemics; Virawala raised all kinds of difficulties, real and imaginary; he egged on the minorities, the Muslims and Bhayats of Rajkot, to press their claims. Confronted with this confusion, Gandhi began to wonder whether he had made any progress at all in converting his opponents. He had come on a mission of peace to Rajkot, but he had only succeeded in increasing the bitterness of the Thakore and his minister. Introspection revealed to him a cardinal blunder he had committed by his appeal to the Viceroy for intervention. His fast was intended to melt the heart of the Thakore. If he had persevered in the fast he would have either succeeded in winning over the errant ruler, or else perished in the attempt. The intervention of the Paramount Power through the Viceroy had vitiated the spiritual value of the fast and was thus a lapse from the high ideal of non-violence which he set before himself.

As a result of this 'silent court of inquiry' within himself, Gandhi took some decisions which astounded his colleagues. He decided to forgo the advantages which the award of the Chief Justice of India conferred on the party of reform; he apologised to Lord Linlithgow and Sir Maurice Gwyer for the inconvenience caused to them, and he implored the Thakore Saheb of Rajkot and his minister to give the best possible deal to the people of Rajkot.

These decisions raised a storm of protest. Was this the way to conduct political movements? Had Gandhi a right to play fast and loose with the fate of the 75,000 inhabitants of Rajkot? Was the party of reform in the State to fritter away its hard-won political gains because the Mahatma had lapsed from a self-erected moral pedestal? Gandhi was unmoved by these criticisms. If he was to conduct or guide a movement, he could not but follow the logic of Satyagraha in which truth was more important than any short-term or long-term political advantage. A Satyagrahi aimed at the conversion of his opponent by love. Gandhi confessed, however, that in the heat of the controversy he and his closest colleagues, had harboured ill feeling towards the Thakore and his minister. It was because they had departed from the high principles of Satyagraha that they had failed to make any headway with their opponents. He recalled the skill of a blind musician whom he had heard as a child in the streets of Rajkot and added, 'there are chords in every human heart. If we only know how to strike the right chord, we bring out the music'.

When a child heckled him and asked, 'What is there in Durbar Virawala to draw out?' Gandhi retorted, 'What is there in you? Well, if there are any virtues in you, even so there are in Durbar Virawala. And if I hug you as my own child why should I not hug Durbar Virawala as a member of the family?

'I was weighed in my own scales in Rajkot and found wanting,' was Gandhi's verdict on this episode, which was important not only as a spiritual crisis for the Mahatma but revealed the inflammable situation in the States. The people of the States, for no fault of their own, lacked the necessary discipline and organizing ability for waging a non-violent political agitation. And political agitation, throwing as it did a challenge to their entrenched authority, seemed to bring out the worst in some of the Princes and their advisers, who attempted to crush the agitation by every conceivable method, fair or foul. The Political Department which alone could call the Princes to order, was indifferent, if not hostile, to the peoples' movements. The real danger was that the terrorism of the Princes might provoke the counter-terrorism of the people, thus dashing to the ground Gandhi's hopes of effecting a peaceful transition from autocracy to democracy.

Gandhi appealed to the people of the States to hasten slowly; they had to wait awhile for popular government. He explained that: 'Responsible government, which is a gift without the will and the power of the people behind it, will be a mere paper responsibility hardly worth the paper on which it may be printed. If it is a fact that the atmosphere for immediate self-government among the States is not propitious, and that the people are not ready to pay the price, it follows that they should have the proper training for it. I am not likely lightly and in the near future to advise mass Satyagraha anywhere. There is neither adequate training nor discipline among the people.'

He asked the people of the States to confine their agitation to the minimum demands which the rulers could be expected to grant—freedom of speech, association and Press, peaceful propaganda, and equality before law through an independent judiciary.

Rajkot had been to Gandhi, 'a priceless laboratory'. He stiffened in his demands upon would-be Satyagrahis; they had to be truly non-violent in action, as well as in thought. If a rigid application of this exacting standard reduced his followers to a handful, he did not mind.

BOOK IV

THE LAST PHASE

Chapter 44

NON-VIOLENCE ON TRIAL

THE clouds of war were hovering over Europe in 1938. The World War of 1914-18 had not proved 'a war to end war'; the peace treaty created more problems than it solved. The system of 'collective security' through the League of Nations had belied the hopes built on it. The League was handicapped by the absence of the United States, the exclusion of Russia and the reluctance of its members to subordinate national interests to international considerations. The first challenge of national defiance from Japan had revealed the helplessness of the League. The invasion of Abyssinia by Italy, the occupation of the demilitarized zone, and the annexation of Austria by Germany and the foreign intervention in the Spanish Civil War revealed that the law of the jungle was being applied to international relations. Political democracy and individual liberty were at a discount. Authoritarian governments, which had crushed all opposition at home, and regimented their resources for war, were preparing for adventures abroad. The smaller nations of Europe lived in daily dread, not knowing when and where the next blow would fall. A thick pall of fear seemed to settle over the civilized world and men wondered if a new dark age had set in.

How did nationalist India react to these events? Internationalism, writes Jawaharlal Nehru, develops in a free country as 'subject condition is like a cancerous growth inside the body politic which not only prevents any limb from becoming healthy but is a constant irritant to the mind and colours all thought and action'. That Indian nationalism, as represented by the Indian National Congress, was sensitive to what was happening on the world stage was largely due to Nehru himself, who had, by study and travel, kept himself abreast of developments abroad. Nehru had reacted sharply to the make-believe diplomacy of the period of 'appeasement', and discounted hopes of buying off dictators with concessions. Under his inspiration, the Indian National Congress had denounced every act of aggression by Japan, Germany and Italy, and condemned the suppression within these countries of civil liberties, the stifling of intellect and conscience, the persecution of religious and racial minorities, the liquidation of political opponents and the brazen display of naked force for the coercion of weaker neighbours.

In 1931, during Gandhi's visit to England, the *Star* had published a cartoon which showed him in a loin cloth beside Mussolini, Hitler, De Valera and Stalin, who were clad in black, brown, green and red shirts respectively. The caption, 'And he ain't wearin' any bloomin' shirt at all' was not only literally, but figuratively true. For a man of non-violence, who believed in the brotherhood of man, there was no facile division of nations into good and bad, allies and adversaries. This did not, however, mean that Gandhi did not distinguish between the countries which inflicted and the countries which feared violence. Briefed by Nehru in international affairs, it was only natural that his sympathies should be with the victims of aggression. But Gandhi's own life had been one long struggle against the forces of violence. For more than thirty years he had been evolving a technique which, while eschewing violence, would nevertheless be effective in solving individual and group problems.

Gandhi's ideas on non-violence, and his technique of Satyagraha had matured over many years. In the Boer War and the First World War he had raised ambulance units and collected recruits for the British Indian Army. The fact that he had not handled a gun himself made no material difference. As he confessed later: 'There is no defence for my conduct only in the scales of non-violence (Ahimsa). I draw no distinction between those who wield weapons of destruction, and those who do Red Cross work. Both participate in war and advance its cause.

Both are guilty of the crime of war. But even after introspection during all these years, I feel that in the circumstances in which I found myself, I was bound to adopt the course I did.'[1]

The Indians whom Gandhi led in the battlefronts of the Boer War, or whom he exhorted to join the British Indian Army in 1918, did not believe in non-violence; it was not repugnance to violence, but indifference or cowardice which had held them back from participating on their own in the war. Believing, as he did in those days, in the British Empire as a benign institution, Gandhi also considered that, as citizens of the Empire, Indians had duties as well as rights, and one of those duties was to participate in the defence of the Empire.

In the two decades which spanned the first and second World Wars, Gandhi's faith in the British Empire had been irrevocably shaken; his own belief in the power of non-violence had grown with greater reflection and experience, and the people of India, thanks to three major Satyagraha campaigns and his extensive countrywide tours, had become familiar with the cult of non-violence. Such was the emphasis which Gandhi had placed on non-violence in the struggle for political freedom that it sometimes looked as if he regarded the means as more important than the goal. In November 1931 he had gone so far as to say: 'And I would like to repeat to the world, times without number, that I will not purchase my country's freedom at the cost of non-violence. My marriage to non-violence is such an absolute thing that I would rather commit suicide than be deflected from my position.' He wished India to give a successful demonstration of non-violence and to set an example to the rest of the world.

As the threat of war grew and the forces of violence gathered momentum, Gandhi reasserted his faith in the efficacy of non-violence. He felt more strongly than ever that at that moment of crisis in world history he had a message for India and India had a message for the bewildered humanity. Through the pages of *Harijan* he expounded the non-violent approach to military

[1] *Young India*, September 13, 1928.

O•

aggression and political tyranny. He advised the weaker nations to defend themselves not by seeking protection from better-armed States, nor by increasing their own fighting potential, but by non-violent resistance to the aggressor. A non-violent Abyssinia, he explained, needed no arms and no succour from the League of Nations; if every Abyssinian man, woman, and child refused co-operation with the Italians, willing or forced, the latter would have to walk to victory over the dead bodies of their victims and to occupy the country without the people.

It may be argued that Gandhi was making a heavy over-draft upon human endurance. It required supreme courage for a whole people to die to the last man, woman and child, rather than surrender to the enemy. Gandhi's non-violent resis-tance was thus not a soft doctrine—a convenient refuge from a dangerous situation. Nor was it an offer on a silver platter to the dictators of what they plotted to wrest by force. Those who offered non-violent resistance had to be prepared for the extreme sacrifice.

Early in 1939, Gandhi told Dr Kagawa, a Japanese expert on co-operatives who claimed to be a pacifist, that it was his duty, if he felt that the war against China was unjust, to declare himself against it and to face the consequences: 'I would declare my heresies and be shot. I would put the co-operatives and all your work in one scale, and put the honour of your nation in the other, and if you found that the honour was being sold, I would ask you to declare your views against Japan and in so doing make Japan live through your death.' One wonders what Kagawa thought of this advice; the mantle of a Socrates does not fit everyone. The melancholy fact was that while millions could be persuaded to kill or be killed in war, not even a few hundred pacifists were willing to die for their convictions in peace.

The fact that the governments and the peoples of the world could not bring themselves to accept Gandhi's technique did not in his eyes detract from its value. Few of his critics under-stood the implications and the potentialities of this technique.

Unfortunately the word non-violence was an inadequate English translation of Gandhi's ideas. Questioned by some visitors in January 1939 as to whether non-violence had a positive quality, Gandhi explained: 'If I had used the word love, which non-violence is in essence, you would not have asked this question. But perhaps love docs not express my meaning fully. The nearest word is charity. We love friends as equals. But the reaction that a ruthless dictator sets up in us is either that of awe or pity according respectively as we react to him violently or non-violently.'

Those who offered non-violent resistance and refused to return violence with violence, or hatred with hatred, posed a problem to the opponent. He might at first mistake this restraint for cowardice, but before long he would discover that he was being made to fight on a new ground which was not of his choosing. The reaction of the aggressor to successful non-violent resistance would be progressively one of surprise, ridicule, indignation, and finally of inner doubt and conversion. In a non-violent struggle there are no victors or vanquished; the object is not to humiliate the opponent but to convert him; there is no aftermath of anger, hatred, or revenge to breed fresh conflicts. Satyagraha thus viewed offers a superior alternative to war for resolving disputes and making adjustments inevitable in a dynamic world-order.

The events of 1938-39 had put the faith of many pacifists in Europe to a severe test. G. D. H. Cole eloquently expressed the anguish of his soul in an article in the *Aryan Path:* 'Until two or so years ago, I believed myself opposed to war, and death-dealing violence under all circumstances. But today, hating war, I would risk war to stop these horrors. I would risk war, and yet even now that second self of mine shrinks back appalled at the thought of killing a man. Personally, I would sooner die than kill. But may it not be my duty to kill rather than die?'

New horrors were being let loose on humanity. The engines of destruction were being progressively perfected; the aeroplane had extended the range of attack. Yet, however terrible the instruments of war, it was a human hand which wielded them and it was a human mind which directed that hand. Those who plotted war did so for a definite purpose—to exploit men and materials of the territories they set out to conquer. The aggressor's effort was to apply terrorism in a sufficient measure to bend the adversary to his will. 'But supposing,' wrote Gandhi: 'a people make up their mind that they will never do the tyrant's will, nor retaliate with the tyrant's own method, the tyrant will not find it worth his while to go on with his terrorism. If all the mice in the world held conference together and resolve that they would no more fear the cat but all run into her mouth, the mice will live.'

Gandhi was aware of the apotheosis of violence which Nazi and Fascist régimes represented, but he did not accept that Hitler and Mussolini were beyond redemption. A fundamental assumption in the non-violent technique was that human nature in essence was one and must ultimately respond to love. 'If the enemy realized,' wrote Gandhi, 'that you have not the remotest thought in your mind of raising your hand against him even for the sake of your life, he will lack the zest to kill you. Every hunter has had this experience. No one has heard of anyone hunting cows.'

When Czechoslovakia was blackmailed into submission in September 1938, Gandhi commended his non-violent method to the unfortunate Czechs: 'There is no bravery greater than a resolute refusal to bend the knee to an earthly power, no matter how great, and that without bitterness of spirit and in the fulness of faith that the spirit alone lives, nothing else does.'

To those who considered such heroism impossible, Gandhi's answer was that they were underrating the powers of the human spirit. The line between the possible and the impossible was, moreover, not a fixed one. Gandhi was fond of giving an analogy from his school days: 'Till my eyes of geometrical understanding had been opened my brain was swimming as I read and re-read the twelve axioms of Euclid. After the opening of my eyes, geometry seemed to be the easiest science to learn. Much more so is the case with non-violence. It is a matter of faith and experience not of argument beyond a point.'

Non-violence was, moreover, not merely a method to meet aggression; it represented a way of life. The motive power of Nazi and Fascist militarism was the desire to carve new empires, and behind it all was a ruthless competition to annex new sources of raw materials and fresh markets. Wars were thus rooted in the overweening greeds of men, as also in a purblind tribalism which enthroned nationalism above humanity. If the world was to get rid of this recurring menace of war, it had to shake off not only militarism, but the competitive greed and fear and hatred which fed it.

In an article in the *Aryan Path* in September 1938, John Middleton Murry described Gandhi as the greatest Christian teacher in the modern world and wrote: 'Assuredly I see absolutely no hope for western civilization except the kindling of a vast and consuming flame of Christian Love. The choice appears to be between that or a mass-murder on a scale at which the imagination sickens.'

In fact there was no kindling of a flame of Christian Love. The lights went out one by one until the war broke out in September 1939.

Chapter 45

INDIA AND THE WAR

ON September 3, 1939, the Gazette of India carried a grave announcement: 'I, Victor Alexander John, Marquess of Linlithgow, Governor-General of India and ex-officio Admiral, therein being satisfied thereof by information received by me, do hereby proclaim that war has broken out between His Majesty and Germany.'

One man, and he a foreigner, writes Jawaharlal Nehru in the *Discovery of India,* plunged four hundred millions of human beings into war without the slightest reference to them. Since the federal part of the Government of India Act of 1935 had not yet become operative, and the ultimate responsibility for the governance of India was vested in the British Parliament, the declaration of Lord Linlithgow was unexceptionable from the constitutional point of view, but tactically it was a great blunder. India, unlike the Dominions of Australia, New Zealand, Canada and South Africa, lacked the mechanism of responsible government at the centre, but there was nothing to prevent the Viceroy from consulting the popular governments in the Provinces and the leaders of the political parties in the Central Legislature. Already, during the summer, as a protest against the despatch (as a precautionary measure) of Indian troops to Malaya and the Far East, the Congress Party in the Central Legislative Assembly had abstained from the session which carried through the Defence of India Act and conferred far-reaching powers on the executive for the conduct of the war. The chain of suspicion and mistrust which was to bedevil Congress-Government relations throughout the war had been forged.

That this should have happened was the more unfortunate because the sympathy of the Indian National Congress was overwhelmingly in favour of the Allies. The 'foreign policy' of the Congress was largely shaped by Nehru, whose opposition to totalitarian régimes admitted of no compromise. In the summer of 1938 Nehru was in London during the critical days preceding the Munich crisis, and in a letter to the *Manchester Guardian* had bitterly criticized the policy of 'appeasement'. Gandhi himself had reacted to Munich with his characteristic sensitiveness: 'Is it a triumph of organized violence? Has Herr Hitler discovered a new technique of organizing violence which enables him to gain his ends without shedding blood?'

The Indian National Congress had consistently sympathized with the victims of the totalitarian aggression, even though some of its influential members, such as Subhas Chandra Bose, doubted the wisdom of antagonizing powerful nations such as Germany, Italy and Japan for the sake of Abyssinia, Czechoslovakia and China, whose fate seemed in any case to be sealed.

There was thus a great reservoir of sympathy for the Allied cause on which the British Government could have drawn. The Viceroy had failed to take Indian leaders into confidence before declaring India a belligerent, but he endeavoured to make up for this omission soon afterwards. He telegraphed to Gandhi to see him. Gandhi took the first train to Simla. He told Linlithgow that his sympathies were with England and France. As a man of non-violence, the utmost he could offer to the Allied cause was his moral support. As he discussed the war and pictured the possible destruction of the House of Commons and Westminster Abbey he broke down. Violence seemed triumphantly on the march.

His heart, under the first impact of war, was heavy: 'I have become disconsolate. In the secret of my heart I am in perpetual quarrel with God that He should allow such things to go on. My non-violence seems almost impotent. But the answer comes at the end of the daily quarrel that neither God nor non-violence is impotent. Impotence is in men.' He saw the futility of violence in countering violence. His line was cast: 'Whether I act as a guide of the Working Committee, or if I may use the same expression, without offence, of the Government, my guidance will be for the deliberate purpose of taking either or both along the path of non-violence, be the step ever so imperceptible.'[1]

Thus at an early stage in the war Gandhi's own position was anchored to his pacifism. He was conscious that the proposal that India should defend herself against foreign aggression with non-violence was one which few Congressmen would accept as a practical proposition. For him, however, there was no other course; he could not give up his faith in non-violence at a time when it was being put to the hardest test: 'My position is confined to myself alone. I have to find out whether I have any fellow traveller along my lonely path . . . Whether one or many, I must declare that it is better for India to discard violence altogether even for defending her borders.'[2]

If politics are the art of the possible, as Bismarck once defined them, Gandhi's attitude at this time was not that of the politician, but that of the prophet. The intensity of his own faith seemed sometimes to blur the distinction between the ideal and the real. In the midst of a global war, when countries were mere pawns in the plans of strategists, he affirmed that free India could have no enemies; the suggestion ignored the cynical, land-hungry and power-mad régimes which stuck at nothing to achieve their aims of world domination. He went on to suggest that if the people of India learnt resolutely to say 'No', foreign armies would not have the courage to invade her soil; that India's economy could be remodelled so as to remove all temptations from a political aggressor. But where was the time to remodel India's economy, and how could a people, which had failed to muster enough true non-violence (by Gandhi's own standards) to evict the British Government, suddenly acquire non-violent strength to repel armed attack? Only a few months earlier, during the Rajkot episode, the Mahatma had acknow-

[1] *Harijan*, September 30, 1939.
[2] *Harijan*, October 14, 1939.

ledged that conditions were not propitious for a large-scale
non-violent movement and that the people lacked adequate
training and discipline. If a non-violent campaign, under his
own supervision, for securing civil liberties in a small principality
bristled with difficulties, the feasibility of applying the non-
violent technique to foreign aggression was obviously doubtful.

The Indian National Congress was not a body of pacifists;
it had accepted non-violence in the struggle for freedom, but
not as a creed for all times and in all situations. Prominent
Congressmen, including Motilal Nehru, had interested them-
selves in the Indianization of the officers' cadre of the British
Indian army, and few of them had imagined that an independent
India would be able to dispense with the police and the military.
Most Congressmen viewed the war, not from the angle of non-
violence, but from that of Indian self-government. In the First
World War, Tilak, Annie Besant and other ardent nationalists
had demanded political freedom as a condition precedent to
India's unreserved participation in the war-effort. A quarter
of a century later, with greater awakening in the country, it
was scarcely to be expected that nationalists would ask for
less. There was an obvious contradiction in Indians fighting
to hold aloft the banner of freedom and democracy in
Czechoslovakia or Poland, while their own country was in
bondage. There was yet another consideration which weighed
with those who felt keenly for the Allied cause. Wars were
no longer bouts between professional armies in distant battle-
fields; whole nations had to be mobilized as workers or soldiers;
unless Britain released India's energies by treating her as an
equal partner in a common struggle, it was hardly possible for
her to play her full part in the world struggle.

In its resolution of September 14, 1939, the Congress Working
Committee expressed its sympathy for those who were resisting
Nazi aggression and offered its co-operation in the war against
Nazism. Co-operation was, however, to be 'between equals
by mutual consent for a cause which both consider to be worthy'.
The committee invited the British Government to declare in

unequivocal language its war-aims in regard to democracy and imperialism, and in particular, how these aims were going to apply to India: 'the real test of any declaration is its application in the present, for it is the present that will govern action today and give shape to the future.'

The Congress thus posed two basic problems to Britain: to define the shape of the order for which the war was being waged, and to give India a foretaste of that freedom and democracy for which she was being called upon to fight. To British statesmen such queries smacked of an unpractical radicalism, if not of a cynical opportunism. How could far-reaching constitutional changes be attempted in war-time? Was it prudent or practicable to reopen the question of India's constitutional future and to expose the country to fierce debate and dangerous unrest? How could the British Government and Parliament find time for that gruelling process which had preceded the passage of the Government of India Act of 1935? How were the claims of the Congress to be reconciled with those of the Muslim League, which questioned the basic premises of the Congress? These and other criticisms of the Congress position seemed to influence the British reaction to the Congress demand in 1939. From the British point of view there were certainly difficulties in meeting the Congress demand, but a little imagination and a little courage in the first few weeks of the war might have reversed the process of mistrust which made an agreement impossible later.

However, neither the British Cabinet headed by Neville Chamberlain, nor the Government of India led by Lord Linlithgow, was capable of an imaginative stroke of policy. In 1939-40 their minds had not moved one yard from where they were in 1937 or, for that matter, in 1935. As a British journalist put it:

'We hope in the event of victory to bring liberty to the Austrians. It would never enter our heads to draw up a constitution for them at Westminster or in Paris . . .

'But in the case of India it is fixed as an obstinate principle in our rulers' minds that God's Englishmen must plan the house in which Indians are to live. Our civil servants will do the drafting. Our Parliament, clause by clause, will debate the Bill. The votes of white men responsible to Clapham and Cardiff shall decide whether India shall have two chambers or one, a wide or propertied franchise.'[1]

In his long-awaited statement of October 17, 1939, the Viceroy expressed his inability to elaborate the war aims beyond what the British Premier had already done: that Dominion Status remained the goal of British policy, that a review of the Government of India Act of 1935 could be undertaken after the war, and that an Advisory Council to associate Indian opinion in the prosecution of the war could be set up. These 'concessions' were hardly calculated to inspire enthusiasm in India. The Viceroy's reference to the problem of minorities (in which he included the Princes and the Europeans) exasperated the Congress leaders and brought forth an acid comment from Gandhi: 'Communal differences have been used by the British Government to thwart Indian aspirations. Even now the ugly spectacle of playing off the League against the Congress seems to be going on. I had expected that the stupendous European crisis would bring better perception to English statesmen.'[2]

The Muslim League had demanded that Muslims alone should determine what their place was going to be in a future constitution of India, and that the Muslim League should be recognized as the sole representative organization of the Muslim community. The war had raised the bargaining power of the League and Jinnah was taking the fullest advantage of his position. A series of conferences in November 1939, between the Viceroy on the one hand and the Congress and League leaders on the other, failed to break the political deadlock.

A fresh incentive for a way out of the impasse came in the summer of 1940, when Nazi armies overran Western Europe. The spectacle of the island of Britain, fighting single-handed

[1] Brailsford, quoted in *Harijan*, March 16, 1940.
[2] *Harijan*, November 11, 1939.

against heavy odds, evoked widespread sympathy as well as admiration in India. It was also evident that if Britain failed to stem the German tide of conquest, nothing could stop Hitler from dominating the Mediterranean and marching into India. The imminence of the peril dictated a new approach, and the Congress Working Committee declared that if the British Government made an unequivocal declaration of Indian independence after the war, the Congress would immediately join in a provisional National Government for the effective defence of the country. This offer was considered as a climb-down by some Congress leaders, including Jawaharlal Nehru; its only justification was the emergency created by the menace of German militarism.

That the Congress was in dead earnest is shown by the fact that in making this offer of co-operation to the British Government it agreed to part company with Gandhi. We have already seen that, in spite of his detestation of the regimentation and violence which Nazism represented, in spite of his sympathy for the Allies, Gandhi believed that violence could only be effectively neutralized by non-violence; he wished the Congress to declare that it would meet even armed aggression with non-violent resistance. Most Congressmen did not believe in the feasibility of this advice. So long, however, as the Congress did not decide to co-operate with the Government the question as to what form—moral or material—that co-operation should take, did not arise. When the Congress offered to enter a provisional government for the better prosecution of the war, Gandhi felt he could not associate himself with a policy in which he did not believe. The Congress Working Committee recognized the divergence of ideals which had necessitated the severance of Gandhi's connection with the Congress: 'While the Working Committee hold that the Congress must continue to adhere strictly to the principle of non-violence in their struggle for independence, the Committee . . . have come to the conclusion that they are unable to go to the full length with Gandhiji but they recognize that he should be free to pursue his great ideal.'

Chapter 46

THE WIDENING RIFT

THE Congress leaders believed in that critical summer of 1940 that they had brought down their terms for co-operation with the Government to the lowest pitch. They had gone the length of forgoing the leadership of Gandhi. In return, they expected a bold and imaginative gesture by the British Government— 'a pleasant psychological shock'—which would wipe out past suspicion and generate a new enthusiasm among the people.

They looked in vain for this gesture in the announcement which the Viceroy made on August 8th on behalf of His Majesty's Government. The view that the framing of the new constitutional scheme should be primarily the responsibility of the people of India was conceded, but with the qualification that this could not be undertaken at a time when Britain was engaged in a struggle for existence. There were the familiar references to the responsibilities which Britain's long association with India had imposed upon her and of which she could not divest herself. There was the significant statement that the British Government 'could not contemplate transfer of their present responsibilities for the peace and welfare of India to any system of government whose authority is directly denied by large and powerful elements in India's national life. Nor could they be parties to the coercion of such elements to such a government'. An affirmation of this kind was hardly called for; nobody expected the Government to coerce 'large and powerful elements' in the country's national life. To use such phraseology, whether its authors willed it or not, was calculated only to increase the intransigence of the Muslim League, and to make more difficult a Congress-League concord, which the Government professed was a *sine qua non* for the transfer of substantial authority to Indians.

The immediate constitutional changes included the expansion of the Viceroy's Council to include some 'representative Indians' and the establishment of a War Advisory Council consisting of representatives from the Provinces and the States and other interests 'in the national life of India as a whole'.

The Congress leaders' reaction was one of profound disappointment. The promise of freedom after the war was much too vague; the phrase 'constituent assembly' seemed to have been deliberately avoided. Would the constitution-making body of the future repeat the history of the Round Table Conferences of the early thirties? In an article, entitled 'The Parting of the Ways', Jawaharlal Nehru observed: '[After the war] we shall have (or so it is proposed but destiny may dispose otherwise) a noble company of bejewelled Maharajas, belted knights, European industrialists and communal magnates, big landlords and talukdars, Indian industrialists and representatives of the Imperial Services, and a few commoner mortals, all sitting together, possibly under the presidentship of the Viceroy, drawing up the Indian constitution. Thus will India exercise her right to self-determination.'

The decisions of such a body were to be subject to Britain's 'special responsibilities' in respect of the Princes, the Minorities, Defence and the position of the Secretary of State's Services. In the immediate future the country was not getting a National Government with real power, but an enlarged edition of the Viceroy's Council, in which there would be more Indians who represented hardly anybody except themselves and might well spend their energies in neutralizing each other.

The 'August Offer' was the maximum which the British Government felt able to make to India in the summer of 1940, but it fell short of the minimum which the Congress was prepared to accept. That even, in a supreme crisis, the Government should fail to respond to appeals for co-operation stung Congress leaders. Their disappointment was all the greater because many of them were really anxious to co-operate in the emergency which faced the Government and the country. In the article, already quoted, Nehru wrote: 'I am told that the British Government has been led to believe that we shall tamely submit to their decrees because so far we have been quiescent. In this world of bombing aeroplanes, tanks and armed men, how weak we are. Why trouble about us? But perhaps even in this world of armed conflict, there is such a thing as the spirit of man and the spirit of a nation which is neither ignoble nor weak and which may not be ignored save at peril.'

It was inconceivable that, at a moment when Britain was fighting for survival against heavy odds, the British Government could have any interest in baiting Indian leaders. The British Government were anxious to secure the co-operation of the Congress, but the 'August Offer' was just the limit to which they felt able to proceed, without, as they believed, jeopardising the war-effort or alienating the Muslim League. The feeling in official circles was that the Government was getting all the men, money and materials it needed for the war; that Congress participation in the Government could even prove a liability. Since the demand for a National Government was also criticized by Jinnah, it is difficult to say, in the light of subsequent history, whether a composite government including the Congress and League could have been formed at this time and whether it would have worked smoothly.

That the Government themselves did not set a high store by the 'August Offer' may be inferred from a secret letter which the Viceroy addressed to the Governors on August 8, 1940, the very day the proposals for the solution of the political deadlock were announced:

'The Home Department have just sent to the Chief Secretaries of all Provincial Governments a letter enclosing draft of a Revolutionary Movement Ordinance . . . Your Government will probably notice that the letter is couched in very general terms and refers throughout to a Revolutionary Movement without specifying the nature of the movement, of the party or parties responsible for promoting it.

'As indicated in paragraph one of the letter, this is deliberate. The original intention was to refer specifically to the Indian National Congress and a Civil Disobedience Movement directed by that body . . . Your officers, I am sure, will have no difficulty in reading between the lines where necessary—for of course, the situation primarily envisaged is still a clash with the Congress —but there are two particular points on which it is necessary to supplement the official letter. I have chosen this way in which to do so, and would ask you to convey what follows to your Chief Secretary by word of mouth.

'In the first place it will be remembered that on the occasion of the last Civil Disobedience Movement, Congress as a whole was not declared an unlawful association; and the view may be held that it would be sufficient to confine the Notification under the Criminal Law Amendment Act to the Working Committee and the Provincial and other local committees of the Congress in each Province. Apart, however, from the fact that action against the Congress as a whole has a merit of simplicity, I feel very strongly that the only possible answer to a declaration of war by any section of the Congress in present circumstances must be a declared determination to crush that organization as a whole. In that view I hope you and your Governments will concur.

'In the second place there is the question of Gandhi's arrest and his treatment after arrest. In the circumstances envisaged there is no intention of exempting him from the action that will have to be taken against other leaders, but in view of his special position and of what has happened before, it will almost certainly be desirable to detain him at Poona under the arrangements made on previous occasions. Where he will be arrested, under what particular law he will be detained, and other details of this nature need not be settled for the moment.'

In planning a knock-out blow at the Congress in the event of 'hostilities', Lord Linlithgow had taken a leaf out of his predecessor's book. The draft of the ordinance which had been sent to the Provincial Governments was an omnibus document which embraced almost every sphere of public activity and conferred sweeping powers on the executive. The letter forwarding this draft indicated that any movement against the Government was to be tackled in two stages. In the 'preparatory stage' the opponents of the Government would be engaged in organizing themselves for action, though they might not have declared hostilities; some forbearance at this stage was permissible, but even here a point might be reached 'when without waiting for an open declaration of war it may be prudent for the Government to take the offensive in order to prevent further demoralization of the public . . . In this respect (as also in regard to activities which are definitely prejudicial) all (provincial) governments are in a stronger position than in normal times, since the Defence of India Rules now exist, and provide various powers of preventive action including in particular preventive detention'.

When the movement of defiance of authority was actually initiated, it was to be regarded as 'hostile action intended to assist the King's enemies'. Past experience had shown 'the advantage of depriving the organizers of such a movement of the initiative at the earliest moment, and it is the intention of the Government of India that as soon as such a movement becomes recognizable, the whole resources of the Government should be employed to crush it at the outset, and to prevent it from obtaining any momentum whatever'.

The ordinance sought to give to the Provincial Governments and its officers authority to arrest, detain and control 'suspected persons', to search persons and places, to confiscate money, buildings, documents, movable property, to control publications, dramatic performances, cinematograph, public utility organizations, posts and telegraphs, telephones, wireless and broadcasting, to impose curfew, to post additional police, to impose collective fines, to take action against volunteer organizations and so on. The offences which were to be punishable under the ordinance included the dissemination of rumours, and contents of proscribed documents, mock funerals and boycott of specified goods or articles. There was a significant hint on the preventive detention of leaders in the letter to the Provincial Governments: 'It is the intention that all persons capable of leading or organizing the movement should be arrested directly the active stage has been reached and it is important that this action should be prompt and complete in order to disorganize the movement at the outset.'

It is important to remember that the draft of this omnibus ordinance was issued to the Provincial Governments on August 2nd, less than a week before the Viceroy had announced his proposals for the solution of the constitutional deadlock; the Viceroy's personal letter to the Governors was issued on the very day on which 'August Offer' became public.

If the Government at this time expected Gandhi to lead the Congress into a mass movement it was guilty of a gross miscalculation. Gandhi was genuinely anxious not to embarrass the Government during the war, and the Congress leaders were so apprehensive about the fate of the Allied cause that a mass movement at this stage was not on the cards. Nevertheless, such was the profound frustration among Congressmen at the attitude of the Government as disclosed in the 'August Offer' that there was a powerful impulse for action of some kind.

An eloquent expression to this frustration was given by Jawaharlal Nehru in the article from which excerpts have already been quoted. 'The declaration of the British Government,' he wrote, 'means the final breaking of such slender bonds as held our minds together.' The All-India Congress Committee met in September 1940 at Bombay and affirmed its total rejection of the Government's proposals. Since there was no prospect of a co-operation with the Government in furtherance of war-effort, the argument as to whether this co-operation could or could not be based on non-violence became irrelevant. There was now no occasion for Gandhi and the Congress to pursue divergent ways; the Congress therefore called upon him to resume its leadership. The Congress wanted to lodge a protest against the policy of the Government and looked up to Gandhi for guidance.

It was a political issue—the refusal of the British Government to give adequate assurances of Indian freedom in the future, and practical evidence of its intentions in the present—which had widened the gulf between the Government and the Congress. But it was not on a political but a pacifistic plank that Gandhi initiated his campaign of protest. His argument was that if the British could not grant or guarantee independence to the people of India, they could at least grant the right of free speech, including the right to preach against India's participation in the World War, and indeed against all wars.

Gandhi resisted the pressure exerted by some of his colleagues and left-wing Congressmen for the launching of a mass movement. He decided to confine civil disobedience to selected individuals. The instructions which he issued for the Satyagrahis and sportingly communicated to the Viceroy ruled out public excitement and harassment to the authorities; they are remarkable for the restraints imposed on his followers. Gandhi insisted on personally approving the lists of Satyagrahis, who were enjoined to advise the district magistrate in advance of the time and place for the performance of Satyagraha. Public meetings were to be discouraged in towns. The Satyagrahis were to repeat the following slogans: 'It is wrong to help the British war-effort with men or money. The only worthy effort is to resist all war with non-violent resistance.'

He directed that Satyagraha was to be offered singly and not in groups; there were to be no demonstrations. Constructive organizations of the Congress were not to offer Satyagraha. Congressmen were to make it clear 'in their speech and their action' that they were neither pro-Fascist nor pro-Nazi, but that they were opposed to all war or at least to war conducted on behalf of British imperialism. If the Congress organization was declared unlawful, it could, explained Gandhi, make no difference: 'I shall conduct the movement so long as I am free. In the event of my arrest, the movement shall become self-acting if the people have imbibed non-violence. Congressmen should remain calm and unperturbed. Each one will act on his or her own initiative. If he or she feels like offering civil disobedience the way is clear. If he or she is unable to offer civil disobedience, the alternative is to pursue the items of constructive programme.'

The whole conception of individual civil disobedience was devised so as to achieve the object of a 'token protest', without seriously embarrassing the Government. Gandhi warned against the exploitation of the peasants, mill workers and students for political purposes. It would almost seem that Gandhi was only providing in this movement a safety-valve for the pent-up frustration in the country. He renewed the emphasis on the constructive programme in which he listed such activities as spinning and cloth weaving, Hindu-Muslim unity, prohibition, basic education, village industries, adult education, the uplift of women, elementary instruction in health and hygiene, prop-agation of Hindustani and reduction in economic inequalities. This programme appeared to him as important as civil dis-obedience; in fact, as he put it, the handling of civil disobedience without the constructive programme was like a paralysed hand attempting to lift a spoon. As Gandhi explained: 'Those who think that the major reforms will come after the advent of Swaraj are deceiving themselves as to the elementary working of non-violent Swaraj. It will not drop from heaven all of a sudden one fine morning. But it has to be built brick by brick by corporate self-effort.'

From a political standpoint, individual civil disobedience with the constructive programme as an alternative seemed a curious and somewhat anaemic mode of agitation in time of war. The movement had begun on October 17, 1940 with an anti-war speech by Acharya Vinoba Bhave at Paunar, a village near Wardha; he was arrested four days later. Jawaharlal Nehru had been chosen to follow Vinoba Bhave on November 7th, but he had been arrested a week earlier on his way to Allahabad and sentenced to four years' imprisonment. In the middle of November the second stage of the campaign began with what Gandhi called the 'representative Satyagraha'. Satya-grahis were selected from groups such as the Congress Working

Committee, the All-India Congress Committee and the Congress members of the Central and Provincial Legislatures.

By the end of the year nearly 400 Congress legislators, including twenty-nine ex-ministers, were in gaol. Early in January 1941 the third stage in the campaign was initiated with lists of Satyagrahis prepared by the local Congress Committees and approved by Gandhi. The fourth stage of the campaign in April 1941 witnessed the enrolment of rank and file Congressmen. By May 15, 1941, according to official records, 25,069 convictions had been made for individual civil disobedience. There was, however, very little excitement, thanks to the manner in which Gandhi had conducted this 'symbolic' campaign; he would not agree to its extension into a mass civil disobedience movement: 'There is neither warrant nor atmosphere for mass action. That would be naked embarrassment and a betrayal of non-violence. What is more, it can never lead to independence. Mass action without communal unity is an invitation to civil war. If civil war is to be our lot, it will come; but if I know the Congress mind, it will never come at the wish or invitation of the Congress.'

When the *Hindu* pointed out that the movement had produced no appreciable impression on the war-effort, Gandhi replied that it was not intended to hamper the war-effort. The Secretary of State for India, Mr Amery, said the movement was 'as regrettable as it is irrational', and described it as proceeding 'languidly and without evoking much interest'. That the self-imposed restraint of the individual civil disobedience campaign was a pleasant surprise to the Government is evident from a letter sent by the Government of India on January 29, 1941 to the Provincial Governments. Gandhi's studied moderation had rendered it unnecessary to use the drastic powers which were to be assumed in an 'emergency'; the Government felt confident that individual civil disobedience could be met with measured doses of repression: 'The present policy may be restated as consisting in a determination to enforce the letter of the law as a matter of routine against those who deliberately

break it but to avoid any sensational or vindictive action . . .
In other words the object should be to keep the popular
temperature as low as possible and to give the impression that
the Government are merely carrying out their duty in circumstances which leave them no alternative but to do so.' The
Provincial Governments were therefore advised to continue
the policy of awarding mild sentences to the Satyagrahis and
avoid provoking any excitement in the hope that public interest
in the movement would decline.

The Bombay Government had suggested that the Government
of India take the initiative to 'lift the movement out of the
channel it is wearing for itself':

'If, for instance, all selected Satyagrahis convicted or detained
in respect of purely symbolic speeches are released to the
accompaniment of a carefully worded communique which
explained that the Government was recognizing the symbolic
character of the movement by a symbolic and unconditional
gaol delivery, the effect on public opinion and even on the
Congress may be considerable. But it would be essential to
the success of the gesture that it should be made when the
movement is at a low ebb. In other circumstances it would
be misconstrued as born of weakness.'

The Government of India did not deny that this proposal could
'upset Mr Gandhi's calculations', but felt that it could be considered only on a future occasion 'as an accompaniment to some
new and important move in the wider political field.'

The occasion came when the war began to take a menacing
turn, towards the close of 1941. Three days before the Japanese
attack on Pearl Harbour, the Government of India, to quote
from the official communique, 'confident in the determination
of all responsible opinion in India to support the war-effort
until victory is secured', announced that it had decided to release
those convicted for individual civil disobedience.

Chapter 47

THE CRIPPS MISSION

THE entry of Japan in the war brought it almost to India's door. With the American fleet crippled, the Japanese swept quickly through the Western Pacific. On February 15, 1942 Singapore fell and the Bay of Bengal lay exposed to the Japanese fleet. The British command of the sea had gone. The tide of Japanese conquest, after overwhelming Malaya and Burma, threatened to engulf eastern and southern India. The rapidity with which the Japanese advanced was evidence not only of their superiority in numbers and strategy, but also of the lack of will to resist in the countries invaded by them.

There was very little pro-Japanese sentiment in India. A small minority, influenced by the broadcasts of Subhas Chandra Bose, did not disdain foreign aid to win Indian freedom, but the great majority of the Indian intelligentsia was anti-Nazi, anti-Fascist and anti-Japanese. Gandhi had condemned the Japanese slogan of 'Asia for Asiatics' and even favoured the boycott of Japanese goods as a mark of sympathy with China. Nehru's sympathy for China was well known. The danger was, therefore, not so much of active collaboration by sections of Indians with the Japanese, as of defeatism and passivity on the part of the people which might enable the Japanese to consolidate themselves if they managed to land and to win an initial battle or two. The demand of the Indian National Congress that the people should be given a stake in an all-out resistance to the Axis Powers acquired a new urgency.

Gandhi's first reaction to the Viceroy's gesture in releasing prisoners convicted for individual civil disobedience at the beginning of December 1941 had been far from enthusiastic;

it did not, he declared, 'evoke a single responsive or appreciative chord' in him. The Congress Working Committee met at Bardoli on December 23rd, acknowledged the gravity of the war situation, but noted that: 'the whole background in India is one of hostility and of distrust of the British Government, and not even the most far-reaching promises can alter this background, nor can a subject India offer voluntary or willing help to an arrogant imperialism which is indistinguishable from the fascist authoritarianism'. The Committe went on to uphold its programme of symbolic civil resistance which it had authorized in September 1940.

Events, however, moved fast, faster than anticipated by the Congress and the Government. In the winter of 1941-42 the war situation was as critical for the Allies as it had been in the summer of 1940 after the fall of France. Once again, a section of Congressmen led by Rajagopalachari favoured an immediate settlement with the British Government for a united front against the Japanese. Most of the Congress leaders were prepared to throw the weight of the Congress against the Japanese peril, provided the Government made a reciprocal gesture. During the discussions at Bardoli, Gandhi noted that what prevented them from co-operating with the Government in the prosecution of the war was not non-violence, but suitable terms for co-operation. 'I found to my astonishment,' wrote Gandhi to Maulana Azad, the President of the Congress, 'that most members (of the Congress Working Committee) differed from my interpretation and held that the opposition (to the war) need not be on the ground of non-violence.' There was a good reason why these differences between Gandhi and the Congress Working Committee came to a head at this time. The vicissitudes of war had brought the danger perilously near to India and the question as to whether invasion was to be met with armed force or non-violent resistance had again become a live issue. As in the midsummer of 1940, so in the midwinter of 1941-42 Gandhi found that the majority of the Congress leaders, acknowledging as they did the moral superiority of the non-violent technique, lacked the courage to apply it to defence against external aggression.

Meanwhile, the war situation had made its impact upon the British Government. Prime Minister Churchill's views on Indian independence have already been discussed;[1] in 1941 they were no different from those he had held in 1931. In December 1941, when Churchill visited Washington, President Roosevelt referred to the Indian problem. 'I reacted so strongly,' Churchill has recorded, 'and at such length that he never raised it verbally again.' It was not only American pressure but the pace of the Japanese advance which was to persuade Churchill to seek a way out of the Indian political deadlock. On February 25th, ten days after the fall of Singapore, he appointed a sub-committee of the War Cabinet to study the Indian problem and to suggest a solution. Of the members of this study group Simon and Attlee had been members of the Statutory Commission, James Grigg and John Anderson had held high office in India, Stafford Cripps was well acquainted with Indian leaders and politics, and Amery was the Secretary of State for India. On March 11th Churchill was able to report to the House of Commons that the War Cabinet had come to a unanimous decision on the Indian question, and that Stafford Cripps, the leader of the House of Commons, was proceeding to India to discuss the proposals with Indian leaders.

No better choice could have been made than that of Stafford Cripps for this momentous mission. His sympathies with the cause of Indian freedom were known and he personally knew the front-rank leaders of Indian opinion. He had thus good reason to be optimistic when he arrived at New Delhi on March 22nd. The 'Draft Declaration' which Cripps brought with him and discussed with prominent officials and leaders contained the British Government's proposals for the solution of the Indian political problem. Immediately after the war elections were to be held to provincial legislatures, and members of the lower houses of these legislatures were to elect a

[1] Chapter 34.

P

constitution-making body. The Indian States were to be invited
to nominate representatives to this assembly, which was to
be charged with framing a constitution for a 'Union of India',
a full-fledged Dominion 'with the same full status as the other
Dominions'. The Union of India was to have the right to opt
out of the British Commonwealth. The British Government
undertook to implement this constitution subject to: '. . . the
right of any Province of British India that is not prepared to
accept the new Constitution to retain its present constitutional
position, provision being made for its subsequent accession
if it so decides.

'With such non-acceding Provinces, should they so desire,
His Majesty's Government will be prepared to agree upon
a new Constitution giving them the same full status as the
Indian Union, and arrived at by a procedure analogous to that
here laid down.'

A treaty was to be negotiated between the constitution-
making body and the British Government, *inter alia,* to provide
for the protection of racial and religious minorities. As regards
the Indian States, it was laid down that 'whether or not an
Indian State elects to adhere to the Constitution, it will be necessary
to negotiate a revision of its treaty arrangements, so far as this
may be required in the new situation'.

Mr Attlee has recorded in his memoirs that the 'Draft
Declaration' was a bold plan, and 'reflected credit on those
members of the Government who were not sanguine as to
the feasibility of Indian self-government and especially upon
the Prime Minister whose views were very strong'. In his
broadcast on March 30, 1942, Cripps declared, 'the British
Government want to make it clear beyond doubt that we and
the British people desire the Indian people to have full self-
government'. The very fact that Cripps had agreed to 'sell'
this plan to Indian leaders was proof enough of the conviction
of friends of Indian freedom in Britain that at long last the
British Government had taken one full stride to meet Indian
aspirations.

As against this exuberant confidence of the British leaders may be set the grave misgivings with which the plan was received by Indian leaders. Gandhi (whom Cripps had summoned from Wardha by telegram), after reading the proposals, advised Cripps to take the next plane home. Jawaharlal Nehru confessed to a 'profound depression' when he read the proposals for the first time; the more he read them and pondered over them, the more depressed he felt. It was true that India's right to self-determination had been definitely conceded by the British Government for the first time, and both the time and the machinery for exercising this right had been clearly specified. But the right of non-accession to the Provinces and the Indian States threatened to convert the country into a political chequerboard containing scores of 'independent states' which could make short work of India as a political and economic entity. The right of non-accession was given to Provinces evidently to meet the Muslim League's demand for Pakistan half-way. 'If you want,' Cripps said in one of his broadcasts, 'to persuade a number of people who are inclined to be antagonistic to enter the same room, it is unwise to tell them that once they go in there is no way out.' The Congress leaders felt that the Cripps' offer (1942) had gone one step further than Linlithgow's August offer (1940) to encourage Jinnah to persist in his separatist line. In March 1940 Pakistan had seemed a phantom; in March 1942 it had become a political possibility.

Alarming as was the prospect of non-accession to the Indian Union of Muslim-majority provinces in the east and the west, the grant of a similar right to the Princely States filled Congress leaders with dismay. Dependent for their privileges and their very existence on the sufferance of the Political Department, were these Princes to blossom into independent rulers with whom the new Indian Union was to negotiate for co-operation? The Indian constitutional problem had already resolved itself into a problem of reconciling the irreconcilables, the Congress and the League; if the Princes were to be brought in the tangle was likely to become inextricable. Another five years were to pass before the British Government recognized this fact and decided to leave the Princes to find their place in the polity of an independent and democratic India without distorting its structure.

The Congress leaders were thus unable to accept the long-term solution of the Indian political problem which Cripps had brought. However, the war situation was fast deteriorating. During the three weeks Cripps spent in India, the Japanese had scored a number of victories. Toungoo was evacuated on April 1st and Prome on April 3rd; bombs fell on Colombo on April 5th, and on Vizagapatam and Cocanada on the following day. Even though Cripps had presented his proposals as a 'package deal', and even though the long-term proposals were the 'bold' part of the plan, the Congress leaders suggested that the long-term proposals be shelved for the time being and an agreement sought on immediate arrangements for the defence of India. There were a series of discussions between the Indian leaders on the one hand, and Cripps and the Viceroy on the other, regarding the functions of an Indian Defence Member of the Viceroy's Council. On April 3rd Cripps met General Wavell, the Commander-in-Chief, at the Army Headquarters and announced that he had postponed his departure for England. 'I think,' he said, 'that I can possibly do something useful next week. I think one may generally say that the points of difficulty are coming down to fairly narrow limits and with common goodwill we may be able to solve the difficulties.' Next day, Cripps introduced Nehru and Azad (the Congress President) to General Wavell, and left them to talk over the scope of the portfolio which was to be entrusted to the Indian Defence Member of the Viceroy's Council during the war. The Congress leaders accepted the need for keeping the control of technical aspects of war-effort in the hands of the British Commander-in-Chief; they argued, however, that in war-time defence impinged on every aspect of national life, and to exclude it entirely from the purview of the Indian Defence Member was to defeat the very purpose of a popular interim government, namely the effective prosecution of the war.

These discussions, in which Colonel Louis Johnson, the personal envoy of President Roosevelt, also joined, broke down not on the demarcation of duties between the Indian Defence Member and the British Commander-in-Chief, but on a much wider issue —the nature and authority of the interim government as a whole.

Article E of the 'Draft Declaration' which Cripps had brought referred to interim arrangements during the war: 'During the critical period which now faces India and until the new constitution can be framed His Majesty's Government must inevitably bear the responsibility for and retain control and direction of the defence of India as a part of their world effort, but the task of organizing to the full, the military, moral and material resources of India must be the responsibility of the Government of India with the co-operation of the people of India . . .'

On his return to England, Cripps asserted that from the outset he had made it clear to all those whom he had seen that it was not possible to make any constitutional changes—except of the most insignificant kind—prior to the new constitution, which was to come into operation as a result of the labours of the constitution-making body after the war. According to Cripps, he had made it clear that the formation of the new Government, how the members of the Viceroy's Council were to be treated, and how its business was to be transacted, were matters for decision by the Viceroy, who had to carry on the Government of India, and not for him (Cripps) a member of the War Cabinet on a visit to India.

This may have been Cripps' intention from the outset, but the Congress leaders nevertheless received a contrary impression. During the negotiations he had used such terms as 'National Government' and 'Cabinet', which had led the Congress leaders to hope that the new Government would function, by convention if not by law, as a Cabinet with full powers and with the Viceroy as a constitutional head. The misunderstanding may have been due to assumptions which the 'Draft Declaration' did not justify; as Nehru wrote later, their (the Congress leaders') eagerness for a settlement may have fed their optimism. Or perhaps there had been a change of front on the part of Cripps. Robert E. Sherwood, in his *Roosevelt and Hopkins*, quotes Churchill's remark to Hopkins that 'Cripps had presented a new proposal to Nehru without consultation with the Governor-General'. It was this new proposal which narrowed the differences between the Congress and the British Government on the formation of a National Government. According to Hopkins, the Viceroy telegraphed Churchill, and Churchill pulled up Cripps for stepping beyond his brief, with the result that Cripps had to break off negotiations and return home.

The comment of an Indian paper, the *National Herald* of April 24, 1942, that 'the Cripps mission was the result of American pressure. It was a stage-managed show to buy off world opinion and to foist preconcerted failure on the people of India' was an index to the Indian frustration at the failure of the Cripps Mission, but did less than justice to the British Government. For the first time that Government had recognized unequivocally India's right to self-government, and this, coming from a Government led by a Premier who made no secret of his distrust of Indian nationalism, was certainly a step forward. Unfortunately, the constitutional proposals were framed as a half-way house between two irreconcilable objectives, the creation of a free and democratic India and its fragmentation into endless segments in deference to Muslim separatism and the vested interests of the Princes. Thanks to Jinnah's ideology and tactics, the Indian political problem had become too complicated to be solved by a formula hurriedly hammered out in London by a sub-committee of the War Cabinet. The fact that the proposals were not subject to any major amendment—the 'take it or leave' condition attached to them—made chances of success still more remote.

Such was the gravity of the war situation, however, that, in spite of serious objections to the long-term constitutional proposals, nationalist India was willing to put that compli-

cated problem in cold storage and to concentrate on the immediate
task of mobilizing the country against the Japanese peril.
Unfortunately, the critical war situation which had provided
the main impulse for the despatch of the Cripps Mission was
also responsible for wrecking it. The Congress leaders (who
had parted company with Gandhi on non-violent defence of
India) were thinking in terms of a last ditch fight against the
Japanese, of building up new armies, militias and home guards.
In his last letter to Cripps, the Congress President had written:
'No one has suggested any restrictions on the normal powers
of the Commander-in-Chief. Indeed we went beyond this
and were prepared to agree to further powers being given to
him as War Minister. But it is clear that the British Government's
conception and ours in regard to defence differ greatly. For us
it means giving it national character, and calling upon every
man and woman in India to participate in it . . . The Government
of India do not realize that the war can only be fought on a
popular basis.'

Roosevelt, who had been anxiously watching the progress
of Cripps' negotiations and was receiving first-hand reports
from his personal envoy at New Delhi, sent a message to
Churchill through Hopkins that the American public could
not understand why, if there was willingness on the part of the
British Government to permit the component parts of India
to secede after the war from the British Empire, the British
Government was unwilling to permit Indians to enjoy during
the war what was tantamount to self-government. Roosevelt
had suggested that another effort should be made to set up
a nationalist government 'in essence similar to our own form
of government'. 'I was thankful,' writes Churchill, 'that events
had made such an act of madness impossible.' Cripps had already
left India.

'To us and to all Indians,' the Congress President had written
to Cripps, 'the dominant consideration is the defence and safety
of India.' Paradoxically, the consideration which made Congress
leaders call for a National Government weighed with the

British in the determination that there should be no substantial transfer of power to Indian political parties during the war. Many senior officers in the Government of India and the provinces felt (to quote Philip Woodruff[1]) that 'not another shell, not another pair of boots, not another recruit, could be contributed by Congress support of the war-effort. As early as January 1942, Churchill had written that the idea that they (the British Government) could get more out of India by putting the Congress in charge at that juncture was ill-founded. 'Bringing hostile elements into the defence machine,' he added, 'will paralyse action.' In March 1942 the British Premier had been persuaded to agree to the Cripps proposals as a long-term solution of the Indian political problem, but his distrust of the Congress (as Congress distrust of him) persisted. Turning down President Roosevelt's last minute plea for yet another effort by Cripps for reconciliation with the Congress, Churchill had recorded that he could not take the responsibility for the defence of India 'if everything had again to be thrown into the melting pot at this critical juncture'.

On his return to England Cripps blamed the failure of his mission on Gandhi. He went so far as to suggest that the Congress Working Committee had passed a resolution accepting the Cripps proposals, but that Gandhi had intervened and the resolution was reversed. Gandhi had been reluctant to come to Delhi. He had agreed to meet Cripps at the latter's insistence. He had made no secret of his misgivings, but he had left Delhi at an early stage of the negotiations. The final decisions were taken by the Working Committee; its members were aware of Gandhi's unfavourable reactions but the Committee also knew that Gandhi would not stand in the way of any decision it took.

Gandhi had been quoted as having remarked that the Cripps offer was a post-dated cheque on a crashing bank. 'I had of course,' Gandhi told a friend, 'said nothing of the kind. But the criticism on the score of its being a post-dated cheque

[1] Woodruff, Philip: *The Guardians*, p. 305.

is absolutely correct.' The whole approach, the reluctance to
rectify the present and the emphasis on the future left him
cold. And he had his own way of judging a policy by its results
in the present. If the British had really accepted India's right
to freedom, or (to use Gandhi's terminology) if they had
undergone a change of heart, he expected to see it not only in
state documents but in day-to-day administration. Of this he
saw no sign.

Chapter 48

QUIT INDIA

GANDHI had taken little interest in the Cripps Mission but its failure was a great disappointment to him. That even a friend of India like Stafford Cripps could have misunderstood or misinterpreted the position of the Congress was something of a shock. It was clear that there was little prospect of a political settlement so long as the war lasted. The Government were preoccupied with the critical war situation. The Indian army was being rapidly expanded and reinforced with troops and military equipment from Britain and America.

What a defence in depth could do in a vast sub-continent had been learnt, at a heavy cost, by Japan in China and by Germany in Russia. India was also a vast country, not easy to occupy quickly. In India, however, unlike China and Russia, the war had not evoked an upsurge of patriotism. There was hardly any unity of purpose between the Government and the people. The distrust of the British had become almost pathological. In the coastal districts of Orissa, which were threatened with invasion, Gandhi's disciple Mirabehn (Miss Slade) noted that the people were confused but that their dominant feelings were those of fear and distrust of the Government. Throughout the country public opinion had been estranged from the Government by the tales of racial discrimination which Indian refugees had brought from Malaya and Burma and by the first experiments in 'scorched earth' policy in Bengal, where thousands of small boats, vital to riverine communication, were destroyed.

While the Government were in touch with the small minority which had thriven on the new avenues of employment and contracts opened by the war, Gandhi's hand was on the pulse of the people. He noted that their mood in the face of grave peril was not one of resolute defiance, but of panic, frustration and helplessness. If India was not to go the way of Malaya and Burma, something had to be done and done quickly. Gandhi became convinced that only an immediate declaration of Indian independence by the British Government could give the people a stake in the defence of their country. He knew that he had dropped a bombshell: 'I know that the novelty of this idea and that too at this juncture has caused a shock to many people. Even at the risk of being called mad, I had to tell the truth if I was to be true to myself. I regard it as my solid contribution to the war and to India's deliverance from the peril.'

Lord Hardinge, who was Viceroy of India during the years 1910-16, has recorded in his memoirs that on one occasion he had asked Gokhale, 'How would you like it if I were to tell you that all the British officials and troops would leave India within a month?' 'I would be very pleased to hear that news,' replied Gokhale, 'but before you had all reached Aden, we would be telegraphing you to return.' Public opinion had advanced much since the days of Hardinge and Gokhale, but a total British withdrawal in the midst of a global war was certainly a startling suggestion. Gandhi was asking not for the physical withdrawal of every Briton from India, but for the transfer of political power from British to Indian hands. To those who said that the time was inopportune for such a step, his answer was: 'This is the psychological moment for recognition (of Indian independence). For then and then alone can there be irresistible opposition to Japanese aggression.'

For more than twenty years Gandhi had argued that the independence of India was impossible without Hindu–Muslim unity. He had, however, seen communalism raise its ugly head higher and higher, and was driven to the conclusion that only in a climate of freedom could the antagonistic claims of the communities be reconciled. 'Quit India' was thus Gandhi's solution for the two perils of Japanese invasion and internal

disunity which confronted India in the summer of 1942. The
charge that this solution was 'defeatist' and a homage to the
rising sun of Japan derived from a complete misunderstanding
of his views. In February 1942, when the Japanese were advancing
in the Far East with lightning speed, he had publicly discounted
fears of a British collapse. Britain had, he wrote, suffered reverses
in several wars, but she had a knack of surviving them and
turning them into stepping stones to success. In unambiguous
language he declared himself against a change of masters: 'I
have no desire to exchange the British for any other rule. Better
the enemy I know than the one I do not. I have never attached
the slightest importance or weight to the friendly professions
of the Axis powers. If they come to India they will not come
as deliverers but as sharers in the spoil.'

In a letter dated May 31, 1942, he gave hints to Mirabehn,
who had gone to Orissa to prepare the people for a non-violent
resistance to the Japanese if they managed to land on the eastern
coast: 'Remember that our attitude is that of complete non-
co-operation with the Japanese army. Therefore, we may not
help them in any way, nor may we profit by any dealings with
them . . . If, however, the people have not the courage to resist
the Japanese unto death and not the courage and capacity to
evacuate the portion invaded by the Japanese, they will do the
best they can. One thing they should never do—to yield willing
submission to the Japanese. That will be a cowardly act, and
unworthy of a freedom-loving people. They must not escape
from one fire to fall into another and probably more terrible.'

Clearly, if the Axis Powers had any collaborators in India,
actual or potential, Gandhi was not one of them. It was pointed
out to him by some foreign correspondents that the sudden
withdrawal of British troops would have the inevitable result
of exposing India to a Japanese invasion and of immeasurably
weakening the defence of China. He recognized that he 'could
not guarantee fool-proof non-violent action to keep the Japanese
at bay'; subsequent discussions with Jawaharlal Nehru led him
to elaborate the proposal for the withdrawal of British power,

so as to fit it into the realities of the international situation. He agreed that the Allied troops should remain on Indian soil during the war, and one of the first acts of a National Indian Government should be to enter into a treaty with the United Nations for defensive operations against the Axis powers. This was a striking departure from the position Gandhi had consistently held since September 1939.

Ever since the outbreak of the war, Gandhi had been commending to his countrymen non-violent resistance even to an invading army; he wished the Congress to adhere to the same method for the defence of the country which it had employed in the struggle for freedom. Twice he had parted company on this issue with the majority in the Congress Working Committee. When, therefore, he agreed to the whole-hearted participation of the Congress in the Second World War, he did something which went deeply against the grain. Only the critical turn which the war had taken, and the passion for Indian freedom reconciled him to this deviation from a principle which was dearer to him than life itself.

'British Rule in India must end immediately,' the Congress Working Committee declared after a meeting at Wardha on July 14, 1942. The Committee pointed out that the failure of the Cripps Mission had resulted in a rapid and widespread increase in ill-will against Britain and a growing satisfaction at the success of Japanese arms. In order to make India 'a willing partner in a joint enterprise', the Committee considered it essential that Indians should feel 'a glow of freedom'.

If there was no response to the appeal for the immediate withdrawal of the British rule, the Committee forecast a civil disobedience movement 'which would inevitably be under the leadership of Mahatma Gandhi'. The final decision on this momentous issue was left to the All-India Congress Committee a meeting of which was summoned at Bombay on August 7th.

The following three weeks were full of hectic activity and breathless tension. The 'Quit India' proposal had caught the imagination of the rank and file of Congressmen but it had its critics. The Punjab Premier, Sir Sikander Hyat Khan, feared that the proposal would lead to 'pandemonium'. 'It was an attempt,' charged Jinnah, 'to coerce the British Government to surrender to Congress *Raj*.' The National Executive of the British Labour Party declared that the proposed movement would imperil the fate of all freedom-loving peoples and thereby destroy all hopes of Indian freedom. C. Rajagopalachari observed that 'the withdrawal of the Government without simultaneous replacement by another must involve the dissolution of the State and society itself'.

Gandhi answered this criticism through articles in *Harijan* and interviews with Press correspondents. The fact that he had implored Britain to leave India to her fate, 'to God, or in modern parlance, to anarchy', did not mean that he expected anarchy as an inevitable consequence of the acceptance of his proposal. On the contrary, he had no doubt that, faced with real responsibility, the Indian parties would come to an agreement and see the country through the crisis. The British withdrawal, so far from weakening the defence against Japan, was intended to strengthen it. The transmutation of ill-will into good-will towards Britain was, argued Gandhi, 'worth all the battleships and airships', and the immediate recognition of India's independence was a 'war measure of first-class magnitude'.

The 'Quit India' resolution was passed by the All-India Congress Committee at its Bombay meeting. Shortly after midnight, Gandhi addressed the assembled delegates: 'The actual struggle does not commence this very moment. You have merely placed certain powers in my hands. My first act will be to wait upon His Excellency the Viceroy and plead with him for the acceptance of the Congress demand. This may take two or three weeks. What are you going to do in the meanwhile? There is the spinning-wheel. I will tell you . . . but there is something more you have to do . . . Every one of you should, from this moment, consider himself a free man or woman and even act as if you are free and no longer under the heel of this imperialism . . .'

'After my last night's speech,' Gandhi told his secretary as he went to bed in the early hours of August 9, 1942, 'they will not arrest me.' But the Government had long since made up its mind. We have already seen how, exactly two years earlier to a day, in a communication to the Governors, the Viceroy had expressed his determination to crush the Congress if it dared to throw an open challenge to the Government. Ordinances conferring sweeping powers on the executive had already been drafted and had only to be pulled out of top-secret pigeon holes of the Secretariat. If these powers had not been assumed earlier, it was because of Gandhi's studied moderation in the conduct of individual civil disobedience during 1940-41.

That the Government of India were aware of the risks of strong action may be judged from a letter addressed by them to the Provincial Governments in January 1941, in which they reviewed the individual civil disobedience movement: 'Only one Province (Provincial Government) has urged that Gandhi's arrest should take place at once as being the only way to stop the movement. Others, while recognizing the illogicality of leaving Mr Gandhi at liberty while arresting those who carry out his orders, seem to be of opinion that his arrest now, so far from stopping the movement, would be much more likely to intensify it and produce that atmosphere of popular excitement in which alone a mass movement can hope to flourish . . . The general opinion also is that everything possible should be done to avoid a fast by Mr Gandhi while he is in captivity.'

These considerations the Government of India cast to the winds in August 1942; their mood was no less desperate than that of the Congress. From his own point of view, Lord Linlithgow had been patient for three long years; in December 1941, he had made a gesture to the Congress by effecting a gaol delivery, but he had failed to win its co-operation. The 'Quit India' proposal had already raised the political temperature; if a mass civil disobedience movement was actually launched, it might paralyse civil administration and endanger the war-effort. For strong preventive action the Viceroy had the full support of the British Cabinet. In London the feeling was that in the Cripps Mission the Government had gone as far as it could in meeting legitimate Indian aspirations, and that any action by the Congress which could jeopardize the conduct of the war at that critical juncture had to be met with the sternest measures. It is noteworthy that the final approval of the thorough-going offensive against the Congress was given, not by Prime Minister Churchill, who was away to Cairo, but by Mr Attlee. Not only was there an identity of views between the Labour and Conservative parties on this point, but the British Government could reasonably hope to carry with them, in the name of the war, the Government and public opinion of the United States.

Gandhi, Jawaharlal Nehru, Maulana Azad and other Congress leaders were arrested in the early hours of August 9, 1942. The news of these arrests produced violent reactions. In several provinces, particularly in Bihar, U.P., Bengal and Bombay, the fury of the people burst the dykes and turned on the instru-ments and symbols of British rule. Post offices, police stations and courts were burnt; railway lines, buildings and rolling stock were damaged; telephone and telegraph wires were cut. In his last speech before the All-India Congress Committee Gandhi had stressed non-violence as the basic premise of the struggle which he proposed to launch, but this advice remained unheeded between the frenzy of the people and the hammer blows of the Government. Though many British officials and non-officials recalled the Mutiny of 1857, the outbreak in 1942 was the result of a violence as spontaneous as it was suicidal. The Government hit back with all its might; mobs were dispersed with firing and even machine-gunned from the air.

'The Congress Party,' Churchill told the House of Commons, 'has now abandoned the policy in many respects of non-violence which Mr Gandhi has so long inculcated in theory and has come into the open as a revolutionary movement.' In India and abroad official propaganda attributed violence to a plot carefully laid by Congress leaders. Within a week of his imprisonment in the Aga Khan Palace, which had been improvised as a gaol for him, Gandhi wrote to the Viceroy complaining of the 'slaughter of truth' in the official version of the sequence of events. He would have strained every nerve, he said, to reach a settlement with the Government if he had not been arrested; neither he nor his colleagues had at any stage envisaged violence as part of the campaign. He charged the Government with precipitating the crisis by the wholesale arrests of the leaders. The Viceroy repudiated this analysis with some asperity and arraigned the Congress movement and Gandhi 'as its authorized and fully empowered spokesman' for what had happened. 'There is evidence,' wrote Lord Linlithgow, 'that you and your friends expected this policy to lead to violence; and that you were prepared to condone it; and that the violence that ensued formed part of a concerted plan, conceived long before the arrest of Congress leaders.'

Gandhi was arrested before he could unfold his detailed plans to the All-India Congress Committee, but on August 7th he had prepared for discussion with the members of the Congress Working Committee a 'draft of instructions' for the people, if negotiations with the Government failed and a movement had to be launched. A one-day *hartal* (cessation of all business activity) was envisaged; the day was to be observed by a twenty-four hour fast and prayers. Meetings were to be held only in villages where the fear of disturbances was appreciably less than in towns. Those employed in government offices, government factories, railways, post offices, etc. were not to participate in the *hartal*, because 'our object is to make it clear that we will never tolerate Japanese, Nazi or Fascist invasion, nor British rule'. Congressmen who were members of the central and provincial legislatures, or municipalities and other public bodies were to resign their seats, and students above sixteen were to leave schools. Salt was to be manufactured in contravention of the Salt Laws, and the land tax was to be refused. While it was not the intention to hinder military activities, arbitrary high-handedness was to be resisted. There was a significant reference to the nature of the struggle:

'A final word: no one should think that those whose names are on the Congress register are the only Congressmen. Let every Indian who desires the freedom for the whole of India and fully believes in the weapon of truth and non-violence for the purpose of this struggle regard himself a Congressman and act as such. If anybody has the spirit of communalism or harbours hatred or ill-will in his heart against any Indian or Englishman, he will best help the struggle by keeping aloof.'[1]

Gandhi did not get an opportunity to discuss these instructions with the Congress Working Committee, but they give a glimpse of the working of his mind at that time. He was trying hard to balance his passion for Indian freedom with his desire not to embarrass the Government during the war. If he had not been arrested it is likely that his programme would have been conditioned by the latter consideration. It is certain that his weight would have been thrown against any violent outbreak. He knew how to bring unruly mobs to order; when appeals failed he could bring them back to sanity by undertaking a fast.

The responsibility for the '1942 disturbances' formed the subject of a long and somewhat acrimonious correspondence between Gandhi (still a prisoner) on the one hand and the Viceroy and his advisers on the other. That Lord Linlithgow (whom Gandhi considered a friend) should have questioned his *bona fides*, and even his belief in non-violence, was more than the Mahatma could bear. He sought 'a soothing balm' for his pain in a twenty-one day fast which began on February 10, 1943. The fast, which the Government of India had dreaded so long had come, but it is an index to their hardened attitude that they took a risk which they had never taken before—that of Gandhi's death in prison. There was an emotional upheaval in the country, as the doctors' bulletins grew gloomier; three members of the Viceroy's Executive Council resigned; leaders of various parties, whatever their other differences, united in appeals

[1] *Gandhiji's correspondence with the Government 1942-44*, Ahmedabad, 1945, p. 357.

to the Government to release Gandhi and to save his life. But the Viceroy, backed by the authorities at home, did not budge an inch; he described the fast as 'political blackmail'; whatever satisfaction such an epithet may have given him, it only stung Indian public opinion the more.

While the fast did not immediately melt the hearts of Gandhi's opponents, it certainly helped to re-educate Indian opinion in the principles on which the Satyagraha campaign would have been run if Gandhi had the time to launch it. So long as Gandhi was a prisoner, he stubbornly refused to pass verdicts on popular violence because he had only a one-sided version, i.e. from official sources. He had never hesitated to condemn violence; but in 1942 he had a suspicion that the Government deliberately played up the misdeeds of the people and minimized its own repression in order to distract the attention of the world from the real issue of Indian freedom. It was not until his release from gaol in the summer of 1944 that Gandhi gave his considered verdict on the events of 1942. There was, he said, something to be said for the fact that the people had not remained supine under the blows of the Government, but it distressed him to find that those who professed to follow him should have forgotten his fundamental principle of non-violence.

When the Congressmen of Midnapore (Bengal) recounted to him how the people had captured police stations, burnt courts, and paralysed communications in 1942, he told them: 'This is not the technique of non-violent action. People committed the mistake of thinking that all that did not involve killing was non-violence. Sometimes killing is the cleanest part of violence. If you kill the mischief maker outright there is an end of it so far as he is concerned. But harassment is worse. It did not put out mischief. On the contrary it brought mischief on our heads. The authorities became vindictive. Perhaps you will say that they would have been vindictive anyhow; but that is not what we should desire or aim at. It does not pay us to let them go into panic. In August 1942, the authorities became panicky. We gave them that excuse.' It was also a fallacy, added the Mahatma, that evil resided in bridges and roads and not in men; the destruction of bridges and roads could not change the hearts of men.

That Gandhi 'put the match to the train carefully laid beforehand by himself and his colleagues. That he was forced to do so prematurely was not his fault but our fortune'—this charge by Sir Reginald Maxwell, the Home Member of the Viceroy's Excutive Council, was part of the official indictment which represented Gandhi and the Congress as saboteurs of the Allied struggle against Japan. This propaganda held the field for a time, but not for long. 'It is sheer nonsense,' Field Marshal Smuts told a Press Conference in London in November 1942, 'to talk of Mahatma Gandhi as a fifth columnist. He is a great man. He is one of the great men of the world.' The attempts to erase him from political life by excluding his photographs and even a mention of his name from the Press were doomed to failure. The courage with which he stood up to the Government, the indomitable faith which he asserted in non-violence at a time when violence seemed to have triumphed all round him, the tenacity with which he attacked the cobwebs which official propagandists spun round the events of 1942—all this raised him further in the esteem and affection of millions of Indians. He became the symbol of a nationalism bloody but unbowed.

Now that the deep emotions which the events of 1942 aroused have somewhat faded, it should be possible to see the events of that year in clearer perspective. When we recall the emphasis which Gandhi had placed on the training of the people for non-violence since 1934, when we recall his anxiety at the growth in the pre-war years of indiscipline and the spirit of violence, and his studied restraint in conducting the individual civil disobedience movement of 1940-41, we wonder how he could have permitted what was certainly a dangerous plunge in the surcharged atmosphere of that period. He knew the risks inherent in a mass movement in the midst of a global war which had brought the Japanese to the gates of India. But he also saw the passivity of the people and the possibility that they might succumb to the Japanese invader. To rouse them to a final assertion of their national self-respect without hatred or violence required a miracle, but miracles had happened before. Within a few months in 1930 Gandhi had succeeded in electrifying political India, with remarkably little racial bitterness and violence. Twelve years later, however, the conditions were different; both the people and the Government were keyed up to a high pitch of tension. With the fortunes of the war trembling in the balance, the Government were less inclined to wait on events, while large sectors of the population were seething with discontent. The political situation in 1942 bore greater resemblance to that of 1919 than to that of 1930. In 1919, as in 1942, Gandhi had sensed the temper of the people, but he was hopeful that he could sterilize it of hatred and violence through a Satyagraha movement. Satyagraha had, however, no chance in the face of the popular terrorism and official counter-terrorism which followed the arrest of Congress leaders.

Gandhi had no right to expect the Government to play the game according to his rules, but the Government equally had no right to blame him for the consequences of the policy it adopted. Lord Linlithgow had acted in accordance with the viewpoint common among experienced British administrators, that the only means of mastering Gandhi's movements was to deliver telling blows at the initial stages. This was the policy which Lord Willingdon was believed to have adopted with signal success. The ostensible gains of such a policy, however, tended to be transient; repression, with its resultant bitterness, recoiled on those who practised it. In 1932 Lord Willingdon inflicted what he believed to be a crushing defeat on the Congress; five years later the Congress swept the polls in the first elections under the Government of India Act of 1935. In 1942 Lord Linlithgow won what was, from his point of view, a decisive victory over the Congress; in 1947 the British rule came formally and finally to an end. It is a strange irony of history that Lords Willingdon and Linlithgow, who dealt the strongest blows to the Indian national movement, unwittingly served as catalytic agents in the political liberation of India.

From the nationalist point of view, the events of 1942 were to prove an embarrassing legacy. It was almost the first large-scale outbreak in which wrecking and burning were indulged in a spirit of misconceived patriotism. It lowered the standards of mass behaviour and set a dangerous precedent when in 1946-47 communal feeling replaced patriotism as the principal ingredient in the popular ferment.

Chapter 49

NO DEFEAT

WITHIN a week of his imprisonment in the Aga Khan Palace, Gandhi lost his private secretary, Mahadev Desai. Competent, industrious and modest, the ever-smiling, 'M.D.' had been for twenty-five years the Mahatma's inseparable assistant. 'Son, secretary and lover rolled into one'—this was how the Mahatma once described Mahadev, who had joined him in 1917, after graduating in law from Bombay University and trying his hand at a few odd jobs. Mahadev's fine handwriting, alert mind, and undivided loyalty made him an efficient secretary, but Gandhi's secretary had to be something more than an amanuensis. In the years preceding the first non-co-operation movement, when Gandhi was not so well known, Mahadev Desai was often his sole companion during his country-wide tours; he made his bed, cooked his food and washed his clothes, besides performing the secretarial functions. As public life increased its demands on Gandhi, Mahadev Desai's burdens grew too; he sorted and dealt with an enormous mail, received and looked after guests, warded off unwelcome visitors, kept accounts, pored over railway guides and maps to arrange itineraries, recorded speeches and conversations and edited journals. As a good deal of his writing was done in third-class compartments of moving trains, he carried candles with him so that, if lights failed in the compartment, the dispatch of the 'copy' to the press was not held up.

The readers of *Young India* and *Harijan* looked forward avidly to an abundant weekly fare from 'M.D.', whose style had a charm all its own. This is how he described Dr Bose, a nature-curist, 'one of the delightfullest of men' who 'would pay Gandhiji a fee every day for taking up his time and treating him! On the day he left he sent a note saying, "This currency note must go to you. It should have gone to you yesterday but remained with me. I am sending it on to you with a hope that I may follow one day . . ." I should not be surprised, if true to his word, he finds his way one day to Segaon.'

Here is an account of an interview with Lady Emily Kinnaird, who described to Gandhi how the heathen in the remotest part of the world, who knew not a syllable of English, had been agreeably surprised to see God's message in his dialect: ' "That proves nothing," said Gandhiji again laughing. Lady Emily also laughed, quite unperturbed by the fact that what she was saying was pouring so much water over a duck's back. The very first qualification of a preacher is unperturbed serenity. "But why all this quarrel about labels?" added Gandhiji, "Cannot a few hundred thousand Indians or South Africans live the message of Christ without being called Christians . . .?" As usual with such battles this was a drawn one, and Lady Emily parted in the greatest good humour.'

There was hardly a word which escaped Gandhi's lips but was not recorded by his indefatigable secretary (who scribbled notes on margins of newspapers, on currency notes, or even on his nails) to be shared later with the public in one of his articles, or transcribed in his 'journal', which he kept almost till his last day. As a chronicler of the activities and utterances of his master, Mahadev Desai has been compared with Boswell. However, Gandhi's secretary had to be something more than a devoted diarist; he had to practise the hard discipline which Gandhi imposed on himself. Mahadev devoted all he had, his painstaking scholarship, his unremitting industry, and his amiable personality to one ambition, that of lightening the daily burdens of his master. He constituted a perfect one-man secretariat, expounding and implementing Gandhi's instructions, keeping in touch with hundreds of public workers, and doing all that he could to save the Mahatma from any avoidable strain. He drove himself too hard in the process; his sudden death in August 1942 was due not only to the terrific strain of the months which preceded the passage of the 'Quit India' resolution, but also to a gnawing fear that the Mahatma would fast unto death in gaol.

Another shadow fell upon the Aga Khan's Palace. Kasturba's health had been causing concern for some time; she was treated by the 'family doctors', Gilder, Dinshaw and Sushila Nayar, and then by Shiv Sharma, an Ayurvedic physician from the Punjab, but she did not rally. On February 22, 1944 she passed away in the lap of her husband. 'I am going now,' she said to him, 'we have known many joys and many sorrows.' One of her last wishes was that she should be cremated in a *sari* made from yarn spun by him.

'We were,' wrote Gandhi in reply to a letter of condolence from Lord Wavell, 'a couple outside the ordinary.' The sixty-two years of their married life had been a period of continual growth. In spite of the immense intellectual gap between them, he had learnt to respect her opinions and to let her take her own decisions. In South Africa she had chosen to go to gaol in the last phase of the Satyagraha struggle. In India she had sought imprisonment during the civil disobedience movements; at the age of seventy she had courted arrest during the Rajkot agitation, and her last imprisonment was to end with her death.

It was not in the political field, however, that her real work was done. To a vast circle of disciples and co-workers of her husband she was 'Ba', the mother; they were her family and the Ashram was her home. She was the picture of contentment when she sat in her husband's hut, fanning him while he ate his lunch, or when she massaged his feet as he dozed off to sleep. She could read and write in Gujerati and had picked up scraps of spoken English in South Africa, which she occasionally practised with more innocence than expertness. 'I know my husband,' she told a European Superintendent of Prisons when he protested that Gandhi himself was responsible for his under-feeding; 'he always mischiefs.' In the Aga Khan Palace, Gandhi resumed his efforts to fill up gaps in her education. It was amusing to see this lady of seventy-four pace up and down her room committing elements of geography and general knowledge to memory. But when the time came for the lessons her memory played her tricks. 'Lahore' she would say, 'is the capital of Calcutta.'

Kasturba's major disappointment was her eldest son Harilal; a problem child, he had rebelled against his parents and lost his moorings. In 1925 Gandhi received a letter from Lyallpur in the Punjab that a company, 'All-India Stores Limited', with his eldest son as one of the directors had turned out to be a bogus concern. The Mahatma hastened to dissociate himself publicly from his reprobate son: 'For me the law of Satyagraha, law of love, is an eternal principle. I co-operate with all that is good. I desire to non-co-operate with all that is evil—whether it is associated with my wife, son or myself.' Dissociation from even such a son was easier for the father than for the mother. Once, when she heard that Harilal had been convicted for having been found drunk in public, she wrote to him to reform himself for the sake of 'a weak old woman who cannot bear the burden of this sorrow'. But Harilal was unreformed and irreformable. A day before her death, he was brought—drunk —to her bedside; the sight upset her and he had to be removed from her presence hurriedly.

After the death of his beloved secretary and wife, the Aga Khan Palace had sombre associations for Gandhi. He was also tormented by the feeling that this improvised gaol, with its large staff and military guards, was costing the country too much. There did not appear to be an early prospect of his release and he prepared himself for a long term of incarceration. But his health began to cause concern to the Government early in 1944. He had contracted malaria and had been running a high temperature. The tide of the war had already turned in favour of the Allies, and the risks of Gandhi's release seemed to the Government immeasurably less than those of a possible death in gaol.

His release (on May 6, 1944) did not please Gandhi; he even felt ashamed that he should have fallen ill in gaol. He was taken to Juhu, a sea-side resort near Bombay. It turned out that he was suffering not only from the after-effects of malaria, but from hookworm and amoebic infections, which had resulted in acute anaemia. He ascribed all illness to a lack of faith in God, the 'Master-Physician'; his known antipathy to drugs did not make it easy to treat him. Nevertheless, before many weeks were over he was well enough to attend to the problems which faced the country.

In the summer of 1944 India had not yet fully recovered from the shock of the 1942 'rebellion'. Overt political agitation had been suppressed and even the underground activities had declined. Popular frustration and discontent still struggled for expression, but the grave peril from Japan, which had provided the main impulse for Gandhi's 'Quit India' demand as also for the Government's sharp reaction to it, had definitely receded. There was thus no question in 1944 of starting the mass civil disobedience campaign which he had planned, but had been unable to launch two years earlier. Nor was there any point in continuing underground activity, as all secrecy was taboo in Satyagraha. Even so, in 1944 India was far from being tranquil. The impact of the war on the economy of the country was being felt. Famine or near-famine conditions prevailed in several parts of the country. With the largest political party beyond the pale of the law, with the constitution in abeyance in most of the Provinces, and with an Executive Council consisting only of the Viceroy's nominees at the centre, the need for a new political move was obvious.

Gandhi knew that his stock in official circles was not high, that his own *bona fides* and those of the Congress were questioned, that with a British Cabinet presided over by Churchill the scales were heavily tipped against him. Nevertheless, he took the initiative to break the political deadlock between the Government and the Congress. On June 17, 1944, he wrote to Lord Wavell, seeking permission to see the members of Congress Working Committee. The Viceroy turned down this request; nor did he see any advantage in a meeting with Gandhi 'in consideration of radical differences' in their viewpoints. In an interview with Stuart Gelder of the *News Chronicle*, Gandhi suggested the formation of a National Government at the centre, chosen by the elected members of the Central Legislative Assembly; this proposal was described by the Viceroy 'as quite unacceptable to His Majesty's Government'. Lord Wavell was only adhering to Lord Linlithgow's policy that there could be no truck with the Congress until it withdrew the 'Quit India' resolution and its leaders offered apologies for the past and guarantees for the future.

On July 17, 1944, Gandhi wrote to Churchill, appealing to him 'to trust and use me for the sake of your people and mine and through them those of the world'. The appeal was addressed to the wrong man and at the wrong time; so long as the war lasted, and so long as Churchill remained at the head of the British Government, the prospects of a conciliatory policy towards the Congress were slim indeed. Moreover, it seemed to the Government that Gandhi's peace overtures stemmed from a sense of political defeat and from a desire to retrieve the prestige of the Congress from the wreckage of the 1942 'rebellion'. Such an assumption was quite in line with the common canons of politics, but Gandhi's reasons were different. He was following the logic of Satyagraha, in which an honourable peace with the opponent is welcome at any time, irrespective of the relative strength or weakness of the combatants. He also recognized—what the Government were to recognize a year later—that only a national government could cope with the difficult economic problems which the war had created or aggravated. In 1931 he had agreed to a truce with the Government when civil disobedience was on a high tide, because he believed in the sincerity of Lord Irwin. In 1944 he sought a reconciliation even though ostensibly the position of the Congress was weak.

It was the contention of British statesmen that the crux of

the Indian problem was not the willingness of the British Government to hand over power to India but the lack of agreement among Indians themselves. The political deadlock, thus viewed, was not so much between Britain and India, as between the Indian National Congress and the All-India Muslim League. The latter had since 1940 taken its stand on 'Pakistan'. We have already seen that Gandhi considered this demand neither in the interest of the country nor of Muslims themselves. At the same time, swearing as he did by non-violence, he could not *a priori* reject such a demand if it commanded the support of a large section of the Muslim community. In April 1942 the Working Committee of the Congress had acknowledged the principle of self-determination and declared that the Congress could not conceive any part of the country being compelled to remain in the Indian Union against its will. In 1942, before his arrest, Gandhi had suggested that if the British Government called upon the Muslim League to form a National Government, the Congress would welcome it. Jinnah did not take the proposal seriously. From gaol, in response to a public statement by Jinnah, Gandhi had written a letter to him which the Government had withheld. Jinnah's comment was that Gandhi was trying to 'embroil' him with the Government. The Muslim League leader had, of course, no intention of being embroiled with the authorities. The arrest of the Congress leaders in August 1942 had given him a welcome opportunity to dominate the political scene and to exploit the official exasperation with the Congress for consolidating the position of his party in the Provinces.

Having failed in breaking the deadlock between the Government and the Congress after his release from gaol, Gandhi sought an accord with Jinnah. The Mahatma did not accept the two-nation theory, but he was prepared to recognize the psychology which had commended this theory to the Muslim intelligentsia. The basis on which he proposed to negotiate with Jinnah was 'the Rajaji formula', devised by Rajagopalachari, the ex-Premier of Madras, and one of the keenest intellects in the Congress.

Rajagopalachari had suggested that if the Muslim League endorsed
the Congress demand for national independence and for the
formation of a provisional government during the war, the
Congress would agree to a demarcation of contiguous Muslim
majority districts in the north-west and north-east of India
and to a plebiscite of all adult inhabitants in these areas to decide
whether they would prefer to remain in a free United India
or in separate states. And if ultimately separation was agreed
upon, the two states were to devise mutual agreements for
defence, communications and other essential matters.

The Rajaji formula was a bold move, the first recognition
of the Pakistan idea by an eminent Congressman. It was also
the first serious attempt to reduce Pakistan to concrete terms,
but it was summarily dismissed by Jinnah. In spite of this rebuff
to Rajagopalachari, Gandhi decided to meet Jinnah. On July 17,
1944 he wrote a letter to 'dear brother Jinnah'. 'Do not regard
me,' he pleaded, 'as an enemy of Islam or of Indian Muslims.
I have always been a servant and friend to you and mankind.
Do not disappoint me.'

The Gandhi-Jinnah talks began on September 9, 1944 and
concluded on September 27th. The optimism which they aroused
at the time did not derive from any real prospects of an agreement between the two leaders, but only reflected public weariness
of the political deadlock, and an almost universal desire for
concord between the League and the Congress. On his return
from the first interview, Gandhi was asked if he had brought
anything from Jinnah. 'Only flowers,' he replied. The subsequent
meetings registered no more tangible gains. Jinnah questioned
Gandhi's credentials; it was true that the Mahatma had since
1934 ceased to be a member of the Congress, but Jinnah knew
very well that Gandhi's weight in the counsels of the Congress
did not depend upon a membership card or on the holding
of any office. The Muslim League leader's approach was
doctrinaire. He wanted Gandhi to recognize that the All-India
Muslim League had the exclusive right to speak on behalf
of Indian Muslims. He wanted the principle of Pakistan to be

conceded before he could define its geographical boundaries or discuss its details. He would not hear of non-Muslims in Muslim majority provinces participating in the plebiscite which was to determine their future; the right of self-determination in these areas could only be exercised by Muslims.

Gandhi suggested that while the principle for the demarcation of boundaries and the plebiscite could be decided in advance, the actual partition, if it became inevitable, should follow and not precede the transfer of power from Britain to India. He hoped that, after the departure of the British, the communities would learn, in the bracing climate of freedom, to make mutual adjustments and the need for the partition of the country might never arise. What was Gandhi's hope was Jinnah's fear; the Muslim League leader did not want to take any risks and so made partition the pre-condition of Indian independence. Jinnah also rejected the proposal for treaty arrangements between the two states for defence, communications and foreign affairs as affecting the sovereignty of the new states. To Gandhi the prospect of two states carved out on the basis of religious affiliations, 'with nothing but enmity in common between them', was disconcerting; the search for cultural and economic autonomy was legitimate enough, but some safeguards were necessary to prevent an armament race and an armed conflict between the two states.

While these conversations were no more than a kind of re-education for Gandhi, to Jinnah they brought an accession of political strength. The fact that Gandhi had knocked at his door raised Jinnah's prestige. For four years the Muslim League leader had not swerved an inch from the position he had adopted in March 1940; events had shown that intransigence paid dividends. The 'Rajaji formula', which had formed the initial basis of the negotiations, did not concede all that Jinnah demanded, but at least it recognized the possibility of the partition of the country. The fact that the Mahatma, who had once described the division of India as a sin, had relented so far as to discuss the machinery for the exercise of the right of self-determination was a feather in Jinnah's cap. Viewed in the long-term strategy of the campaign for Pakistan, the Gandhi-Jinnah talks were another milestone, marking further progress from the offer of Lord Linlithgow in August 1940, and the Cripps Mission in March 1942.

The interest of the next two attempts to break the political deadlock also lies in how far they fitted into Jinnah's strategy. In 1945 Bhulabhai Desai, the leader of the Congress Party in the Central Legislative Assembly, and Nawabzada Liaquat Ali Khan, Deputy Leader of the Muslim League Party, discussed the proposal for an interim National Government in which the Muslim League and the Congress were to have equal representation. To Bhulabhai Desai's chagrin Liaquat Ali denied that any agreement had been reached. The idea of a parity between the Congress and the Muslim League had, however, been introduced in political parleys and was to receive an official recognition in the Simla Conference which Lord Wavell convened during June-July, 1945. Lord Wavell had recently returned from England with the concurrence of the British Cabinet to a proposal for the reconstitution of his Executive Council in consultation with Indian leaders. A conference of the Congress leaders (recently released from gaol) and the Muslim League leaders led by Jinnah was held at Simla to discuss the Viceroy's proposal. Gandhi was not a delegate to the Conference, though he was consulted by the Viceroy and the Congress Working Committee. Lord Wavell had suggested a parity of representation in the Executive Council, between the 'caste Hindus' and Muslims, but by the time the conference was over Jinnah was demanding parity between Muslims and all the other communities. The conference actually broke down on the insistence of Jinnah, that the Muslim League should have an exclusive right to nominate Muslim members of the Viceroy's Executive Council. This was something which the Congress could not concede without repudiating its national composition and outlook. The conclusion is inescapable that at this time Jinnah was not interested in a compromise; he did not think the time for an agreement was opportune; in any case, an understanding with the Congress had little attraction for him when he hoped to get better terms from the Government.

As the war drew to a close, the need for a fresh move in India was keenly felt. The Simla Conference was a recognition of this need. The war in Europe had ended in May and Japan surrendered in August. The first post-war elections in Britain returned the Labour Party to power. The new Secretary of State for India, Lord Pethick-Lawrence, spoke of equal partnership between Britain and India. The Viceroy had already announced that elections would be held 'as soon as possible' to the Central Legislative Assembly and Provincial Legislatures which had been in existence since 1934 and 1937 respectively. In September 1945, after a visit to London, the Viceroy announced that in the spirit of the Cripps offer the Government proposed to convene a constitution-making body. The announcement did not arouse much enthusiasm. The Labour Government decided to send an all-party British Parliamentary Delegation to study the situation in India and to convince her people that self-government was within their grasp.

Chapter 50

THE COMING OF INDEPENDENCE

IN January 1946, when Gandhi visited Srinivasa Sastri, the veteran Liberal leader, the conversation veered to the British Parliamentary Delegation which was touring India. 'We know,' commented Sastri who was on his death-bed, 'nothing can come out of it. Labour or Conservative, so far as India is concerned, they are all one and the same.' That this melancholy judgment should have been passed at a time when the transfer of power was about to take place, and by one who had always been considered a friend of the British connection, was significant and showed that the representatives of the British *Raj* in India gave hardly any inkling of an early departure.

On a superficial view, the British position in India at the close of the Second World War could not have been stronger. There had never been more British troops on Indian soil. The Congress organization was banned and, with the exception of Gandhi, almost all nationalist leaders were in gaol. The Muslim League was campaigning for Pakistan, but its target was the Congress, not the British Government. In six provinces constitutional government was in abeyance; in the remaining five provinces ministries more or less friendly to the Government were in power. The repressive measures adopted in 1942 had brought a welcome respite to the British officers who had slogged at their desks for six years. The civil servants were hard-working men who did their duty according to their lights, but, as Gokhale put it, 'their lights are dim. And even as regards efficiency my own conviction is that it is impossible for the present system to produce more than a certain very limited amount of efficiency and that standard has now been reached'. Gokhale had spoken in 1905; forty years later the dynamics of national awakening and economic change had accentuated these deficiencies. Few of these conscientious civil servants could see in 1945 that the old order, which they had known and shaped and loved, had been largely, even if imperceptibly, eroded.

The war had accelerated this process of erosion. It had brought easy money to a few, but in the minds of millions of Indians it was synonymous with scarcity and high prices. A terrible famine, to the making of which man and nature conspired, had ravaged Bengal; the people did not know and perhaps did not care how far the tragedy was due to ministerial neglect and corruption in Bengal and how far to the constitutional propriety or inertia which prevented timely intervention by the Central Government. Shortages of food and cloth were endemic almost throughout the country, and efforts to control and ration supplies had brought corruption in their wake. The war had lowered moral standards; it tempted too many people to make hay while the brief sun of war-time prosperity shone.

In any case, the transition from war to peace was going to be a necessarily slow and painful process. The demobilization of an army which had swelled in number from 189,000 to 2,250,000 was a stupendous task. The Indian soldier was no longer the raw peasant whom the recruiting officer had picked up from the village; he had fought in the battle-fronts of Malaya, Burma, the Middle East and Italy; he had seen empires topple and he had learnt to ask awkward questions. The Government was not entirely oblivious to the strains and stresses created by the war. A number of post-war plans had been framed in the central and provincial secretariats, but these plans had an air of unreality about them. The civil servants, while at home in the mysteries of the land revenue tenures and the Indian Penal Code, were prone to view ambitious blue-prints with scepticism. As in politics so in economics, the official dictum was that swift changes were neither possible nor desirable in India. And in any case, such changes called for not only higher taxes, but also inroads into the privileged position of the very classes—the Princes, the landlords and the rich industrialists —who were loyal to the British *Raj*.

It must be stated, however, that whatever their difficulties the morale of the majority of the British officers in India was high, and that they had not lost confidence in their ability to govern India for many years to come. If, within a year of the end of the war, large strides had been taken towards Indian independence, it was due not so much to any weakening on the part of representatives of the *Raj* as to the change of political climate in Britain and the determination of the Attlee Government to come to terms with Indian nationalism.

British historians are inclined to regard the events of 1947 as a logical climax of the policy outlined in the declaration of August 1917. Lord Chelmsford who, as Viceroy of India, had pleaded for this declaration had himself suggested that 'it should be accompanied by a very clear declaration that this is a distant goal'. One is reminded of Morley's comment on his talks with Gokhale: 'He made no secret of his ultimate hope and design— India to be on the footing of a self-governing colony—I equally made no secret of my conviction that for many a day to come —long beyond the short span of time that may be left to us— this was a mere dream.' 'Not in my lifetime', seems to have been the verdict on Indian independence of Lloyd George and Montagu, MacDonald and Benn, Baldwin and Hoare, Churchill and Amery. British statesmen were conscious of the long process of conflict and evolution through which parliamentary government had passed in Great Britain, and of the time taken by Canada and Australia to attain political maturity. That this process should have taken even longer in an Oriental country, with its variety of creeds and cultures, was axiomatic to them.

From 1917 the policy of the successive British Governments towards India was 'self-government by stages'. The trouble about this mode of advance was that each instalment tended to become out of date by the time it was actually granted.

The Reforms of 1919 might well have appeased political India in 1909; the Reforms of 1935 would have evoked enthusiasm in 1919, and an equivalent of the Cripps offer in 1940 could have opened a new chapter in Indo-British relations, halted the process of estrangement between the Congress and the Government and between Hindus and Muslims.

To this step-by-step advance Gandhi dealt a mortal blow in 1920. His promise of 'Swaraj in one year' was no make-believe; since slavery was, in his view, essentially a state of mind, a nation began to liberate itself the moment it resolved to be free. Satyagraha, his technique of non-violent resistance posed a difficult problem for the British. If they ignored it, it gathered momentum. If they attacked it, it enlisted sympathy in India and abroad. Repression was not only ineffective in the long run; it was also repugnant to the democratic conscience of England. The British people took only a fitful interest in Indian affairs, but they were too proud of their liberal tradition to agree to 400 millions of Indians being governed against their will. As each successive Satyagraha campaign revealed the strength of the nationalist opposition in India, it weakened the plea of the official apologists that only a minority of malcontents was against the *Raj*.

It was World War II which helped to mature British public opinion on India. The war changed the map of the world and the balance of power, but it also changed the minds of men. The intellectual and social ferment, of which the Labour Party's triumph in 1945 was an expression, helped in reassessing the merits of the traditional policies. Ideologically, the Labour Government was prepared for a new policy, but the facts of the Indian situation also drove it in the same direction. Speaking on March 6, 1947 in the House of Commons on the condition of India in November and December 1945, Mr Alexander, a member of the Labour Cabinet who was closely associated with the process of transfer of power, observed: 'It might be said that the Indian authorities were literally sitting on the top of a volcano, and as a result of the situation which had arisen after the war, the outbreak of revolution might be expected at any time.'

The opening months of 1946 confirmed the correctness of this estimate. Such was the irascibility of the popular temper that there were violent outbreaks at the slightest provocation, and sometimes without any provocation. In February 1946, a Muslim demonstration at Calcutta against a court-martial verdict on a Muslim officer of the Indian National Army degenerated into general lawlessness in which shops were ransacked and tramcars and buses burnt. There were instances of indiscipline in the Air Force and a major naval mutiny in Bombay. In several Provinces there were signs of disaffection spreading to the police. The instruments of law and order, on which British rule ultimately depended, were proving broken reeds.

In the face of this diminishing respect for authority what was needed was an immediate strengthening of the administration, but the war had, from the British point of view, led to a lamentable dilution of the 'superior services'. There had been a tremendous expansion in sphere of governmental activity, while the recruitment to the Indian Civil Service and the Indian Police Service had been kept in abeyance during the war. Not only were there fewer Europeans to man key jobs; their ranks were likely to further thin down in the next few years when the senior officers retired.

That the run-down condition of the administration should have figured prominently in the explanations of British ministers was only to be expected; but the emphasis on this factor seems to have derived from the habit of empiricism which makes the British stress the practical rather than the ideological aspect of a solution. The transfer of power from Britain to India would not, however, have been a significant event in world history if it had been only a recognition of a political necessity. Not merely the compulsion of events, but a measure of idealism went into the policy which Prime Minister Attlee initiated and carried through during the years 1946-47. And in so far as the British Government was impelled by this idealism, by a desire to open a fresh chapter in Indo-British relations, it was a victory for Gandhi, who had pleaded for nearly thirty years for a transformation of the relationship between the two countries. Among the advocates of this transformation were several English men and women, Hume and Wedderburn, C. F. Andrews and Horace Alexander, Brailsford and Brockway, Laski and Carl Heath, Muriel Lester and Agatha Harrison, who never wavered in their sympathy for the Indian cause. In their own day they represented a tiny and not-too-influential minority, but in the fulness of time their opinions became the national policies of their country.

Whatever the reasons for the change in British policy, the arrival of the Cabinet Mission in March 1946 went a long way to convince India that the British Government was in earnest. Of the three Cabinet Ministers on the Mission, Lord Pethick-Lawrence and Sir Stafford Cripps were well known to Gandhi. The Mission consulted him frequently during their stay, both formally and informally. They interviewed no less than 472 'leaders', though it was clear from the outset that the only parties which mattered were the Congress and the Muslim League, and the crucial question was whether India was to remain united or to be split up. The Congress was opposed to the partition of the country but was prepared to go to the farthest limit in conceding cultural, economic and regional autonomy. A conference at Simla failed to resolve the Congress-League differences. The Cabinet Mission then offered a compromise plan in their statement of May 16th. They sketched a three-tier constitutional structure for India. On the top was to be a Union of India embracing British India as well as the Indian States, but dealing only with foreign affairs, defence and communications. The bottom tier was to consist of Provinces and States in which were to vest all residuary powers. The intermediate tier was to comprise groups to be formed by Provinces (if they chose) to deal with certain common subjects. It was laid down that the Constituent Assembly (consisting of representatives of Provinces and States), after a preliminary meeting was to divide up into three sections; Section A consisting of Madras, Bombay, United Provinces, Bihar and Orissa; Section B comprising Punjab, Sind and North-West Frontier Province, and Section C consisting of Bengal and Assam. Each section was to decide whether the Provinces covered by it were to form a group, and if so, what were to be the subjects which were to fall within the jurisdiction of the group executive and legislature.

Gandhi's initial reaction to the Cabinet Mission's proposals was favourable. 'After four days of searching examination,' he wrote in *Harijan* of May 26, 1946, 'my conviction abides that it is the best document the British Government could have produced in the circumstances.' There were, however, several features of the scheme which disturbed him. The difficulty of settling individually with 562 States (in view of the fact that the Paramountcy of the Crown was to lapse) was obvious enough. But it was the clause about the grouping of Provinces which jarred on him. This clause had been introduced in the Cabinet Mission Plan as a concession to the Muslim League. The shrinking of the authority of the central government to three minimal subjects, and the vesting of the residuary authority in the Provinces weakened the future Union of India. The creation of groups as intermediate tiers was likely to be another centrifugal force. But even this price would have been worthwhile if it could guarantee the unity of the country. Unfortunately, the Muslim League, even while it accepted the Cabinet Mission's Plan, made no secret of its hope that the grouping of Provinces was but a step towards Pakistan rather than a substitute for it.

To understand the shifting and somewhat confused political situation which developed after the departure of the Cabinet Mission, it is useful to sum up briefly the attitudes of the British Government and the two major parties on the eve of the transfer of power. Mr Attlee was anxious to retain the initiative he had so boldly taken; his one anxiety was to make the transfer of power not only speedy but smooth. To the British Government the Indian constitutional problem was a political problem which was capable of solution by compromise and a spirit of 'give and take'. They were thus committed to no one solution; they were prepared to accept any workable arrangement on which the Congress and the League could agree.

Gandhi's view was different; the transfer of power was not a problem of expediency or power politics, but one which called for and admitted of a just and moral solution. He wanted the majorities to go far to meet the anxieties of the minorities, but he was not prepared to be stampeded into partition, which in the long run might do more harm than good to India and the two communities themselves. He was disturbed by the understandable anxiety of the British Government not to alienate Jinnah. He advised the Congress not to accept any arrangement in a hurry, which they might have to repent at leisure; at the worst, Congressmen were to be prepared to go once again into the wilderness. This advice did not appeal to Congress leaders, who (like the British) tended to judge the situation in terms of political necessity, and feared a drift to a civil war through vacillation or delay. Somehow their dread of civil war was greater than Gandhi's, who believed that after the British departure a few days of blood letting were likely to bring the parties back to sanity. Recent history of civil wars in China and Spain did not support this optimism. The Labour Government at any rate were under no doubt that neither the Parliament nor public opinion in Britain would endorse a solution which did not promise an orderly transfer of power.

It seemed to Gandhi that, the declaration of the British Government notwithstanding, quite a few people in India seemed to think and behave as if the British were really not going. Only a dramatic gesture, such as the immediate withdrawal of the British troops, or the immediate revocation of the Paramountcy of the Crown from the States, could jolt the various political parties and interests out of the grooves in which they had moved too long. Ever since it became apparent to him that the British had decided to quit, the one

Q*

question which had exercised Gandhi incessantly was: how would the people of India, after centuries of servitude, react to the shock of freedom? He told Brailsford, a British journalist, in April 1946: 'This time, I believe the British mean business. But the offer has come suddenly. Will India be jerked into independence? I feel today like a passenger who has been hoisted in a basket chair on a ship's deck in a stormy sea and has not found his feet.'

He anxiously observed the vast crowds which came to greet him at railway stations or attended the meetings which he addressed. Some of them were orderly enough, but others were unruly. He was worried at the growing indiscipline, which was partly a hangover from 1942 and partly a symptom of the post-war malaise. In February 1946, in an editorial in *Harijan* on 'How to canalize hatred', he wrote: 'Hatred is in the air and the impatient lovers of the country will gladly take advantage of it if they can through violence to further the cause of independence. I suggest that it is wrong at any time and anywhere . . . The result will be deeper hatred and counter-hatred and vengeance let loose on both sides . . . And yet if truth is told as it must be, our non-violent action has been half-hearted. Many have preached non-violence through the lips while har-bouring violence in the breast.'

The prime dangers, as Gandhi saw, were hatred and violence, which were finding expression in anti-British feeling or in the communal riots that were again beginning to disfigure the towns. For the riots the Hindus blamed the Muslims, the Muslims blamed the Hindus, and both blamed the hooligans. 'Who are the hooligans?' Gandhi asked and replied, 'We are the makers of the brand.' It was when the intelligentsia spilled venom and whipped up excitement that the hooligans got their chance. He revived the suggestion which he had made in the late thirties for the formation of 'peace brigades', consisting of men sworn to non-violence and ready to die in the noble task of restoring the rioters to sanity. Meanwhile, the one thing which was needed was restraint in speech and writing so that the great changes which were imminent could be ushered in peacefully.

Unfortunately, the very reasons which impelled Gandhi and the Congress to seek a lowering of the political temperature led Jinnah and the Muslim League in the opposite direction. For the latter it was a question of 'now or never'. The long negotiations with the Cabinet Mission had revealed that not only was the Congress opposed to Pakistan but the Labour Government seemed to prefer a solution which kept the Congress and the League within the framework of a single constitution. Only a civil war, or the threat of a civil war, seemed likely to beat down the objections of the Congress and the scepticism of the British Government towards partition. The Cabinet Mission plan was a compromise but it did not really bring the two parties together. The result was that questions, presumed to have been settled by the Cabinet Mission, were reopened soon after the return of its three members to England.

Controversy rose to a fever pitch on two crucial questions, that of the grouping of Provinces and the composition of interim government. On July 27, 1946, the Muslim League Council withdrew its acceptance of Cabinet Mission Plan, decided to boycott the Constituent Assembly and announced a programme of 'direct action' to achieve Pakistan. Jinnah declared that Muslims had bid good-bye to constitutional methods. 'We have forged a pistol,' he said, 'and are in a position to use it.' When asked whether the movement would be violent or non-violent, he refused to 'discuss ethics'. Some of his lieutenants in the League were even more forthright. Angry words and impatient gestures were, however, a poor preparation for 'direct action', if the object was a peaceful agitation.

At a time when tension was mounting it was imperative that the country should have a strong and stable government at the centre. The Cabinet Mission had failed in the formation of a national interim government. In July the Viceroy, Lord Wavell, once again took the initiative and asked Nehru to form the Government. Jinnah, who was approached by Nehru but refused to co-operate, was bitterly critical of what he described as 'the caste Hindu Fascist Congress and their henchmen' who sought 'to dominate and rule over the Mussalmans and other minority communities of India with the aid of British bayonets'.

This bitterness boded ill at a time when exemplary restraint was necessary to pull the country through a critical period. The 'Direct Action Day', which was celebrated by the Muslim League on August 16th, touched off a chain reaction of violent explosions which in the succeeding twelve months shook the country.

Chapter 51

QUENCHING THE FLAMES

THE Muslim League observed August 16, 1946, as the 'Direct Action Day'. On that day Calcutta witnessed a communal riot, the scale and intensity of which had never been known in living memory. For four days, bands of hooligans armed with sticks, spears, hatchets and even fire-arms, roamed the town, robbing and killing at will. The 'Great Calcutta Killing' —to use the grim epithet coined by the *Statesman*—took a toll of more than five thousand lives besides the fifteen thousand or more who were injured.

Bengal was ruled by a Muslim League ministry led by H. S. Suhrawardy. 'In retrospect,' wrote the *Statesman* 'it is the Muslim League's conduct before the riots that stands open to inference—not only by its political opponents—that it was divided in mind on whether rioting of some sort would be good or bad.' Charges were in fact levelled against the Provincial Government that it did not provide against the outbreak which it might well have anticipated, and that Suhrawardy deliberately prevented the police from acting promptly and impartially when the riots broke out.

If, as was suggested at the time, the outbreak was intended to serve as a demonstration of the strength of the Muslim feeling on Pakistan, it proved a double-edged weapon. The non-Muslims of Calcutta reeled under the initial impact, but then, taking advantage of their numerical superiority, hit back savagely. The impression went abroad that, in spite of a Muslim League ministry in Bengal, the Hindus had won in this 'trial of strength' in Calcutta. Two months later reprisals followed in the Muslim-majority district of Noakhali in East Bengal where, taking advantage of poor communications and encouraged by fanatical priests and ambitious politicians, local hooligans burnt the Hindus' property, looted their crops and desecrated their temples. A shocking innovation was the forcible conversion of Hindus and kidnapping of Hindu women. Thousands of Hindus fled from their homes. In that year of growing lawlessness, East Bengal did for rural India what Calcutta had done for the towns; it showed what inhumanities could be practised in the name of religion and ostensibly for political ends.

Gandhi was in Delhi when the news from East Bengal came through. He was particularly hurt by the crimes against women. He cancelled all his plans and decided to leave for East Bengal. Friends tried to dissuade him. His health was poor; important political developments, on which his advice would be required, were imminent. 'I do not know,' he said, 'what I shall be able to do there. All that I know is that I won't be at peace unless I go.'

At Calcutta he saw the ravages of the August riots and confessed to a 'sinking feeling at the mass madness which can turn man into less than a brute'. He made a courtesy call on the British Governor, met Premier Suhrawardy and his colleagues, and Hindu and Muslim leaders of Bengal. He made it clear that he had not come as a prosecutor or a judge. He was interested not in fastening guilt on any community or individual, but in creating conditions which would enable the two communities to resume their peaceful life. Suhrawardy was at first agreeably helpful: he deputed a minister and two parliamentary secretaries to accompany Gandhi.

The atmosphere in East Bengal was charged with fear, hatred and violence. In a statement, Gandhi declared that he found himself in the midst of exaggeration and falsehood: 'I am unable to discover the truth. There is a terrible mutual distrust. Oldest friendships have snapped. Truth and *Ahimsa*, by which I swear and which have, to my knowledge, sustained me for sixty years, seem to fail to show the attributes I have ascribed to them. To test them or better to test myself I am going to a village Srirampur . . .

Of the 200 Hindu families of Srirampur village in Noakhali district, only three had remained after the recent disturbances. He dispersed his entourage in the neighbouring villages. Pyarelal, Sushila Nayar, Abha, Kanu Gandhi and Sucheta Kripalani— each of them settled in a village. At Srirampur Gandhi's only companions were his stenographer Parsuram, his Bengali interpretor Prof. Nirmal Kumar Bose and Manu Gandhi. For the next six weeks a wooden bedstead, covered with a mattress, served as his office by day and his bed by night. His working day extended to sixteen and sometimes twenty hours. He slept little and ate little, made his bed, mended his clothes, cooked his food, attended to his enormous mail, received callers and visited local Muslims. For several years he had been maligned in the League Press, as the 'enemy number one' of Indian Muslims. He let the Muslims of Srirampur judge for themselves.

The restoration of confidence between the two communities was, however, a slow and difficult process. Gandhi did not agree to the demand of the Hindus for forming Hindu 'pockets' in Muslim areas, and for police and military reinforcements. The only protection, he maintained, which a minority could really count on was that given willingly by neighbours to neighbours. Nor did he accept the specious pleas of Muslim politicians that the accounts of the riots in East Bengal had been fabricated by the Hindu Press to discredit the Muslim League ministry; thousands of people were hardly likely to become homeless and penniless simply to spite the ministers in Calcutta. He lifted the issue of peace from the plane of politics to that of humanity; whatever the political map of the future, he pleaded, it should be common ground among all parties that standards of civilized life should not be thrown overboard.

Gandhi's presence acted as a soothing balm on the villages of East Bengal; it eased tension, assuaged anger and softened tempers. His success would have been more spectacular were it not for the sustained propaganda against him in the Muslim Press, which continued to suspect a 'deep political game' in his mission. Under pressure from local party bosses and perhaps from the League High Command, Premier Suhrawardy became critical of Gandhi's tour, and joined the outcry that Gandhi should quit Bengal. Gandhi was not dismayed by this perverse opposition; he argued that, if he could not command the confidence of the Muslim League leaders, the responsibility was his own. He was in a mood of self-examination, almost of self-castigation. An entry in his diary dated January 2, 1947, reads: 'Have been awake since 2 a.m. God's grace alone is sustaining me. I can see there is some grave defect in me somewhere which is the cause of all this. All round me is utter darkness. When will God take me out of this darkness into His light?'[1]

The same day he left Srirampur on a village to village tour. At Chandipur village he discarded his sandals and, like the pilgrims of old, walked bare-foot. The village tracks were slippery and sometimes maliciously strewn with brambles and broken glass; the fragile bamboo bridges were tricky to negotiate. He saw gaping walls, gutted roofs, charred ruins and remnants of skeletons in the debris—the handiwork of religious frenzy. A song from Tagore, which he liked to hear, expressed some of his anguish:

Walk Alone.
If they answer not to thy call, walk alone;
If they are afraid and cower mutely facing the wall,
O thou of evil luck,
Open thy mind and speak out alone.
If they turn away and desert you when crossing the
      wilderness,
O thou of evil luck,
Trample the thorns under thy tread,
And along the blood-lined track travel alone.
If they do not hold up the light when the night is
      troubled with storm,
O thou of evil luck,
With the thunder-flame of pain ignite thine own
      heart,
And let it burn alone.

[1] Pyarelal: *Mahatma Gandhi, The Last Phase*, Vol. I, p. 470.

On March 2, 1947, he left for Bihar, where the Hindu peasants had wreaked a terrible vengeance on the Muslim minority for the events in Noakhali. Gandhi had first heard of the Bihar riots when he was on his way to Noakhali in the last week of October 1946. He had made it known that, if peace did not return at once, he would embark on a fast unto death. This warning, coupled with the stern measures adopted by the Bihar Government and a visit by Jawaharlal Nehru, helped in restoring order quickly. The loss of life, however, had been colossal, and problems of relief and rehabilitation were stupendous.

In Bihar Gandhi's refrain was the same as in East Bengal: the majority must repent and make amends; the minority must forgive and make a fresh start. He would not accept any apology for what had happened, and chided those who sought in the misdeeds of the rioters in East Bengal a justification for what had happened in Bihar. Civilized conduct, he argued, was the duty of every individual and every community irrespective of what others did. He collected subscriptions from Hindus for the relief of Muslim sufferers, and encouraged the Bihar Government to prepare an elaborate scheme for the resettlement of Muslims displaced by the riots. Conditions in Bihar began to improve; they would have improved more quickly but for the fact that communal tension in 1946-47 was a reflection of the political situation which continued to oscillate continually and violently.

While Gandhi had 'buried' himself in the villages of East Bengal and Bihar, the political landscape had undergone bewildering changes. As we have already seen, the Cabinet Mission's Plan, prepared with such infinite patience and skill had, soon after its departure, failed to work. The Muslim League withdrew its acceptance of the plan, and launched a 'direct action campaign' to achieve Pakistan. The savage rioting in Calcutta touched off a chain reaction in East Bengal and Bihar. Minor riots went on in most other provinces. Alarmed by this increasing lawlessness, Lord Wavell brought the Muslim

League into the Interim Government, but the formation of
this coalition—which for seven years had been talked of as
a panacea for India's political ills—fanned political controversy
instead of putting it out. The Constituent Assembly was
summoned to meet on December 9th, but the Muslim League
had declared that its representatives would not participate.
The constitutional impasse looked complete when, in the last
week of November 1946, in an eleventh hour bid to bring the
parties together, the British Government invited the Viceroy,
Nehru, Jinnah, Liaquat Ali Khan, and Baldev Singh to London.
The discussions proved abortive but the British Government
issued a statement on December 6, 1946, to clarify the disputed
clauses about the grouping of provinces in the Cabinet Mission
Plan. Though this clarification largely met its objections, the
Muslim League did not remove its boycott of the Constituent
Assembly.

The year 1947 dawned with the darkest possible prospects
on the political horizon. India seemed to be sliding into an
undeclared, albeit confused, civil war with the battle lines passing
through almost every town and village. The Central Government, split from top to bottom, was unable to set an example
of cohesion or firmness to the governments in the Provinces.
The Viceroy, Lord Wavell, seemed to have been completely
outplayed in the face of divergent pressures which he could
neither reconcile nor control; he even suggested the desperate
expedient of a British evacuation of India province by province.
To check the drift to chaos, Premier Attlee came to the conclusion
that what was needed was a new policy and a new Viceroy to
carry it out. He announced in the House of Commons on February
20, 1947 that the British Government definitely intended to
quit India by June 1948, and if by that date the Indian parties
did not agree on an All-India constitution, power would be
transferred to 'some form of Central Government in British
India or in some areas to the existing Provincial Governments
or in such other ways as may seem most reasonable and in the
best interest of the Indian people'. Simultaneously, it was

announced that Lord Mountbatten would succeed Lord Wavell as Viceroy.

'Wise and courageous' was Jawaharlal Nehru's comment on the statement of February 20th. Jinnah, however, was impressed not so much by the bold sweep and the abounding faith which inspired this historic declaration as by the possibility envisaged in it of transferring power in June 1948 'to the existing Provincial Governments'. Apparently, the Muslim League could, by staying out of the Constituent Assembly, frustrate an All-India constitution, and get power for the Provinces in the east and west which it claimed for Pakistan. Of these Provinces, Bengal and Sind had already Muslim League ministries and Baluchistan was centrally administered. There were Congress ministries in Assam and the North-West Frontier Province, and a Congress-Akali Unionist coalition in Punjab; the immediate Muslim League strategy was to dislodge these three ministries and to replace them by Muslim League governments. 'Direct Action' campaigns were launched or intensified in these three provinces. The results, particularly in the Punjab, were disastrous. The Hindu and Sikh minorities in the West Punjab went through the same horrors as those suffered by the Hindu minority in East Bengal and the Muslim minority in Bihar. A semblance of order was restored with the help of the military, but tension continued. The first two towns of the Province, Lahore and Amritsar were caught up, however, in a strange guerilla warfare in which shooting, stabbing, and arson went on in the midst of police patrols and curfew orders.

Gandhi was in Bihar when he received the news of the trouble in the Punjab. Since October 1946 he had been wandering from one Province to another in a vain attempt to stem the tide of violence. While his work was unfinished in one Province, there was an outbreak in another. There were some who shrugged their shoulders and said that anarchy was only to be expected with the departure of the British, who alone had prevented Hindus and Muslims from flying at each other's throats. 'The fearful massacres,' said Churchill in September

1947, 'which are occurring in India are no surprise to me. We are, of course, only at the beginning of these horrors and butcheries perpetrated upon one another with the ferocity of cannibals, by the races gifted with capacities for the highest culture, and who had for generations dwelt side by side in general peace under the broad, tolerant and impartial rule of the British Crown and Parliament.'

To Gandhi the violence of 1946-47 was a shocking and even a bewildering phenomenon. All his life he had worked for the day when India would set an example of non-violence to the world. The chasm between what he had cherished in his heart and what he saw was so great that he could not help feeling a deep sense of failure. His first impulse was to blame himself. Was his technique faulty? Had he been unobservant, careless, indifferent, impatient? Had he failed to detect in time that while the people had, on the whole, refrained from overt violence in the struggle against foreign rule, they had continued to harbour ill feeling against the British? Was communal violence only an expression of the violence which had smouldered in the breasts of those who had paid lip service to non-violence?

It was only natural that he should have sought an explanation of this tragedy in terms of his own philosophy and of his part in India's political struggle. In retrospect, it would appear that he was exaggerating his own responsibility and the failure of non-violence. It would have been too much to expect that even in thirty years one single leader, however great, could have sterilized completely the hate and violence of 400 million people inhabiting a vast continent. It was remarkable enough that in the several Satyagraha campaigns he had led, violence had been reduced to negligible proportions, and India's millions received a nationalist awakening without that dose of hatred which is usually associated with resurgent nationalisms.

While it is possible that the lawlessness which followed the arrests of the Congress leaders in August 1942 lowered standards of mass behaviour, the real explanation for the violence of 1946-47 is to be sought in the tensions which the movement for Pakistan aroused both in its protagonists and antagonists. The basic premise of this movement was that Hindus and Muslims had nothing in common in the past, present or future. Large sections of the population were siezed with vague hopes or equally vague fears. No one could say with certainty whether India would remain united or be divided into two or more states, whether the Punjab or Bengal would retain their boundaries or be split, whether Indian states would be integrated into an independent India or become autonomous. The Adivasis of Central India and the Nagas of Assam found champions for an independence which they had never claimed before; there was talk of a Dravidistan in the south and a thousand mile corridor to link the two wings of future Pakistan. The 'balkanization of India', once an ominous phrase, had become a real danger. All this excited popular fantasy; the turbulent elements in the society saw in the coming transfer of power a period of vacuum such as had occurred in the eighteenth century during the twilight of the Mogul Empire.

In the face of these perils the Central Government was a house divided against itself, and the Provincial Governments were facing increasing demoralization. The impending termination of their careers had embittered some British officers; moreover, few of them had the will or the ability to cope with the volcanic violence which erupted everywhere. Indian officers, when themselves free from prejudice, were not always able to restrain their subordinates from petty tyranny. The growth of private armies, the Muslim League National Guards, the Rashtriya Swyamsevak Sangh, and others, showed that popular faith in the instruments of law and order had been shaken.

Gandhi had sensed the explosive possibilities of this situation. 'We are not yet in the midst of a civil war,' he had commented on the Great Calcutta Killing, 'but we are nearing it.' From the end of October, when he had left Delhi for Noakhali, he had made the assuaging of communal fanaticism his primary mission. He knew as well as anybody else that a settlement between the political parties could help in restoring stability. But he also saw that not only was political settlement not in sight, but violence might influence the nature of the political settlement. He wondered whether the people might be persuaded to agree, if their leaders could not. His tours of Bengal and Bihar succeeded in re-educating the masses, but he was handicapped by the fact that his voice did not carry the weight with the Muslim middle class which it once had done. The Hindus were also restive and critical of what they believed to be his policy of 'unilateral disarmament', but he could still sway them.

If Gandhi's efforts at restoring communal peace had been supplemented by someone who commanded the allegiance of the Muslim middle class, his task would not have been half so difficult. In 1946-47 Jinnah was at the zenith of his influence with the Muslim intelligentsia; he was the *Qaid-i-Azam*, the Great Leader, whose every nod was obeyed. If Jinnah had toured East Bengal or West Punjab, he might have helped in stopping the rot. Such a suggestion would, however, have been simply laughed away by the Muslim League leader, whose political instinct rebelled against fasts and walking tours.

Lawyer and parliamentarian as he was, it is difficult to believe that Jinnah could have believed in force. But he seemed to have believed in threats of force. We have already seen how, in 1938, he had warned the Congress that the Muslims could disrupt the unity of India, as the Sudeten Germans had broken up Czechoslovakia. After the 'Great Calcutta Killing' and the disturbances in Bengal and Bihar, communal violence became the strongest argument in his brief for Pakistan; if India was not divided, he warned, worse things would happen. Though he obliged Wavell and Mountbatten by signing appeals for peace, he did little to restrain his bellicose lieutenants; he himself issued double-edged statements which extenuated the violence they purported to condemn.

Chapter 52

VICTORY OF THE VANQUISHED

THE British withdrawal from India had been decided and dated by the February 20th statement. 'How can we hope,' Churchill had asked in the House of Commons, 'that the thousand year gulf which yawns between the Muslim and the Hindu will be bridged in fourteen months?' To those who knew the facts of the Indian situation, fourteen months seemed not too short but too long a period for a successful withdrawal. From Mr Attlee's window in Downing Street, the darkest aspect of the Indian horizon was the threat of a civil war. He has recorded in his memoirs that though he did not think that the chances of an orderly change-over were very good he felt there was one man who 'might pull it off'. The man was Rear-Admiral Lord Mountbatten, who succeeded Lord Wavell in March 1947.

One of the first acts of the new Viceroy was to invite Gandhi for a discussion. The Mahatma interrupted his peace mission in Bihar and travelled by train to New Delhi. He advised Mountbatten to dissolve the Congress-League coalition government and to ask Jinnah to form a cabinet. Evidently, Gandhi's object was to disarm Jinnah's suspicion of the Congress and the Hindus with one supreme gesture. To the British Government, however, the suggestion looked far-fetched. The Congress leaders had lately seen enough of their Muslim League colleagues in the Interim Government to want to give them a *carte blanche*; the time for gestures was past. When Jinnah met Mountbatten he reiterated his demand for the division of India.

The Viceroy's task was made easier by a reorientation of the Congress attitude to partition. Hitherto the Congress had insisted that partition should, if at all, follow and not precede political liberation, that (to use a famous expression of Maulana Azad) there could be no divorce before marriage. But a few months of stormy courtship in the Interim Government had cured the Congress leaders of all desire for a closer union. In the spring of 1947 the choice seemed to them to be between anarchy and partition; they resigned themselves to the latter in order to salvage three-fourths of India from the chaos which threatened the whole.

The stage was thus set for the June 3rd Plan, under which power was to be transferred by the British to two successor states on August 15, 1947. The final proposals, which took the Viceroy ten weeks of tireless negotiations and taxed to the full his ingenuity and diplomatic skill, represented the lowest common denominator of agreement between the Congress and the League; though they left the ultimate decision to democratic processes—voting by members of provincial legislatures or by referendum—the partition of India, as also the partition of the Punjab and Bengal, were foregone conclusions.

What Gandhi had feared had come to pass. India was to be divided, but partition was not to be imposed; it had been accepted by Jawaharlal Nehru, Vallabhbhai Patel and a majority of the members of the Congress Working Committee. Gandhi had no hand in the final negotiations, but his opposition to partition was an open secret. His reasons were the same which he had given several times before: 'We are unable to think coherently whilst the British power is still functioning in India. Its function is not to change the map of India. All it has to do is to withdraw and leave India, carrying out the withdrawal, if possible, in an orderly manner, may be even in chaos, on or before the promised date.' The very violence, which in the opinion of his Congress colleagues and that of the British Government provided a compelling motive for partition, was for him an irresistible argument against it; to accept partition because of the fear of civil war was to acknowledge that 'everything was to be got if mad violence was perpetrated in sufficient measure'.

With such strong views on partition, it might well have been expected that Gandhi would oppose the Mountbatten Plan. The Viceroy had indeed some anxiety on this score, and Alan Campbell Johnson records how Mountbatten faced an interview with the Mahatma with some 'trepidation'. Gandhi had no intention, however, of blocking a settlement which was accepted by leaders of the Congress and the League as well as the British Government. At the meeting of the All-India Congress Committee which debated the Mountbatten Plan, he made no secret of his own misgivings but threw his weight in favour of its acceptance. By this act of self-abnegation he saved a split in the Congress at a crucial moment, without compromising his own independence.

Partition having become a *fait accompli*, Gandhi's efforts were henceforth directed to mitigating its risks. He welcomed Jinnah's promise of equal rights and privileges to the Hindu minority in Pakistan, and urged the future Indian Union, as 'the major partner', to set an example to its neighbour in treating the minorities not justly but generously.

A becoming pageantry was to mark the transfer of power from Britain to India on August 15, 1947, but Gandhi was in no mood to think of bands and banners. The day for which he had longed and laboured had come, but he felt no elation. Not only was India's freedom being ushered in at the cost of her unity, but large sections of the population were uneasy about their future.

Early in August, after a brief visit to Kashmir, Gandhi passed through West Punjab and saw the havoc which the recent disturbances in that province had wrought; then he left for East Bengal, where the Hindus of Noakhali feared a fresh wave of disturbances after the establishment of Pakistan.

On arrival at Calcutta he found the town in the grip of communal lawlessness which had been its lot for a year. With the exit of the Muslim League ministry and the transfer of the majority of Muslim officials and police to Pakistan, the tables had, however, been turned. It seemed as if the Hindus of Calcutta were determined to pay off old scores. Suhrawardy, now no longer Premier, and therefore somewhat chastened, met Gandhi and urged him to pacify Calcutta before proceeding to Noakhali. Gandhi agreed on condition that Suhrawardy would stay with him under the same roof in Calcutta and also use his influence with Muslim opinion in East Bengal to protect the Hindu minority. The Mahatma's choice fell upon a Muslim workman's house in Belighata, a part of the town which was considered unsafe for Muslims. Hardly had he moved into his new quarters, when, on August 13th, a group of young Hindus staged a demonstration against his peace mission. He explained to them how he had been trying to end the fratricidal strife, and how hate and violence would lead them nowhere. His words fell like gentle rain on parched earth, and the young men returned to their homes converted. Calcutta was transformed overnight. Rioting ceased. On August 14th, the eve-of-independence was jointly celebrated by the two communities. Hindus and Muslims collected in the streets, danced and sang together. The incubus which had pressed down upon the heart of the town since August 1946 was suddenly lifted. On the *Id* day Hindus exchanged greetings and gifts with Muslims. The scenes were reminiscent of the halcyon days of the Khilafat movement in 1920-22. Three to four hundred thousand people attended Gandhi's prayer meetings, where the flags of India and Pakistan flew together. Gandhi was pleased. 'We have drunk the poison of hatred,' he said, 'and so this nectar of fraternization tastes all the sweeter.'

This cordiality had hardly lasted for a fortnight when the news of the massacres and the migrations from the Punjab caused a fresh flare-up. A Hindu mob raided Gandhi's residence in Belighata on the night of August 31st; it was angry, abusive, violent; it smashed the windows and forced its way into the house. The Mahatma's words were drowned in a violent din; a brick flew past him; a *lathi* blow just missed him. Concurrently Calcutta relapsed into rioting.

This was a serious set-back to Gandhi's efforts for peace. His answer was the announcement of a fast from September 1st, to be broken only when peace returned to the town. 'What my word in person could not do,' he said, 'my fast may.' The announcement electrified Calcutta; the Muslims were moved, the Hindus shamed. Not even the hooligans of Calcutta could bear the thought of having his blood on their conscience; truck-loads of contraband arms were voluntarily surrendered by the communal underground. The leaders of all communities pledged themselves to peace and begged Gandhi to break the fast. Gandhi consented, but with the warning that if the pledge was not honoured he would embark on an irrevocable fast.

The Calcutta fast was universally acclaimed as a miracle; in the oft-quoted words of the correspondent of London *Times*, it did what several divisions of troops could not have done. Henceforth Calcutta and Bengal were to remain calm; the fever of communal strife had subsided.

Immediately, Gandhi felt free to turn to the Punjab. In a sense the flare-up in that Province in the middle of August 1947 was only a continuation of the earlier riots in March 1947; the villages and the towns of the Punjab, seized with fantastic hopes or strange fears, had been dreading and at the same time preparing for a battle of the barricades. The administrative paralysis caused by the reshuffling of cadres on a communal basis, and the infiltration of communalism into the police and military had, by the end of August, led to a situation in which it was impossible for the Hindus to stay in West Punjab and Muslims to stay in East Punjab.

The sum of human misery involved in the movement of five million Hindus and Sikhs from West Punjab to East Punjab, and in the movement of an equal number of Muslims in the opposite direction was appalling. The danger, however, was that as the refugees with their tales of woe arrived at their destinations, violence might spread. This is indeed what happened in Delhi in the first week of September. Gandhi found the capital of India paralysed by one of the worst communal riots in its long history. He felt there was no point in his proceeding to the Punjab when Delhi was aflame. The Government had taken prompt and energetic action. Prime Minister Jawaharlal Nehru had declared that violence would be suppressed sternly; an emergency committee of the Cabinet had been formed and troops had been moved into the town. But Gandhi was not content with a peace imposed by the police and the military; violence had to be purged from the hearts of the people. It was an uphill task. The town had a number of refugee camps, some of which housed Hindus and Sikhs from West Pakistan, while others sheltered Muslims fleeing from Delhi for a passage across the border.

The Hindu and Sikh refugees were in a difficult mood. Many of them, uprooted from their homes, lands and occupations, were going through unfamiliar pangs of poverty; some had been bereaved in the riots and all were bitter. They were anxious to wedge their way into the economy of Delhi; their eyes were riveted on Muslim houses and shops to replace those they had left behind in Pakistan. They could not understand the Mahatma's advice to 'forget and forgive' and to bear no malice in their hearts for those at whose hands they had suffered. They even blamed him for the division of India; his non-violence, they said, had been outclassed by violence. When he suggested that one day they would return to their homes in Pakistan, they smiled incredulously: he had not seen what they had seen; he had not suffered as they had suffered. Little did they know how the tragedy weighed upon him. As he sat down to his frugal meal, he thought of those who were going hungry. At night, when he heard the gentle patter of rain on the roof of Birla House, where he was staying, he lay awake thinking of those who were without adequate shelter. The tales of woe he heard burned themselves into his soul, but he did not falter in his conviction that only non-violence could end this spiral of hate and violence. In his prayer speech every evening, he touched on the communal problem. He stressed the futility of retaliation. He wore himself out in an effort to re-educate the people of Delhi; he heard grievances, suggested solutions, encouraged or admonished his numerous interviewers, visited refugee camps, remained in touch with local officials. It was an exhausting and sometimes a heart-breaking routine.

Gandhi had a half-serious and a half-humorous way of saying that he aspired to live for 125 years, which, according to the Hindu tradition, was the full span of human life. He was, however, so unhappy at the communal riots which began with the 'Great Calcutta Killing' that he repeated time and again that he did not want to 'be a living witness of the fratricidal strife'. Congratulated on his birthday he asked, 'Where do congratulations come in? Would condolences be not more appropriate?' When the *Diwali*, the festival of lights, came he said he could not celebrate it when the light of love had gone out in the hearts of men. When his English disciple, Mirabehn, invited him to visit her *Ashram* in the Himalayas in March 1948 he answered, 'What is the good of counting on a corpse?'

One wonders whether he had a presentiment of an early end, or whether these remarks were no more than occasional glimpses of the torture of mind and spirit which he suffered during this period. 'Life and death' he once described as 'the faces of the same coin'. He spoke of death as an 'incomparable friend'. There were several occasions when his life had hung by the slenderest thread. He was only twenty-seven when he was nearly lynched in the streets of Durban; eleven years later he was belaboured in Johannesburg by a rugged compatriot; in 1934 a bomb narrowly missed him while he was on his way to the Poona municipal hall. Several of his fasts brought him to the verge of a collapse; in at least two of them his survival seemed a miracle. As a soldier of non-violence, he had probably run more hazards than many a general had done in the battlefield.

On January 13, 1948 he began a fast. 'My greatest fast,' he wrote to Mirabehn. It was also to be his last. The fast was not to be broken until Delhi became peaceful. The town was ostensibly quiet; thanks to the stern measures taken by the

Government, the killings had stopped. But the peace for which Gandhi had been working for four and a half months was not 'the peace of the grave', but a peace symbolizing the reunion of hearts. Of the latter there was little sign. Muslims did not dare to move about freely in the town; reports reached the Mahatma that the refugees from West Pakistan were applying subtle methods to oust local Muslims from their shops and houses. The argument that Hindus and Sikhs were equally unsafe throughout the whole of West Pakistan struck him as irrelevant.

The fast had a refreshing impact on Pakistan, where it punctured the subtle web of propaganda which for ten years had represented Gandhi as an enemy of Islam; warm tributes were paid to him in the West Punjab Assembly by Muslim League leaders. In India there was an emotional shake-up. The fast compelled people to think afresh on the problem on the solution of which he had staked his life. There was a sense of urgency; something had to be done quickly to create conditions in which he could end his fast. The Government of India paid out to Pakistan, at his instance, and as a gesture of goodwill, Rs. 55 crores (£44 million) which were due as part of united India's assets but had been withheld on account of the conflict in Kashmir. On January 18, 1948 representatives of various communities and parties in Delhi signed a pledge in Gandhi's presence that they would guarantee peace in Delhi. Before breaking the fast, the Mahatma told them, what he had told the signatories of the peace pledge at Calcutta in September 1947, that if they did not honour the pledge he would fast unto death.

After this fast the tide of communal violence showed definite signs of ebbing. Gandhi felt freer to make his plans for the future. He had promised the refugees from West Pakistan that he would not rest until every family had been rehabilitated in its native town or village. But he felt he could not go to Pakistan without the permission of the Government of that country. Meanwhile, he thought of returning to his *Ashram* at Sevagram. For several months almost all his time had been taken up by the communal problem. However acute this problem was, in a wider perspective it was only a red herring across the path of the country's onward march. The real problems of India, the social and economic uplift of her people had never been absent from his mind. On some of them he had been thinking aloud in his speeches at the evening prayer meetings. He dwelt upon the shortage of food in the country. 'We have,' he argued, 'plenty of fertile lands and large man-power. If we utilize both there would be no necessity of continuing controls.' As for cloth, he had no doubt that the millions in the villages could spin and weave for their needs in their own cottages during their hours of enforced leisure. He thought of the tasks ahead. Constitution-making would soon be over. He had no thought of entering the Government or active politics in independent India, but he could do his bit to strike out new channels for constructive work. In December 1947 he had convened a conference of the representatives of the various constructive organizations which had been founded under his aegis; each of these organizations had its own chosen sphere, such as removal of untouchability, propagation of basic education, *khadi* and village industries. He discussed the possibility of unifying all the constructive organizations for the realization of the non-violent order which was their common aim.

Political freedom having become a fact, Gandhi's mind was switching more and more on to social and economic reform, and to the refurbishing of his non-violent technique.

However, he was destined neither to go to Pakistan nor to pick up the threads of his constructive programme. The first warning came on the evening of January 20th, when a bomb exploded in Birla House a few feet from where he was addressing his prayer meeting. He took no notice of the explosion. Next day he referred to the congratulations which he had received for remaining unruffled after the explosion. He would deserve them, he said, 'if I fall as a result of such an explosion and yet retain a smile on my face and no malice against the assailant'. He described the bomb-thrower as a 'misguided youth' and advised the police not to 'molest' him but to convert him with persuasion and affection. Madan Lal, a refugee from the Punjab who had been arrested, was in fact a member of a gang which had plotted Gandhi's death. These highly-strung young men saw Hinduism menaced by Islam from without and by Gandhi from within. When Madan Lal missed his aim, a fellow conspirator, Nathuram Godse, a young journalist from Poona, came to Delhi. With a pistol in his pocket he hovered round Birla House, where Gandhi stayed and held his prayer meeting.

Vaguely suspecting a conspiracy, the local authorities had increased their vigilance. Gandhi would not, however, permit the police to search those who came to attend his prayer meetings. 'If I have to die,' he told the police officers, 'I should die at the prayer meeting. You are wrong in believing that you can protect me from harm. God is my protector.' On the evening of January 30th he left his room in Birla House for the prayer ground. It was only two minutes' walk, but he was a little late that day, having been detained in a meeting with Sardar Patel. With his forearms on the shoulders of his grandnieces, Ava and Manu—walking-sticks as he called them—he walked briskly. As he approached the prayer ground the congregation of five hundred made a passage for him; many rose, some bowed low in reverence. He said he was sorry for being late, lifted his hands and joined them in a *namaskar* (salutation). Just at that moment Godse edged forward through the crowd, bent low as if to prostrate himself at the Mahatma's feet, whipped out his pistol and fired three shots in quick succession. Gandhi fell instantly with the words '*Hé Rama*' (Oh, God).

It was a strange irony that the apostle of non-violence should have met a violent end. The dark forces of hate seemed to have won; but theirs was a pyrrhic victory. The bullets which passed through Gandhi's chest reverberated in millions of hearts. The very wickedness of the crime exposed, as if in a flash of lightning, the fatuity and futility of communal fanaticism. The flames which reduced the Mahatama's body to ashes on the banks of the Yamuna on the evening of January 31, 1948, proved to be the last flicker of that conflagration which had enveloped the Indo-Pakistan sub-continent since August 1946. Gandhi had fought this fire with all his strength while he lived. His death was to finally quench it.

EPILOGUE

WITHIN five years of his return from South Africa Gandhi became the dominant figure in Indian public life. By 1920 most of the front-rank politicians had joined his banner and the others had practically ceased to count. Rarely had a political conquest been more spectacular or more complete. During the next three decades there were periods when his opponents wrote him off as a spent bullet. But this proved to be a case of the wish being father to the thought; Gandhi staged a resounding come-back at a moment of his own choosing and with his influence undiminished.

Part of the explanation for his meteoric rise and enduring influence lay in the impact which he made upon the imagination of the Indian masses. The cult of the Mahatma had its practical inconveniences; it turned his tours into a terrible ordeal for him, but it also made his prestige independent of the immediate success or failure which attended his movements.

There were also other reasons for this pre-eminence. The struggle in South Africa had matured him; he had outgrown the diffidence which had dogged him as a student in England and as a young lawyer in India, and learnt to combine a tremendous confidence with a disarming humility. Those who came under his spell and changed the very texture of their lives included men and women of vastly dissimilar talents and temperaments: great lawyers and parliamentarians like C. R. Das and Motilal Nehru, humanitarians like Madan Mohan Malaviya and Rajendra Prasad, realists like Vallabhbhai Patel and Rajagopalachari, idealists like Jawaharlal Nehru and Jayaprakash Narayan. They saw in his non-violent technique the only practical alternative to speech-making and bomb-throwing between which Indian politics had so far ineffectively oscillated.

They turned their backs upon personal comfort and professional ambitions and spent the best part of their lives in railway trains or in British prisons. They did not share all his ideas on politics and economics; few of them shared his religious outlook, but they were tied to him by a deeply emotional bond. He was not only the leader, but the *Bapu*, the father who deserved affection and respect. With his immense appeal to the masses, and his peculiar relationship with Congress leaders, Gandhi symbolized in his own person the basic unity of Indian nationalism over a quarter of a century, thus providing a prophylactic against the fatal tendency of nationalist movements towards schism. With other political parties, he stressed the points of contact rather than those of conflict; he did not ridicule or denounce those with whom he differed. With the three Liberal leaders, Tej Bahadur Sapru, M. R. Jayakar and Srinivasa Sastri he corresponded frequently, often thinking aloud with them and seeking their candid reactions. 'Your truthfulness,' he wrote to Srinivasa Sastri, 'is more important to me than your co-operation.' If he could not develop a similar equation with the Muslim League leaders, it was not for want of trying.

The real significance of the Indian freedom movement in the eyes of Gandhi was that it was waged non-violently. He would have had no interest in it if the Congress had not adopted Satyagraha and subscribed to non-violence. He objected to violence not only because an unarmed people had little chance of success in an armed rebellion, but because he considered violence a clumsy weapon which created more problems than it solved, and left a trail of hatred and bitterness in which genuine reconciliation was almost impossible.

This emphasis on non-violence jarred alike on Gandhi's British and Indian critics, though for different reasons. To the former non-violence was a camouflage; to the latter it was sheer sentimentalism. To the British, who tended to see the Indian struggle through the prism of European history, the professions of non-violence seemed too good to be true; their eyes were riveted on the stray acts of violence rather than on the remarkably peaceful nature of Gandhi's campaigns. To the radical Indian politicians who had browsed on the history of the French and Russian revolutions or the Italian and Irish nationalist struggles, it was patent that force would only yield to force, and that it was foolish to miss opportunities and sacrifice tactical gains for reasons more relevant to ethics than to politics.

Gandhi's critics were too prone to apply to his non-violent campaigns yardsticks pertinent to violent warfare. Satyagraha was not designed to 'seize' any particular objectives or to 'crush' the opponent, but to set in motion forces which could lead to his conversion; in such a strategy it was perfectly possible to lose all the battles and win the war. In fact, victory or defeat inadequately describe the object of a Satyagraha campaign: a peace honourable to both parties.

The battles for Indian freedom under Gandhi's leadership were thus waged on the moral, or what is the same thing, the psychological front. 'Even under the most adverse circumstances,' he wrote in January 1920, 'I have found Englishmen amenable to reason and persuasion, and as they always wish to appear just, it is easier to shame them than others into doing the right thing.' The process of conversion was twofold. Indians, no less than the British, needed a change of heart. Gandhi said many hard things about British rule in India, but he said harder things about the evils which divided and corroded Indian society from within.

The final consummation in 1947, the transfer of power, was due to the interaction of numerous national and world forces, but there is no doubt that the timing and the method of British withdrawal were influenced by what Gandhi had said and done for a quarter of a century. In retrospect, it would seem that the three major Satyagraha campaigns in 1920-22, 1930-32 and 1940-42 were so well spaced that they gave time for second thoughts and for that conversion of the British conscience which was Gandhi's ultimate aim. And it is well to remember that in August 1947 it was not only that the Indian felt a load had fallen off his back, but the Briton in India also felt really free for the first time.

Though his role in the political liberation of India inevitably loomed large in the eyes of the world, the mainspring of Gandhi's life lay not in politics but in religion. 'What I want to achieve,' he wrote in his autobiography, 'what I have been striving and pining to achieve these thirty years—is to see God face to face, to attain *moksha*. I live and move and have my being in pursuit of this goal.' His deepest strivings were spiritual. Finding him in a political deputation, Montagu, the Secretary of State for India, had exclaimed, 'How have you, a social reformer, found your way into this crowd?'

Gandhi explained that participation in politics was only an extension of his social activity: 'I could not be leading a religious life unless I identified myself with the whole of mankind, and that I could not do so unless I took part in politics. The whole gamut of man's activities today constitutes an indivisible whole. You cannot divide social, economic and purely religious work into watertight compartments.' He did not know, he said, any religion apart from human activity; the spiritual law did not work in a field of its own but expressed itself through the ordinary activities of life. To be truly religious one did not have to retire to the Himalayas nor shrink into the security of the home or a sect.

The dissociation between politics and religion, between state-craft and ethics has lasted so long, however, that neat minds revolt against any mixture of the two. Truth, charity and love are considered virtues applicable only in the domestic and social spheres. In politics expediency seems to be the prime mover. Gandhi's whole career was a protest against this double morality. He did not divorce the sacred and the secular. His interest in politics derived from the fact that he developed a technique—Satyagraha—which sought to introduce the spirit of religion into politics. The question was often asked by Western observers whether Gandhi was a saint or a politician; he was a saint who did not cease to be one when he entered politics.

Gandhi himself considered the word saint too sacred to be applied to him. He was 'a humble seeker after truth', who had caught 'only the faintest glimmer of that mighty effulgence'. He was, he said, making experiments about some of the eternal verities of life, but could not even claim to be a social scientist because he could show no tangible proof of scientific accuracy in his methods nor such tangible results of experiments as modern science demands. He made no claims to infallibility, and let all the world know when he was groping in the dark. If he thought or spoke of himself as if he were an instrument of God, it was not as a chosen instrument with a special revelation of God's will. 'My firm belief is,' he said, 'that He reveals himself to every human being, but we shut our ears to the still small voice within.' When someone represented him as an incarnation of Lord Krishna he described it as a sacrilege. He had often to restrain his admirers when their adoration outran their common sense. During one of his tours, the inhabitants of a village told him that his auspicious presence had made the village well miraculously fill with water. 'You are fools,' he reproved them, 'beyond a doubt it was an accident. I have no more influence with God than you have. Suppose a crow sits on a palm tree at the moment when the tree falls to the ground. Will you imagine that the weight of the bird brought down the tree?'

His humility was not a cultivated virtue, but sprang from a ceaseless struggle for self-mastery in which he remained engaged from his childhood to the last day of his life. 'For him,' wrote his secretary Mahadev Desai, 'the struggle with the opponent within is keener than with the opponent without.' He described himself as an average man with less than an average ability. 'I admit,' he remarked 'that I am not sharp intellectually. But I don't mind. There is a limit to the development of the intellect but none to that of the heart.' One cannot resist the impression that, in exalting the goodness of the heart at the expense of mere intellectual brilliance, Gandhi tended to foster the idea of his own intellectual mediocrity. He did not care much for book learning, but his occasional imprisonments helped him to catch up with his reading, and what he read he turned to good account. His autobiography and his history of Satyagraha in South Africa are proofs of a retentive memory, and both his colleagues and opponents bore testimony to his keen intellect. Nevertheless, it is a fact that he considered reasoning a poor guide beyond a certain point unless it was controlled and directed by his intuition. The truth he sought was not a static but a dynamic entity which endlessly continued to unfold its myriad facets. When charged with inconsistency, he retorted that he was consistent with truth not with the past. He went on modifying, correcting and enlarging his ideas in the light of fresh experience. One can discern a process of evolution even in his daily prayers; beginning with recitations from Hindu and Christian scriptures in South Africa, they came to incorporate verses from the Zend Avesta, the Koran, and Buddhist and Japanese scriptures. A few hours before his death he wrote out his last exercise in Bengali, a language which he had started learning a year earlier so that he could serve riot-torn Bengal the more efficiently. To the end he retained the zeal and humility of a student.

Since he was continually elaborating his ideas on every subject, it was easy to confront him with his own earlier pronouncements on caste, machinery or *khadi* and point out the discrepancies. In the glare of the ruthless publicity in which he lived, every one of his gestures and words was public property, but he willingly shared with the world even an ignoble thought if it happened in a dream to flash across his mind. What he wrote of Tolstoy is equally true of him: 'Tolstoy's so-called inconsistencies were a sign of his development and passionate regard for truth. He often seemed inconsistent because he was continuously outgrowing his own doctrines. His failures were public; his struggles and triumphs private.'

Rabindranath Tagore once aptly described Gandhi as essentially 'a lover of men and not of ideas'. Though he loved to reduce all problems to his moral algebra, Gandhi did not ram his opinions down anybody's throat. 'Never take anything for a gospel truth,' he warned, 'even if it comes from a Mahatma.' *Hind Swaraj*, his first political testament, included a scathing attack on modern civilization and all its appurtenances of schools, railways and hospitals, but Gandhi no more tried to foist this philosophy on his followers than he compelled them to change into the loin-cloth. Agatha Harrison has recorded how he used to lecture her on the evils of tea drinking, but whenever she accompanied him on his tours, tea was invariably served to her at 4 p.m. Thousands of people in India and abroad who met him or corresponded with him treasured small acts of courtesy and affection for which, in spite of all his preoccupations he was never too busy. He aspired to identify himself with 'the least, lowliest and the lost'. He used a stone instead of soap for his bath, wrote his letters on little bits of paper with little stumps of pencils which he could hardly hold between his fingers, shaved with a crude country razor and ate with a wooden spoon from a prisoner's bowl. All this austerity, while it may have satisfied some of his own inner needs, was primarily a means to an emotional identification with the Indian masses whose poverty and misery always haunted him; it provided the motive power for all his political, social and economic activities; it gave him his unique hold over the people, and it also, not unoften, created barriers between him and the town-bred Indian intelligentsia.

Gandhi's asceticism sat lightly on him; it did not make of him a killjoy. He had the gaiety of a child. Every one of his visitors could expect to be entertained to a joke or two. 'Do you suffer from nerves?' he was asked by a woman visitor. 'Ask Mrs Gandhi,' straight came the reply, 'she will tell you that I am on my best behaviour with the world but not with her.' 'Well,' continued Mrs Miles, 'my husband is on his best behaviour with me.' 'Then,' retorted Gandhi, 'I am sure that Mr Miles has bribed you heavily.' Asked why he was uncharitable to those who drank, Gandhi answered: 'because I am charitable to those who suffer from the effects of the curse.' 'How many children have you,' he asked a sailor. 'Eight, sir, four sons and four daughters.' 'I have four sons,' said the Mahatma, 'so I can race with you half-way.' He could extract mirth out of the most unpromising situations. In September 1932, when the Hindu leaders met in Yeravda prison under the shadow of his Poona fast, he sat at the centre of the table and chuckled, 'I preside'.

Gandhi devoted the best part of his life to one crucial problem: how to perfect and extend *ahimsa* (non-violence) in human relationships. On several occasions he declined invitations to tour Europe and America as he saw the absurdity of preaching non-violence abroad before there was a successful demonstration at home. And when at last the British decided to transform Indo-British relations on a basis of equality, as Gandhi had long urged, and a bloodless revolution was in the offing, India was caught in a vicious chain of communal fanaticism and bloodshed. Gandhi saw the fabric of national unity, which he had cherished, shiver into pieces before his eyes. Even as he struggled to guide the forces of violence into the paths of peace, he was haunted by a deep sense of failure. His popularity had not diminished. He was hailed as the Father of the Nation. The leaders of the Government paid him homage. He continued to draw huge crowds which shouted 'Victory to Mahatma Gandhi'; these words had always grated on his ears but now they cut him to the quick. For there could be no victory for him when parts of India were given over to fear and violence. The tragedy stemmed from several causes, some of them rooted in recent Indian history and others in a political-cum-religious movement which had temporarily unhinged the minds of men. Gandhi lived long enough to witness two spectacular triumphs of his method; his fasts shamed Calcutta and Delhi into peace. And his death achieved, what he had tried so hard in his last days to achieve, the return of sanity to the Indo-Pakistan sub-continent.

For Gandhi, however, the validity of non-violence was even independent of his own success or failure. His criticisms of Western materialism and militarism in *Hind Swaraj* were made six years before the outbreak of the First World War, when

R*

Europe was at the zenith of its prestige and power. These criticisms may have appeared quixotic fifty years ago; today, as the world trembles on the brink of a Third World War, they seem prophetic. By spurning material progress at the cost of moral values, and by irrevocably renouncing violence, Gandhi took a line in direct opposition to the two dominant ideologies of the twentieth century, capitalism and communism. He visualized and worked for a society which would provide for the essential needs of the community (and no more), and in which the decentralization of economic and political structures would minimize the incentives for exploitation within and conflict without. Such a society could, he believed, dispense with the coercive apparatus of the modern state, and depend upon non-violent techniques not only to maintain order but to protect itself against external aggression.

It is difficult to say whether Gandhi's dream will come true. Nations, like individuals, are tempted to continue along the beaten path, even though it may end in a blind alley. Gandhi knew the difficulties of translating his non-violent dream into the world of reality. But he refused to compromise on what he held to be the fundamentals. To the last he affirmed that even good ends do not justify dubious means; that our real enemies are our own fears, greeds and egotisms; that we must change ourselves before we can change others; that the laws of the family, of truth and love and charity, are applicable to groups, communities and nations; and above all, that 'non-violence is the law of our species, as violence is the law of the brute'. To those who are charged with the destinies of nations, all this may sound a very desirable but a very distant ideal. Yet, in the thermo-nuclear age, if civilization is not to disintegrate into a mass of torn flesh and molten metal, the premises of Gandhi have an immediate relevance.

GLOSSARY

Ahimsa: Non-violence; love.

Ashram: a retreat or place for community living.

Brahmacharya: observance of chastity or continence 'in the quest of Truth that is God'.

Charkha: spinning-wheel.

Darshan: sight of a venerated deity or person.

Dharma: duty.

Fakir: a recluse.

Guru: teacher.

Harijan: literally child of God; a name coined by Gandhi to describe the so-called untouchables.

Hartal: suspension of work as a mark of protest or mourning.

Himsa: violence.

Khadi: hand-spun and hand-woven cloth.

Lathi: a wooden staff, a long stick.

Mahatma: a great soul.

Mandir: temple.

Maulana: a title of respect applied to Muslim priests or scholars.

Sadhana: striving; practice.

Sadhu: a recluse; mendicant.

Sanyasi or *Sannyasi:* a recluse.

Sari: a long piece of cloth worn by Indian women.

Sarvodaya: universal good.

Satyagraha: literally holding on to truth; truth-force or soul-force.

Swadeshi: of one's own country.

Swaraj: self-rule.

Talukdars: hereditary revenue collectors created under the early British rule in India.

Vaishnava: votary of the cult of Vishnu.

Zamindar: a landlord.

SELECT BIBLIOGRAPHY

ALEXANDER, H. G.: *The Indian Ferment*; Williams and Norgate, London, 1929. *India Since Cripps*; Penguin, London, 1944.

ALBIRUNI, A. H.: *Makers of Pakistan*.

AMBEDKAR, B. R.: *Ranade, Gandhi and Jinnah*; Thacker & Co. Ltd., Bombay, 1943. *What Congress and Gandhi Have Done to the Untouchables*; Thacker & Co. Ltd., Bombay, 1945.

ANDREWS, C. F.: *Mahatma Gandhi's Ideas*; Allen & Unwin, London, 1929. *Mahatma Gandhi: His Own Story*; Allen & Unwin, London, 1930. *Mahatma Gandhi at Work*; Allen & Unwin, London, 1931.

ANDREWS, C. F. and MOOKERJI GIRIJA: *The Rise and Growth of the Congress*; Allen & Unwin, London, 1938.

ARYAN PATH: Special *Hind Swaraj* Number, Theosophy Co., Bombay, September 1931.

AZIM HUSAIN: *Fazl-i-Husain*; Longmans, Green & Company Ltd., Bombay, 1946.

BERNAYS, ROBERT: *Naked Fakir*; Victor Gollancz, London, 1931.

BURNES, A.: *Colour Prejudice*; Allen & Unwin, London, 1948.

BESANT, ANNIE: *How India Wrought for Freedom*; Theosophical Publishing House, Madras, 1915.

BIRLA, G. D.: *In the Shadow of the Mahatma*; Orient Longmans Ltd., India, 1953.

BOLITHO, HECTOR: *Jinnah*; John Murray, London, 1954.

BOLTON, GLORNEY: *The Tragedy of Gandhi*; Allen & Unwin, London, 1934.

BOSE, NIRMAL KUMAR: *Studies in Gandhism*; Indian Associated Publishing Co., Calcutta, 1947.

BOSE, SUBHAS CHANDRA: *The Indian Struggle*; Wishart, London, 1935.

BRAILSFORD, H. N.: *Rebel India*; Victor Gollancz, London, 1931.

BROCKWAY, FENNER A.: *The Indian Crisis*; Victor Gollancz, London, 1930.

CAMPBELL-JOHNSON, ALAN: *Mission with Mountbatten*; Robert Hale, London, 1951. *Viscount Halifax*; Robert Hale, London, 1941.

CATLIN, GEORGE: *In the Path of Mahatma Gandhi*; Macdonald & Co., London, 1948.

CHINTAMANI, C. Y.: *Indian Politics since the Mutiny*; Allen & Unwin, London, 1939.

CHATURVEDI and MARJORIE SYKES: *Charles Freer Andrews*; Allen & Unwin, London, 1949.

CHURCHILL, WINSTON: *The Second World War*; Vol. I, III & IV, Cassell & Co. Ltd., London, 1948, 1950, 1951.

COATMAN, J.: *India in 1925-26, 1926-27, 1927-28, 1928-29*; Calcutta.

COUPLAND, R.: *The Constitutional Problem in India; India; a Restatement*; Oxford University Press, London and Bombay, 1944.

DANTWALA, M. L.: *Gandhism Reconsidered*; Padma Publications, Bombay, 1944.

DESAI, MAHADEV: *The Diaries*; Navajivan Publishing House, Ahmedabad. *1953. The Epic of Tranvancore*; Navajivan Press, Ahmedabad, 1937. *The Gita According to Gandhi*; Navajivan Press, Ahmedabad, 1946. *Maulana Abul Kalam Azad*; Allen & Unwin, London 1941. *Nation's Voice*; Navajivan Press, Ahmedabad, 1932. *A Righteous Struggle*; Navajivan Publishing House, Ahmedabad, 1951. *The Story of Bardoli*; Navajivan Press, Ahmedabad, 1929.

DESHPANDE, P. G.: *Gandhiana*; Navajivan Publishing House, Ahmedabad, 1948.

DHAWAN, G. N.: *The Political Philosophy of Mahatma Gandhi*; Navajivan Publishing House, Ahmedabad, 1951.

DISORDERS INQUIRY COMMITTEE (HUNTER COMMITTEE): Report, Calcutta, 1919-20.

DIWAKAR, R. R.: *Glimpses of Gandhiji*; Hind Kitabs, Bombay, 1949. *Satyagraha—Its Technique and History*; Hind Kitabs, Bombay, 1946.

DOKE, JOSEPH J.: *M. K. Gandhi*; G. A. Natesan & Co., Madras, 1909.

DUNCAN, RONALD: *Selected Writings of Mahatma Gandhi*; Faber & Faber, London, 1951.

DUTT, R. PALME: *India Today*; People's Publishing House, Bombay, 1947.

ELWIN, V. and WINSLOW, J.: *The Dawn of Indian Freedom*; Allen & Unwin, London, 1931.

FISCHER, LOUIS: *A Week with Gandhi*; Duell, Sloan & Pearce, New York, 1942. *The Life of Mahatma Gandhi*; Harper & Brothers, New York, 1950.

GANDHI, M. K.: *Bapu's Letters to Mira (1928-48)*; Navajivan Publishing House, Ahmedabad, 1949. *Constructive Programme*; Navajivan Press, Ahmedabad, 1941. *Delhi Diary*; Navajivan Publishing House, Ahmedabad, 1948. *Economics of Khadi*; Navajivan Press, Ahmedabad, 1941. *Ethical Religion*; S. Ganesan, Madras, 1922. *For Pacifists*; Navajivan

Publishing House, Ahmedabad, 1949. *Gandhiji's correspondence with the Government*; Navajivan Publishing House, Ahmedabad, 1945. *A Guide to Health*; S. Ganesan, Madras, 1921. *Harijan*; Navajivan Press, Ahmedabad, 1933-40, 1942, 1946-48. *Hind Swaraj*; Navajivan Press, Ahmedabad, 1938. *Indian Opinion* 1904-14 Natal; *Non-Violence in Peace and War*; Navajivan Publishing House, Ahmedabad, Part I, 1945, Part II, 1949. *Rowlatt Bills and Satyagraha*; G. A. Natesan & Co., Madras, 1919. *Satyagraha*; Navajivan Publishing House, Ahmedabad, 1951. *Satyagraha in South Africa*; S. Ganesan, Madras, 1928. *Self-Restraint v. Self-Indulgence*; Navajivan Publishing House, Ahmedabad, 1947. *History of Satyagraha Ashram*; *From Yeravda Mandir*; *Cent Per Cent Swadeshi. Speeches and Writings*; G. A. Natesan & Co., Madras, 1933. *The Story of My Experiments with Truth*; Navajivan Publishing House, Ahmedabad, 1945. *To Ashram Sisters*; Navajivan Press, Ahmedabad, 1952. *To a Gandhian Capitalist*; Hind Kitabs, Bombay, 1951. *To the Students*; Navajivan Publishing House, Ahmedabad, 1949. *Unto this Last*; Navajivan Publishing House, Ahmedabad, 1951. *Women and Social Injustice*; Navajivan Press, Ahmedabad, 1942. *Young India*; Navajivan Press, Ahmedabad, 1919-32. *Young India*; Ganesan, Madras, Volumes I, II & III (1919-22, 1924-26, 1927-28).

GANDHI, MANUBEHN: *Bapu—My Mother*; Navajivan Publishing House, Ahmedabad, 1949.

GEORGE, S. K.: *Gandhi's Challenge to Christianity*; Allen & Unwin, London, 1939.

GOVERNMENT OF INDIA: *Congress Responsibility for the Disturbances (1942-43)*; New Delhi, 1943. *Gandhian Outlook and Techniques*; New Delhi, 1953. *Homage to Mahatma Gandhi*; New Delhi, 1948. *Speeches by Lord Irwin*, Vols. I and II, Simla, 1930 and 1931.

GREGG, RICHARD B.: *A Discipline for Non-Violence*; Navajivan Press, Ahmedabad, 1941. *The Power of Non-Violence*; Navajivan Press, Ahmedabad, 1938.

HARDINGE: *My Indian Years*; John Murray, London, 1948.

HINDUSTAN TIMES: *India Unreconciled*; Delhi, 1943.

HINDUSTANI TALIMI SANGH: *Basic National Education*; Syllabus, Sevagram, 1939. *Educational Reconstruction*; Sevagram, 1940.

HINGORANI, A. T. (edited and published at Karachi by): *To the Students*; 1935. *To the Hindus and the Muslims*; 1942. *To the Princes and their People*; 1942. *To the Protagonists of Pakistan*; 1947.

HOYLAND, JOHN S.: *Indian Crisis*; Macmillan, New York, 1944.

INDIAN OPINION: *Golden Number*; (Passive Resistance Movement in South Africa, 1906-14), Phoenix, Natal, 1914.

JACK, HOMER A. (edited by): *The Wit and Wisdom of Gandhi*; The Beacon Press, Boston, 1951.

JAYAPRAKASH NARAYAN: *Gandhiji's Leadership and The Congress Socialist Party*; 1940.

JONES, E. STANLEY: *Mahatma Gandhi: An Interpretation*; Hodder & Stoughton, London, 1948.

JONES, M. E.: *Gandhi Lives*; David Mckay Co., Philadelphia, USA, 1948.

KALELKAR, KAKA: *Stray Glimpses of Bapu*; Navajivan Publishing House, Ahmedabad, 1950. *To a Gandhian Capitalist*; (Gandhi's correspondence with Jamnalal Bajaj). Hind Kitabs, Bombay, 1951.

KANJI, DWARKADAS: *Gandhi ThroughMy Diary Leaves*; Bombay, 1950.

KIRPALANI, K. R.: *Tagore, Gandhi and Nehru*; Hind Kitabs, Bombay, 1947.

KIRPALANI, J. B.: *The Gandhian Way*; Vora & Co., Bombay, 1938.

KRISHANDAS: *Seven Months with Mahatma Gandhi*; S. Ganesan, Madras, 1928.

LAJPAT RAI, LALA: *Ideals of Non-Co-operation*; S. Ganesan, Madras, 1924. *Unhappy India*; Banna Publishing Co., Calcutta, 1928.

LUMBY: *Transfer of Power*; Allen & Unwin, London, 1954.

LESTER, MURIEL: *Entertaining Gandhi*; Ivor Nicholson & Watson, London, 1932.

MASANI, R. P.: *Dadabhai Naoroji*; Allen & Unwin, London, 1939.

MARQUESS OF READING: *Rufus Isaacs, First Marquess of Reading*; Hutchinson & Co., London, 1945.

MASHRUWALA, K. G.: *Gandhi and Marx*; Navajivan Publishing House, Ahmedabad, 1951.

MEHTA, ASOKA and PATWARDHAN, ACHYUT: *The Communal Triangle in India*; Kitabistan, Allahabad, 1942,

MITRA, N. N. (published by): *Indian Annual Register*; Calcutta.

MIRABEHN: *Bapu's Letters to Mira*; Navajivan, Ahmedabad, 1949.

MONTAGU, EDWIN S.: *An Indian Diary*; William Heinemann, London. 1930.

MUKERJEE, HIRENDRANATH: *Indian Struggle for Freedom*; Kutub, Bombay, 1946.

NAG, KALIDAS: *Tolstoy and Gandhi*; Pustak Bhandar, Patna, 1950.

NAIR, C. SANKARAN: *Gandhi and Anarchy*; Tagore & Co., Madras, 1922.

NAYYAR, SUSHILA: *Kasturba*; Wallingford, Pennsylvania, Pendle Hill, 1948.

NEHRU, JAWAHARLAL: *An Autobiography*; John Lane, London, 1936. *The Discovery of India*; Signet Press, Calcutta, 1941. *Eighteen Months in India*; Kitabistan, Allahabad, 1938. *The Unity of India*; Lindsay Drummond, London, 1941.

PARIKH, NARHARI D.: *Sardar Vallabhbhai Patel*; Navajivan Publishing House, Ahmedabad, Volume I, 1953.

PATEL, G. I. *Vithalbhai Patel (Life and Times)*; Books I and II, Bombay, 1950.

PATEL, MANIBEHN: *Letters to Sardar Patel*, Navajivan, Ahmedabad, 1950.

POLAK, H. S. L., BRAILSFORD, H. N., PETHICK-LAWRENCE: *Mahatma Gandhi*; Odhams Press, London, 1949.

POLAK, MILLIE GRAHAM: *Mr Gandhi: The Man*; Allen & Unwin, London, 1931.

PRASAD, RAJENDRA: *Gandhiji in Champaran*; S. Ganesan, Madras, 1928. *India Divided*; Hind Kitabs Ltd., Bombay, 1947. *Autobiography*; Bharti Sadan, Muzaffarpur, 1947, *Satyagraha in Champaran*; Navajivan Press, Ahmedabad, 1949.

PUNJAB SUB-COMMITTEE, INDIAN NATIONAL CONGRESS: *Reports*, Vols. I and II, Lahore, 1920.

PYARELAL: *The Epic Fast*; Navajivan Press, Ahmedabad, 1932. *Mahatma Gandhi, The Last Phase*; Volume I, Navajivan Press, Ahmedabad, 1956.

RADHAKRISHNAN, S. (edited by): *Mahatma Gandhi: Essays and Reflections*; Allen & Unwin, London, 1939.

RAJAGOPALACHARI, C.: *The Nation's Voice*; Ahmedabad, 1932.

RAMACHANDRAN, G.: *A Sheaf of Gandhi Anecdotes*; Hind Kitabs, Bombay, 1946.

RAO, R. V.: *Gandhian Institutions of Wardha*; Thackers, Bombay, 1947.

ROLLAND, ROMAIN: *Mahatma Gandhi*; Allen & Unwin, London, 1924.

SETALVAD: *Recollections and Reflections*, Padma Publications, Bombay, 1946.

SHEEAN, VINCENT: *Lead Kindly Light*; Cassell & Co. Ltd., London, 1949.

SHRIDHARANI, K.: *War Without Violence*; Harcourt Brace & Co., New York, 1939.

SHERWOOD, ROBERT E.: *The White House Papers of Harry L. Hopkins*; Vol. II, London, 1949.

SHUKLA, CHANDRASHANKER (edited by): *Incidents of Gandhiji's Life*; Vora & Co., Bombay, 1949.

SIMON: *Retrospect*; Hutchinson, London, 1952.

SITARAMAYYA, PATTABHI: *History of the Indian National Congress*; Volumes I & II, Padma Publications, Bombay, 1947.

SMUTS, J. C.: *Jan Christian Smuts*; Cassell & Co. Ltd., London, 1952.

SMITH, W. C.: *Modern Islam in India*; Victor Gollancz, London 1946.

TEMPLEWOOD, LORD: *Nine Troubled Years*; Collins, London, 1954.

TENDULKAR: *Mahatma*; Volumes I to VIII, Times of India Press, Bombay.

TENDULKAR, D. G., CHALAPATHI M. RAU, MRIDULA SARABHAI and VITHALBHAIK JHAVERI (edited by): *Gandhiji: His Life and Work*; Karnatak Publishing House, Bombay, 1944.

THOMPSON and GARRATT: *Rise and Fulfilment of British Rule in India.*

TUKER, Lt.-General Sir FRANCIS: *While Memory Serves*; Cassell & Co. Ltd., London, 1950.

VISVA-BHARATI QUARTERLY: Gandhi Memorial Peace Number; Santiniketan, 1949.

WOODRUFF, PHILIP: *The Guardians*; Jonathan Cape, London, 1955.

WALKER, ROY: *Sword of Gold;* Indian Independence Union, London, 1945.

YAGNIK, INDULAL K.: *Gandhi as I knew Him*; Delhi, 1945.

ZACHARIAS, H. C. E.: *Renascent India*; Allen & Unwin, London, 1933.

INDEX